EXPLORING HIGHLANDERS OF TRIPURA AND CHITTAGONG HILL TRACTS

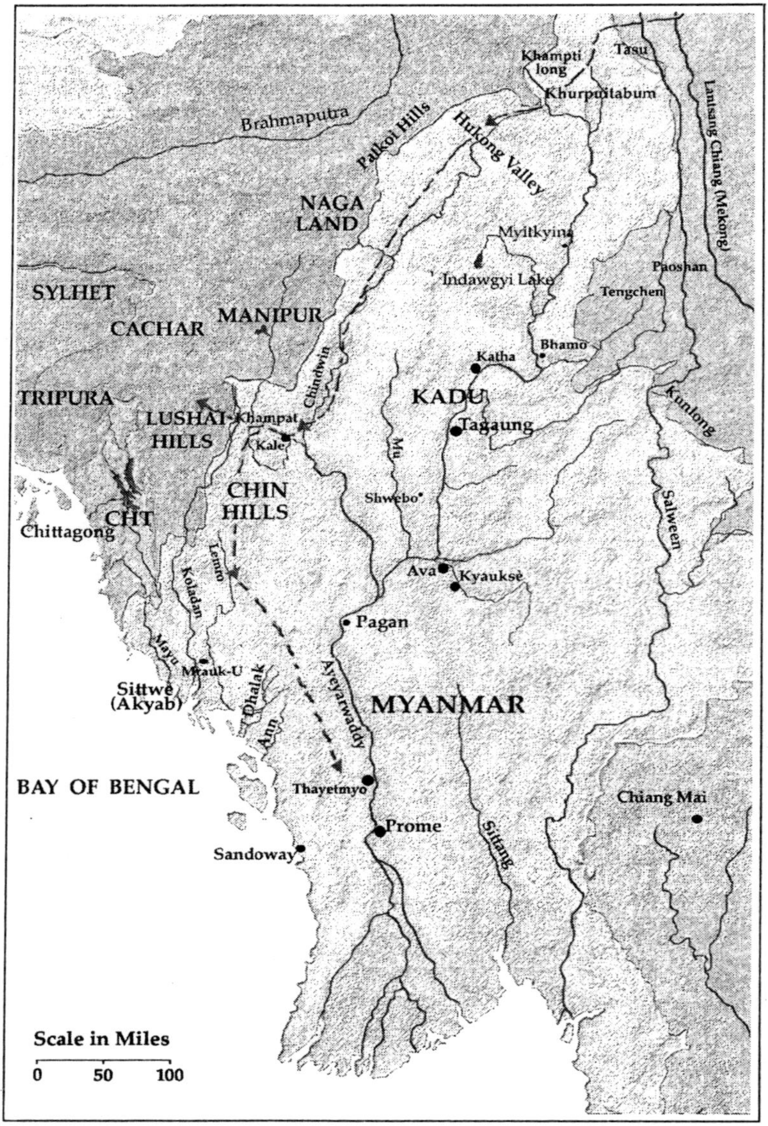

Khampti long
Tasu
Khurputtabum
Brahmaputra
Patkoi Hills
Hukong Valley
Lantsang Chiang (Mekong)
NAGA LAND
Myitkyina
Indawgyi Lake
Paoshan
Tengchen
SYLHET
CACHAR
MANIPUR
Bhamo
Katha
TRIPURA
KADU
Kunlong
LUSHAI HILLS
Khampat
Chindwin
Kale
Tagaung
Mu
Salween
CHIN HILLS
Shwebo
CHT
Chittagong
Lemro
Koladan
Ava
Kyaukse
Pagan
Mayu
Mrauk-U
Sittwe (Akyab)
Dhalak
Ann
Ayeyarwaddy
MYANMAR
BAY OF BENGAL
Thayetmyo
Chiang Mai
Prome
Sittang
Sandoway
Scale in Miles
0
50
100

Exploring Highlanders of Tripura and Chittagong Hill Tracts

Rupak Debnath

AKANSHA PUBLISHING HOUSE
NEW DELHI • GUWAHATI • VISAKHAPATNAM

AKANSHA PUBLISHING HOUSE
4649-B/21, Ansari Road
Darya Ganj, New Delhi - 110 002
Ph.: 23263193 / 9811582579 / 09435116718
Fax: 011-23263193
Email: ektabooks@yahoo.com
www.akanshapublishinghouse.com

Exploring Highlanders of Tripura and Chittagong Hill Tracts

First Published 2010

ISBN 978-81-8370-214-0

PRINTED IN INDIA

Published by Akansha Publishing House, New Delhi and Printed at S.N. Printers, Delhi.

To
Rahel, Shounak and Shravasti

Contents

Acknowledgements

Acknowledgement is due to a large number of individuals from the different tribes who as informants gave me sufficient time and happy accommodation to be interviewed, sometimes even re-interviewed for new queries that came up in preparing a seamless narrative out of the experiences accumulated during fieldwork. I have taken the opportunity to express my gratitude to them and include their names within the body of the work itself. Happily, the credits for information are due to my knowledgeable informants.

A lot of photographs were taken during fieldwork. I took some shots while the credit for taking several pictures is due to my friends, Dinanath Tanchangya and Goutam Borua. Unavoidable constraints have compelled the inclusion of only a few photographs in greyscale in the present work. Perhaps, sometime in the future an exhaustive picture gallery would find a place in another publication.

—Rupak Debnath

Preface

It is almost a decade now since I began to work on the Tibeto-Burman tribes of Northeast India and the Chittagong Hill Tracts. The experience is very different from any of those I had when I began my early schooling in Nagaland and then moved on to Meghalaya before settling in Tripura. Many Naga, Khasi, Garo, Darlong, Bru and Mizo boys were my friends and during my school and later on college and university days, they aroused in me no additional interests than good friends did. Interests in ethnicity, tribes and races did not matter at that time. To them, I was more of a school or college friend than a Bengali or an ethno-racial competitor. The same old relationship continues even today and when occasions allow friends to meet, we spend most time in talking of the good old school and college days, about our teachers, our favourite footballers and the heroes of the 1980s and the 1990s.

In most ethnographic accounts, I find authors claiming to have spent five, ten or fifteen years in contact with the groups that arouse their interests. Undeniably, that is part of research methodology, which seeks participant observation through frequent, interactive contacts and extended interviews, structured or unstructured, whichever is feasible for generating maximum information within a short period of time. In writing this account, too, a planned study has been carried out in different villages and hamlets of Tripura and the Chittagong Hill Tracts. Among the distinct advantages I enjoy over many ethnographers and socio-anthropologists are an innate familiarity with the region and a wide network of contacts that I could build over the years through my good old friends. There is no need to make extra efforts to secure reliable contacts to carry out investigations; the only thing needed is to go out of the house and walk into the unexplored recesses of the hills and look for folks who still remember something of the olden days. Ethnic strife, insurgency activities often force suspension of my explorative activities, thanks to the good people who in such situations advise me to postpone work for a couple of months or so. When things begin to settle down, the invitation is made in the most familiar terms, 'When are you coming?' and I get to work again. Today, new friends have grown from old connections and I earnestly hope to enjoy my share of their company for many more years to come.

During the last ten years, I have learnt that my school and college friends come from different ethnic communities, which though coexisting and interacting, differ from one another in linguistic, racial and cultural terms. The kaleidoscopic variation within those communities is vast and, more importantly, in much need of genuine appreciation of the many good things they have, preservation of the positive residual aspects of their fast transforming material cultures, and extension of welfare measures to the economically excluded or marginalised sections. Insurgency in Tripura and the Chittagong Hill Tracts is no doubt the outburst of long denied or repressed aspirations in the wake of Bengali expansion. But there is also another force, that of the dominant valley-dwelling tribes, which has perpetrated counter-hegemony of the Tibeto-Burman type, causing exclusion of the demographically peripheral highlanders from socio-economic and political participation. Though some issues do not come exactly under the present concerns of this work, there is always a humanistic necessity to remove all systemic discriminations against the under-privileged highland tribes and create productive synergies across ethnic intolerance and repression.

The present work deals with the highland tribes of Tripura and the Chittagong Hill Tracts, documenting the distribution of different ethnic communities, their origins, the traditional and material aspects of life, their social structures, their notions of sex and gender, family and village, and so on. My personal concerns and the methodology adopted in this work are summarised in the introductory chapter, and it would be redundant to explicate the same here again. Accuracy of documentation has been earnestly attempted and available information analysed with impartiality. I hope that the book will interest the readers and encourage researchers to make extensive socio-anthropological studies on many tribes that remain unreached until the present day.

—Rupak Debnath

1
Introduction

The primary concern of this work is to generate a fair understanding of ethnic, economic and socio-political systems of the Kuki-Chin and other highland tribes settled in Tripura and the Chittagong Hill Tracts. Specific tribe-based studies on Mru, Bawm and Lushai have been carried but works on the other tribes constitute the undone vast; hence, a common socio-anthropological framework is adopted for the highland tribes of the selected region. Invariably, all highlanders are hill-dwellers but not every hill-dweller can be called a highlander. In terms of ethnic stock, the hill men of Tripura and the Hill Tracts are Tibeto-Burmans of the Sino-Tibetan family, but within the Tibeto-Burman population, one finds two distinct divisions. On the one hand, we have the valley dwelling Tippera, Chakma, Sak, Marma and Tanchangya; on the other, we find the highland Kuki-Chin tribes, besides the Bru (Riang) and the Mru.

The Region, Its Physical Aspects

The region selected for this study constitutes the extreme northeastern part of the Indian Sub-Continent, between 20.10° and 24.32° North latitudes and 91.50° and 93° East longitudes. In terms of political boundary, it is divided between India and Bangladesh. Tripura is one of the seven sister states of Northeast India with an area of 10,492 square kilometres and a total population of 3,199,203 in 2001 (compared to 2,757,205 in 1991). The total area of the Chittagong Hill Tracts (abbreviated to CHT) is 12,181 square kilometres and in 1991, it had a population of 974,445 individuals. As part of the eastern Himalayas, the region is rich in tropical rainforests, into which ecosystem diverse tribes are integrated. Viewed from the coastal plains of Bengal, the land is amassed into eastward undulations until the chains of the tropical Himalayas are reached. These chains that mostly run north to south break into ravines and patches of lowland along riverbanks. The hills are covered with tropical rainforests and have an abundance of bamboo and creeper jungles. Precariously steep slopes are seen at several places around the Keokradaung (4054 feet) on the CHT-Myanmar border; otherwise, in most places, the hills are generally low running with the average declivity favouring swidden cultivation. In the northern and the eastern parts of the Hill Tracts and in the tri-junction of Tripura, Mizoram and CHT, mountain summits also rise to considerable heights. The Betling Sib in the Jampui range on Tripura-Mizoram border is 3100 feet from the sea-level.

The Deo and the Manu rivers of North Tripura flow in north-south direction; the Gomati of South Tripura District flows west past Udaipur and Comilla towns into the Meghna while another river of the same district, the Muhuri, initially moves west, then turns south through the centre of the Belonia subdivision to feed the Feni, which marks the political boundary of Tripura and Bangladesh. In the Chittagong Hill Tracts, the Karnaphuli (Kynsa Chaung) is the major river; it is fed by the Rainkhyoung (Rain Chaung) from the south, and the Chengri and the Kassalong rivers from the north. The Maini merges with the Kassalong around Langadu while at Barkal, the Subalong joins the Karnaphuli. From the Jampui Hills, the Sajek (Tuipui) runs south past Tlabung (Demagiri), then turns a little west at Barkal to fall into the Karnaphuli; from the opposite direction flow the Thega and the Tuichang, demarcating the flanks of the Chakma Autonomous District Council of Mizoram. In the southern part of the Hill Tracts, small streams like the Bomu, the Lama Chaung and the Tein Chaung (Tain Chhari) form the principal tributaries of the Matamuri (Marit Chaung), which is also fed by the Harbung river in the Chittagong district. The Sangu (Ragri Chaung) flows due north up to Ruma, then turns northwest to reach Bandarban, after which it runs west into the Bay of Bengal.

The warm humid tropical monsoon climate of the region is conducive to both *jum* and wet-rice cultivation. In summer, the temperature soars to 35°C, while it is around 18°C on average between December and February, occasionally sinking to a low 4 to 5°C on the coldest day of the season. In the higher altitudes, the temperature is usually two or three degrees lower than the average. Between October and February, dense fogs are seen at sunrise and sunset. The prevailing wind is southwesterly but in winter, a strong northerly wind blows, sometimes bringing showers and cyclones. In early March, the morning fog begins to turn thin, and it becomes thinner by mid-April; if during this time, the nights are clear and starlit, one finds dew deposits on the morning grass. But April is also the time of the terrible Northwester (called *Kal Vaisakhi* in Bengali); every year, its devastative fury leaves many trees uprooted, scores of houses destroyed and their roofs blown. Around the last week of April, the weather begins to get dry; with the showers now becoming very intermittent, the average temperature and the human discomfort rise steadily until the monsoons bring some relief in the early part of June. The average precipitation in the monsoon months is 250 cm.

Famine is almost unknown in the hills but food shortages occur when the rains play truant. Besides, during bamboo flowering, which invariably occurs once in several years, rats arrive in hundreds and thousands, and cause much damage to the crops. Diseases attributable to the climate include common fever and malaria, rheumatism and dysentery. Malaria is also particularly acute in the hills. Between January and March 2009, there was in the Longtrai Hills of Tripura an outbreak of meningitis epidemic that killed more than a hundred people. The hill folks, men and women are all inveterate smokers, which habit makes them vulnerable to respiratory diseases like tuberculosis and whooping cough. Skin diseases too are fairly widespread, in addition to which people often suffer from intestinal worms and stomach ulcers. A tendency to partial amnesia is found in ageing swidden farmers.

People of the Region

The people inhabiting the selected region belong to opposed stocks, Tibeto-Burman speaking Mongoloids on the hills and Indo-Aryan speaking Bengalis on the plains. For several centuries, the latter cultivated with the plough, their mode of economy favouring extensive agricultural operations on lowlands, permanent settlement and trade, and steady revenue to sustain a centralised polity. On the contrary, the hill groups subsisted on swidden farming, in which mode returns became constrained when the population exceeded the carrying capacity of the environment. As already mentioned, the Tibeto-Burman stock can be divided into valley-dwellers and highlanders, the former having originally occupied the river valleys while the latter lived apart from them in the interior spaces of the hills. This highlander and valley-dweller distinction is drawn on Lewin (1869: 28) who in classifying the tribes of the Chittagong Hills Tracts used the generic Mranma term 'Toungtha' or the "Children of the hills" as opposed to 'Khyoungtha' or the "Children of the river."

There are similarities in the material cultures and the economic strategies of the two hill type peoples but there also some telling disparities between them. Proximity to Bengal allowed the valley-dwellers (Tippera, Chakma and Marma) to enter into politically beneficial arrangements with the rulers of the plains, initially the Mughals and subsequently the British, which led to restructuring their traditional tribal organisations after the centralised polities of the plains. The native *Rajas* or Chiefs betook upon themselves the vital function of privileged tax-collectors and paid annual tribute to the plains' rulers and enjoyed in return territorial powers. Most highland societies have, on the contrary, lived not too long ago in village-based communities, as either band-type egalitarians or cohesive tribes under hereditary Chiefs. Some like the Halam who came under Tippera domination paid yearly revenue. Families of the valley-dwelling tribes paid regular taxes to the Circle Chiefs or their native *Rajas* through the heads of kinship groups initially and through the nominated headmen in later times. A highland family was not required to pay tax to the Chief but he was offered a yearly bottle of rice-beer and a hind leg of a hunted animal in acknowledgement of his right to everything in his village. Besides, most highland tribes recognised no centralised authority above their own tribal Chiefs. But around the mid-19th century, some eastern tribes began making murderous forays into the territories of the valley-dwelling Chiefs and *Rajas*, compelling the British to send punitive expeditions against them. By the close of the 19th century, all highland Chiefs were subjugated and their chiefdoms annexed to the British territory.

Demographically, the highland tribes of Tripura and the Hill Tracts comprise small, marginalised communities, living mostly in far-flung villages and hamlets with little access to the basic amenities of health and education. In Mizoram, the Lushai is the largest ethnic entity within the Mizo group of tribes which returned a total of 646,117 individuals (about 77% of the total population) in 2001. Their population in CHT is around a thousand souls (against a return of 662 in 1991). In Tripura, Lushai is clustered with Darlong, Betu, Puitu, Tirthu, Saimar, etc. under 'Any Kuki Tribe' with a population of 11,674 in 2001. The total population of the Halams, presently a composite of more than a dozen tribes of the Old Kuki, is 47,245 souls or 4.8% of the tribal population of Tripura in 2001, while the combined population of the Khyang and the Khumi tribes of the Hill Tracts is estimated around only 6,000. In the 1991 Census of Bangladesh, there were 1,241 Khumis and 1,980 Khyangs in CHT. The total for Pangkhua against the same year in CHT was 3,227 while the Bawm numbered 6,431. In the same census, a higher figure (22,167) is given for the Mru but the tribe is economically backward and educationally deprived. The Bru or Riang of Tripura (with a larger population of 165,103 in 2001) gets some economic support from the Government of India following their inclusion within the Primitive Group category.

Among the valley groups, the most numerous are the Tippera with 543,848 individuals living in Tripura and an estimated one hundred thousand in CHT in 2001. The total number of Chakmas is around 400,000 (out of which only 64,293 live in Tripura) excluding 71,283 souls now living in Mizoram. As far as the Marma is concerned, their estimated number in CHT and Tripura is not more than 200,000, the precise figure for Tripura being 30,385 in 2001. In the Bangladesh Census of 1991, there were 239,417 Chakmas, 142,342 Marmas and 61,174 Tipperas in CHT. The valley-dwellers are dominant not only in numeric terms within the tribal populations of the Tripura and the Hill Tracts but they also play an active role in policy-making, political power-sharing and contentious competition with the hegemonic Bengali (who constitute almost 68% of the total population of Tripura and about 50% of the CHT total) and, most significantly, in securing the benefits of reservations meant for the overall uplift of all tribal and backward communities. In their creed, the valley-dwelling tribes profess a mainstream Indian religion; the Tipperas are still predominantly Hindus while the Chakma and the Marma follow Buddhism. Most Kuki-Chin tribes are now Christians though some like the Mru and the Khumi continue to be largely Animists. In very recent times, an indigenous Mru religion called Krama has found partial favour with the tribe. The Khyangs are in the main Buddhists, but a section of their people embraced Christianity in the early part of the 20th century. As for the Bru and the Halam, they were

Hindus up to the mid-20th century but their pecuniary circumstances compelled many families of these tribes to convert to Christianity during the last fifty years. A current passion for Judaism is found among a section of the already Christianised Kuki-Chins.

Previous Studies and Present Concerns

At the outset, it must be frankly admitted that there is scantiness of literature on the small highland communities of Tripura and the Chittagong Hill Tracts. An early seamless narrative on the dwellers of the Chittagong Hill Tracts by Lewin (1869) is a first-hand document on the hill tribes, mainly the valley-dwellers with some observations on the highland Mru, Khyang, Khumi, Bawm and Pangkhua tribes. No considerable note of the highlanders of CHT was taken before German anthropologists (Speilmann, Brauns and Löffler) carried out some extensive work especially on the Mru and the Bawm in the 1950s and 1960s. However, Lewin's account on the Lushai, the Thangluah clan in particular, is vivid and insightful. In Hutchinson's (1909) book, the ethnographic sections are partly derived from Lewin (*Ibid.*) and partly from his personal experiences, while an older work by Buchanan (1798) has interesting observations on the social life of the hill tribes and their relations with each other. Phayre's (1841) paper on the tribes of North Arakan is brief but informative; it also contains an early note on the emergence of the Bawm's ethnic system.

Perhaps, the most inspiring work on the Lushai and other tribes of Mizoram is Shakespear's (1912) account of the Kuki-Lushai clans, which besides furnishing detailed observations on highland customs and manners, accounts vividly for the absorption of different Kuki-Chin tribes and clans by the Lushai. McCall (1949) takes a humanistic approach in analysing the transitional aspects of the Lushai society, as also in detailing the consequences of their exposure to other cultures. Lehmann (1963) adopts the techniques of Leech (1954) to illustrate that the existing social structures of the Chins are the consequences of their long-standing exposure to the neighbouring societies. Carey and Tuck (1896) furnish valuable information on the complex ethnic situation in the Chin Hills. In the 1960s, Bernot took some notes on the highland tribes but his interests were chiefly centred on the Marma and the Sak. Some preliminary observations were also made on the Khyang. An excellent ethnographic study on the Mru was done by Brauns and Loffler (1990); it illustrates in telling details the diverse aspects of the Mru's material culture, as well as their kinship structures and feasts of merit. Spielmann's (1968) view of the social structure of the Bawm is idealised but the work is an indispensable document for socio-anthropologists working in the region. Changes in the socio-political structures of the highland and the valley-dwelling tribes in the colonial and post-colonial situation in the Hill Tracts are pertinently analysed by Mey (1984) and the work will continue to inspire future researchers, particularly political anthropologists interested in the Hill Tracts.

On the highland tribes of Tripura a brief but effective account is furnished by Rawlins (1792). For the history of Tripura, the chief secondary sources consulted are the *Rajmâlâ* or the 'Royal Chronicle of the Tippera Kings,' Administrative Reports of the late 19th century and the *Tripura State Gazetteer* of 1975. Besides, some ethnographic information is available in the *Census of Tripura* 1931 and in tribe-specific accounts of later times. As the bibliographic material at the end of the present work shows, there are some works on the Bru and the Kuki tribes of Tripura, furnishing partial pictures of the social organisations and the life-cycle ceremonies of those tribes. However, traditions of origin and migration, as also several social and cultural aspects of highland life remain ineffectually explored. Frankly, there remains a lot to be done if any researcher is keen on appreciating the kaleidoscopic components of the highland cultures found in the region. The present author does not claim to have a pristine understanding of the highland tribal life of Tripura and the Hill Tracts but an in-progress ethno-linguistic field study on the Halams has provided opportunity for acquaintance with this group as also with other tribes allied to them, besides the Bru (Riang), Uchai, Murasing and disintegrated clans of the Central Chins, many of whom are now officially designated as 'Kuki.' Some understanding of Khyang life, both past and present, is humbly claimed after extensive fieldwork in the Hill Tracts. But frankly, as far as the Khumi and the Pangkhua are concerned, the unexplored vast lies beyond familiar domains. In a year or two, the book on the Khyang will be published. In the meantime, it is hoped that there will come another opportunity to go to the Hill Tracts and interact extensively with the Khumi as well as the Pangkhua.

In course of this study, sufficient time in several phases was spent interacting with the highland tribes. The method of unstructured, participant observation with direct and consented interaction was adopted in collecting field notes from suitable informants and verifying those notes with other informants from the same community living in the same village or in different villages. Notes were also taken of cases wherein different versions of a single tradition existed. To gain access to a selected research setting, permission of village gate-keepers was sought. Also, the rights-based approach as envisaged by the Social Research Association of Great Britain was adopted and respect for informants providing information ensured. At no point were informants compelled to provide any information they were unwilling to provide. Most importantly, to ensure commitment and motivation of informants, they were familiarised with the research background, as well as with the significance of the study. As already stated, information obtained from a particular informant was not automatically presumed as correct; it was subsequently verified with other informants. The last part of the technique helped make possible stronger generalisations as well as ensure checks on reliability and validity. Extant information on historical and cultural aspects of the tribes as found in secondary data was rechecked through pertinent inquiries and notes taken accordingly. In the process, new information was gathered. Emphasis was also given on folk traditions, tales of dispersion and notices on the customs of particular tribes as also on the things that the neighbouring tribes said of those who were being investigated. Gatekeepers were responsive and no hurdle was encountered in gaining access to potential informants.

As stated at the outset, this work attempts to furnish a reliable account on the highland societies of Tripura and the Chittagong Hill Tracts. Ethnic subdivisions in terms of tribal groupings and clusters, linguistic affiliations, clan structures and functions, as well as traditions of origin, causes of ethnogenesis, etc. are analysed in an early chapter. Earlier writers had accounted for the origin and migration of the Kuki-Chin tribes mainly in fragments; in the present work, the origin and the probable route, time and causes of Kuki-Chin dispersion and their arrival at the places of present settlement are proposed on the basis of extant traditions, as well as available historical accounts. Aspects of highland life and dwelling, their attitudes to sex and gender are examined against socio-economic developments in time and space. A separate chapter on head-hunting is incorporated for better understating of a most significant aspect of the tribal past of communities locked in at internecine feuds. The concluding chapter accounts for social changes or transitions in the highland societies of the region.

Credits for Ethnographic Information

Foremost, I owe a debt of gratitude to my family and friends without whose moral support this book would not have been possible. For valuable criticisms and timely suggestions, I am grateful to Rev. Tamborlian Halam, Nirphunjoy Halam (Bagbasa, North Tripura), Laxmidhan Murasing (Patichhari, South Tripura), Thoysafrue Khyang

(Chandraghona, Chittagong), Kaingwai Mru (Chini para, Bandarban) and Basa Khyang (Gunguru Para, Bandarban).

Many of them were my hosts. To Debendra Molsom (Gantachhara, Ambassa), I remain particularly indebted for providing much valued information and for helping to make a much required network of contacts in the Longtrai Range. My old friend, Nirmal Chakma, helped me access the Bru informants in South Tripura.

I would most sincerely acknowledge my thanks to individuals who helped collect information –Zohmingliana Rokhum (Hawaibari, Teliamura), Amrit Kuki, Chintamanik Kuki (Hawaibari, Teliamura), Nathan Bawm (Rangamati), L. Rama Halam (Zoitang, Dharmanagar) Birendra Halam (Dharmanagar, North Tripura), Angthui Khyang, Aungsau Mongchaw Khyang (Chandraghona), Hlabai Khyang (Dhupchhari, Chandanais), Gideon Molsom, Ramkumar Molsom, Baigo Molsom (Arundhatinagar, Agartala), Rev. Lalrema Darlong, Puranjoy Reang (Arundhatinagar), Parendra Reang (Adipur, South Tripura), Rajendra Reang (Devipur, South Tripura), Bhiksu Aksayananda (Benuban Buddha Bihar, Agartala), Upendra Rupini (Bhrigudas, Jirania), Senacharan Rupini (Rumber Para, Hawaibari), Rajnarayan Rupini (Sanlang Para, Hawaibari), Indramanik Koloi (Brahmachara, Teliamura).

I am grateful to the library staff, National Library (Kolkata), Asiatic Society (Kolkata), Chittagong University Library (Chittagong), and the Tribal Research Institute (Agartala). Acknowledgement is also due to the Curator-in-charge, Tripura State Government Museum, and I am most happy to thank Pritiranjan Tanchongya (Bangalkhali), Dinanath Tanchongya (Rajasthali, CHT), Angmak Prue (Hta-Htae-Kaung, Kyauktaw) and S.T. Somokanta Singh (Imphal, Manipur) who helped me during fieldwork in CHT, Arakan and Manipur.

2

The Highland Tribes

The highland tribes of Tripura and CHT belong to the Tibeto-Burman branch of the Mongoloid stock. As we shall see later in the reconstruction of the migration of the Kuki-Chin tribes, during the Spring and the Autumn Periods (c. 770–476 BC) of Zhou China, their ancestors lived in the upper reaches of the Hwang-Ho. From there, they came down to South-western China, thence moved to north Burma, into the area of the present Kachin State. Later, with Kachinic incursions into that area about the middle of the first millennium AD, they followed the course of the Chindwin to reach the Chin Hills, from where some moved southwards into Arakan while some others crossed over to Mizoram. The term 'Kuki-Chin' as assigned to most of these tribes distinguishes them from the other Tibeto-Burmans of the Assam-Burma branch, *viz.*, Bara, Naga, Kachin-Lolo and Mranma. Unequivocally, they believe that they belong to a primordial race that sprang from the bowels of the earth once upon a time. As for the Mru, their present-day language shows affinities with Burmic, Baric, Naga and Kuki-Chin while the Bru (Riang), whose language is now a dialectical variant of Kokborok (the Tippera language), differs from the Tippera in most other aspects.

Old Kukis

Commonly, the Kuki-Chins tribes are classified into four broad linguistic divisions: Northern Chin, Central Chin, Old Kuki and Southern Chin (Grierson 1904: 2). The

Northern Chins (Thado, Sokte, Siyin, Ralte, etc.) are not found in Tripura and the Hill Tracts, except for disintegrated sections of Ralte that merged with some of the Halam tribes sometime in the 19th century. I shall refer to the Southern Chins later in this chapter. As for the term 'Old Kuki,' it designates the early tribes that left the Chin Hills and entered Mizoram but were driven out of that country by the Ralte, the Thado and their allied tribes, who, in their turn, had their own communities dispersed when the Lushai arrived. However, their own traditions, as we shall note, associate them with the Central Chins (Tashon or Shuntla, Zahau, Lente, Khaulsim, Lushai, etc.). Grierson (*Ibid.*) concedes that the term 'Old Kuki' is retained 'for want of a better word to denote a language which we know in many dialects, such as Rangkhol, Bete, Aimol, Hallam and others.' Perhaps, with reference to their dispersal from the Chin Hills or their arrival in Mizoram, one may as well refer to them as Early Chins.

The appellation 'Kuki' was allegedly coined by plainsmen to refer to several but allied Tibeto-Burman highlanders living precariously on the eastern frontiers of Bengal. Ethnically, they are allied to the Chins of the Chin Hills and the Lushai of Mizoram. A century ago, the term 'Kuki' was not used by these people (Soppitt 1893: 2). But today, it is ethnically most relevant for the Kuki National Assembly, an organisation that operates from the hills of Manipur and endorses to resource competition aimed at securing the overall uplift of the Kuki peoples of Northeast India. For the decimated population of Betu, Puitu and Tirthu of West and South Tripura, the term 'Kuki' is not just surname but a designation inseparable from their culture and distinct ethnos. In Tripura, the Kuki-Chin tribes and clans not included under the 'Halam' group are officially 'Kukis'; in the decennial census reports of the state, even the Lushai is included under 'Kuki Tribes.'

The ethnonym 'Halam' covers several allied tribes of the Old Kuki that came under Tippera domination. Of these, the more cohesive tribes are also referred to as '*Alian*' while the smaller or disintegrating units constitute the '*Asin*.' Officially, the number of Halam tribes varies. The group claims that originally, twelve tribes composed the *Baro Halam* 'Twelve Halams' but again their names are not very convincingly recalled. In the Census of 1931, eighteen tribes are mentioned – Koloi, Kulu or Khulang, Korbong, Kaipeng, Koireng, Chorai, Chaimal [Saimar], Dab [Dap], Thangachep, Sakachep, Nabin, Bongshel [Bongcher], Marchum [Molsom], Murchakhang or Murasing, Hrangkhawl, Rupini, Langgai [Langkhai] and Langlu [Ranglong]. Yet, in a footnote, the Saimar is identified as Kuki while the Murasing is described as Nowatiya (Debbarma 1934: 81). An older account, the *Krishnamala*, identifies the following Kuki tribes as the subjects of the Tippera *Raja* – Sakachep, Khamachep [Thangachep], Chorai, Rangrung [Ranglong], Rangkhol, Saibem, Chaite [Chothe?], Chaimar [Saimar], Bong, Langgai, Rupini, Elpui and Kung [Kom or Kawm]. Early findings of an ethno-linguistic study on the Old Kuki, which I am still working on, point to the twelve tribes – Molsom, Kaipeng, Hrangkhawl, Koloi, Korbong, Bongcher, Langkhai, Mawrsephang, Chorei, Rupini, Ranglong and Dap – as constituting the original Halam group. Soppitt (*Ibid.*: 4) was of the view that Ranglong and Sakachep were off-shoots of Hrangkhawl: 'The Langrong [Ranglong] are the Kukis inhabiting the Tippera Hills and are identical with the Rangkhols. The Sakajaibs [Sakacheps] inhabit the North Cachar Hills.' As far I am convinced, the Ranglong is a distinct tribe and the cultural traits they share with the Hrangkhawl are common to most Old Kuki tribes. Within the Ranglong tribe, one finds the Achep clan that in former times performed the role of *kanta* ('the junior in ceremony'), assisting the chief priest of the tribe from the Sanghuipu clan. The Acheps got divided into the *Sakachep* and the *Thangachep*. Ethnic divisions often blur in time and dispersed groups intermix with other communities to imbibe new cultural traits. In the North Cachar Hills, many Ranglongs affiliate themselves with the Khelma Kuki, and not many years ago, if one trusted native assertions, the number of Acheps exceeded the total of the other clans of Ranglong living there.

The term 'Halam' is not Kuki-Chin but Baric in origin, *ha* meaning 'earth' and *lam* 'path.' Their own name for themselves is *Hriam* (pronounced '*Riam*') or more specifically *Mi-Riam* or *Riam-mi*. Here *mi* denotes 'man' while *riam* seems cognate with Lushai *ram* meaning 'land' or 'country.' When compounded into a single term, *Mi-Riam* is the native equivalent of 'highlander.' Tipperas who gave them the name Halam also speak of them as the original dwellers of the hill kingdom. In 1873, the British fixed the Longai river between the Jampui and the Haichek ranges as the eastern boundary of Hill Tripura; a century before that, or prior to the arrival of the Lushai, it extended beyond the Tlawng (Dhaleswari river) up to the Tuivai (Tipai) on the Manipur border and compassed a great part of the Lushai country. The Halams, on their part, claim to have known their subjugator long before they came to present Tripura. One Ranglong tradition narrates that in former times, when the Hriams lived in the Tuivai country, they had a king (*Hriam-reng*, 'the Hriam *raja*') who one day developed infatuation for his own daughter. Soon people came to know of it; so the Hriam *raja*, in utter humiliation, jumped into the river. But as he fell, he was miraculously changed to a rock. The place acquired the name Tamlung, which literally means 'the Jumping Rock'; it lies south of Senbaum. His crown slipped and fell into the Tuivai and as it was being carried downstream, a Tippera chieftain (*Vai-reng-te*, 'the small *raja* of the Vais') picked it up and put it on his head. The Hriams, having no king of their own at that time, made the Vai (Tippera) their ruler and helped him build *Reng-pui-ram* or 'the land of the big king,' the Kuki-Chin name of Tripura (Debnath 2008b: 30).

Each tribe within the Halam group has several clans (*panchi*) that are neither purely exogamous nor strictly endogamous; among them, kin group endogamy is allowed after the third descending generation from a point of reckoning. Some clans are further subdivided into lineages. The Mapu clan of Molsom recognises three lineages – Mapu Sen ('Red Mapu'), Mapu Vom ('Black Mapu') and Daurai Mapu. Similarly, the Tara clan of the Ranglong contains the Chieru Tara, the Polpa Tara and the Khol Tara lineages.

A remarkable feature of the Halam traditional economy was the recognition of distinct, clan-based roles. The Hrangkhawl tribe has thirteen clans, of which eight clans – Saitawl, Rwipu, Vaplom, Chawnbak, Khawngpol, Dorja, Laikai and Lawkatangya – performed core village-functions. Saitawl is literally 'the owner of rice,' and in the ideal Hrangkhawl village, members of this clan were in charge of the common granary, and they also controlled the ration of rice in some form. The allocation of the cotton crop and, later on, the collection of cotton from families for payment of revenue were done by the Chawnbaks. In the past, the village shifted periodically, on the exhaustion of available *jum* plots, and a chief task of the Rwipu clan was to find new sites for settlement, even seek out fresh plots for swiddening. The Khawngpol and the Dorja acted as village 'drum-carriers' and 'drummers' respectively while the Laikai performed the duty of the herald. During social ceremonies, the Vaploms arranged hospitable feasts with gayal meat and rice-beer. The Lawkatangyas rendered clientele services to their Saitawl and Rwipu masters. Of the other five clans of the Hrangkhawl, the early Chiefs of the Malalkhak enjoyed all privileges, but one day a certain Chief turned degenerate and the whole clan earned a bad name for his action. The Drawmkha, the Dabder, the Khawram-rawsang and the Sairang lived mostly as village layabouts.

Rupinis too allotted useful functions to the apical ancestors of different clans. The Kazari performed a role identical with that of the Hrangkhawl Rwipu while the Marsawdengsa harvested chilli and the Sutar controlled distribution of the essential commodities of everyday use. The Tior excelled as judgs, the Pharute as village guard, the

Phungchao as messenger, and so on. Another tribe, the Koloi allows specialised activities like raft-making and bamboo transportation to its Wakbur clan and the production of *jum* vegetables to the Bukang clan but the other clans are now identified either according to their physical types or in terms of likely connections to other ethnic stocks. Interestingly, both Koloi and Rupini are Kokborok-speaking tribes but many things suggest connections with the Old Kuki.

Some relic of the old clan-based division of labour is found in the Molsom too. The members of its Mapu clan 'went ahead of the others to select village sites and plots for swidden cultivation'; they performed a role was similar to that of the Hrangkhawl Rwipu. However, the other clan-names – Leingman, Sungphun, Nokham, Nampawr, Lourak, Singar Lungthung, and Uisa pertain to physical attributes or behavioural idiosyncrasies of their apical ancestors. With the Singar clan, one may hypothesise some connection with non-human object (*singar* is the 'lynx cat') but no ritual for multiplication or preservation of totem species is now recalled. The probable plant emblem in the name Mawrsephang is strengthened by the tribe's claim to have originated once upon a time from a very hot species of chilli that grows plentifully in Manipur and in the neighbouring Cachar Hills. In Halam, *mawrsaw* means 'chilli' while the specific variety referred to by the Mawrsephang is probably the one that Meitheis call *o-mawrok*. The tribe today has a small population, roughly estimated to less than 250 souls; their dominant neighbour, the Molsom tribe, attributes the Mawrsephang's reduced number to a violent strain in their character, which in former times led to frequent clashes among the clans and disintegrated the tribe. At present, they recall only three clans – Achersa, Derbarkha and Raisawnguawk. Sometime in the past, a section of this tribe assimilated into the Ranglong to eventually become the *Mawrsephang panchi*; some families which merged with the Rupini have their descendents in the *Marsawdengsa panji*.

Small and decimated groups like Korbong and Bongcher have very few clans. The Bongcher clans are – Bongpui, Vatok, Hakmung, Chorai, Irying and Ronte. Of these, the Hakmung clan has only two families that now live in the Hawaibari area of Teliamura, isolated from the tribe that has small hamlets in the Longtrai Hills and the upper reaches of the Gomati. The Bongpui clan which functioned as selector of new village sites (Sailo 1992: 11) could be one of the original clans of the tribe while most of the other clans merged with the Bongpui in the late 18th or the early 19th century following their dispersion from the Lushai Hills. A large section of the Ralte (a Northern Chin tribe) underwent subjugation under the Lushai while small groups merged with the early tribes as the Ronte clan. Some migrated north and later on merged with the Hmars, some others went west and assimilated into the Darlong, and still others took a south-easterly route with the Bongpui to reach Amarpur. Sometime in the mid-19th century, some Ronte families joined the Molsom who at that time lived around the Dumbur Falls. My Korbong informants told me that once their village was raided by the Khosak (Lushai) and they were ruthlessly massacred. Only two members of one family, a brother and a sister survived and from them descended the two *adeks* ('branches') – Korbong or the brother's *adek* and Bongcher or the sister's *adek*. The Bongchers could not confirm this tale but from what we have known about them, some clans of the Bongcher suffered at the hands of the early Lushai clans that were pushed westwards by the later and the more powerful Sailos. A Rupini tale about the Korbong says that in former times, they were skilled practitioners of witchcraft but were so much addicted to drinking that their skill failed when a *Sikam chauba* (Kuki raid) occurred. Many were killed and most corpses that lay scattered in the village had no heads; some Korbongs escaped by entering a Rupini village strongly pallisaded on a hilltop. Interestingly, the Korbong tribe has now three clans, *viz.*, Kazari, Sutar and Phungchao that are also found among the Rupini *panjis*.

The Halams, with the exception of Rupini and Koloi, recall a rural community in Arsien Khuasak and a sad *rawnrui* or break in their connection with the old community. *Arsien Khuasak* becomes *Arsiem Khuapui* in the Hrangkhawl dialect. Literally, *arsi* is 'star' and *em* 'the sea' while *khuapui* refers to a large settlement; whence, a place where people were as numerous as stars in the sky. The Molsom tradition recalls that nine-times-twenty-and-nine types of Hriams lived in Arsien Khuasak, which was close by the *Twi-bum* river (the Chindwin?). About its extent, the same lore metaphorically states that if one walked from one end of the village carrying a sizeable homespun ('*pawnpui*'), sopping wet, he found it bone-dry by the time he reached the other end. One day, it so happened that *Rulrengnu*, a huge snake, entered the village and began devouring children every day. The people were at a loss, knowing not what to do, but then the Kamchikao's own daughter went missing, and a thorough search was conducted to get the culprit. At last the god Sangrak learnt about it and in order to punish *Rulrengnu*, he took the form of a giant snake. In their folly, the villagers cut the god into pieces and distributed his meat to the villagers. A widow who lived in the outskirts of the village was given the head of the snake, which, shortly before dawn, spoke in a human voice and told her to leave Arisien Khusasak before sunrise, for a flood would destroy the village. The widow conveyed the warning to the village and as the people prepared to leave, the rains came down. Soon, the Twi-bum swelled and water started entering the village. People scrambled up a ridge from where they threw bark ropes to the other side of the river and made a bridge. After a section had crossed to the other side, the bridge collapsed and many were left stranded; it is not known what became of them.

Central Chins

In the northern hills of Tripura, on the Jampui range, lives a small population of Lushai or Duhlien; their major concentration is, however, in the neighbouring state of Mizoram. Some Lushais also live in the Hill Tracts. The Bawm and the Pangkhua tribes are concentrated in the Hill Tracts with a couple of villages of recent times in the southern parts of Mizoram.

Pangkhuas have seventeen clans – Seval, Leihang, Seizang, Laibowr, Laiswa, Chawngnam, Leisate, Rama, Simla, Palow, Laitelyang, Danzang, Bongkhuai, Khualring, Sathang, Dawn and Rwipachei. Several of these clans are sections of older tribes that lived between the Tashon and the Zahau settlements in the Chin Hills. Sometime in the late 18th century, they moved southwest and crossing the Chimtuipui river (part of the Koladan in South Mizoram) entered the Hill Tracts. Around the same time, a section of Zahau and Sunthla too moved to the upper reaches of the Bawinu (Chimtuipui) river and got involved in conflicts with the Mru and the Khumi. The tribal group known as Bawm uses the affix *-zo* in the same ethnic sense, as *Sho* or *Cho* is added to some Chin appellations. In British accounts, they are referred to as *Banjogi* with *ban* meaning 'a forest' and *jogi* 'a wanderer' (Hutchinson 1906: 159), which is an Aryanised rending of *Bawm-zo*. In 1798, Buchanan was informed of an 'independent tribe, named Bonjoogy' by a 'Mussulman of ... [Company's Hut in Chittagong], who pretended to be well acquainted with the Country to the east' (van Schendel 1992: 27-8). Phayre (1841: 707) was told by a *Hleng-tchyo* [Hlawnceu] *toung-meng* that several generations ago, 'a portion of his clan coming from the N.E. subdued the *Lung-khes* [Lungkhuas] and *Boung-jwes*.' The Bawm imbibed several societal traits of their Lai-zo (Shendu) masters and evolved for themselves a rigidly stratified social-system with two distinct classes, the Sunthla and the Panghawi, each comprising a number of clans that used to be strictly exogamous.

Sunthla : Aineh, Bawitlung, Cheulai (Ceulai), Cheurek (Ceurek – Hlawnceu), Cinzah, Dawitlung, Hauheng, Khenglawt, Lawnsing

(HLawnching), Hlawnceu (Lawnceu), Laitak (Leitak), Lalnam, Laikeng, Leihang, Maram, Milai, Rengbe, Rualleng, Runkual, Sando (Chando), Siarlawn, Tenu, Thangtu, Thilum, Thluathang, Tongir, Vandir, Zahau and Zathang.

Panghawi : Amlai, Buiting, Charang (Carang), Demrawng, Khualring (Khualhring), Kongtaw, Komlau, Lengtawng, Milu, Mitaw, Nakaw, Ichia, Palang, Pawngkeng, Rakha, Repeche, Rupichai (Ripichei), Sailuk, Sakhong (Sakhawng), Satek, Sangla, Samthang, Sangthing, Shalu, Siahro, Tipileng, Talaksa, Thangming and Thangthing.

The Sunthla clans evolved through an ethnic fusion of the Hlawnceu with the vanquished Lungkhua, while several clans that the Lungkhua had subjugated earlier became the Panghawi group within the newly constructed Bawm society. Small groups of Mru and Khumi also assimilated into the Panghawi clans. Before their conversion to Christianity in the early 20th century, the Shuntlas avoided all marital alliances with the Panghawis.

Like all Chin groups, the Bawm and the Pangkhua believe that their ancestors came out of a stone covered hole or cave among the rocks. The Bawm tale is retold by Lewin (1869: 95) in these terms: 'Formerly our ancestors came out of a cave in the earth, and we had one great Chief, named Tlandrok-pah. He it was who first domesticated the guyal; he was so powerful that he married God's daughter.... The cave whence they came out is in the Lhoosai country close to Vanhuilen's village, of the Burdaiya tribe; it can be seen to this day but no one can enter. If one listens outside, the deep notes of the gong and the sound of men's voices can still be heard.' My Bawm informants told me that the cave was not in the Lushai country but somewhere in China from where their ancestors originally came. In addition to this tale of the origin of man, the Bawm retains, as does the Old Kuki, the memory of a primeval Chin village but their version has undergone localisation of the type now found among the Khumi.

The Lushai came very late to Mizoram. Around the close of the 18th century, they had began to move out of Tlankna, which lies to the north of Falam, in the Chin Hills, where they had a chief called Thangura (Shakespear 1912: 3). Jealous rivalry with other Chin tribes like Zahau, Fanai, and the eponymous Hualngo and Hualhang (Howlong) over the possession of land for their self-sustaining swidden-economy had forced Lushai migration in about 1780, and as they moved into present Mizoram, they dispersed the earlier Thados (*or* Khongzais), Biates, Hrangkhawls and other Old Kuki tribes from the region. By tradition, several clans, viz., Rokhum, Zadeng, Thangluah, Pallian, Rivung and Sailo, composed the Lushai, and all these clans descended from the apical Chief, Thangura. Shakespear (*Ibid.*) also mentions a seventh clan, named Chengkhual, born of a concubine by the same Chief. For sometime, these clans fought each other in unpredictable alliances. In early 19th century, Lushai or Thangur chiefs of the Zadeng and the Pallian clans combinedly resisted the Hualhangs but when the feud ended, the Zadengs allied with the Sailos and ousted the Pallians. Later, the Zadengs themselves were vanquished by the Sailos. In 1851, Sailo chief Vuta destroyed a Rivung settlement on the west side of the Chengri River, and several families of that clan escaped to safety in Hill Tripura. The most powerful of the Thangluah Chiefs, Rothangpuiya (Ruttonpuiya) secured himself against the Sailo and the Hualhang by befriending the British in 1861.

Different clans of the Lushai followed their independent chiefs. The Rokhum occupied the Sylhet-Tripura frontier, the Zadengs settled in the north around the Tlawng (Dhaleswari) and the Pallians to the northwest of the Zadeng, while the Rivungs and the Thangluahs took a southwestward course to settle in the Tlabung (Demagiri)-Barkal area (Shakespear *Ibid.*: 3-5). The Sailos, who entered the Lushai Hills in 1810 led by one Lallula (McCall 1949: 35f), became undisputed masters of North Lushai Hills by the mid-19th century; they subjugated the non-Sailo chiefs, even extended their control over several older tribes of the region.

In pre-Christian Lushai, the vanquished Raltes did not enjoy equal social footing with the Lushai. The Lushai who assumed primacy of status and wealth, considered the Ralte as outcaste and avoided alliances with them. In their clientele-system, influential Lushais took 'clients' from ethnic groups they had vanquished in war; these clients rendered useful services to their masters. Those social restrictions were abandoned when the Lushai adopted Christianity and undertook extensive missionary campaigns to admit into Christian fellowship all Kuki-Chin tribes in the Lushai Hills, including the subjugated groups.

In the Census of Tripura for 2001, the Lushai is included under 'Kuki,' which group also includes Betu, Puitu, Tirthu and Darlong. The first three are mainly Chin clans that got dispersed with the advent of the Lushai; a section followed the Rokhum into Tripura. In Tripura, the first settlement recalled by the Betu and the Puitu is Halva in the Ampi area (under Amarpur Block of South Tripura), from where they went to live at Havakhua, a village named after Hava Kuki, their Chief. Havakhua is today's Hawaibari in Teliamura Development Block of West Tripura, and the Chin clans living in this area are also referred to as Hava Kuki. Some families of the same clans also live at Dhuptali under Kakraban Development Block of South Tripura while sections of their people who once lived in Tuirong are now assimilated into the Hmar and the Darlong. The Darlong acknowledges ethnic connections with the Hmar of the North Cachar Hills. Interestingly, many clans of the Darlong occur among the Hmar too. Linguistically, they share affinities with the so-called Old Kuki; culturally, they are close to the Central Chins, owing to an early Rivung domination some Old Kuki clans endured while living at Darlawngtlang (now in North Mizoram). One native writer (Darlong 1995: 42f.) traces the pedigree of the Darlong Chiefs to Thangura, the ancestor of Lushai. An early Pallian influence on some clans of the tribe cannot be denied. When all non-Sailo clans were ousted from the Lushai Hills by the Sailos, the Old Kukis of Darlawngtlang too got dispersed; a section migrated northwest with the Pallians into Cachar and Sylhet hills while another accompanied the Rivungs into CHT and thence migrated to Tripura.

The Darlong's ethnic system emerged in the late 18th or early 19th century after small groups of Old Kukis were absorbed into the Lushai clans that came as vanguard of the Sailo; sections of other Chins such as the Ralte merged into them. My Ranglong informants of North Tripura told me that the Darlongs were originally like them but they are now different. On their part, the Darlongs say that before the beginning of chieftainship, seven clans – Chawngkhal, Fenkawi, Chawmnel, Invung, Rawnte, Tlukte and Tualngen – managed their traditional village system (*Ibid.*: 53). The Darlong's newly emerged social system was not as rigidly stratified as that of the Bawm but clan-ranking and marriage restrictions existed among them for some time until Christianity removed those differences in the early 20th century. Within the tribe, the highest ranking clans were those of the Chief ('Lal') whose Rivung and Pallian connection ultimately traced their pedigree backwards to Thangura. The lowest-ranking or *lalchi loi* clans formed of fragmented clans of the Old Kukis provided clientele service to the high-ranking *Lal* clans. Between the *Lal* and the *lalchi loi* were the *nusum parual* clans that gave advisors and assistants to the Darlong hereditary Chiefs.

As for the tale of the origin of man, the Darlongs say that Sinlung or a rock covered cave was the place where their ancestors originally lived. One day, they began to come out of the cave, one after another. When the turn of the Fatlei clan came, they made so much noise that the god of

Sinlung, fearing that the world had grown too populous, sealed the mouth of the cave with a huge rock. But many people were left inside in the cave. Those outside waited for them to come out; for many days, they distinctly heard the voices of people inside the cave and the knoll of the gong (Darlong *Ibid.*: 13). No one knows what became of them.

Southern Chins

The Khyang and the Khumi tribes belong to the Southern Chin, which group includes Chinme, Chinbok, Welang, Shendu, Chinbon, and Taungtha, besides the marginalised communities of Anu, Bwetsi, Twisip Chin, Kyaw, Sabawng, Bwake and Yalang. A small number of Khumi and Khyang live in the Chittagong Hill Tracts. In Tripura, no Southern Chins tribes are found. Early British accounts consistently refer to a tendency in the Khyang to imitate the Mranma (Trant 1828: 261; Spearman 1880b: 262). Phayre (1841: 684) and Hodgson (1853: 15) were of the opinion the Khyang was of the same lineage as the Mranma. One Khyang tradition even makes the Mranma the elder brother of the Khyang. The Mranma view of their nation being formed of a hundred and one races is echoed in the Khyang myth of *Hli-nu* ('mythical earth-born mother') who laid 'one hundred eggs... from which sprung one hundred human beings, the progenitors of the different races of men. She then laid another egg which was beautifully coloured as if by the hand of some skilful artist' (Spearman *Ibid.*:261). The son born of the last egg was the Khyang.

Khyang, of course, is the Burmese pronunciation of *Chin*: the term *Khyan* occurs in old Burmese inscriptions of the 12th-13th century (Luce 1931: 298). But the Khyang of the Chittagong Hill Tracts calls himself *Hiou*, which is a variant of Sho or Asho, the appellations which sections of their people in Myanmar use in the ethnic sense. Several clans ('*shawng*') are recognised by the tribe; specifically, in CHT, I found eleven clans: *Hokchaw*, *Khepchaw*, *Laibreshaw*, *Mawnglamshaw*, *Lithushaw*, *Mawngchaw*, *Nünchaw*, *Pechaw*, *Shamchaw*, *Shechaw*, and *Yaungchaw*.

In the mid-19th century, Khyang settlements in Myanmar extended 'along the Yoma range (which runs nearly N.N.W. and S.S.E.) from about the nineteenth to the twenty-first degree of North latitude' (Hodgson 1853: 15). Another tradition speaks of their early occupation of the region between Ava and Pegu under a powerful ruler until a horde of 'Tarters' invaded the land, deposed their king and killed most chieftains, compelling the survivors to seek refuge in the mountains (Trant *Ibid.*: 263). Clearly, the allusion here is to the Mranma, for the tradition which makes him the elder brother of the Khyang also mentions of a continual repression of the Khyang by the former. It is said that though *Hli-nu* loved her youngest son most, she could only give him the Roma Mountains as inheritance. To this, fowls and domestic animals were added but the Khyang was naïve and the Mranma systematically robbed him of every possession.

Besides the traditions already mentioned, there are at least two tales, or two versions of a single tale that probably alludes to a flood of the Chindwin and the subsequent migration of the Khyang. In the first tale, it is recalled that during a great flood, the king of the land arranged for twelve large vessels but as the Hiou were too numerous, not everyone could be accommodated in the vessel. The Muyu Khyang (the name by which the Khyangs of CHT also refer to themselves) were left behind and having no place to go save the Pondaung Hills, they lived there for sometime. At a later period, they went down to Kyaukpu where they lived before moving into the Hill Tracts. In the second tale, the vessel in which the Hiou were sailing also carried their king and his queen. After travelling for several days, they came to a place where there was yellow sand and dry leaves. The queen mistook a pile of leaves for a sleeping deer and asked the king to bring her the creature. But the king said that it was only a pile of leaves. As the queen would not be corrected, a quarrel ensued and it was agreed that whoever was right would take the vessel away, leaving the other behind. The poor queen lost but as she was pregnant at that time, the king took pity on her and gave her a few Hiou retainers to attend to her needs. In the years to come, those retainers were called the Muyu Khyang, meaning 'those who were abandoned.'

The Khyang first immigrated to the Chittagong Hills in the late 18th century, in the wake of Burman occupation of Arakan (1784) but at that time, they were not numerous enough to be distinguished from Marma, the principal target of Burman oppression. While inhabiting Arakan, a section had intermixed with the Marma, following which the *Laibresha* clan was created. Bohmong Kaung-hla-pru is a familiar name among them but the tribe sadly recalls that when they came to the Hill Tracts there was much fighting among the immigrants for land; in the end, the Khyang was left landless. Lewin (1869: 94) was aware of a small number of Khyangs inhabiting 'the spurs of the great hill range separating the Hill Tracts from Arracan.' Forty years later, Hutchinson (1909: 45) figured out their number in CHT to be 500 and living 'in the most inaccessible places.' In the early 1960s, Khyang settlements existed in the Chemni Mouza between the Sangu and the Karnaphuli (Bernot 1964: 162). Thoysafrue Khyang of Chandraghona told me that the upper region of the Harbung in the Cox's Bazaar District was where Khyangs first settled when they came from Arakan. In the Hill Tracts, the present Khyang population is only 3,500; they live mostly at Chandraghona, Rajasthali and Chandanais; besides, they are also found around Rowangchhari, Ruma, Thanchi and Kukyachhari.

As far as the Khumi is concerned, there are two major divisions among them. The Awa Khumi who, like Mru, is one of the older tribes of the upper Koladan, while the Aphya Khumi (also called *Ahraing Khumi*) came into that area around the late 17th century, having been driven by Shendus out of their older habitat in Saphodaung on the Roma Mountains. The arrival of the Aphya Khumi led to the dispersal of the older settlers, the Awa Khumi and especially the Mru to Mrauk-U, Ponnakyun and Maungdaw (Ba Thin 1931: 249). A section of the Awa Khumis immigrated with the Mru to the Chittagong Hills, settling in the upper reaches of the Sangu and the Matamuri rivers; they have intermarried with the Mru and are now largely absorbed in the latter. Interestingly, the Khyang calls both Mru and Awa Khumi by the same term, *Mra*. The Awa Khumis had frequent clashes with the Aphya Khumis in course of the 19th century; the Mru too recalls bloody feuds with the Aphya Khumi. Some differences exist in the material cultures and the religious practices of the two groups.

The Burmese pronunciation of Khumi is *Khye-mi*, meaning 'dog-race,' and the term contains also an allusion to the latter's way of so wearing the loincloth that a loose end hangs down at the back in the manner of a tail. But when the native calls himself *Khumi*, the term is used in the ethnic sense. *Mi* is Tibeto-Burman for 'man' while *khu* seems cognate with the Kuki-Chin generic affixes *Sho*, *Zo*, *Cho*, *Kho*, etc. Traditionally, the Awa Khumis managed themselves on the lines of democracy; the Aphya Khumis, on the contrary, had a distinct chieftain class, and each faction had its own hereditary *Ahraing* who derived no revenue from the faction village but received from each family a yearly basket of rice and a bottle of rice-beer. On his part, the *Ahraing* gave feasts and organised fortune war parties; in addition to which, he also performed such essential tasks as selecting suitable sites for frequently shifting villages, acquiring provisions for his clansmen in times of crises, etc. Their bitter rivalry with the Shendu continued up to as late as the end of the 19th century. Lewin (1870: 306-7) writes of a Khumi *toungmeng*, Young, who once burnt a Shendu village, and, in retaliation had his own village burnt on two occasions by the Shendu. At the close of the 18th century, they had some villages in the southern parts of the Hill Tracts, in the upper Matamuri valley. Today, there are some Khumi hamlets in the interior parts of Thanchi, Ruma and Rowangchhari. Their present population in CHT is not more than 2000 individuals.

The Southern Chins have little memory of the places they lived before coming to Myanmar. We have seen that the Old Kukis recall a primeval village named Arsien Khuasak where the ancestors of the Chins lived and we have also seen how the village was destroyed. In the Khumi tradition, the locale is shifted from the unremembered past to the familiar neighbourhood of the Voga Kain, a lake that lies to the northeast of Remakri, south of the Rainkhyoung Forest Reserve. In trying to catch a huge snake that everyday devoured their domestic animals, the Khumis managed to cut off only its enormous tail and distribute the snake meat throughout the village. Everyone except for a couple ate the meat. At night, the tailless serpent visited them in a dream and told them to leave their homes before dawn, because a devastative surge would come down on the village. They soon conveyed the news to everyone but none believed them. Sadly, the next morning the serpent's curse came true, and only the couple lived thereafter to see the water of the Voga Kain replace a flourishing Khumi village. In the Bawm tale, a lover is betrayed by his ladylove into entering a snake-hole and getting killed. But before he died, he told an old couple who adored him like their son that he would take a serpent's form to destroy the village wherein the girl who betrayed him lived. The old couple tried to warn the villagers but everyone laughed at them. Shortly after the lover died, a snake emerged out of his body and quickly became so large and ponderous that its weight crushed everything under it, even split the earth into parts. Soon water gushed out through the split and drowned the village, thus creating the Voga Kain.

Other Highland Tribes

The most numerous of this group is the Bru who identify a place called *Maini-tlang* as their early habitat. *Tlang* is Kuki-Chin for 'hill'; the place so named refers to the upper reaches of the Maini river in the Khagrachhari Hills District (CHT). One tradition (Hutchinson 1909: 36) also points to

Riang settlements further south on the hills overlooking the Matamuri. In 1798, Buchanan was told that '[t]he Reang... live near Oodapour [Udaipur], upon the banks of the Gomooty [Gomati] and the Moory [Muhuri] rivers' (van Schendel 1992: 126). More than a dozen clans are recognised by the Bru, and *Riang*, the appellation now officially applied to the whole tribe, is merely one of the clans.

What then is the Bru's ethnicity? Hutchinson (*Ibid.*) believed that they were of Kuki origin while Debbarma (1931: 73) considered them an admixed group of Kuki and Tippera. Probably they came as the vanguard of the Kuki-Chins and, as we shall note in a subsequent chapter, moved westwards to reach Maini-tlang. In dress and personal decoration, they differ much from the Tippera. The clan-name *Riang* looks like a variant of *Hriam* or *Riam*, which subgroups of the Halam apply to themselves in the ethnic sense. Another clan *Molsoi* seems to have some connection with Molsom, a Halam tribe. In the 15th century, the Bru came under Tippera domination and assimilated into them; they even adopted the latter's language. But the Tippera considers them an inferior people. In the Arakan annals, Tipperas are consistently referred to as *Mroung*, which term in the ethnic sense would apply specifically to the Bru and the Uchai than to their subjugator. Later, in course of the 16th century, when the Tipperas penetrated into the southern parts of the Hill Tracts, the Bru moved with them, their hamlets spreading from the Matamuri valley southwards to the borders of Arakan. Hutchinson (*Ibid.*) says that two Riang brothers, Kilay and Manglay, 'were Karbaris or managers on behalf of the Tippera Raja Udaigiri [Uday Manikya (1567-73) ?].' At the close of the 16th century, Arakan king Meng Phalaung made captives of the Mrungs and settled them on the Lemro in Sittwe 'with a view I suppose of cutting off their retreat to their own country; but when *Arakan* became convulsed in consequence of the invasion of the Burmese [in 1784], they gradually commenced leaving the *Lé-myo* [Lemro], and returning through the hills towards their own country. For a time they dwelt on the *Kola-dán*; now none are to be found in any part of Arakan, save on the *Mayú* in its upper course, and only a few stragglers there' (Phayre 1841: 684).

A parallel version of Bru migration might be gleaned in an Uchai tradition, which says that a certain king of Arakan captured their people and settled them in the hills around Maungdaw, where they lived peacefully for a long time under their own kings. Then, one day, some people came from the west and their king sought to befriend the king of Maungdaw and invited him to a dinner. But the latter was served poison with his food, on eating which he dropped dead. In the meantime, a messenger was sent to Maungdaw to ask the people to show their allegiance to the new king, failing which, they were threatened with a punitive expedition against them. When they refused to comply, several hundreds of men, women and children were ruthlessly murdered. Only two brothers, Ringsa and Uchya, managed to escape. But they were apprehensive of a pursuit; so, they divided the survivors in two groups. Ringsa, the elder, reached Tripura earlier than Uchya. The present-day Uchais claim that they are descended from the younger brother, Uchya, while the Riangs originated from the group that went ahead of them.

Ethnically, Uchais are the closest of the Bru, and, like the latter, they too saw an early Tippera domination. In the Chakma tradition of empire expansion by Bijoygiri, the Uchai are referred to as *Hai-chai Tippera*, and an army of this people is said to have accompanied Bijoygiri during the Rowang (Arakan) expedition. The group was led by a Bru commander, Kunjadhan Riang (Debnath 2008b: 63).

The ethnicity of the Mru of Chittagong Hill Tracts has vexed researchers. Hodgson (1853: 17) noted that *Mru* is 'used by the Arakanese as generic term for all the hill tribes of their country.' When Buchanan toured the Chittagong Hills in 1798, he found that in 'their features and accent they [Mru] entirely resemble the Rakain. They are quite naked, except a small bit of cloth used for the sake of decency.... They inhabit the banks of the upper part of the Edgong river, and are subjects of Kaung-la-pru: but have a Ru[a]-sa of their own tribe' (van Schendel 1992: 63-64). Culturally, the Mru shares affinities with the Awa Khumi, and they are also largely intermixed with the latter. Linguistically, Mru has many things in common with Burmese, Bodo, Naga, and Kuki-Chin (Grierson 1904: 380). Shafer (1955: 103) classified Mru language under a distinct *Mruish* section of the Burma branch. Mru did not have any written characters until 1985, when a native, Menlay Mru evolved a writing system with thirty-one graphemes.

About the Mrus' origin almost nothing is known, but they branched off from 'the Tibeto-Burman family at an early date, before the modern groups such as Bodo, Naga, Kuki-Chin, etc. had been developed' (Grierson *Ibid*: 381). One Arakan chronicle associates a Mru named Marayu with the mythical founding of Dhagnyawaddy (Phayre 1844: 33-4); again, in the 10th century AD, a Mru chieftain named Amatyo and his nephew Pyobo are said to have briefly ruled over parts of Arakan (*Ibid.*: 37-8). But these notes occur in contradiction to the Mru's own socio-political organisation that does not indicate to the existence of a centralised authority over the whole group at any time. Nevertheless, it may be said with some certainty that Mrus (spelt *Mro* in Marma) were already in upper Koladan when the first wave of Mranma reached in Arakan in the 11th century AD. Much later, in the 17th century, when they were driven out their habitat by the Aphya Khumi coming down from Saphodaung, a section crossed over to the Chittagong Hill Tracts. In the 18th century, the Mru lived in the Matamuri valley; the majority were across the border in the hilly parts of Saingdin and Ponnakyun Township.

Another group that may be included in this category is the Murasing of South Tripura. They share a common language with the Tippera; ethnically, however, they differ from the group whose language they speak and deserve a distinct standing. There are several tales of origin, one of which tells that once some revenue collectors of the Tippera king went to a village where they found the houses decorated with the horns of the gayal. The village had no name and the people no identity; so the king's men on returning to the court spoke of them as *kuthuyni bawkrawngbai nawk sajawgnairawg*, meaning 'they who decorated their houses with dead horns.' A dead horn in Bengali is *mara-sing*, whence the people who decorated their houses with the horns of dead animals became *Murasing*. Another tale recounts some swidden-farmers once presenting to the Tippera king the horns of a cow or gayal that perished in *jum* fire and earning for themselves the appellation *Murasing*. A third tale associates a certain *raja* of the *Khongdai* clan (Thado-Khongzai?) leaving Mogle (Manipur) in much shame and settling in the eastern hills of Comilla. The time of the above tales does not go beyond the late 18th century. When the Lushai arrived in Mizoram, most tribes of older immigration dispersed and those lacking cohesion disintegrated rapidly. In the melting-pot situation that emerged, new ethnic formations took place following intermixture of different tribes and ethnic stocks. In the Murasing's case, the Bara element is reinforced by their present linguistic affinity with Tippera but they also have appreciable traces of Kuki-Chin. Joking relationship among the different divisions ('*Khil*') of the tribe indicate to ethnic intermixture. In physical type, the *Mawsbang* is heavily built, yellow-skinned and having low, flattish nose with broad tip; he is temperamentally irascible, like chilli, which he is fond of eating. Etymologically, *Mawsbang* is explained as a compound formed of *masha* ('chilli') and *kabang* ('excessive'); the interpretation is identical with that of Mawrsephang, a Halam tribe. In the Census of Tripura for 1931 (Debbarma *Ibid*.: 81), a parallel appellation for Murasing is given as 'Murchakang.' The proper *Murasing Khil* has assimilated into it other clans like *Khongdai* and *Twimukdawk*, the former having a tradition of their ancestors taming the gayal; in physique, they are tall, slim, well-built and brown skinned with a flat nasal bone but high and broad tip. As for the *Dawngraw Khil*, the males are as tall as the *Murasing* proper but have light-brown skin with the bridge of the nose almost level with the forehead. They consider themselves as early dwellers of the Dumbur Falls area in Amarpur Subdivision of South Tripura. Symmetric joking makes the *Totram* the most loquacious of the Murasing *Khils*; the average male is of medium stature with light yellow skin and sharp nose. These neat physical types are no longer conspicuous today, owing to intermixture among the *Khils*; nevertheless, tales of physiological differences still prevail within the tribe.

In the construction of the Murasing ethnic system, the Tippera played a core role, giving the assimilated people a common language and the Vaishanvite cult. As we shall see in the concluding chapter, the socio-administrative head of the Murasing community was the *Rai* but his activities were monitored by the *Misip* who was invariably a Tippera of royal blood.

3

Origin and Dispersion of Kuki-Chins

In *Siji* 116, Sima Qian (Ssu-ma Ch'ien) wrote that in the 2nd-1st century BC, the southwestern part of China was inhabited by the *Xinan-yi* or 'Southwestern barbarians.' Roughly, they lived in the area comprising today's Sichuan, Yunan, Guizhou, and Guangxi. Distinguished from the Man ('Southern barbarian'), the ethnic groups and subgroups of the *Xinan-yi* are known by various names in Chinese records. During the Qin Dynasty (221-206 BC), we hear of the Di Qiang groups, Zhou, Xia, Shu and others; in the Han period (206 BC –220 AD), the prominent groups are Sui, Kunming, Qiongdu, Dian, Zhadu and others. Some of them such as Sui and Kunming were nomads and pastoralists; others like Dian, Yelang and Qiongdu were of the settled type, having centralised polities and powerful local chiefs (Watson 1961: 295; Ping 2006: 540-41). The Di-Qiangs or the Ch'iang tribes were the ancestors of not only the Chins but all Tibeto-Burmans. It has already been indicated earlier that during the Spring and Autumn Period of Eastern Zhou China, corresponding to 770-476 BC, the Di Qiangs were located in the upper waters of the Yellow River (Hwang Ho). At a later period, waves of migration brought them to Guizhou, Yunan, Sichuan (Ping *Ibid.*); by the close of the Christian era, they had peopled today's southwestern China, some had even penetrated into the northern parts of Myanmar.

Early dispersion and Chindwin connection

Why did the Di tribes leave the Yellow River? Perhaps, the political mayhem that came with the collapse of the Eastern Zhou Dynasty (770-476 BC) compelled them to move out. The later Zhou Emperors had made several assaults on the Di Qiang and dislocated some communities but their exodus from the Yellow River occurred in the Warring States Period (475-222 BC). Lehmann (1963: 22) opines that when the Tibeto-Burmans first set out on their long migration, they did not move as distinct social and cultural units. Though the presently existing cultural and linguistic divisions within the Tibeto-Burman family in terms of Bara, Naga, Kachin, Mranma, and Kuki-Chin are consequences of not too old developments, different levels of socio-cultural attainments did exist among the early migrants. The Sui and the Kunming were 'barbarians'; they had neither permanent homes nor centralised polities; but the Dian, the Yelang and the Qiongdu of the *Xinan-yi* were noted even by the Han Chinese for their advanced socio-economy based on farming and stock-rearing.

Of particular interest to Myanmar history is the Qiongdu that in subsequent periods came to be called Kantu and Kadu; they were among the early Tibeto-Burmans to reach Myanmar. Ancient chronicles of Myanmar consistently refer to 'Thet' or 'Thek' (Sak), Pyu and Kanran as the early races of that country. *Sak* or *Asak* was what the Kadus called themselves. Besides the organised Qiongdu, some pastoral or egalitarian groups related to the Sui or the Kunming might as well have entered Myanmar at an early date and passed quietly southwards following the course of the Chindwin River. The Bru (or Riang) and the Mru came as the vanguard of the Kuki-Chins. The former moved west from the Chindwin and crossed Mizoram to reach Maini-tlang or the upper reaches of the Maini in the northern parts of the Hill Tracts; the Mru moved further southwest to settle in the upper Koladan. At least up to the late 14th century, the Bru was probably the only tribe in the hills between the

Maini and the Karnaphuli rivers. The Mru lived in the upper Koladan up to the close of the 17th century, around which time, the Aphya Khumi, coming down from Saphodaung, drove them out.

The ancestors of the Kuki-Chins entered Burma sometime after the Sak and centuries before the Mranma came. As we shall see subsequently, they preceded the Kachin. They might have had some connection with the Sui of Han China or the older Shu of the Qin period but between Shu or Sui and 'Sho,' 'Asho,' or 'Hiou,' the name by which the Khyang knows himself, there is an interregnum period of more than a thousand years, which makes my opinion no more than a conjecture. However, in the course of their long migration, the Tibeto-Burman tribes of Han China got fragmented and restructured into new groups. Probably, the Kuki-Chins did not stem until some of the older groups had migrated to the Chindwin, thousands of miles from Sichuan. Lehmann (*Ibid.*: 22) connects the beginning of the Chin history with the foundation of the Mranma civilisation. It is not easy to asses the precise relation the Mranma had with the Chins. Strategically, friendship with the Chins (Luce 1959: 89) would have given them some advantage over the Sak-Kadu, with whom the Mranma had historical enmity stretching up to as late as the 14th century AD (Debnath 2008b: 50f.). But a Khyang tradition also says that the Khyang people were so systematically oppressed by the Mranma that they had to abandon their old settlements, which extended as far as Ava and seek refuge in the Arakan and the Pegu Romas. The Sak had entered Myanmar through Bhamo and settled between the Chindwin and the Ayeyarwaddy (with Tagaung as their capital); the Mranma took a route between the Nam Hka and the Salween and made Kyauksè their earliest base in the 9th century AD. As far as the Kuki-Chins are concerned, their ancestors took a northerly route, entering Myanmar through the passes around Tasu and, leaving the Kadu to their left, moved westward close to Khamptilong, from where they descended into the Hukong Valley. We shall know more about their migration in connection with Khurpuitabum. For the present it would suffice to say that Kachinic incursions about the middle of the first millennium AD forced them to move southwards into the Chindwin Valley.

The Mranma name for Chin is *Khyan* and the term occurs in old Myanmar inscriptions of the 12th-13th century AD, though Luce (1931: 298) indicates that the word, 'without "tonal" marks, has several senses in Old Burmese, and is not easy to say if one of these is ethnic.' However, the name Chindwin ('*Khyantwan*' or '*Khlantwan*') occurs several times and indicates to the valley through which the river of the same name flows (Luce *Ibid.*). In Phayre (1883: 08), Chindwin is spelt as 'Khyengdweng.' Whether the Chins gave their name to the Chindwin or they got their own name from the valley is less important than the fact that the ethnicity of Chins is inseparably merged with the Chindwin. Around this place, the Chins developed their ethno-cultural and linguistic differences with the other Tibeto-Burman groups – the Mranma on the east and south, the Naga and Kachin on the north and the Bara to their west. It occurred between the 8th and 13th century AD. In the previous chapter, I had referred to a Molsom tradition that recalls a primeval Chin village in Arsien Khuasak with nine-times-twenty-and-nine types of peoples living there. Though present identities and ethnonyms used by Kuki-Chin tribes of Northeast India and the Hill Tracts were constructed long after they had left the Chindwin and with reference to interacting groups and geo-political divisions of later times, they remain affiliated to the tribes of the Chin Hills in terms of preserving pan-Chin elements in language and culture.

When the Khyang migrated to the south, they took with them reconstructions of the Chindwin but in the subsequent centuries developed some distinct traits of their own through extended interaction with the Mranma. The Hriams had their ancestral groups named after the places they settled in the Cachar-Mizoram-Manipur frontier. Some of those groups interacted with the Tippera and became the Halams. Tribes like the Bru (Riang) and the Mru had older connections with the same groups of the Di-Qiang that settled in the Chindwin but they migrated elsewhere long before the 8th century AD, around which time the Chins actually began to shape their distinct culture and language with reference to the site of the Chindwin river and its valley. I have already indicated to a possibility of the term 'Riang' being cognate with 'Hriam.' A distinct Bru culture did not develop until they had interacted over an extensive period first with the Old Kukis and then with the Tippera who subjugated them. In almost identical manner, the Mru culture was constructed through social interaction with other tribes, especially the Awa Khumi.

As for the Lushai, the Pawi and the Lai-zo (Shendu) tribes of Mizoram, they came to the Sub-Continent at a recent date as thoroughbred Chins.

Chinlung and Khurpuitabum traditions of origin

One tradition which binds all Kuki-Chins is that of man emerging once upon a time from the bowels of the earth. The term that most Chin tribes associate with the cave whence their ancestors came out is *Chinlung* (Vomson 1986:3; Sailo 1992: 4; Darlong 1995:13), also pronounced *Chinglung*, *Sinlung*, *Singlun*, *Sirlung*, *Jinlung*, etc. In most traditions, the same cave is covered with a stone. For instance, in the Darlong tale, we are told that when it was the turn of the Fatlei clan to come out, they made so much noise that the god of Chinlung, fearing that too many people had gone out, sealed the mouth of the cave with a rock (Darlong *Ibid.*).

The cave motif is undoubtedly primordial but in the telling, one finds such modifications as are attributable to later times when different Kuki-Chin tribes created their distinct ethnic identities with reference to their immediate levels of social interaction. In the Koireng version (Grierson 1904: 243), the Khongzai tribe and the Kabui Nagas emerged quietly but the Koirengs made so much noise that the god of the cave shut the mouth with a stone, whence not all Koirengs could come out and they were outnumbered by the two groups that preceded them. A Shendu version of the same tale narrated by Parry (1932: 4) makes reference to the Lushai; it says that when Lushai clans began to come out of the cave, only the first man out announced his name and the god of the cave, thinking that there were very few men in the world, gave the Lushai a longer time and they poured out in large numbers. But when the Shendu's turn came, each clan announced its name and their clans being numerous, the god of the cave feared that too many people had gone out of the cave and he promptly sealed the mouth. In the Lushai tale, as recounted by Shakespear (1912: 94), after the Lushai clans had come out, it was the Ralte's turn, and the first two Ralte who emerged began chattering at once, which made Pathien think that there were many men out in the world and he closed the cave with a stone.

Various places between southwest China and Chindwin have been identified as the location of Chinlung, and one Mizo historian (Zawla 1976: 2f.) associated it with the confinement of the Chins within the Great Wall of China and suggested a correlated date (about 225 BC) when the Chins defied the Chinese Emperor Chin Shih Huang and came out of Sinlung. But the hypothesis goes uncorroborated in the face of the fact the Chin national identity did not quite evolve before the 8th century AD. The Halam tradition of *Khurpuitabum* indicates to the Kachin State as the place wherein the Chin ancestors lived after coming down from Sichuan and before migrating south to the Chindwin Valley.

In the Molsom tale, there was a large cave ('*Khurpui*') and many people lived in it. When they first tried to come out, an *Awkpol*, 'dragon-bird' began to devour them. This continued for long; then one day, the *Ulyin* ('the traditional chief') planned a strategy to take his people safely out of the

Khurpui. He selected two *Zhou* warriors, equipped them with spears ('*sei*'), and took up them on his shoulders; then, he put a cock on his head and instructed his dog to lead the way. No sooner did they come close to edge of the hole than the dog ran out, barking loudly. When the monster-bird swooped down on the dog, the cock flew in the opposite direction, crowing and distracting it. In a flash, the two *Zhou* warriors sprinted into the open and nailed the *Awkpol* to the ground with their spears. They would have cut off its head but the bird pleaded for clemency. The *Ulyin* granted the creature its life on the condition that it shall never grow bigger than the size of its fluff (whence, the *Awkpol* was metamorphosed to the crow). Thereafter, the Hriam (pronounced '*Rem*' in Molsom) ancestors, their women and children came out of Khurpui and they went to built Arsien Khuasak on the *Twi-bum* [Chindwin?].

In another version, that of the Ranglong, the details differ; it is stated that the Hriam ancestors came from *Khurpuitabum*. The place is identified somewhere 'in the hills north of Manipur' (Debbarma 1931: 80). Literally, *khur* is 'a hole' and *pui* means 'big' or 'great,' whence *Khur-pui* 'the big hole.' It becomes *Khul-pui* in the Chorei dialect. Several Naga tribes like Anal, Monyon, Monsang and Tarao have traditions of migration through *Khulpu* or 'hole in the earth.' In one Meithei tradition, Poireton and his people travelled through a subterranean passage to reach a village where the entrance was blocked by a stone that no man could move. At last, the great Nongdom Ox ('the gayal') accompanying the party was asked to push aside the stone with its horn. In the Ranglong tale, the holy *Syel* ('gayal') helped to gore the stone that sealed the mouth of *Khurpui*. There were two alternative paths which the Hriams could have chosen as detour but one of those went down to a river whose depth no one knew while the other went through mountains covered with so dense fog that one could barely see an outstretched hand. In the Meithei tale, a tiger waylaid the men whom Poireton led out of the cave. Among the Kom tribe too, a tiger waylaid the people who tried to come out of Khurpui; so, they devised a means to rid themselves of the tiger. Karongpa or the apical Chief of the Karong clan put on a tiger's skin and befriended the tiger; the head of the Saiche clan the took the opportunity to kill the tiger, after which the *Rems* (the Kom pronunciation of 'Hriam') came out of the cave and went to settle at Chung-khuapui. In the Ranglong tradition, the Hriams settled in the village they found at the end of the Khurpui but some time afterwards the *Bak* came and drove them out of that village and then they went to live at Arsien Khuasak (also Arsien Khuapui in Hrangkhawl). Perhaps, Ranglong *Bak* is allegorised in the Molsom tale as *Awkpol*; phonologically, *Awk* would be a dialectical variant of *Bak*, the bilabial stop undergoing yodisation and then elision.

Increased Kachinic movements in the Upper Chindwin valley around the middle of the first millennium AD caused dispersal of the groups that evolved in later times as Kuki-Chin. As for the people identified as *Bak* by the Ranglong, a reference to the same occurs in Leech (1954: 208-09): 'A number of early Chinese works published at various dates between A.D. 350 and A.D. 1000 make references to "the wild and troublesome b'uok tribes" living apparently in the mountains to the west of Yung Ch'ang... This seems to be a population inhabiting the Kachin Hills Area, and though language and culture may have changed, the tribal name has stuck. Modern Maru call Jinghpaw speakers *p'ok;* the Shans of Hkamti Long used to refer to their Kachin serfs as *kha-p'ok* (serf p'ok); Jinghpaw itself might well be written as *ing-p'ok;* modern Chinese refer to the modern Kachins as *p'u man* – the *p'u* being written with the same character as the earlier *b'uok*.' An old Chorei song, 'Kachin ulien sakol raza' (Chorei 2004: 25) recalls early settlement in the Kachin State. Interestingly, in the Kachin language, the familiar term for 'hill' is *bum*. The corresponding term in Kuki-Chin is *tlang* or *tang* after reduction of the initial cluster. Hence, Old Kuki *Khurpuitabum* would generally mean 'a large subterranean passage through the hills'; more specifically, it would indicate to a place in the Kachin State, perhaps not far from the Hukong Valley.

Apparently, the two terms *Sinlung* and *Khurpuitabum* would convey identical sense but close scrutiny shows that they originated under different circumstances and their meanings are different. The cave motif is part of the collective memory of all Kuki-Chins (as also of some Naga tribes) and it could as well be part of a primitive socio-economic stratum prior to the setting up of periodically shifting villages. But for the *Khurpui* group of the Old Kukis, *Khurpuitabum* is a subterranean world from which their ancestors came out while *Chinlung* refers to the Chin Hills area. In the Molsom tradition, *Sirlung* is a place between *Arsien Khuasak* and Rihli-Champhai. After the flood in *Arsien Khuasak*, the Hriams passed through *Sirlung* to arrive at Rihli. Pertinently too, the Halam know the Lushai as *Khosak* who came down from *Chintlang* or *Chintang*, the Chin Hills. 'Chin' is, of course, a collective identity while 'lung' connotes 'stone,' and based on such cognate forms as *Chintlang* and *Sirlung* found in Old Kuki, it seems but logical to postulate that *Chinlung* referred to the Chin Hills but at a later time, its meaning expanded by absorbing the older cave-motif. For the Halams, *Chintlang* and *Khurpuitabum* still continue to be different places.

Later dispersions and ethnic identities

From extant Myanmar inscriptions and references to the Chins (Luce 1959: 79f.), it may be inferred that during the early part of the Pagan period (1044-1287 AD), they were in the Chindwin Valley. In the native traditions of Old Kukis, we saw that after coming out of Khurpuitabum, their ancestors settled at Arsien Khuasak, a primeval Chin village by a big river called Twi-bum. The Mranma may not have had direct confrontation with the Chins but by the close of the 10th century, a section of the Mranma penetrated into the lower Chindwin and in Arakan. Their growing presence must have hindered the continuity of Chin settlement on the Chindwin and they moved westwards. The Khyang says that systematic oppression by the Mranma (identified as the Khyang's 'elder brother') caused their migration into Arakan and Pegu Romas. For sometime, a section of the people had lived in the Pondaung Range.

Mranma movements may have affected an eastward expansion of the Chins but the exodus from the Chindwin into the Kale-Kabow Valley was perhaps caused by natural calamities. The Old Kuki tradition of Arsien Khuasak attributes the destruction of the Hriam's riverside settlement to a deluge. Similar tales of flood prevail among the Betu, Puitu, Tirthu and Rokhum clans of West and South Tripura. The Betu in particular associates their ethnic appellation to the flood that destroyed the ancient settlement of the Mi-Hriams. It is retold in a humorous gesture that when water began to enter the village, their people scrambled up the hill. One man whom the widow had cursed for giving her the head of the serpent slipped over and would have fallen into the river but he survived by clinging on to a pea-plant. *Betu* in their dialect means 'the pea pant,' whence his descendents got the name Betu and the clan is still known by that name. Traditions of flood are also recalled by the Khyang and the Khumi.

In the 13th-14th century, the Shan made inroads into the Chindwin and the Kale-Kabow valley and they were probably responsible for pushing the Chins further westward from Khampat into the Lotha and Pondaung Ranges. And by the time, the city of Kalemyo was built (in 1395) to mark Shan domination of the region, a westward migration of the Chins had already occurred. The Ranglong tale indicates that the Hriam in course of their migration reached a place called Tahan where lived the three Great Chiefs of the Chins – Hmarbwangkhup in the North, Lersi in the South and Luopui in the centre (Debnath 2008: 31). This division as mentioned in their oral tradition corresponds to the present ethnic and linguistic division of Kuki-Chin into Northern,

Central and Southern Chin. It is learnt from the same tradition that looking west from Tahan, one saw the sun going down at Champhai. Before leraving Tahan, Luopui planted a banyan sapling, predicting that one day this will grow so huge that branches from the top will hang down to touch the root; on that day, the living descendents of the three Great Chiefs will unite into a single nation. In the Hmar tradition (Dena 2008: 13-14), the three Great Chiefs who lived in the Kabow Valley were Lersi, Zingthlo and Luopui. The traditions agree in that Luopui planted the banyan tree at Khampat.

The early section of Chins to enter Northeast India were the Old Kukis; the Ranglong believe that they belong to the group that followed Luopui while the Khongzai (Thado) and the Ronte (Ralte) who came after them were in the group that Hmarbwangkhup led. The Khosak (Lushai) too descended from the Loupui group but they stayed back in Chintlang. The early wave recalls having crossed the Tyao and entered Mizoram through Champhai; an old song tells that on their way, the Hriams had seen the water in Rihli. Another old song recalls prosperity in Rihli-Champhai. After crossing Champhai, some followed the north course of the Tuivai to reach Ruongle-vai-shua (Tipaimukh), 'the junction of three rivers' which became their home; others continued to live at Champhai and Tuivai, and still others crossed the Tuivai and came to as far as the Longai. From the Longai, the Molsom and the Kaipeng turned south to reach the upper waters of the Maini river where they found the Bru. In the late 14th or the early 15th century, a section of the Hriams was subjugated by the Tippera and they were called 'Halam.' Many ethnonyms that the Old Kuki tribes use now indicate to the different places they settled after leaving the Chin Hills. The appellation 'Ranglong' is attributed by the tribe to the Tui-ruong while the Langkhai retain memories of their settlement on the Longai river. Another tribe, the Rupini associates its origin to the Tui-rupa or Rupini river on the Tripura-Cachar frontier. The ethnic system of the

Rupini emerged following amalgamation of some Old Kuki clans with a section of the southward migrating Tipperas. In the year 1712, Arjun Das and Ratna Kandali, the two emissaries of the Ahom King Rudra Singha then travelling to Tripura found the Rupinis on the bank of the Rupini river while the Rangrung (Ranglongs) lived not far away.

The Lushai migration started towards the close of the 18th century and the consequence of their arrival has already been discussed in the previous chapter. For the present, it would suffice to say that the Thado and the Ralte tribes of Northern Chin had entered Mizoram before the Lushai and began a process of establishing themselves by expelling the Hrangkhawl and other Old Kuki tribes but their own effort at territorial domination of that country was snapped by the Lushai who quickly drove them out. Wars with the Thado saw the Hrangkhawl divided into two groups, one settling in the Cachar Hills and another migrating to Tripura. In the late 18th and the early 19th century, there was much restructuring within the Kuki-Chin societies of Northeast India, the impact of which on different tribes has already been discussed in detail. The ethnogenesis of Darlong also occurred at the same time. A laudable aspect of the Lushai, more properly Sailo expansion in Mizoram in the 19th century was preparing the ground for a common Mizo fulcrum. Later on, Christianity too fostered the common 'Mizo' fellowship. '*Mi*' is Tibeto-Burman for 'man' while the affix '*zo*' in *Mizo* occurs as a generic variant of *Sho*, *Zo*, *Yo*, *Cho*, *Kho*, etc.; it is used in the ethnic sense. For the Old Kuki, the term *Mi-Riam* indicates to an older Chindwin-Chin Hills descent through the Rihli-Champhai line of Kuki-Chin dispersion.

In the South Lushai Hills, Shendu movements became very conspicuous from the early 19th century, leading eventually to a Lai domination in the South. Earlier, in the late 17th century, they had driven the Aphya Khumi out of Saphodaung; at subsequent time, a section of the Shendu amalgamated with the Lungkhua to evolve the social system of the Bawm of the Chittagong Hill Tracts.

The Khyang was the earliest of the Lersi group of Kuki-Chins to have moved to the south. Some went to live in the Pangoung Range but later on took a south-westerly direction to enter the North Arakan Hill Tracts; others followed the eastern course initially of the Chindwin and then of the Ayeyarwaddy to inhabit the Arakan Romas, spreading southwards to Thindwe (Sandoway) and Hendaza and also penetrating south-eastwards into Pegu. Formerly most Southern Chins inhabited the tract of the country south of the Haka division along both sides of the Rongkhlang Range and extending into the Pokkhu Chin Hills. Small tribes like Chinme, Chinbon and Chinbok are still found living within that tract. They had probably moved out of the Chindwin with the Khyang but remained in the Chin Hills while the latter migrated to the other parts. The old fashioned tattooed faces of Chinbon women could be closely connected to the same circumstances that long ago compelled the Khyang to tattoo the beautiful faces of their women in black. To this must be added the fact that the older Chin appellation *Khyan* is not unfamiliar to them: '... whatever they may be called by their neighbours, all call themselves Khan or Chan (hence "Chin") meaning "human being"' (Rigby 2000: 130).

A section of the Khumi, the Awa Khumi, migrated from the Chin Hills to the upper reaches of the Koldan where they found the Mru and, in course of time, a section of the tribe migrated with the Mru to Chittagong Hill Tracts and got assimilated into them. The remaining sections of the same tribes were driven from the older habitat, as I have already noted, by the Aphya Khumi in the late 17th century. Outside Chittagong, the Mru and the Khumi are found in the hilly parts of Sittwe (erstwhile Akyab); their population is Myanmar is several times higher than it is in the Hill Tracts of Chittagong.

Israel Origin and Judaic Ancestry

The question of identity and the search for old roots often lead to erroneous inferences, especially when cultural entities are reconstructed on the basis of accidental variations. In the context of Kuki-Chin origin, one Hmar writer (Songate 1956) developed a hypothesis in the mid-20th century of their descent from an old Jewish line. His views literally echoed Mason (1843: 73) who had earlier traced the Karen tradition on the origin of man to the Old Testament. Much later, in 1937, Scottish missionaries to China sought, as part of their zealous campaign, to connect the newly converted races to lost tribes of the Old Testament and, thus, give traditionally animist groups persuasive ground for accepting Christianity. Also, among the millenarian missionaries, there was spirited quest to discover the Ten Tribes of Israel that the Assyrian king Shalmaneser had placed at Halah, Habor, Hara and Medes after the conquest of Samaria in 722 BC, 'so that they would lose their identity and mix with the local populations' (Guthrie & Motyer 1970: 361). The Ten Lost Tribes of Israel (1 Chronicles 4:24–5:26, 7:1–40) were the descendants of Simeon, Reuben, Gad, Manasseh, Issachar, Dan, Zebulun, Naphtali, Ephraim and Asher.

The argument in support of old Israelite connections is that Manmasi, a Hmar-Mizo-Chin name chanted during a pre-Christian rite of offering fowls to spirit deities, is none other than the biblical Manasseh, and that Manmasi is a 'corruption' of Manasseh (Dena 2008: 11). In sheer contradiction to extant records and native traditions, it assumes the Kuki-Chin dispersion from Israel to China through Afghanistan, and their subsequent settlement in Myanmar and parts of Northeast India. DNA tests on the Kuki-Mizo tribes conducted at the Central Forensic Science Laboratory, Calcutta, showed a few samples with the haplotype of a Jewish community in Uzbekistan but those findings were contradicted by a laboratory report of the Jewish Genetic Project, Haifa, Israel, which tested 300 samples from Hmar, Kom, Hualngo, Zohte and other Kuki tribes of Manipur and found that the DNA samples were 'all within normal Tibeto-Burman parameters' (*Ibid.*). The possibility of any Lost Tribe migrating to China in the long past is not supported by epistemological studies. As for the Jewish people of Uzbekistan, they are the offshoot of an Iranian community, not a section of the Lost Tribes; they are, like the Jews of China, an enduring fascination for local economy thriving much on tourism (Zhou 2005: 79). Nevertheless, missionary enterprises in China and Burma in the 19th and the 20th century continued to find the Lost Tribes and bring Christian redemption to them. The latest find of Manasseh descent are Mizos, Hmars and all Kuki-Chins ethnically allied to them.

Kuki-Chin adherents to the notion of Jewish ancestry consider the pre-Christian rites and rituals of former times as the relics of their Judaic past. Some informants even preposterously associated native traditions on the Chindwin flood with the biblical deluge that made Noah build his Arch of Covenant and save the world from extinction. To the same adherents, the Hmar winter festival, *Sikpui kut*, has a deep meaning (Dena *Ibid.* 9-10); it allegedly connects their ancestors with those Israelites whom Moses had led across a divided Red Sea. When the Jesuit missionaries described Kuki-Chin villages as old Jewish places, they did so with the fervour of discovery and a consequent reaching out to the unredeemed communities that failed to see the Messiah in Jesus Christ. Evidently, they had failed to foresee that among the tribes that accepted the New Testament, there would emerge a group of reactionary Zionists eager to forsake Christianity for Judaism. In recent times, several hundred Kukis and Mizos from Manipur and Mizoram have immigrated to Israel.

4

Village and Dwelling

Formerly, highland villages were built on the principle of expediency. Since the mode of living favoured periodic shifting of village sites, no labour was misspent in making the dwelling house permanent. The occurrence of a village at a certain site depended on the rate at which available *jum* lands in the surrounding got exhausted. Other factors compelling abandonment of old sites were epidemic outbreaks and inter-village feuds. Yet, within the brief periods of settlement, measures were taken to protect villages against possible raids by enemies. Topographic elevation along with a penchant for rough paths difficult of ascent gave villages an extra edge over the enemy. Some tribes had specific clans to warrant the suitability of the selected sites. Typically, a village was perched on an extensive ridge, surrounded with stolid bamboo and timber palisade along the slope and had specific paths for exit and entry. As a rule, the site was selected with reference to a water source, which hopefully would not dry up in the tropical summer. The closer the stream, the easier and safer it was for the women to carry water to the uphill village.

The Village

Villages varied in size and composition. Cohesive tribes with powerful chiefs built larger villages than those that had pronouncedly egalitarian strains in them. The Lushai village was very large with several hundred houses. At the time of the British expedition against the Eastern Lushai

(1872), the village of Lenkhama had 832 houses, that of Tankama 722 while the combined villages of Chileya and Bungteya had 683 houses (Debnath 2008a: 10-11). Around the same time, the total of *vengs* under the three minor sons of Poiboi was about a thousand houses. Those settlements were very compact. In 1872, Lalburha's village stretched only a thousand yards on the spur of the Seswang Hill but had as many as 474 houses. Mru, Bawm, Darlong and the *Alian* tribes of Halam were familiar with large villages. An old Molsom tradition recalls a large rural community in *Arsien Khuasak*, which accommodated nine-times-twenty-and-nine types of people in it. Smaller tribes like Korbong and Mawrsephang lived in small settlements; the former had a tendency to continual disintegration while the latter thrived with some dependence on their more organised neighbours. The Korbong attributes their lack of cohesiveness to an ancient curse that allegedly spelt disaster on their village every time the total of houses exceeded a hundred and twenty. Today, they live as a decimated, impecunious tribe in two hamlets – the Champabari Korbong Para (under Jirania PS, West Tripura) with 18 families or 69 souls and the Purnachandra Korbong Para (under Rupaichhari Panchayat, Telimura Block, West Tripura) with 9 families or 40 individuals.

In the prevailing practice, a village is named after a Chief or some headman but sometimes it is also known by its nearest water source, an identifiable hillock or some distinguishable feature of the landscape. Formerly, the name of a village known after its Chief tended to change when the old Chief died and a new Chief took his place, the mode of periodic shifting of sites giving legitimacy to the new names. But after the permanent settlement of the highland tribes, that practice has been abandoned; today, there is a tendency to name a village or a hamlet after its original founder.

Organised villages often endorsed their internal social units to manage the core activities of settlement, cultivation, warfare, supervision of village granary, etc. Among the Molsom, the chief task of the *Mapu* clan was to select sites for their periodically shifting village. A similar function was performed by the *Rwipu* clan of the Hrangkhawl. In the Lushai's case, village elders and priests carried out the task of site selection, though the Chief's consent was imperative to finalising it. For a tribe engaged in constant warfare, the site had to be strategically gainful. Besides it was also necessary to be convinced that the site was auspicious and had no disabilities as would affect the settlers. In the Molsom rule, the *Mapu* elders spent the night at the new site taking with them a cock and hoping that it would crow at dawn-break. If the contrary happened, the site was abandoned and a fresh search undertaken. A similar custom existed among Lushais. 'Before final selection, the elders would sleep the night at the site, taking with them a cock. If it did not crow like a good lusty cock should one hour before dawn, it was taken as a bad omen' (McCall 1949: 165-66).

For groups lacking cohesion, the purity of a village site was secondary to the exigency of finding new hillock to build houses, especially when the human load in their familiar habitat increased. The Bru recalls a practice of the village elders taking home a lump of earth from the site of a would-be village and finalising the choice after auspicious signs in dreams. Yet, my Bru informants of South Tripura told me that many hillocks have been chosen and hamlets built thereon without reference to their customary practice.

As already pointed out, the traditional site of highland Kuki-Chin village was a ridge-top with some difficulty of access. The path leading to the village was left rough, without any conspicuous effort in altering the ruggedness of the ground. At many places, it was overgrown with jungles that were cleared only after the laborious ascent to the ridge-top. Not far from the settlement was the chief water source, usually a perennial stream or river. If *jums* were located on the other side of the stream, a log thrown over the stream served as bridge. Where the gap between the two banks of a river was too wide, long bamboo poles were tied with stout bark ropes and a bamboo hand-rail added to the structure to make the crossing safe. In times of war, the bridge was destroyed to make the approach of an enemy difficult. Paths connecting the village to the cultivation site were not of a permanent nature and little effort, unless necessary, was made to cut the jungle, simply because shifting of *jum* plots at the end of the harvest could also necessitate changing the old paths.

Within the village, the houses were laid out in two rows on either side of a central pathway, which lead to a high point of the ridge where one found open space. The principal house here was that of the Chief and close to it were the houses of his advisors. Egalitarian way of life did not permit the Bru to endorse to the notion of a village granary but the more cohesive of the Kuki-Chin tribes constructed their common granaries in open spaces in the village, as a precaution against fire. It was constructed quite close to the age-set residence, for purposes of easy protection. To return to the lay-out, topographic constraint of the ridge-top site allowed the village to extend lengthwise more comfortably than to swell out sidewise. Between two houses were open spaces, and each house had its natural backyard where small quantities of vegetables could always be grown. In some open space away from the village granary, normally at a viewable distance from the Chief's house, was the sacrificial pole. The Ranglongs performed their annual gayal-sacrifice on this spot. In the same place, the Khumi performed their cattle-killing ceremony. Mru villagers plant a bamboo pole in a cleared space and atop the pole, they nail the cut off tongue of the cow sacrificed during the *Chia-shat-pay* ('cow-sacrificing ceremony'), in a symbolic gesture at punishing the primeval cow that swallowed the scripture God had written for them, leaving the tribe, as they are now – unlettered, unenlightened.

Head-hunting tribes like Lushai and Darlong built villages with stockades at significant points along the approach. Continual strife among the Lushai clans as also their rivalry with other tribes taught them to seriously consider the matter of defence. Naturally, in the face of external aggression they put up better resistance than the egalitarian tribes did. Col. Shakespear (1900: 20) recalls that when the British first occupied the Lushai Hills, 'every village was surrounded by one or more lines of stockade made of timber, with several rows of bamboo spike outside it. At each gateway was a block house, and others were built at suitable places on the roads along which enemies were expected to come, and were occupied whenever an attack was apprehended.' On the contrary, the Bru showed little preoccupation with the protection of their villages. Their egalitarian ways caused existing villages to split into smaller hamlets and then disintegrate into vulnerable clusters of five or six houses on isolated hillocks. No doubt, there were ethnic and historical compulsions behind the Bru's lack of cohesive force. They had settled in the northern parts of the Hill Tracts several centuries before other ethnic stocks immigrated to the region and in having faced no threats to their occupation for long, their society remained weakly synchronised. When the head-hunting tribes began foraying into the Hill Tracts and the southern parts of Tripura in the 19th century, the Bru suffered much at their hands.

The Khumis were egalitarians. Long ago, when Khumi villages were raided, the people defended themselves by either running away or climbing tree-houses and chopping off the accessible ladder. As late as in the 19th century, the Mru too followed the same practice (Spearman 1880b: 67); incidentally, a section of the Khumi tribe, the Awa Khumi is today integrated into the Mru. Another section, the Aphya Khumis, following a long-standing rivalry with the Lai or Shendu in the 17th-18th century, strengthened their defence-system with walled enclosure round the village, leaving gateway houses near the approach and restricting the movements of women and children. The Ranglongs of North Tripura viewed the *khanam* outside the palisade with suspicion; women and children were forbidden to go out alone. Typically, a Ranglong village had two strong wooden gateways with beams that were lowered to closure; the gateway in front was the *thang satan* while the one at the rear called *sak satan*. Besides providing defence in times of war, the enclosure served other purposes. Once a year, during the *Kwapathien* ceremony (the equivalent of the Tippera's *Ker* festival), the village was closed to outsiders. Of course, villagers could go out to attend any urgent business after the stars appeared the sky. When a cholera or small-pox epidemic broke out in the neighbourhood, the entire village was put in quarantine, which lasted for several days. Sacrifices of fowls were made to spirit deities believed responsible for the epidemic. The Khumis killed monkeys to offer to the *Nats*, and after consuming the meat, they hung up the bones on trees in the belief that the act would prevent the disease from entering the village.

Despite the palisade and difficulty of ascent, most villages were vulnerable to attacks by stronger and organised groups used to a similar mode of living. Some villages' had concealed paths that were used, during war time, to move villagers to safety. Usually, raids occurred before dawn, and if the defending tribe found itself in a disadvantageous position, they used the concealed path and the cover of darkness to escape. It was preferable to bear leech bites in silence, even die of snakebite than get killed by the enemy and have the heads chopped off. For the head-hunting Lushai and Darlong, the tally of human heads was important and no compassion was shown to the enemy, not even to the old and decrepit abandoned by their relatives in the raided village. Captives were also carried off by the raiders to work for their families during the *juming* season.

The gory days of ethnic feuds are now a thing of the past, and with the fear of head-hunting raids gone, village palisades and other defensive precautions have been abandoned. Today, in remote areas, some coarse fencing is usually done to protect human and domestic animals from leopards and other wild cats.

Age-set system

In most Kuki-Chin villages, there existed in former times, a social grouping of unmarried males, which included the unmarried boys of the village. They were segregated physically from their families and made to live together at night in a large hall-type house built of bamboo, timber and thatch grass. Cohesive groups had strong and rigidly organised men's houses. The Lushai called it *Zawlbuk* and the Darlong *Bukpui*. No sub-division within the age-set is recalled but young boys in the age-group twelve to fifteen were never assigned tasks expected of older lads of eighteen or twenty.

The house in which the age-set resided was constructed with the combined labour of the men of the village. It resembled the traditional house on stilts but was larger in size and had a spacious inside without any partition. Villages with large population had larger men's house than those with ten or fifteen families. An elderly lad was in charge of the age-set and he enjoyed the position as long as he remained unmarried. Cases of juvenile delinquency were decided by him and the delinquents were, according to the degree of offence, either by flogged or confined within the residence without food for a day or two. It was no offence on the part of a lad to sneak out at night to meet his beloved but if the girl's father complained against him for violating his daughter's bed, the lad was rebuked for sheer indiscretion. He was expected to come out of the girl's house without waking her father. However, if he indulged in any incestuous relationship, the infringement was severely dealt with. No one interfered with the activities of the age-set.

Typically, an age-set chiefly imparted group discipline to a young generation of males who would eventually be required to carry out different social duties. In times of inter-ethnic warfare, the Lushai and the Darlong chiefs recruited strong and able-bodied warriors from the village *Zawlbuk* or *Bukpui*. As they had little domestic obligations to meet, they readily responded to the Chief's call to war. Sometimes, young warriors of one village also volunteered their services to other Chiefs who were favourably disposed towards their village. During Lalburha's war with the British in 1892, about 400 warriors from Poiboi's village had come over to Seswang Hill to reinforce Lalburha's men; besides, there were also Lushai men from Bungteya and Lenkhama (Debnath *Ibid.*: xxi). Not all unmarried males went out on the war-path; small boys of the village age-set volunteered in house building, *jum* work, distributing meat of hunted animals, etc. If there was no work at hand, they always found some means to recreate themselves. Generally, a boy became a warrior at seventeen or eighteen years of age. When the British went out to subjugate the Lushai, they resorted to some basic strategies, one of which was to cut off the village from its source of ration and another to dismantle the *zawlbuk*. Later when Christianity came to the Lushai, missionaries also favoured its abandonment; they were quick to perceive that the *zawlbuk* was the centre of the Lushai's community life.

Community Bonds and Feasts of Merit

A sense of belongingness to the village community comes through feasts that families organise for their neighbours, even for the entire village on special occasions. For the commoner, the life-cycle ceremonies provides opportunities to reinforce kinship ties. The closet kins are always invited; however, if one has had a good harvest and an occasion for celebration comes immediately after it, a point is made in the house to invite as many people of the village as possible. Usually weddings are expensive and the hill men often incur debt from lavish expenditure on such occasions. Even a birth in the family anticipates a feast. In pre-Christian Lushai, childbirth was an occasion gayal sacrifice and a feast of meat along with rice-beer (Rawlins 1792: 163). Among the Khyangs, the invited guests always bring fowls and rice-beer with them during the *Opel* or 'name-giving ceremony' and thus save a poor kinsman from any embarrassment at his inability to provide generous feasts to relatives and friends.

Of greater social significance were the old feasts of merit, which the rich and the well-to-do organised with great financial extravagance. It re-emphasised the feast-giver's bond with the larger village community and, at the same time, earned him a socially privileged present life and a happy, untroubled afterlife. For three months before the Lushai *Khuangchawi* ceremony, the feast-giver employed wood-collectors and when their work was done, he rewarded each of them with at least a goat, if not a gayal. The *Khuangchawi* feast, which lasted four days, gave no power to the feast-giver but he earned the privilege to wear special clothes and to cut a window in the house wall (Shakespear 1912: 89-90). In the *Ahraing-Chyeng* feast of the Aphya Khumi, the giver enjoyed great social prestige and he earned the right not only to keep a window by the hearth but also to make other alterations in the house layout and raise monoliths in the place of sacrifice. As a rule, he was required to perform the *Ahraing-Chyeng* ceremony two times in life. If a man died after giving only one feast, it was binding on his son to give the feast for the father in absentia. The feast lasted seven days, and no Khumi family in the village cooked food at home on those days. The feast-giver's position was enviable and his lifetime achievement an object inspiration for other men of his village.

Among Old Kukis, the annual gayal-sacrifice was celebrated as community event. It was meant to secure the prosperity of the whole village, not of a single individual. Of course, individuals could also organise feasts of merit, provided they had the means to do so. A common practice for the Ranglongs was to have their village Kamchikao take the responsibility of organising the gayal-sacrifice at the end of the *juming* season. He engaged people to collect subscriptions and ensured that the five original clans carried out the roles expected of them. Their celebrations lasted a whole day and the meat of the sacrificed gayal was eaten in a community feast on the same day. The Uchai too celebrated their buffalo-killing ceremony in almost identical manner, the chief difference being that the Uchai observed the ceremony outside the village, on a river bank. Individuals could earn little merits by bringing goats to the priest for sacrifice and giving a feast of the meat to their relatives or to some neighbours on the following day.

Today, the feasts of merit are rarely held. The highland villages no longer exist as compact and cohesive units as they used to do in former times. Restrictions on swiddening and a consequent changing over to other modes of subsistence have adversely affected their traditional life-style. Religious conversion when total as among the Lushai, led to the abandonment of old practices considered wild and savage under the tenets of their new faith. On the other hand, partial conversion as now found in the Old Kukis has affected collective participation. The Christian section of these tribes deliberately keeps itself aloof from all their erstwhile Animistic rituals and Hinduised practices.

Common Funeral Ground

When a Khumi dies, the corpse is taken to a less frequented place outside the dwelling area of the village and burnt on a pyre. A small hut is built on the site of cremation; the ashes of the dead along with the clothes used and the mat on which the dying took the last breath are kept inside. Other things such as drinking cups, bamboo baskets, a bottle of rice-beer, etc. are also given to the dead. The Mru too follows the same practice, giving the dead some tokens of the things useful in life (Brauns & Löffler 1990: 198). In former times, villages shifted periodically, and in the new site a common funeral ground was made of the place wherein the first person dying of a natural cause was disposed. The choice of the site found endorsement by other families subsequently disposing their dead on or about the same place. Traditionally, a small hillock isolated from human haunt was for the Khumi the ideal place to build a dead man's hut, in a symbolic gesture to impress upon the living that the land where the soul journeys is removed from the familiar world of everyday activities. Normally, the fear of spirits kept people away from the funeral site, so much so that even if one side of the same hillock had a lusty bamboo growth for *juming*, none dared burn it. Today, a jungle near the village is a good place to build the dead man's hut. Between the village and its common funeral site, there is a stream where mourners returning after the obsequies take a refreshing bath.

The Bru and the Halam tribes prefer to cremate their dead by a stream, in keeping with the Hindu belief of the soul's transportation through the water route. Most villages now have permanent cremation grounds on river banks; sometimes, two or more villages use the same site. Christianised sections of these tribes as of the other Kuki-Chins resort to the common burial grounds outside the living area of their villages. In pre-Christian Lushai, the corpse of a Chief or an influential man was preserved about the house for several weeks. Most clans left the corpse on a bamboo platform for the sun to dry it; the head was subsequently removed and the body stuffed in an earthen pot and buried in the funeral site occurring at the furthest end of the village area. In the Hualhang practice, the Chief's corpse was hung up on a house-beam for seven days, during which time the deceased's wife sat under it spinning (Lewin 1869: 109). The old Pangkhua rule was to place the corpse inside a coffin and then have it carried to the jungle and hung from a tree. Almost daily for about a year, some member from the deceased's family would turn up to smoke the corpse with a slow fire underneath. On completing a year, the coffin was reopened, the bones taken out, washed and interred in the village graveyard. Among the Bawm, the village now has a common burial ground; but before their adoption of Christianity, the low-ranking Panghawi clans were not allowed to bury their dead in the same graveyard the Sunthla used.

When a child not older than three months dies, the body is buried in a place other than the common funeral ground. But this rule is normally also applied to older children up to the first year. In an old Thangluah practice, also endorsed by most clans of the Lushai, the corpse of a child was wrapped in homespun and stuffed inside an earthen pot, which was then buried under the platform of the family dwelling house. Between death and the journey to Mithi-khua (literally, 'the dead man's village'), the soul hovers about the places of its living kinsmen, seeking sustenance. Rice-beer is offered along with other articles of food to the soul of an adult dead but in the case of a child, the sustenance is boiled rice with milk. Before stuffing the child's corpse inside a pot, an egg was put in one hand and a piece of cotton soaked in his mother's milk in the other. A dead child's soul was believed not to know the way to Mithi-khua, whence the egg slipping out of his hand rolled on and the soul crawled after it to reach its destination. Some clans of the Bongcher endorse a similar practice (Sailo 1992: 34) but in this tribe, the prevailing custom is to bury a dead child on a river bank outside the village, not under the house platform as in old Lushai.

With tribes that cremate their dead, there is also the provision for burial on river banks. It is resorted to when death comes of unnatural causes such as animal attacks, accidents, epidemics, etc.

The Dwelling house

House repairs and patchwork are usually done before the rainy season but in constructing new houses, the favoured time is between the close of a harvest and beginning of the next *juming* season. Renovation of existing houses is carried out without any formality but in constructing new houses, the auspicious signs about the plot are ascertained in a manner analogous to those observed while setting up new villages. In building the traditional house, stone or concrete blocks are never used. Bamboo, timber and thatch grass comprise the common materials resourced from the rainforest environment. Commonly, the Kuki-Chin house is oblong shaped, the face shorter than the side, with a front door directly under the ridgepole and having bamboo floors raised to a considerable height from the ground and supported on bamboo uprights. The main posts are sometimes the trunks of tropical hardwood trees. By varying the lengths of the bamboo uprights, the height of the platform is adjusted to the uneven terrain. This choice of elevated platform helped avoid the additional labour of levelling the surface soil, which the plains' people painfully undertake to make the low ground-floor. A raised platform has several advantages; it keeps the interiors dry in the rainy season; it provides safety from prowling animals, and, as we shall note later, it also helps the family manage its domestic waste. In the space under the platform floor, pigs are kept, though, in the drier part of the space, bundles of firewood can also be stocked.

House walls are of matted bamboo, and the material for the roof is thatch-grass or bamboo leaves. A part of the platform extends outward in front with a corresponding lengthening of the roof over a cosy portico. The Central Chins, as also the Old Kuki tribes will leave the platform extended and hypaethral in the rear part of the house for purposes of drying and winnowing paddy. Water is usually stored in the front part of the house, sometimes also inside, in large earthen pots or gourd vessels. The Bru and Uchai retain the open-air platform in the rear, the latter sometimes constructing a room on one side of that platform to give space and privacy to the newly married daughter and her groom during the latter's tenure of residential bride-service. Southern Chins like the Khyang avoid the rear platform but they keep a small, walled *tongleng* ('space for toilet') in the rear part of the *buhim* (kitchen room) so that old folks and pregnant wives may use it at night for micturition and defecation. In general, there is no provision for an in-house toilet in the highland stilt-house.

Among the Marma, the house has wider face with two front doors and shorter sides, one of which cuts a door into the kitchen extension; the interior of the dwelling house is divided into compartments with partition walls of matted bamboo. Mru and Khyang houses make a compromise between the Chin and the Marma types. The Chin type of a large, undivided hall with a central hearth occurs in the Khyang house as a medium-sized front hall called *imnu*, used by the householder and his wife, while the rear part of the house is partitioned in the Marma way to allocate separate compartments to other members of the family. A partition wall is absent inside a Khumi house. The Khyang keeps a single front door, not two doors as in the Marma house. Guests are accommodated on one side of the *imnu*. In the Mru house, the interior consists of a large single room, the *kimtom*, and a hearth that occurs slightly in the rear. Most Kuki-Chins, as also the Bru do their cooking in the central hearth of the undivided hall; the Khyang, on the contrary, follows the Marma practice of constructing a separate kitchen called *buhim* on the outer side and laying a thatch roof over it. The Khyang central hearth ('*lai-khawng*') is provisioned with firewood during the winter to keep inmates warm. In the Mru house, a smaller room, the *kimma*, is built against a side wall with door, and it is used for the same purpose as the Khyang *buhim*. Other than for cooking, the *kimma* or the *buhim* can be used to store grains and also to afford privacy to a newly married couple. School goers may also use it to study for some undisturbed hours.

Invariably, the house is accessed by climbing up a log-ladder with rough steps hewn on it. Inside, there is no furniture, not even beds, and the whole family sleeps on the bamboo floor after spreading mats and blankets. Since the traditional house is meant to accommodate the highland joint family, the structure is mostly large, some houses extending thirty to forty feet in length and ten feet in width. In former times, individual families cooperated with each other not only in food production but also in activities like house building. Assistance came on voluntary basis; the householder, in a sign of gratitude, offered meals and rice-beer to males engaged in the work. Today, paid labour is common throughout the hills. Besides, the central hearth, an additional fire-place on one side is used in winter. Formerly, the houses did not have windows; instead, small openings were kept on the outer walls to let in sufficient air and make the interior pleasant during summer. Besides, the gaps in bamboo matted walls also allowed air and sunlight inside and prevented stench. Among the Lushai, a chief privilege of one who performed the *Khuangchawi* ceremony was to have a window in his house.

Household commodities consist of things the family considers essential, such as bamboo baskets of various shapes, sizes and patterns, some used in carrying *jum* products, firewood, forest gatherings, others for storing grains, clothes, etc. Flat baskets and winnowing trays are found lying about large storage bins. Every house has a number of fish traps and fowl cages; these are usually kept outside, tied to bamboo poles or suspended by ropes from the rafters of the roof. To store jewellery and other valuables, women use finely woven cane boxes. Inside the kitchen, the common utensils are earthen pots, gourd vessels, vats and strainers, aluminium bowls and pans, wooden ladles and stirrers, bamboo mortars, forked sticks, cups, spoons, and the *da* or iron chopper. The chief agricultural tool is the *da*, besides which one also finds the digging drills made of pointed sticks or sharpened bamboo. Musical instruments like gong, cymbal, flutes and blow-pipes made of bamboo and dried gourd are among the treasured possessions of the house. Women manage most housework – they collect firewood, cook meals, prepare rice-beer, wash clothes and utensils, and weave the homespun while the men build the house, slash jungle for cultivation, hunt wild beasts, manufacture baskets, etc.

The family eats together squatting on the bamboo floor. Rice is the staple food; it is eaten with boiled vegetables, curry, eggs, meat and a most delicious paste of dry-fish.

Condiments are regularly taken, and these vary from sauce extracted of animal fat to a pounded mixture of dry fish, chilli and onion. At home, highland families eat two meals a day, once in the morning before going out to the *jum* and another after sunset, at the end of the day's work. The morning meal is usually cooked in excess and a small quantity wrapped in banana leaf and taken to the place of work and eaten around mid-day. Home-made rice-beer is consumed freely in private and also used in life-cycle rituals and ceremonies. To this must be added the general habit of betel chewing and smoking. In the highlands there is no taboo against women's smoking.

Waste management

The sanitation configuration of highland houses was suited to its physical and human system; it helped to control the load of faecal pathogens in the environment and block the transmission pathways of common disease vectors. The extended platform was used for washing utensils and cleaning vegetables, the waste water and all kitchen trash, as well as the refuge from meals and all food waste fell underneath through the gaps in the bamboo floor. A part of the same platform also served as unplanned urinal; children, of course, could also defecate from it. At night, old folks and women at advanced stage of pregnancy used it as toilet, to avoid risky climbing up and down the log-ladder. With the pigs around, peridomestic sanitation was maintained and no stench created. Large earthen or gourd vessels with water for washing hands and feet were kept at the point of access to the living quarter. Much attention was given to hygiene at home. Even in places where a couple of these houses still exist, anyone coming from outside must wash his hands and feet before entering the house. Guests too are expected to do the same. Footwear is invariably left outside the door.

The tribes under study were not accustomed to the idea of the in-house toilet. The Khyang, we have already seen, had a *tongleng* for defecation or micturition at night by old parents and pregnant women; ordinarily though, both men and women did their business in the open, making the best use of the slopes around the house compound. Others raised thatched walls around the outside toilet, using bamboo and timber for the floorboard. The hill slope provided natural drainage. Periodic shifting of village sites also contributed to maintaining the sanitation chain.

Permanent settlement of these tribes and a consequent transformation in their dwelling pattern has not been adequately compensated by alternative sanitation facilities, especially in terms of familiarising them with new waste management technologies and infrastructures. Hence, one often comes across instances of the snapping of the normal health chain in many tribal hamlets today, especially those that remain far-flung, isolated or unreached.

5

Swidden and Other Strategies

Traditional economy in the highland societies of Tripura and the Chittagong Hill Tracts was swidden based. The origin of this type of agriculture goes back to the Neolithic period, when the hunting and foraging techniques showed strains in sustaining increasing nomadic populations. Stone-axes were then used to slash patches of rainforest and fire to burn the dried jungle before cultivation. Today, the iron-chopper or axe and the digging hoe made of the same metal are used but the technique remains unaltered. Many communities in Southeast Asia resort to the same procedures that the early Maya people had used in their milpa system. There are some arguments in favour of swiddening and many against it, and we shall take note of those after we have considered the typical aspects of the slash and burn cultivation as practised by small sections of the highland tribes covered under the present study.

Swidden Cultivation

The initial task of the swidden farmer is to find a suitable plot on a ridge face, usually one that has a thick undergrowth of bush and bamboo. It is mainly done by the family heads or experienced males and the preferable time is around late December to mid-February. Selected plots are then marked by planting bamboo poles along the edges to avoid encroachment. In former times, some highland groups had specific clans that performed the task of site-selection. The *Mapu* clan of the Molsom was not only entrusted with the responsibility of finding new sites for periodically shifting villages but also with demarcating an extended outer area of the village wherein their kinsmen could cultivate. As for specific choice of plots within a cultivable area, it was either left to individuals or entrusted upon a select category of the village population to see to the allocation of *jum* plots. The Lushai Chiefs were aided by their own Ramhauls, who like the *Mapu* experts, selected the cultivation site for the village; in return, they were allowed to keep for themselves some of the best *jums*. Bru householders, on the contrary, selected their individual *jums* and seldom did the village council interfere with individual choice unless some dispute arouse with regard to the selected sites.

In the past, when the carrying capacity of the environment was low, families could indulge in the customary practice of determining whether the chosen site was auspicious or not. As a rule, a piece of bamboo used to be split in two halves and tossed. If the splits fell on opposite faces, it meant that the selected plot was suitable for cultivation; if, however, the splits fell on the same faces, it was a bad sign and the cultivator had to seek out a fresh plot. To the highland tribes, land as common property or, at best, it was possessed by some spirit. The practice of propitiating spirits to retain possession of a selected site through the *juming* season perhaps evolved when increased populations put added pressure on the rainforest ecosystem, and sufficient virgin plots for cultivation were no longer available. Generally, fowls were offered to appease spirits. In the past, there was a tradition peculiar not only to the Kuki-Chin tribes of the region but also to the Mru of CHT and the Bru (Riang) of Tripura to begin cultivation on a site after auspicious signs in dreams. From the selected plot, a lump of earth was carried home by the cultivator and put under his pillow. If in his dream, he saw a clear stream, an unmarried maiden, a marriage party, etc. it signified good harvest. But it was considered unlucky to dream of monkeys, boars, funeral parties or broken pots. Since migration is officially restricted and swiddening not quite favoured, bad dreams have now ceased to discourage the hill farmer. If superstitious enough to believe in omens, he does not abandon the site but tries ritualistically to annul its impurities through propitiatory sacrifices of domestic fowls.

The slashing of the jum plot can begin almost immediately after its selection. As for the time needed to complete the task, it may vary considerably depending on the size of the plot and the type of growth on it, as also the number of cutters involved. The typical *huk lambir* of the Murasing extends for miles; the plots are contiguous and families work as a cooperative village community, each helping the other throughout the season. Usually, males in large numbers get into the business; the cutting is done with the common iron-chopper, commencing from the bottom of the hill. The work is toilsome and there is the additional risk of getting snakebites. From the bottom of the hill, the cutters steadily ascend the slope, working in a horizontal line. The low trees are cut on their upper parts, the stumps left standing, while the larger hardwood growths are left in their place after the low branches have been felled. Mature bamboo is felled and carried to the village home; a part of it is used in house repair while the rest sold in the local market.

Then for almost two months, the fallen jungle is left to dry in the sun. Around early April, the dried jungle is fired. Soon everything is reduced to ashes; the fire also burns the soil a couple of inches below the surface. Most of the nutrients are stored in the vegetation; on burning, these return to the soil to give nourishment to the crops subsequently sown. Several days after the fire has died out, pieces of half-burnt wood are collected for use as firewood. But a *jum* fire can cause great devastation unless timely precautions are taken to keep it under control. Usually, the day of setting the dried jungles on fire is decided by a common consent of the swidden farmers of the village, and, once that is done, the information passes on to the neighbouring villages. The

Murasings retell a pathetic tale in which a group of *kirtaniyas* ('carol singers') travelling from one village to another in early April was caught in the fire of a *huk lambir* (contiguous *jums* that extend for several miles) and everyone got charred to ashes. Should a plot be too large, it is fired simultaneously from all sides. Commonly, the area around the *jum* plot is cleared and everything dry and ignitable removed to prevent the conflagration from spreading outside. Besides, as long as the fire is alive, men keep continually moving along the contours, beating down every straying flicker with branches of trees. The firing of dried jungle is a male task, and women and children are asked to keep away from the *jum* at this time

Large trees that survive the fire show their green tops; otherwise, the hillside looks like a desolate waste of ashes with debris of charred wood and half-burnt stumps. The wood is collected in piles for use as firewood. In the coming months, when the cultivator builds a temporary pile-dwelling in the *jum* field to keep watch over the growing crops, his wife will need the firewood to make their meals. Rain showers are usual in this time of the year; it makes the upper soil soft for digging holes. Then whole families, men, women and children, get to work, sowing seeds in vertical rows. Each cultivator has a bamboo basket strapped to the back; it contains a mixture of paddy, melon, pumpkin and cucumber seeds, Indian corn, beans, sesame, chilli, oilseeds, etc. Several varieties of paddy can be produced in the *jum*; hence, on an average, 50% of the mixture is paddyseeds. In the highland rule, one must achieve maximal outcome with minimal labour. With the hand that holds the chopper, the cultivator digs holes in the earth while with the other hand he picks up a pinchful of the mixture from the basket and dibbles it into the holes. As the cultivator moves up the hill, he effortlessly uses his feet to move the loose upper soil and cover the holes. Cottonseeds are never used directly but mixed with clay, rolled into small balls and dried in sunlight. Only dried cotton balls are added to the general mixture of seeds.

Should brief showers aid the human work in the field, germination begins in about a week after the sowing. Celebrations around this time are not uncommon. When the green shoots of the paddy crop begin to sprout, the Khyang farmer performs the *Bugule* ceremony by sacrificing a boar in honour of the residing *nat* of the *jum* field. Friends and relatives are invited to a feast of pork and rice-beer.

From June to October, painstaking labour goes into keeping the *jums* clear of weeds that sprout plentifully. Though the iron-chopper can be used, weeding is mostly done by hand, and it is women and growing children who toil for hours in the field, bending down in rain and sunshine to pull out whole weeds by their stalks. Men of some means who could afford to keep clients always had additional hands while those of modest means had neighbours to assist them on voluntary basis. In their turn, they also helped their neighbours. As the *jum* plots 'are generally situated in propinquity... mutual help and assistance in weeding the crop is given; each one takes his turn to help in his neighbour's joom' (Lewin 1869: 21). During weeding, insect bites are common, occasional snakebites also occur; in addition, there is the risk of catching malaria after mosquito bites. While most tribes perform the drudgery with painful silence, the Brus resort to a means to ease their labour. An elderly drummer called *d'wa* plays the drum with his hands, the rhythm though monotonous to the unused ear, inspires the women to sing weeding songs and happily finish the day's work. The same thing goes on throughout the weeding period.

Wild animals, especially deer, wild boars and monkeys can cause extensive damage to the standing crops and loss to the farmer. In late August, the paddy crop begins to ripe, and flocks of birds are attracted to the feast. To keep watch on the *jum* and protect the crops against these 'nuisances,' small cabin-shelters are built on bamboo uprights. Alternatively, the watch-house can also be put up on a tree. As precaution, many sounding devices made of tin are set up at different points in the *jum*, all connected by a long rope to the cabin-shelter where some members of the family resides in their turn. These tin devices are beaten vigorously to scare away birds and beasts from the field. Besides, traps and snares are also set up in the field for intruding boars and deer. This period of vigilance is not altogether dull work; there is ample leisure for chat and gossip in the evenings. For young folks, it is a good time to select mates and court their future life-partners.

Early cucurbits are harvested in June but additional stocks of vegetable seeds, legumes and more cucurbits are sown simultaneously. The process is repeated with each successive harvest to ensure the family a steady supply of vegetables through the cultivating season. Generally, crops produced in *jum* are sufficient to sustain a family but increased demand for *jum* vegetables in the plains market now makes farmers produce their food crops in surplus. Swidden cultivation is essentially multi-crop, and during the cultivating season, a large variety of crops are harvested, some as early as in July-August. But the cotton crop comes in late September or early October, followed by oilseeds in November and December. Cotton obtained from the *jum* is generally used to make the homespun, unless economic exigency obliges families to sell their produce.

When paddy ripens in September, whole families, men, women and grown-up children get into the act of reaping. Soon the hills reverberate with joyous songs. The compositions are mainly extempore and sung in consonance with the competitive work wherein each harvester tries to overtake the other in the paddy harvest. A line sung by one singer is cheerfully responded to by another singer across the field, and in this the singing spreads from one plot to another. The predominant theme is of love, though among the Kuki-Chins there is also a nostalgic recall of prosperity in the abandoned fields of Rihli-Champhai. For those who cannot sing will join the others in making the joyous hill cry. None would want to be left out from this merriment. After the harvest of the paddy crop, the straw is discarded in the *jum* while the rice collected in bamboo baskets and stored temporarily in the cabin-shelter. Later, it is taken to the village home. In the past, when some villages had common granaries, small quantities of rice were kept at home while the bulk was stocked in the granaries.

Traditional highland villages had thrived as cooperative communities wherein individual families mutually aided each other in everyday activities. Even today, if a woman at leisure sees her neighbour engaged in winnowing, she will readily come up to assist her. Together, they work and share their sorrows and happiness. The cotton crop is carefully treated by removing seeds from the yarn with the ginning machine. When sufficient quantities of cotton have been ginned, the pile is dried in the sun, after which it is carded, spun into thread and then wound on spindles. Extracted cottonseeds are stored for the next sowing season.

Pragmatics of swidden cultivation

Early suggestions to induce plough cultivation among the inhabitants of the Chittagong Hills came up in 1784, when the East India Company sought the opinion of Mr. Irwin, Chief of Chittagong, in that regard (Lewin 1869: 22). The matter was raised again, in 1829, but the Commissioner of Chittagong told the Company that it had no right to interfere with the internal matters of hill chiefs. The picture changed in 1860, when the British annexed the Hill Tracts. Between 1860 and 1880, initiatives were taken to induce hill farmers to adopt a mode of cultivation that differed from the one they traditionally subsisted on. It did not produce the desired results, prompting the British Political Agent of Hill Tripura to dissuade the government from pursuing the same policy in the hill kingdom. Nevertheless, progress was made in the following decades, after the British actively involved the CHT Chiefs. Hutchinson (1909: 69) mentions that in 1900, about 11,000 acres of land were brought under plough cultivation, which fetched the government Rs.14,000 in revenue.

Policy makers in the region have always insisted that *jumed* plots take many years to recoup fertility; they have also argued that replenishment of burnt forests is not possible under reduced *jum* cycles. *Juming* has been viewed as not conducive to rootedness to living places but favouring nomadic habits in the hill men. The British administration and, later on, other post-British governments failed to appreciate the interdependency of forest and cropping; they condemned swiddening as destroying vast areas of rainforests, arresting soil fertility and increasing soil run-off. Their conspicuous lack of understanding of the symbiotic connectedness between the hill-dweller and his environment became evident when vast areas of their habitat were brought under reserved forests and swiddening was banned within the reserves. Ironically, the same governments have exploited reserved forest to procure timber for construction work, to supply tons of bamboo to paper mills and allot hectares of cultivable ridges to ecologically detrimental projects on rubber plantation.

Notwithstanding the condemnation of swidden cultivation, ethnic groups in the region have known their traditional agro-economy as best suited to the ecological environment in which they have been living for several centuries. Even today, without the intrusion of the 'outsider' Bengali into the hills, the ethnic population would have remained within the carrying capacity of its traditional resource system. Most striking is the large variety of crops harvested from the *jum* in course of a single season against the mono-crop pattern of the lowlands. 'In an ordinary year he [the swidden cultivator] will secure an ample supply of rice for his own requirements and a surplus for sale, in addition to yams, pumpkins, melons, chillies and Indian corn to vary his diet and for barter' (Hutchinson *Ibid.*: 67). To be precise, the variety of swidden produce ensures not only quality diet but also generates resources to meet family needs pertaining to dwelling, clothing and ornamentation, as well as ritual and ceremony.

The topographical character of the hills and the problem of communication that comes with it must be pragmatically considered. Efforts to introduce wet-rice cultivation in many places are yet to pay off. Stretches of cultivable lowland lie unexploited along river valleys within the unexplored hills, and it is likely to remain so for at least another decade or until official atavism favouring wet-rice cultivation comes to prevail among the dwellers. Many places lack in terms of a proper network of roads, rendering unfeasible any transportation of technology for alternative modes of production. In those places, *juming* must be pursued to meet the basic needs of living.

This said, the adoption of prophylactic and preventive measures could make *juming* itself an economically viable and ecologically non-detrimental strategy. Most crucially, it would save from extinction the traditional economy of the highland tribes living in the region. In plots having declivity above 45%, soil run-off can be minimised by providing catch-water drains higher up the slope. Fire-terracing of *jum* plots before the dried jungle is burnt, piling of unburnt debris along the contours, and the sowing seeds in horizontal instead of vertical rows (OPHRA 1966: 55) are some measures that could be adopted. To minimise the hazards of forest fires and the loss of nutrients through extensive burning, swidden cultivators could be advised to go for controlled burning and keeping *jum* fires small and low. 'In Bhutan and parts of India (Arunachal Pradesh and Meghalaya), the slashed material is covered with soil before burning' (Kerkhoff and Sharma 2006: 50). The technique would be workable in most parts of Northeast India. A form of composite swiddening, after the practice of minority farmers in North Vietnam (Van Dung *et. al.* 2006: 58), could be taken up in CHT and Tripura; in this mode, single households would continue to cultivate wet-rice on fringeland and, at the same time, go for small, rotating swidden plots on ridge faces.

Hunting, fishing and foraging

With government ban on hunting, an old ecological niche is now abandoned, and the use of most hunting tools of yesteryear forgotten. Except for the aged and the too old, very few highland folks know what a spear-trap looked like. Occasionally though, animals straying into the *jum* are caught with noose traps or killed with sticks and choppers; the meat is partly eaten and the rest sold. In the past, hunting wild animals like boar, deer and tiger was done in groups with bows, arrows and spears and the meat of large animals distributed to the whole village. The Halams were skilled in trapping elephants. One of the twelve tribes, the Rupini, takes great pride in retelling the tale of trapping and taming *Mayung Kuphur*, a white elephant that allegedly roamed in the forests of Maini-harung ('Maini-tlang' of the Bru) once upon a time.

Sometimes Lushai and Darlong men in small groups used hunting dogs but the other tribes hunted together in large groups, driving the game to where it could be killed with poisoned arrows or spears. If a tribe had a hereditary chief, the hunting party would give him, in recognition of his right to everything in the village, a hind leg or the best part of the meat of the hunted animal. The use of bows and arrows by the Kuki hunters began to fall in disuse with their acquiring of guns around the early 19th century. Its impact on traditional hunting is noted by Soppitt (1893: 21) in these terms: 'In late years, the Kukis obtained a comparatively large number of guns, and have in consequence lost a great deal of their skill in setting traps for game.' Today, even licensed guns are no longer allowed, a spate of insurgency in the region has compelled governments to take back old muzzle-loaders that hill men had in their possession until the mid-1970s. Small traps are used by villagers to catch birds, especially the wild fowl. Growing children are sometimes seen roaming in village-side jungles with slings in their hands. When reptiles are encountered, villagers beat them to death with sticks. Snake-meat is eaten by many tribes but some avoid it. Even if snake-meat is not tabooed by a certain tribe, pregnant women avoid it out of the fear of having children with forked tongues.

Fishing is done with traditional tools such as fishing-net, basket traps and the fishing rod. Besides, a variety of hill-growing creeper is used to haul fish from the stream. The technique is simple. Once the creeper is obtained, it is pounded thoroughly and small quantities of the same are soaked at several places within a selected area of the stream. A fish straying into that area gets temporarily paralysed. During winter, when streams grow shallower, bare hand fishing is done. Village-side marshes also abound in several varieties of crabs and tortoises, which all hill men love to eat. Shortage of fish is met by purchase from the local market.

As far as foraging is concerned, the rainforest habitat still produces sufficient varieties of yams, potato, roots, tubers, and especially the tender shoot of the bamboo. Mushrooms are greatly relished, so too are most species of wild banana. The sole tool for food-gathering is the *da* or iron-chopper but when rain-showers make the ground soft, pointed sticks or bamboo can become very handy. While fishing is done by men and women, foraging is chiefly associated with women and children. Males too old for *jum* work can accompany their granddaughters to the jungle to collect leaves and other natural edibles.

Husbandry

Domesticated animals provide families with a steady protein diet round the year. Under the bamboo platform, every house has its pigsty with strong fencing around it. It gives ventilation, natural drainage and overhead shade: besides, the water falling from the platform creates 15 to 25 cm deep wallows, a prerequisite for the pigs during the warm summers. Separate log-sheds along slopes are seen in places where concrete or semi-concrete houses with low floors have replaced the stilt-house. The common village pig (black with patches of erect hair on the shoulder) is most preferred for meat but its poor performance against a steadily rising population has compelled shifting of preference for exotic breeds like the *Large White Yorkshire* (with erect ears) or *Landrace* (white with drooping ears), which bring both meat and money. A boar upgraded with either of these breeds weighs between 275 and 300 kilograms while the sow achieves a litter-size of fifteen.

For poultry, the free-ranging system is practised. During the day, fowls roam freely but are confined at night in fowl-cages or enclosed pens. The commonly domesticated breed is the *Chittagong fowl* with long neck, single short comb, red earlobes and wattles, and long, thick legs. Chicks have scanty fluff but are without any plumage. Under poultry up-gradation programmes, district poultry farms now supply the *Rhode Island Red* known for its high resistance to disease or the *White Leghorn* which has a great laying capacity (about 250 to 300 eggs between short clutch-periods). But during the last five years, recurring bird-flue in the region has greatly affected every kind of poultry. Ducks are still not quite preferred.

In addition to pig and poultry, most plough-cultivating families now domesticate cattle mainly for cultivation and occasionally for selling milk. In former times, the gayal or the hill cow (also called 'gabay') was domesticated. To marry a common Lushai girl, the prospective groom in former times had to give her father at least three gayals as bride-price. Sometimes, a new birth in the family was also celebrated by killing the same animal and giving a feast of the meat. When a man of some means died, his relatives killed a hill cow and gave a feast. Over the years, the creature has become rare; besides, the present way of the highlander's life does not encourage domestication of the gayal.

Manufactures

Every family makes its bamboo and cane baskets, the Bru being something of a specialist in this craft. Their intricately woven baskets are of high quality and durable enough to last for many years. Continual use in the rain and sunshine initially discolours the material before finally turning it blackish-brown. Large baskets are used to store grains while a small or small-medium one is strapped to the back during sowing or suspended by a head strap in carrying *jum* vegetables from the ridge-side plot to the village home and, if the produce be surplus, from home to the nearest market. Baskets are almost never traded. Very small baskets with lid are used to keep women's decorations like earrings, bangles, anklets, necklaces, hairpins, etc. Basket manufacturing is solely a man's job and women are not allowed to engage it.

Smoking has noticeably declined in recent years but about two or three decades ago most hill men were inveterate smokers. There are no restrictions on women's smoking. The valley-dwelling Tippera and Chakma, even the Dimasa prefer smoking the *daba*, a bamboo device made on the principle of the hookah. Some Halams also use it. But for the other highlanders, the smoking apparatus most favoured is the pipe. Easily available *bidis* and cigarettes from the market have now replaced the pipe, but an old Bawm will continue to shun these items as cheap and inelegant. If his old pipe breaks or gets useless, he sits leisurely at home, carving one of a piece of softwood. But if he is in no mood to manufacture a new one, he will go down to Ruma to buy a new one that local traders import from Sittwe. Other male manufactures include the *plung* ('bamboo-fitted gourd pipes') of the Mru and the Khumi, the brass and copper moulding of the Lushai, besides several types of drums, flute-pipes and crude violins that the other tribes make.

Nearly all kitchen utensils are purchased from Bengalis. Clay pots for cooking rice and distilling rice-beer, earthen tumblers or aluminium vessels to carrying water have to be bought from the local markets. A form of indigenous pottery was known to the Lushai in 19th century (Shakespear 1912: 29). Bamboo cylinders may be used to cook small quantities of rice or make special items like condiment of dry fish mixed with chilli, onion and local herbs. Gourd vessels can be used to store water but some time is required to manufacture one. Besides, considerable care goes to clean and dry the inside of the vegetable. Bamboo stirrers, wooden bowls, ladles and spoons too can be locally made with some effort but the same articles of sturdier metal are easily procurable from the markets. Rice is no longer eaten on plantain leaves; the poor now buy cheap aluminium or melamine plates while the rich prefer the more expensive porcelain dishes.

Of late, a manufacture that has tended to fall into much disuse is the exquisite homespun which a woman traditionally mastered after years of practice under the supervision of her mother and grandmother. One chief objection of the early Lushai to girl's education started by British missionaries in the beginning of the 20th century was that they would lack in the essential craft of weaving clothes by the time they became marriageable. Most tribes have their own distinctive attires, and the colours and patterns vary noticeably from one tribe to another. Some like the Mru did not initially weave their clothes; they have interesting tales about the scantiness of the female attire. One tale says that when God started distributing clothes to different races of man, the Mru was working in the *jum*. By the time he learnt of the event, it was already evening, and so he ran and went up to God but there was nothing left save a short piece of the blue coloured cloth bare enough for his wife to tie round the waist and conceal her shame. Another tale says that God one day sent plentiful clothes for the Mru woman but the cow that ate their scripture also swallowed the clothes except for the very short *wanklai* which their women wear. In more recent times, the Mru learnt weaving from their neighbour tribes. Thirty years ago, the Bru female used a waistcloth (*r'nai*) that barely even touched her knee; yet, it is very difficult now to get the Bru to conceding the fact. Today, of course, she puts on a longer piece, which falls to a couple of inches above the ankle.

Preparation for making the homespun begins at home, usually after the last harvest of paddy. As already indicated, the cotton is ginned, dried, carded with a bow and spun into thread. From the leaves of the indigo plant and the barks of jungle trees, various dyes—blue, green, red, black and yellow are obtained and the threads coloured accordingly. Weaving is mostly done on the portico. One end of the warp is fitted to a bamboo beam in the front wall; the other is adjusted by a leather strap that the weaver wears round the back of her waist. To operate the loom, she presses the treadle with her feet. Then, as the heddles start moving, she skilfully passes the spindles through the warp, simultaneously flattening all intersecting threads with a heavy blade of chiselled bamboo. The process is long, and it requires several weeks of uncomplaining labour to make a decent piece of cloth. In the past, she was always assisted by her little daughter who eventually learnt to do the work herself. Today, the same girl goes to school and has little time to assist her mother at home. With a diverse assortment of clothes to be had of the markets, very few young girls show interest in acquiring the traditional craft from their mothers and grandmothers.

Trade and Barter

Though swidden economy was essentially self-sustaining in character, men of some means in the village employed clients to work in the jum to secure surplus and have opportunities to carry on some form of trade or barter. Of course, economic necessity sometimes compelled the poor hill farmer to sell rainforest products like bamboo, honey, roots and unused cotton in nearby markets and buy food, salt, dry fish, etc. Some form of internal trading existed among the hill tribes long before they came into contact with the people of the plains. A basket of paddy seeds borrowed in sowing time was returned after the harvest. Exchanges were always possible – a large gourd vessel against a loan of cottonseeds, an iron spear-head for a pair of egg-laying fowls, and so on. Individual families carried on the barter, and repayment was done by giving back the principal, no interest being charged on the loan. To meet the expenses of marriage in a family, Chiefs or well-to-do persons of the village were approached; generally, these loans were repaid through clientele services, the debtor asking one of his own children or a relative to serve the creditor until the expiry of the loan (Lewin 1869: 34). But in post-contact situation, when hill men started coming down to river-side bazaars, the chief marketers they found were Bengalis who by diverse means made them sell their commodities at throw-away prices. If cash was loaned in one season, it was repaid in the next season by the hill farmer giving away his produce of cotton, oilseeds, and bamboo either free or for a negligible balance that remained after deducting the principal plus the interest on it.

The markets were held on certain week days and, with the control of Bengali traders steadily increasing in course of the 19th century, every form of barter was replaced by cash transaction. Early prosperity coming from the bamboo trade in the Feni country led the well-do-do Bru families to devise one of their cultural artefacts, the *Rangbatang* or an elaborate necklace of silver coins. The use of silver for ornaments, especially the heavy earrings that Bru and Halam women fit into the large holes of their earlobes, predate by centuries their trade interactions with the Bengalis but the *Rangbatang* gained popularity only in 19th century with the silver coins showing the head of Queen Victoria. The frontier tribes like Darlong, Bawm, Puitu and early sections of the Lushai generally preferred trading within their own territories. In their deals with these tribes, the plains' trader paid levies on cotton and oilseeds at collecting stations and in return got the hill produce at prices much lower than it would have fetched if sold directly.

As long as family-tax was payable in cotton, the system favoured the swidden farmers because with some effort, they could easily produce surplus in their own *jums* and pay their dues but after the British extended their fiscal policy to the hills, cash became vital and the swidden-farmer not always having ready money at hand, incurred the debt of the Bengali trader.

The British tried to stop money-lending through legislation and, theoretically at least, some curb was put on the activities of *mahajans* by limiting the amount of interest on debt incurred and appointing supervision officers (Lewin 1869: 24-25). But the practice continued to exist for more than a century after the first laws were made. Government disfavour with swidden farming along with attempts to induce the highlander to adopt plough cultivation did not necessarily ensure their economic well-being. When a section of the Kaipeng initially went over to plough cultivation in the mid-20th century, they failed to produce enough crops to sustain their families for the whole year and thus incurred debt (Bhattacharya 1980: 66). Banking at that time was not adequately developed in Tripura to make unscrupulous money lending ineffectual. One of the many factors responsible behind ethnic riots of 1980 in the state was economic deprivation of the tribes; but since then things have changed. In CHT, on the contrary, Bengalis started to settle illegally in large numbers soon after the British left and their number, despite decades of armed resistance from the Shanti Bahini, has multiplied. Today, they control the major markets in the three hills districts of Khagrachhari, Rangmati and Bandarban, while the tribes carry on small trade in their villages. In Tripura, especially after 1980, Bengalis have stopped trading in the interiors, leaving the hill men to manage their own affairs. However, major transactions are conducted in markets located in the district and the sub-divisional towns.

In all tribal markets, the old character of specific week-day bazaar is retained. Some come down to sell vegetables grown in their *jum*, others the surplus paddy from intensive agriculture on available plain lands and still others their domestic pigs and poultry. Enterprising traders will import from Myanmar diverse articles ranging from mosquito nets to porcelain cups, wooden ladles, etc. Government officials do not mind these cross-border transactions so long as no illegal deals in arms and ammunitions are reported. Tape-recorders, cassettes, mobile phones, rechargeable batteries, charge lights, China-made watches and electronic gazettes can also be had from the more frequented markets. The Burmese *napi* ('powder of dried shrimps') is a valued item among the Chittagong tribes. Women greatly prefer the Burmese *htamin* ('colourful cloth worn like petticoat'), besides fanciful garments and articles of toilet like cologne, freshener, musk, nail polish, hairpins, lingerie, etc. from countries of Southeast Asia. There is always something to buy from these markets.

6

Head-hunting

Blood-feuds were common to most ancient societies, having originated in the attempt to justify the tenet of gore, i.e., blood for blood, and thus binding upon a man the duty to avenge the killing of his kinsman. Reconciliation was possible by compensating in material terms the worth of the dead kinsman, on the pretext of meting out justice in ways other than bloodshed. Head-hunting emerged as the corollary to equally dealt justice and eventually became a means to attainment of temporal as well as spiritual merits. The manner in which the fiercest of Indo-Myanmar tribes carried it out until about the closing years of the 19th century differed little from their own game-hunting expeditions. Their choices were simple – the village for the jungle and the human for the game, with the ascent to fame measured by the number of heads brought home. Cannibalistic feast on human flesh is unknown to the Kuki-Chins. When the head-hunter took part in blood-feuds, he verily reaped multiple merits – justice for a slain kinsman, social acclaim for himself and for his Chief, as also the entitlement to a happy afterlife.

The head-hunting tribes

The Bru appears to make some distinction between the Halams and the later Chins, calling the latter *S'kam* (a variant of Tippera *Sikam*) and holding them responsible for carrying out *chawba* or massacre. In sad tales pertaining to raids on Sing-gang, Maisikhi, Kaitwak, etc. (villages on the southwest side of present Tripura along the Chittagong

Hill Tracts), the Lushai is identified as depredator. Those villages were destroyed and the heads of slain Brus taken as trophies of war. Most Old Kukis have no tradition of head-hunting. Some like the section of the Hrangkhawl living in Cachar Hills appear to have got involved into it during their clashes with the Thado. Among other Halam tribes, the Korbong suffered much despicably from the Lushai raids of the late 18th century AD. As for the Darlong of Tripura, they are recalled as fierce head-hunters who, at the behest of Bir Chandra Manikya, suppressed the Jamatiya revolt of 1864 and took 200 Jamatiya heads to Agartala (Debbarma 1931: 67). In that raid, the Darlongs were assisted by the Hava Kukis. Ngursailoia was the Darlong chief and Haupuilala the chief of the Hava Kukis, and together they had sent six hundred warriors to punish the Jamatiyas who dissented to paying the high family tax imposed on them by the Tippera Raja.

Roughly, the period of head-hunting in Tripura and Chittagong Hill Tracts covers the second half of the 18th and almost the entire 19th century. It became particularly acute after arrival of the Lushai and the Shendu to Mizoram and the North Arakan Hills bordering CHT. The Thado or Khongzai tribe had preceded the Lushai into Mizoram and expelled the earlier tribes like the Hrangkhawl. Soppitt calls the Thado a co-tribe of the Jansen and refers to their head-hunting practice: 'The heads of the foe slain are brought back by the victors or, should these be too numerous, the ears of the slain foe are preserved' (1893: 18). Initially, head-hunting was confined to the independent hill territory on the eastern side of the Tlwang but it gradually penetrated into the Chittagong Hill Tracts and the adjoining territory of Hill Tripura.

In 1777, the Chief of Chittagong commanded Captain Ellesker to send men from the 22nd Batallion of Sepoys 'for the protection of the inhabitants [of the Hill Tracts] against some Kookies' (Lewin 1869: 21). The Tippera chronicle, the *Rajmala* mentions 'Kuchang Kukis' seeking the assistance of Rajdhar Manikya in 1792 against the Lushai on the ground that the latter had invaded their village and massacred men, women and children. Undoubtedly, the Lushais were the most feared for their head-hunting raids; the appellation originally meant 'one with long hair,' and it probably originated in the peculiar way the Lushai male wore his long hair into a bun at the back of the head. But *Lushai* in the sense of 'head-hunter' (*lu* for 'head' and *shei* meaning 'cutting off') gained currency in the early 19th century when raids on the frontier villages of Cachar, Manipur, Tripura and Chittagong Hill Tracts came to be increasingly characterised by a tendency to procure human heads as spoils of victory. In January 1860, the Thangluah clan committed an outrageous foray on 15 villages in Chaglania under Khandal Police Station (now in Noakhali District of Bangladesh), killing 186 people and taking about a hundred captives, mostly women.

Besides the Darlong and the Lushai, the Shendu and the Pawi tribes too were infamous for their head-hunting proclivities. During the later half of the 19th century, the Shendu and the Haulhang raided on several villages in the Hill Tracts. In one incident which occurred in January 1888, not far from Rangamati, a group of Pawis attacked Lieutenant Stewart and his survey party and took away their heads; around the same time, in the upper Chengri valley, a Haulhang raid left thirty one killed and their scalps removed (Hutchinson 1909: 11).

In the simplest form of blood-vengeance, some relative of a murdered man went out to slay the murderer and secure justice for his slain kinsman. If the malevolence was deep-seated, the murderer was killed, his head then cut off and carried home to the satisfaction of the family. This one-to-one equation changed when a man of some standing of a certain village got killed by another man from a different village and a common issue was made out of the private feud and the entire village dragged into a vendetta that called for many heads to offset the loss of one. Inter-ethnic disputes over land for swidden-farming was not new to the Kuki-Chins but about the 17th-18th century AD, when those feuds became increasingly acrid, some of the later Chin tribes generated community consent and made, through the instrument of repetitive action, head-hunting a socially approved practice. At a later period, it was also carried out as mere sport with peaceful villages converted into human hunting fields. As the inevitable result of such action, the measure of a head-hunter's fame came to be seen in computable terms of the total enemy heads he brought home. As corollary to fame followed the conferment of social titles, such as that of the *Raltha* among Darlongs, and the license, as in pre-Christian Lushai, to violate the chastity of many virgins.

Besides private disputes and inter-ethnic rivalry, there were also other social promptings behind the raids. When some powerful Lushai Chief died, his sons procured human heads and stuffed those in their father's grave in the belief that the souls of the vanquished enemy would journey with him to *Mithi-khua*, the village of the dead, and there serve him as clients. Among the Shendu, human heads were demanded as bride-price, especially when the Chiefs sought alliances for their sons or daughters. At the level of the commoner, maidens were easily wooed by young males who participated in raids and brought back human heads. Any male indisposed to head-hunting was considered effeminate and it was difficult for him to get a beautiful wife. So much of emphasis was put on the possession of human heads that with passing time the manner of acquiring it dwindled into dastardly murders. Of course, the Kuki-Chins never carried out their wars with open boldness; there were neither challenges to be thrown to the enemy to meet in face-to-face battles nor naming of the day and time to formally commence hostilities. Everything was carried out through clandestine operations and abrupt, unannounced attacks. It was no shame for a warrior to retreat from an unmatched or stronger warfront. What mattered most was the tally of human heads.

If a young man failed to bring home a head from a raid, he could always sneak into the jungles around his neighbour's village and take chances with the women who came to fetch water from the river. In game hunting expeditions, the sex of the killed animal was never important; in the same way, the head-hunter made no distinction between males and females when he collected human heads. For him, there was also glory in kidnapping a child from another village, taking home the head after throwing the victim's body into the river.

Mode of Expedition

Raids were carried out in the early hours of dawn and the chief strategy was to take the enemy by surprise. The choice of dawn as the time of attack gave the raiders the opportunity of sufficient daylight to return home through the thick jungles, especially in the event of the enemy organising a pursuit after them. As already mentioned, Kuki-Chin raids were never carried out in open boldness but in a quiet, abrupt manner to gain an advantage over the enemy village. The strategy was effective and the warriors acquired for themselves a maximum number of enemy heads. When the number of heads were too numerous to be carried along, only the scalps were collected. If a village under attack became suspicious of any enemy movements outside the defensive palisade, the common recourse was to abandon houses and escape through the concealed paths, leaving behind only a couple of old decrepit to the sheer frustration of the raiders. Sometimes, two warriors would divide the spoil between them, one of them taking the head and his friend the scalp. A Sema Naga who failed to get an enemy head but had helped another warrior to secure one would hang up a gourd or an earthen pot to represent his trophy (Hutton 1921b: 176). But when the Angamis failed to find sufficient human heads in the enemy village, they chopped off the arms and the feet of the few slain and took those pieces back to the village in triumph (Hutton 1921a: 158).

In Kuki-Chin head-hunting, chopped off human limbs were not preferred to the severed head or the scalp.

When a group of warriors went out on the war-path, they were cheered and complimented by their kinsmen. The appearance of a single star close to the moon was a sign that it as war time; various other omens were also consulted but the essential preparation to any expedition consisted of sacrificing an animal by the Chief and giving to his warriors a feast of the meat along with excellent rice-beer. Stimulants extracted from the locally grown hemp plants were also used by the warriors. If the Chief accompanied the party, he went after the ablest warriors of the age-set. Should they achieve victory, he led them triumphantly back to the village but if the enemy proved more powerful, forcing the raiders to retreat, the same Chief as a rule abandoned the field after his warriors had scrambled to the safety of the surrounding jungles. Among the Lushai was a custom not to kill any Chief except in uncontrolled battle fury, because their Chiefs were believed related to each other by ties of consanguinity (Lewin 1869: 100).

Once a party went out on the war-path, the simple code was to put to death as many as possible. Some captives were usually carried away by the raiders to their village where families employed them as clients to lighten the labour of family members during *jum* work. The Thados sometimes sold their captives of war; some Chin tribes of Myanmar too did the same. But the Lushai or the Darlong did not favour such practice. For their Chiefs and men of some means, captives were a means to ensure economic surplus for their families in course of the cultivating season. Powerful Lushai Chiefs often raided villages in Cachar to secure female captives to attend to their newly married daughters.

If a Chief was incapacitated by illness or otherwise, young warriors of the age-set residence of his village brought in a captive so that he could strike off the head with a chopper. A similar practice was followed if the Chief was too young and the regular warriors considered it a risky business to get him into a war. The captive was bound up with ropes and brought before him so that he could cut off the head. After all, the Chief had the right to everything in his village. In an old Rivung practice, the heads of adversaries were stuffed 'into leathern bags; and, if the blood of their enemies be on their hands, they take care not to wash it off. When, after this slaughter, they take their own food, they thrust a part of what they eat into the mouths of the heads, which they have brought away, faying to each of them: "Eat; quench thy thirst; and satisfy thy appetite: as thou hast been slain by my hand, so may thy kinsmen be slain by my kinsmen!"' (Rawlins 1792: 161). To lick the enemy's warm blood from the spear or the chopper was a gory showing off; by itself, the act attached no ritual significance. But when a warrior ate a cut-out piece of the adversary's liver, it was believed to swell his courage and make him more brazen in barbarity. When finally, the enemy's cut off head was stuck on a bamboo pole in the heart of the village, it assured the beholders that the head-hunter had performed an act worthy of simulation. Apparently, the annihilation of an entire village would have blocked the chances of retributive slaughter but in the Lushai's world a Chief always had some blood relative in another village to execute the tenet of gore in the near future by seeking blood for blood and head for head.

Among the Nagas, head-hunting not only enhanced the head-hunter's social prestige but also made the crops better through transference of the soul matter into the soil. Originally, animals were sacrificed by the cultivator to appease the spirit-deities. Later, when animals were replaced by human beings, the mode of sacrifice turned gory. In an old Melanesian custom, the mummified head of the enemy was worn to take possession of the dead man's soul. The Angamis cut off not only the heads of their victims but also the hands and feet merely to put them in the fields and secure good crops (Hutton 1921a: 160). No Kuki-Chin associated head-hunting with soil fertility, but when he ate a piece of the adversary's liver, as it was believed to empower him with the vital energy of the enemy. If the enemy was a sorcerer, the piece of liver was eaten to neutralise any evil spell he might have cast on the warrior while dying. McCall (1949: 72) reports an incident in which Thangvuka, a young man of the Sailo clan murdered a *Dawi-thiam* ('sorcerer') named Keitawna and ate a piece of his liver 'to neutralise the effect of any evil words which Keitawna may have uttered against Thanvuka's welfare.' In a Konyak Naga custom, a slave was fetched so that the Chief's son could cut him down and distribute pieces of the victim's flesh among the young men of the *Morung* or the male age-set of his village (Hutton *Ibid.* : 159). To spear a man and then cut off the head was as effortless as killing deer or jungle boars but for a Kuki head-hunter, human flesh was not the substitute of the meat he got from hunted animals; his zeal never induced him to distribute pieces of human flesh throughout the young warriors of the *Bukpui* or the *Zawlbuk*. The Lotha Nagas of Chingaki were known to eat a part of the flesh of enemies killed in head-hunting raids, selling the rest to their neighbours (*Ibid.*: 160).

As for taking of female heads, Kuki-Chin myths' tend to associate the practice to a later date of head-hunting. In one Rivung tradition, it is recalled that once a certain woman asked her neighbour 'why she came so late to her business of sowing grain: she answered, that her husband was gone to battle, and that the necessity of preparing food and other things for him had occasioned her delay. This answer was overheard by a man at enmity with her husband; and he was filled with resentment against her, considering, that as she had prepared food for her husband for the purpose of sending him to battle against his tribe, so in general, if women were not to remain at home, their husbands could not be supplied with provision, and consequently could not make war with advantage. From that time it became a constant practice, to cut off the heads of the enemy's women...'

(Rawlins *Ibid*: 157). Generally, of course, women were easier prey than men and one could collect their heads or scalps without going out into actual warfare. It would not be far-fetched to suppose connectedness between the slaying of women and the keeping of birth-rate of the enemy low, an argument that Hutton (Ibid.: 164) had advanced in connection with Angami head-hunting, but the Kuki-Chins did not attach any special value to a woman's head as the Angami warriors did by wearing the slain woman's hair as the insignia of achievement. The tally of heads, not the sex of the victim, was the yardstick of fame. Of course, the Kuki-Chin warrior was believed to become party to the providential scheme of things when he acquired two heads out of single human body by slaying a pregnant woman. In a most gruesome practice, the belly of the headless woman was slit open with the *da*, the unborn pulled out and beheaded.

Warriors returning from a raid were welcomed with ecstatic dancing, singing and offering of excellent rice-beer from gourd vessels. When a warrior took out the head of a slain enemy from his bag, his family and admirers uttered jubilant cries, blew the gayal horn and made much noise by beating tin plates and other instruments they had with them. The young warriors were usually attended to by maidens who offered them rice-beer and also washed their blood-stained hands with the same liquor (Rawlins *Ibid*: 162). A few of those maidens were predestined to be ravished by the warriors they had thus welcomed, in fulfilment of an old custom that Lushai braves avidly observed to secure a meritorious afterlife. A warrior with a family would hold out the chopper that cut the enemy head for his growing son to give a gratifying lick on it while the mother of his son offered him rice-beer and washed the blood stains from his hands. For the warrior's wife, it was a special occasion to put on her finest piece of homespun, decorated head-dress and ornaments.

The revellers then went up to the Chief's house and in the open space in front stuck the heads on bamboo poles.

In a community feast that followed, the triumphant return of the head-hunters was celebrated by killing a gayal or a few pigs and eating the cooked meat with rice-beer. Usually, the clientele clans or the domestics of rich men prepared the feast. The man who lacked the pluck to kill an enemy or cowered from going into head-hunting was the object of ridicule, and on the occasion of celebrating manly feats in the village, he was dressed in female clothes to the ample entertainment of the onlookers. At the end of the revelry, the warriors carried some heads to their individual homes, leaving the rest on the poles in front of the Chief's house. In memoriam, a warrior also placed an enemy head on the grave of his father.

Inter-village raids were generally carried out in the months of December and January, at the close of a *juming* season or before the beginning of a new one when clients would be required by highland families for cultivation. Raids in the other seasons were not very usual unless villagers were faced with the exigency of the death of a Chief or the marriage of a would-be Chief, even some uncalled for effrontery by another village. The Bru and the Rupini associate the blossoming of the wood-plum with *Sikam chauba* or Lushai raids. In an old Bru song, it is said that every year when the wood-plum bore flowers, the Sikam made forays into their village and took away men and women. If, in those days, Lushai woodcutters were haply espied in some jungle, it caused so much panic in the neighbourhood that whole villages were abandoned and their population moved to places safe from the raiders. On the war-path, the warriors carried spears, but the most useful weapon was always the *da* or iron-chopper with which the jungle on the way was slashed, the defensive palisade of an enemy village chopped down and, most essentially, the much prized head severed from the adversary's body. In the early 19th century, Lushai and Shendu raiders learnt to wield flint muskets.

Peace-making

When two villages at enmity with each other showed earnestness to making peace, the custom was to send messengers and decide upon a future date when their Chiefs would meet at some place and make a treaty. As a rule, a gayal was sacrificed and the two Chiefs touched each other's foreheads with blood-stained hands. Both then took an oath by the iron-chopper used in cutting off the gayal's head, the summary of the treaty was that if one of them acted false, the other would be entitled to slay him with the chopper. At the conclusion of treaty, there was always feasting and drinking. The group that took the most number of heads usually returned a couple of those to the other group, in a gesture to even out things between them, but the actual equalising act came through an exchange of captives taken in the raids.

If two Lushai Chiefs took the *Saui-tan* oath ('vow of peace after strife'), each was required to eat pieces of the heart and the liver of a sacrificed dog. McCall (*Ibid.*: 50) reports an incident in which Rothangpuia once persuaded an erstwhile enemy, a powerful Sailo Chief called Savunga to eat first, which no sooner done than Rotangpuia left the place, much to the chagrin of Savunga, without eating his portion but having negotiated to his advantage. He is reported to have told Savunga, 'As you, who are the elder, have already eaten it is as though we had both eaten' (*Ibid.*). Under the circumstances of the *Saui-tan* oath, Savunga Sailo became bound never to raid Rotangpuia's village while the latter remained free, at the liberty to follow in own instincts and do what he considered best.

There were other ways in which peace-making oaths could be taken. Among Puitu Kukis, two Chiefs could also conclude a treaty by biting the tooth of a tiger or wild boar, whichever was available, in the belief that if either of them failed to keep his word, he would surely be devoured by a tiger or a boar. The fear of painful death by an attack of wild animals kept things quiet between the villages for some time, but after the death of the old Chiefs, their sons were not bound to uphold old treaties. Besides, the tendency of villages to migrate periodically from one place to another, as also the necessity to abandon old partners and forge new alliances rendered ancient oaths automatically null after some time.

When two unequally matched villages made peace between them, the weaker one usually lost its legitimate Chief and accepted a tributary status under the vanquisher, as the Ronte (Ralte) stood in relation to the Sailo clan, rendering clientele services to the latter.

Head-hunters and territorial administrators

On April 16, 1844, a party of 200 Lushai warriors under Lalchukla and Bawtaia raided Kochabari within the Manipuri territory, carrying off twenty heads and six live captives (McCall *Ibid.*: 40). The heads were taken by the raiders to fulfil a mortuary requirement of Lalchukla's father, Lalrihna. When the British sought the aid of the Tippera Raja, Krishnakishore Manikya, to bring the raiders to justice, the latter's reply that the outrage occurred outside the Tippera territory made the East India Company suspect that there existed some connections between Hill Tripura and the raiding tribes of the east. Tensions between the British and the Tippera *Raja* with reference to Kuki raids did not ease until the raid of 1860 in Chaglania and after investigation, the Judicial Proceedings, November 1860, No. 245-47, identified the chief instigators as 'four Hill Tipperah refugees of royal blood who being driven away by the Raja of Tripura had lived for sometime among the Kukis, and who took advantage of the ill-feeling caused by an attack made by the Raja's subjects on some Duptung Kukis to incite a rising that unfortunately became diverted to British territory' (*op. cit.*, Chakraborty 1964: 50).

Not all Kuki-Chin tribes living within Hill Tripura were subjects of the Raja. The Halams lived as buffer tribes between the hill kingdom and the independent territory across the Tlwang river; the reconciliatory approach of the Tippera king required their families to pay nominal revenue, even enjoy exemption from taxes when their *jum* crops failed. But the Darlong and the Hava Kukis paid no revenue to the Raja; instead, they offered him military service when needed – such was the arrangement. The Raja did not interfere in their internal matters but kept them pacified by conferring on their Chiefs titles like Jung Bahadur. With reference to the Lushai who established their supremacy over a vast territory to the east of the Longai in course of the early 19th century, the Raja's position was not very advantageous. Dissident members of his family coalesced with the independent Chiefs and instigated them to harassing him. When instigations got misdirected into murderous raids on British subjects, the Raja was suspected by the East India Company of complicity in crime. The Tippera's fiscal policy within the hill kingdom caused dissent among tribes like the Bru (Riang) who had to pay a much higher family tax ('*ghar-chukti kar*') than the other tribes did. In 1860, two relatives of the Raja, one Krishnachandra Thakur and his brother Madhuchandra Thakur, who fled from the Tippera court and took refuge in the Hill Tracts, had persuaded a section of Bru dissidents of the upper Feni to join the Lushai in the fierce raid on Chaglania.

Further south, in the Bohmong Circle, the situation began to take a grim turn from 1840, the year in which the Rigresa Chief San-taing-pru died childless and there erupted intense rivalry among his brothers and their sons on the issue of succession. By the time Kaung-hla-ngyo became the legitimate Chief in 1847, albeit with British intervention, the Shendu started their forays on villages within the Bohmong territory. No doubt, some dissident kinsmen of Bohmong Kaung-hla-ngyo had instigated the Shendu to making the raids of 1847 and 1848 with a view to removing him from power. To make matters worse of the Circle Chiefs of CHT, the new tax policy introduced about the same time had much repercussions. In the traditional way of village management, highland families were bound to their own independent, thigh-eating Chiefs; they paid no taxes to either the Chakma or the Bohmong rulers. But under the new regulation, highland families notwithstanding their ethnic affinities or blood ties to appointed village headmen were required to pay family tax through the latter to the Circle Chiefs. That caused resentment in the hill population and sections of them joined the independent tribes to foray on Chakma, Tippera and Marma villages.

Here it might be recalled that in 1760, Chittagong was ceded to the East India Company. The British did not interfere with the internal matters of the hill tribes so long as their internecine feuds and the head-hunting raids remained confined to the tribes themselves and occurred outside the British territory. But from the mid-l9th century the frontier villages and tea-estates began to be repeatedly violated. Initially, the chief motive of Lushai forays was not to attack the British but tribes that had earned their ire and taken refuge in the British territory or in Hill Tripura. However, a number of misdirected raids got the British involved. In 1860, the Hill Tracts was formally annexed and a number of frontier posts created to exert direct control over the tribes. But the raids did not stop until the Lushai were completely subjugated and their independent territory annexed in 1893. That came as a happy culmination to a series of punitive expeditions the British had carried out against them for almost half a century. A proposal for administering the North and the South Lushai Hills under a single charge was made on November 15, 1893; the proposed amalgamation took on April Fools' Day 1898 and the Lushai Hills District was created under the province of Assam and put under the charge of a Superintendent with headquarters was at Aizwal. The creation of the Lushai Hills District affected the section of the Shendu living in the South Lushai Hills, and they got separated from their kinsmen in the Chin Hills. By 1924, their kinsmen in Myanmar too were subjugated.

In British dealings with the head-hunting tribes, aggression was followed up by attempts at befriending the Chiefs who tendered their submission. Diplomacy allowed the British government to induce the independent tribes into becoming peaceful subjects but it was Christian missionary activities that transformed them into a people with broad sympathy and compassion for mankind. In the Baptist Missionary Societies' Report for 1906, John Lorrain wrote these encouraging words – 'Formerly, the Lushais were known only to the outer world as a much-feared savage tribe, whose head-hunting expeditions often brought sorrow, death or slavery to those who were unfortunate enough to have their homes within raiding distance of their mountain fastnesses. Nowadays, prayers and songs of praise are rising to God from many villages in this wild country....' In the early part of 1892, the Lushai had raided the Borunchhera Tea Estate on the Cachar frontier, killing forty-nine persons and taking thirteen captives. Fourteen years later, in 1906, they were contributing money for the relief of earthquake victims of the Kangra Valley.

7

Sex, Gender and Family

Multiple areas of exclusion in the social construct can be conceived of by linking sex or the physiological and visible distinction of genitalia with the social facts of gender inequality, subordination and power asymmetry. In patrilineal societies of mainstream India and Bangladesh, descent and inheritance are reckoned in the male line and there is a very high premium on the social management of female sexuality. The highland tribes of Tripura and Chittagong Hill Tracts too endorse patrilineal descent in that children invariably belong to the father's clan. Though in matters pertaining to love, wedlock and divorce, the individual choice of the highland female was never summarily curtailed in traditional societies, she still suffered gender subordination and asymmetry in the public domain. Until recent times, property and inheritance were controlled exclusively by highland males.

Attitude to female sexuality

After wedlock, highland women are faithful to their partners and indulgence in adultery is rare. Before marriage, adolescent boys and girls freely intermix and it is not sinful of a maiden to yield to the solicitations of her lover. In their world, chastity does not affect the customary flow of bride-wealth from the groom to the bride's father. A Rivung girl might leave a door open for her lover to slip into the house while her unsuspecting parents slept but the boy had to take care not to wake her parents up and, in former times, he had to return to the age-set house before dawn. Among the Bru, a young male who has found favour with a girl's father can reside with her family and take liberties with the girl once her parents are asleep. It is not that the girl's parents do not know of the clandestine affairs carried in their house but so long as a particular match has their tacit approval, they will ignore things. If, however, her family does not fancy the lover, the latter has to take the added caution of giving them no inkling of his movements. To get caught in the act is double disgrace for a boy; he is compelled to pay a customary fine to the girl's father and also to bear the molestations of her brothers or other young men of the neighbourhood.

The extent of free mixing is evinced by the practice of young lads to call on a girl, in the evening, after the day's work and to spend several hours at her house singing, gossiping and drinking. To have multiple suitors is not uncommon for girls but with passing time and familiarity, she takes only the best of them for husband. In the old days, girls preferred brave hearts who killed tigers and other wild beasts, or took part in raids and punitive expeditions, even joined elephant kheddah operations and returned to the village with the tales and trophies of individual success. Men who lacked the courage to wield spear or *da* on animals and enemies were objects of ridicule. With changes in economy and life-style, old preferences have shifted, and though the maiden heart yearns for a brave heart as bed-mate, her head cannot afford to summarily overlook the economic side of wedlock. In a compensatory gesture, a mock display of the suitor's physical strength is made, as among the Murasing, by bringing down a banana plant with a single blow of the iron-chopper. Parental opposition is not a worth deterrent so long as the customary practices of the tribe are upheld, and in such cases, they might resort to persuasion to deter their daughter from match-making with the boy at their discountenance. A highland girl enjoys the liberty to approve or disapprove of any suitor. If, for some reason, her regular lover incurs her displeasure and she decides to take a different man as husband, neither the latter nor his family will make any issue out of her past action after wedlock. Yet, until that time, she must be cautious enough not to offend any of her suitors. Among Darlongs, a real impediment to a girl's marriage is any impolite behaviour at the time courting, which marks her as nasty, uncouth (Darlong 1995: 142). In some head-hunting societies of yesteryears, like that of the Lushai, maidens were often afflicted by the warrior's special privilege to violate the chastity of a certain number of girls and earn spiritual merits from the act. But that wild custom is now abandoned.

Youthful transgressions are not uncommon and if pregnancy is not desired, the abortion services of local hospitals can be availed. There are also other old ways of terminating unwanted pregnancy by twitching of the abdomen, eating of irritant leaves, etc. Sexual excesses indulged in time of festivals and celebrations do not always lead to permanent relationships; mostly, such acts are committed as fleeting passion or ephemeral temptation. Incest is shunned and prostitution unknown. The absence of unmarried mothers in highland villages encourages the inference that abortion is carried out quietly. As already indicated, chastity is not a social impediment to wedlock, but since descent is invariably reckoned in patrilineal terms, the notion of legitimate fatherhood is most relevant. In general, when a girl becomes pregnant, her parents attempt, even enforce compulsions on her lover to marry their daughter. In head-hunting Lushai, a warrior was not required to marry the maiden he ravished but when they abandoned their old ways, they too endorsed the rule of not forcing a girl to have sex against her will. Social fatherhood is allowed to children of legitimate birth by the instrument of adoption, and all cases of housewives adopting the illegitimate children of their unmarried sisters are kept secret. The presence of unmarried mother in a house is considered the greatest disgrace to the family.

As far as management of sexuality is concerned, the customary practices of most tribes are the result of socio-political changes experienced by them. Girls in every society have a natural right to look attractive, but up to as late as the mid-19th century, the Khyang had meticulously scrapped that right of their women by hideously tattooing their faces in black. A similar practice prevailed a century ago, though with falling disuse, among the Chinme and the Chinbon tribes of the Yawdwin Chin Hills. No doubt, it was an attempt to rescind the declining birth-rate of villages affected by inter-ethnic raids that saw the women of weak tribes carried off by their powerful neighbours. In the Khyang tradition, it is recalled that a certain king, who once upon a time conquered the plains of Ava and Pegu and drove the Khyangs to the mountains, imposed an annual tribute on them, in default of which, their women were carried away. As this continued for long, bringing their race to the verge of extinction, it was proposed that women should tattoo their faces and the proposal was readily accepted (Trant 1828: 268). Other Kuki-Chin tribes did not adopt the Khyang practice of their women neglecting the toilet; instead they encouraged maidens to look attractive, giving premium to the natural liberties of youth so long as they stayed in the village but restricting their movements outside the protective palisade in a bid to minimise the chances of their women being carried off as captives, beheaded or scalped.

It has already been stated that married women are faithful to their spouses and adultery in the highlands is extremely rare. Should any such affair be ever discovered, the offenders are punished by the village council according to the customary laws of the tribe. The Khyang lets off the adulteress on payment of penalty that includes forfeiture of the claims to even her personal belongings. In pre-Christian Lushai, a wronged husband could in fit of anger kill an unfaithful wife. But the Lushai's severity was compensated by allowing their woman much freedom of choice in matters of divorce or separation. 'If parents marry her to a man whom she does not like, she generally runs away from her husband, and is not thought to be wrong in doing so' (Lewin *Ibid.*: 101-2). Divorce is easy to get. On diverse grounds of the husband's violent temper, drunken misbehaviour or infatuation for another woman, she needs only to apply to the village council for separation. If a wife is guilty of violating her wedlock vows, her husband claims the bride-price he paid at the time of contacting marriage. He can also demand of the other man a compensatory amount of money equal to the dowry he paid to the wife's father. Should separation come of the husband's fault, the wife is given maintenance until the time she gets remarried.

The only tribe that does not seem to incorporate any specific provisions for formal divorce within their customary law is the Pangkhua. At best, a woman may apply to the village council for *Insen* or the condition to live apart from her husband on the same grounds that her counterparts in other highland societies seek divorce. But while divorce allows a woman to remarry, nullifying old wedlock vows through community consent, in the *Insen* system, neither the wife nor the husband is allowed to remarry as long as both are alive. Should either of them take a lover, it is considered a grave social offence for which the offended party is compensated with a gayal or a reasonable amount of cash. Remarriage of a Pangkhua woman is allowed only after the death of the original spouse.

Comparing the Gender roles

Though considerable freedom is allowed to highland women in matters of mate selection, marriage and divorce, gender asymmetry is conspicuous in the collective process of socialisation that assigns to her the tasks of child rearing, housework and of assistance to the male workforce in the *jum* but excludes her from all economic and political power-sharing. Mythic constructs that prevail in the highlands confine women's wisdom to the immediate water source or mainly her domestic chores. In head-hunting societies of the pre-Christian Lushai and the Darlong, she was subjected to extreme marginalisation; the great emphasis those societies put on warfare and participation of the male force in head-hunting raids reduced her economic status to the parallel level of the client. As already discussed, one aspect of the Lushai raids was to procure clients for *jum* work; the arrangement gave much leisure to the male workforce but they kept their women working side by side with their clients in sowing seeds, weeding and harvesting. Their social status suffered too, and in one old saying, the female is compared to a bamboo fence useful when she is fresh and strong but replaceable when she gets old and worn-out. An old Darlong axiom associates the woman to a doorstep that requires replacement after some years of use.

Among the Halam tribes, the women did not suffer as much degradation as their counterparts in Lushai did, though in the old days, the former too was denied economic rights and excluded from power-sharing. The husband gave some support to his constantly drudging wife in domestic matters by helping her collect firewood, giving fodder to the domestic animals and working by her side in the *jum* field. Though he never did any weaving for her nor expected her to help him in making baskets, he extended a fair measure of support in terms of attending to the needs of their growing children and treating them with affection. The Lushai father too was affectionate towards his children, especially to a growing son who was expected to follow his footsteps by becoming a fierce head-hunter in the years to come, but a general lack of confidence in the Lushai in matters of supportive childcare saw their society practice a form of infanticide in which the infant of a woman who died of complications during child delivery was smothered and buried beside her in the same grave. This practice is unknown to the Old Kuki, the Bru and the other highland tribes of the region.

The notion of inheritance of landed property is comparatively recent among the highland tribes studied herein; it did not evolve before they had settled down in permanent villages, abandoning their former roving nature. But when it evolved, the woman was excluded from inheritance. With reference to social titles and other paraphernalia that come with high social standing, it may be pointed out that Lushai women like Banitangi emerged as powerful Chiefs but such instances are rare. Marriage payments do take the form of bride wealth, but here too the actors involved are invariably males – the husband or the husband's group as the wealth-giver and the wife's father as the wealth-taker. The bride's mother gets only a token milk-price. Banitangi's rise to Chieftainship comes from the particular circumstances of her blood-connection with the strong Lushai Chiefs, Mungpir as her father and Sukpilal as her sibling, as also from her marital alliance with the son of another powerful Lushai Chief, Lalsukla. Her bride-price was exorbitant and Murchuilal needed two years to pay the same and take Banitangi as his wife (Chatterji 1995: 82).

Usually, the Lushai Chief did not consult his wife on economic and socio-political matters but she could extend reprieve to a fugitive or an offender. Lewin (1869: 102) refers to an old Thangluah rule by which a murderer could escape the vengeance by seeking the intervention of the Chief's wife: 'A life is exacted for a life. The murderer will not escape even by taking refuge in the Chief's house; the relatives will cut him down. If however the Chief's wife adopts him as a son, he escapes scatheless.' Among Bawm, the Chief's wife enjoyed many privileges, including, as Spielmann (1968: 73) points out, her husband's prerogative to ride on the back of his clients. Co-wives and other female attendants of the Bawm *Raja* were not entitled to similar prerogatives but they enjoyed a high social status and commanded the respect of his people. Nevertheless, the entitlements also cost them dearly. When a Bawm Chief died, his wife was buried alive with him, so that she accompanied him to the afterlife and attended to his needs. Old folks who had witnessed the burial of the last Bawm

Raja say that two maidens were also buried alive with him, and for several days after the incident, they heard the sound of the gong coming from inside the *Raja's* grave.

From a pacifist's point of view, it might be argued that the highland woman is a social personality – a daughter to one, a wife to another, a mother to a third, a sister to a fourth, etc. – balancing the male roles as son, husband, father, brother and so on. But the actual picture is that she toils everyday from sunrise to sunset, and the so-called division of labour allots to her more work and less leisure than to the men. Growing boys play around their houses or loiter about the jungles with slings in hand but the girl stays at home and begins by helping her mother in her daily chores from a very tender age and learning, in course of time, to cook food, weave clothes, and do all other works about the house. Should a family be large and the women in it few, she works for extra work hours in making clothes for everyone. Weaving is done alongside the regular chores of bringing firewood from the jungle, fetching water from the river to the uphill village, looking after growing children, cooking meals for the family, attending to ageing in-laws, etc. The Chief's wife or the wives of rich family-heads can afford to keep female clients and distribute her everyday chores among them but the commoner's wife dispenses with that luxury. Before marriage, a girl has time to attend to her toilet but after marriage, the added responsibilities of a housewife keeps her busy throughout the day, and she gets little or no time to attend to personal looks, except on socio-religious occasions when she is expected to put on her finery. She usually ages more quickly than her husband does.

Family type

The predominant family type in the highlands is one which connects male members of three generations descended lineally from a common ancestor and includes their wives and unmarried daughters. They are all embedded in the male family head. However, when a man has two married sons, the rule seeks one of them live with his parents while the other son goes out of the family to build a new home. A daughter will leave her father's house on marriage and become a member of her husband's family. Among the family members, they share strong ties and perform their individual roles according to age and gender. Polygamy is not favoured but highlanders are not unfamiliar with the practice of their Chiefs and well-to-do householders keeping several wives. Except among the Pangkhua, an ordinary swidden-farmer can take a second wife in the lifetime of his original wife if the latter suffers from barrenness or any inabilities that deny the male a biological heir.

The highland joint family evolved at a time when the hunting-foraging groups began to practice slash and burn cultivation and spend more time and energy in securing a steady diet throughout the year than rely on the odds of acquiring victuals from animal hunting and gathering of rainforest products. In the oral tradition of the Bru, three distinct stages of social development are identified. The *Bruha-Breha* or the first period is the cave-dwelling stage in which hunting and foraging were the principal subsistence strategies. Among hunters-gatherers, the sharing of meat resources formed the basis of economy, but the individual's responsibility towards family was confined to nurturing children to a certain age. The natural resources of the environment could not always be relied upon to sustain large families. During the *Khichongma-Khichongapha* stage, swidden-cultivation became the chief economic activity supplemented by the older resources from hunting and food gathering. A domestic workforce was essential to ensuring a steady food produce from cultivation; whence, the *Khichongma-Khichongapha* parents sought to merge their nuclear workforce with those of their married children and thus create the joint family. In the *Danguima-Danguipha* stage, dated around the late 15th century AD, the Bru's present ethnic system emerged. They came under Tippera domination.

Without variation, the highland family is patriarchal; the male head is the authority figure and the other members live and work with reference to him. It is, however, different from the Hindu joint family wherein all lineal and collateral kinsmen of the patriarch lived as a single unit, each contributing to the growth of the family's wealth through individual labour and bringing dowry with marriage. The dowry was either moveable things like cash or jewellery and domestic animals or immoveable property like land and house. In the highland type of joint family, married male siblings do not usually stay under the same roof and their marriage payments flow as bride-wealth from the wife-taker to the wife-giver. Besides, the highland patriarch could not afford to be authoritative in which case his married son would abandon him or his wife acquire a divorce. In the Hindu united family, on the contrary, the woman suffered maximal repression, without the right to get legitimately separated from an assaulting husband. Among the Pangkhua too, a wife cannot acquire divorce from her husband but, as already noted, she enjoys the right to live apart from him with the informed consent of the community.

Apart from paying bride-wealth, every highland groom was required to stay for a certain period with the girl's father and provide to her family compulsory bride-service. In matriarchal societies, the favoured rule is uxorilocal residence wherein the son leaves his mother's house to take up residence with his wife or the daughter brings in the husband to her mother's house to compensate the fall in the family's male force occasioned by the departure of her brother. In the highland societies of CHT and Tripura, the custom of compulsory bride-service requires the would-be groom to take up periodic residence with his would-be father-in-law and work for the family to meet the obligations of taking away his daughter. Perhaps, the custom originated from the biological denial of sons to family heads and they were obliged to acquire males for temporary periods from outside. In the Ranglong *maksa* (marriage through compulsory bride-service), the prospective groom must serve his father-in-law for a maximum of four years, beginning the day after finalising the wedlock. Uchai custom requires four years of uxorilocal bride-service while Hrangkhawls insist on seven years of the same obligation and Brus a maximum of seven years but not less than three. For both Mru and Khyang, the tenure is three years.

Dependent members of the family included adopted children or fictive kins and clients. The former was a full-fledged family member who met the shortage of naturally born children and had the right to inheritance. Adoptions were done on the essential condition that the process involved no payment to the genitor or genetrix. There prevails in the highlands, a custom of well-do families adopting children of their poor relatives. As for clients, they were mainly debtors who agreed to repay a loan through physical labour. In the head-hunting societies, there was another category of clientele comprising captives brought from raided villages to do *jum* work and other chores for highland' masters and mistresses. In the Naga society, female captives were usually kept as domestic servants but male captives mostly killed, occasionally sold for execution and distribution of human flesh (Hutton 1921a: 154). In the Kuki-Chin practice, captive clients were as much part of the family as debtor clients were, treated at par with the other family members and living under the same roof and sharing the common hearth. However, the chief restriction that highland families observed with reference to their clients was to forbid adoption and alliance with that category.

Property and Inheritance

Traditionally, the swidden-practising tribes of Tripura and the Chittagong Hill Tracts viewed land as common property; the village and cultivable ridges in the accessible neighbourhood belonged to the community. Individual families used those ridges for their agro-economy as long as the village was in possession of the site. After two or three years, the village shifted to a different site, and individual families then sought out fresh plots in the vicinity of the new settlement. Under the highland system, private ownership of cultivated plots was not tenable but once a family selected a particular plot, it was not usual for another family of the same village to put the issue of selection into contention. Also, if a man died shortly after selecting a plot, the son living with him in the same house cultivated on it. An abandoned *jum* plot could be used by another family but in such cases there was always an interregnum fallow of several years.

When highland villages migrated from one place to another, they took with them only such moveable belongings as were most indispensable to everyday use. Lewin (*Ibid*: 15) describes the sight of a deserted village in these terms: 'there are all the evidences of occupation and recent life, but every living creature has disappeared. Granaries may be half full of grain: large wooden mortars for pounding the grains, the weaving implements of the women, and some half-finished clothes...' Any mortars and weaving implements left behind could be collected at a later time if the new village was not too far removed from the site of the deserted village. The time in which Lewin saw abandoned villages was the period of intense inter-ethnic warfare and head-hunting, when villages were abandoned in the haste of battle or from the rumour of *Sikam* (Lushai) raiders coming down to collect human heads.

The bulk of the moveable property (fowls, livestock, pigs, stock of paddy, cash and other valuables, etc.), besides social titles and endowments passed from the father to the son. Specifically though, among Bawm, Pangkhua and the Lushai clans, the youngest son lived with his parents after his marriage and became the rightful inheritor. Most Halam tribes, on the contrary, accorded the privilege of inheritance to the eldest son in the manner of the Hindus. The Murasing tribe too did the same. Wives and daughters were gracefully allowed to retain their personal jewellery and homespun. A mother could also keep the milk-price she got from the groom at the time of her daughter's marriage. After the inception of money economy, the family's cash earnings were inherited by the son who lived with the ageing father. Even the money earned by the women through physical labour became part of the father's or the husband's wealth. But the Bru women evolved an ingenious way to retain the silver coins they either earned though work or got from fathers or husbands as share of grace, using those to make their elaborate coin necklace, the *Rangbatang*. In the old highland rule, a wife who got divorced from her husband through some fault of the latter was entitled to receive maintenance until the time she remarried. A widow with minor sons acted as the guardian of all immoveable property of the family as long as the son was not mature enough to handle family matters by himself.

The notion of immoveable property gained vogue among the highland tribes around the close of the 19th century. British legislations to wean swidden farmers away from the slash and burn cultivation and to induce them to adopt plough cultivation were the prelude to permanent settlement and the notion of landed property. Restrictions on periodic migrations also affected the traditional way of life. When, in course of the early 20th century, most of the tribes started settling in permanent villages, they sought to modify their customary laws of inheritance by extending the prevailing rules on moveable property to cover immoveable property (the house and the land for wet-rice cultivation) and exclude wives and daughters from inheritance under the same old terms. Initially, landed property was passed from the father to the youngest son or to any other son who took care of the ageing parents. But of late, all sons are allowed some share of their father's immoveable property, though among the Bawm, it is still the youngest son who gets the largest share with reference to his responsibility and the privilege extended to him by old Bawm custom.

The son inheriting the property as well as the social title of the father is also responsible for repayment of every debt incurred by the father. If more than one son inherits parental property, the debt is repayable proportionately by each inheritor. Prior to disintegration of the traditional socio-economic organisation of the highlands, the creditor-debtor relation was chiefly confined to the village and unpaid debt subjected the poor swidden-cultivator to render clientele services to the Chief or some wealthy householder until the time the debt was repaid. Those debtor-clients lived with the creditor as family members and were never exposed to any harsh usage. Once debt was compensated by physical labour in jum work and other family errands, the clients returned home and lived freely. That cordial relationship between the debtor and his creditor was disrupted with the introduction of the plains type of fiscal policy and the consequent interaction of Bengali money-lenders with the hill people. A loan taken in the exigency of marriage or failure of crops increased several folds at the time of repayment. It made many debtors silently suffer 'the galling bondage' of the Bengali *mahajans* (Lewin *Ibid.*: 34); at the same time, it compelled some hill debtors to join in raids on the villages of their creditors to kill them and thus avoid the obligation of debt payment.

Ordinarily, a woman who borrowed vegetables, a small quantity of paddy or a couple of fowls from her neighbour, returned the same after a couple of days or weeks, and these transactions did not increase the dues. As a rule, women were not entitled to inheritance and that absolved even those females who inherited property through parental or spousal grace from the obligation of repaying the dead father or husband's creditors as well as sharing the debt responsibility with the male heirs. She could also postpone repayment of borrowed money as along as she remained custodian of her husband's property but once her son grew up and became a responsible householder, heirship made it incumbent on him to repay the old debt. Should the son die without having repaid a debt, the responsibility passed on to a subsequent heir, the grandson or a kinsman related to the original debtor by consanguineal ties. Usually, if in the absence any lineal descendant, the sum of liabilities far exceeded the sum of assets of the deceased, claim to heirship was not made by blood relatives for the obvious reason of avoiding repayment.

Marriage

Among the Bru, the ideal type of marriage came through parental negotiations and the groom went to live with the father-in-law and render brideservice to his family for at least three years. Lovers challenged by parental disapproval of their romance could initially elope and marry but for socialising the wedlock, it was binding on the boy to provide uxorilocal bride-service to the girl's father. Things are no longer the same today and educated Bru males find the old type of marriage repulsive. Though Bru type marriage by bride-service has now fallen into much disuse, it is not quite obsolete in far-flung remote hamlets. After a suitable girl is found, the boy's family prepares for the *wakha kaimi* or 'initiation of talks.' A day is fixed and the boy's parents go to the girl's house taking along two bottles of *arak* ('rice-beer'), some coconuts and at least two pounds of sugar-cakes. Other relatives and friends of the groom also accompany them to bear witness to the negotiation. If the girl's parents accept the gifts, it means no objection to the match. Should the father of the girl be unwilling, he finds some flimsy ground to refuse the gifts. But since visits of this type are made only after a *yauhkrai* or go-between has ensured the approval of the girl's father, the gifts are accepted and a future date selected for a second visit to discuss the topic of wedlock.

Other highland tribes of the region too carry out negotiations with the approved consent of the girl's parents and by sending intermediaries. The Ranglong term for the rice-beer gift which the groom's party sends to the girl's father through a go-between is *Chawngra kalzu*, and it is literally 'rice-beer for permission to negotiate marriage.' In the Bawm custom, the earnestness to negotiate is shown by sending the *palai* ('negotiator') three times to the girl's parents to finalise a date. Once that is done, the proposal for wedlock is conveyed by *Relpa* and *Relnu*, an elderly couple who, in addition, are entrusted with task of persuading the parents of both the bride and the groom to finalise the day of wedlock. The Pangkhua negotiate through two intermediaries, one from the groom's party and another from the bride's side before the groom's parents go to meet the girl's father. In the Khumi practice, the boy's parents, accompanied by their relatives, will reach a place close to the girl's house usually in the evening and then send an intermediary to girl's father along with rice-beer and some fowls. Should the girl's father see no objection to the match, he accepts the gifts and invites the groom's party to come and spend the night in his house.

Bru marriage payments flow as bride-wealth from the wife-taker to the wife-giver. As a rule, pigs and other domesticated animals are demanded of the groom. But most importantly, the groom is expected to humour his would-be father-in-law by agreeing to perform *chamaroi tungmani* ('uxorilocal bride-service') for at least three years. If in-laws are not satisfied with the services rendered, the young man must abide with the girl's family for a longer period, the maximum tenure not exceeding seven. Bru marriage was a legitimate means for the wife-giver to acquire an additional male to booster the economic activities of the family so long as the hamlet remained at a particular site, their customary preference being a male from an agnatic segment. Hence in the old type wedlock, the ritual was conducted with the bride in absentia and the groom took his wedlock vow sitting on the folded homespun which the bride used as *risa* or breast-cover. Today, of course, both the bride and the groom take their wedlock vows together.

In the Pangkhua practice, uxorilocal bride-service is an alternative to the mode of taking the bride by paying bride-price to the girl's father. A groom who fails to pay *inkai* ('bride-price') demanded of him within an agreed period compensates his failure by rendering physical services to the girl's father. In contrast, the Khyang's economic impoverishment had long ago made families abandon the practice of bride-price and adopt the system of bride-service in which the groom is required to stay with his father-in-law for three years and help the latter in house repairs and *jum* cultivation. At the end of the period, he can take his wife and settle elsewhere or, if he is poor, live close to the father-in-law, who in such cases extends material support to the couple until the first paddy harvest.

Permissible marriage categories show some variations. Cross-cousin marriages are common; the chief argument in its favour is that one marries the children of his parents' affines, not the children of the parents' siblings of the opposite sex. Descent is traced patrilineally, and in a cross-cousin alliance, wedlock is effected in a roundabout with the son or daughter of FZH, not with any cousin born of FZ. In the old Bru society, wherein a strong egalitarian strain had led to agnatic segmentation, parallel cousin (FBC and MZC) marriage was allowable, but with later socio-economic changes affecting their family structures, the older practice has over the years tended to fall out of general favour. Even today, it is not sin for Brus to marry their parallel cousins but in present-day practice, such alliances are seldom contacted.

Strict clan-exogamy existed in former times, but most tribes now disseminate positive marriage rules by distinguishing the marriageable categories from the non-marriageable ones. Except for Bawm, Mru and Khumi, the other tribes in the region are neither purely exogamous nor strictly endogamous as far as the clans are concerned. Consanguinity is an inviolable criterion for any alliance disqualification. If two males are bound by parent or sibling ties, their lineal descendents must avoid marrying within the clan at least up to the third descending generation. But the Bawm continues to practice strict clan-exogamy; thus, within the Sunthla group, a boy from the Hlawnceu clan cannot take a wife from the same clan; he can marry a girl from any of the other clans within the Sunthla, such as Siarlawn or Bawitlung, unless of course the two clans share some blood-relation between them from a point of kinship reckoning. Bawm marriage also has a shade of hypogamy in it and the wife-givers rank higher than the wife-takers. In pre-Christian Bawm, alliances were most rigidly regulated; the high-ranking Sunthla clans summarily avoided intermarriage with the low-ranking clans of the Panghawi group.

Khumis too distinguish their clans as wife-givers and wife-takers and a boy will always marry a girl of higher status. The asymmetric relationship between wife-takers and wife-givers is evident in their manner of laying out feasts. Wife-takers invariably offer chicken to the wife-givers but the later must entertain the former with the more expensive pork. In their exchange of marriage gifts too, the wife-givers try to get as many things as possible from the wife-takers, besides the customary bride-price of a hundred and twenty pieces of silver coin, an uneven number of fowls (usually nineteen) and thirteen spears. In return, the wife-giver gifts a turban and a boar to the groom. As already stated, the Awa Khumis of the Chittagong Hill Tracts are largely intermixed with the Mru and their present-day practices are to a considerable extent influenced by the latter. For instance, in the exogamous Mru society, the wife-giving clans ('*tutma*') rank socially higher than the wife-taking clans ('*pen*') do. No *tutma* can take as wife a girl from *pen*. 'In principal... wife-takers, the *pen* must show respect to the *tutma*, who are wife-givers' (Brauns & Löffler 1990: 170). Within an elaborate network of kinship ties, a clan reckoned as *pen* by another clan becomes *tutma* in its relation to a third clan. Two clans recalling no alliances between them in the past can form a *tainou* or 'ceremonial friendship' at a certain point, after which members of these clans will never intermarry among themselves. Today, a boy of the *Tang* clan cannot marry a *Gripcha* girl because they now share a *tainou* relation between them.

Without exception, the general tendency is towards monogamy but a man or a woman can always marry a second time after the death of the original spouse. Even the Pangkhua has no objection to widow remarriage. Child marriage is absent. Polygyny is not unheard of at the highest level of the tribal Chief. The Lushai *Lal* could also assert filial widow inheritance. To the commoner, except the Pangkhua, a co-wife is allowed when the original wife is incapable of giving him a biological heir. Leviratic and sororatic alliances are restricted to marrying the younger sibling of the deceased spouse.

Highland Women in a Changing World

Initially when Christian missionaries tried to educate Lushai girls, they faced some opposition. In traditional socialising, a daughter began by helping her mother collect firewood from the jungle and fetch water in bamboo tubes or earthen pots from the nearby spring. As she grew, she learnt to husk paddy, cook meals and weave the homespun. When missionaries started girl's education in the South Lushai Hills in the early 20th century, Lushai parents were reluctant to send their daughters to school. In the Annual Report for 1913 of the Baptist Missionary Societies, F.W. Savidge wrote, 'A Lushai girl from the time she is about 4 years of age beings to help her mother.... she is constantly busy and is so useful to her poor hard-worked mother that she cannot possibly be spared to come to school.' The social-cultural interface necessitated adjustments in the form of co-curriculum aimed at training girls in the essential life-skills so that they would not be found to lack in the qualities of a good housewife when they returned home at the end of schooling.

In subsequent times, women's education received much encouragement from government agencies and missionary projects. Structural and functional changes in highland socio-economy have also helped the cause of women's education. In the Census of Tripura for 2001, the female literacy rate of 'Any Kuki Tribe' is 63.8 against the total tribal female literacy rate of 44.6 in the State. For tribal males from same group, the literacy rate is 81.9. The gender gap in literacy is the lowest in Mizoram with male showing 96.8 and the female 94.4 percent literates in the year 2001. Women from the others tribes are yet to match the literacy level of the Lushai women of Mizoram. In CHT, low income of families, absence of schools in most villages, poor communication and tensions following military presence have adversely affected education, and the average literacy rate of highland tribes excluding the Lushai is 33.2 (according to the Bangladesh Census of 1991). Tribe-wise, the Khumi female shows a literacy rate of only 2.7, followed by 6.6 percent for the Mru female. A section of educated highland women, especially in Tripura, also work as teachers, clerks, etc. in some private and public sector offices. In respect of inheritance, highland societies have advanced significantly to allow their women to become legitimate owners of parents' property in families where the householder is denied biological sons. Besides, there are now provisions to include daughters as inheritors along with sons, though in such cases, the old patriarchal trait prevails and the male inheritor gets a larger share.

Yet, in terms of political power-sharing, the male continues to dominate and the participation of the highland female in Tripura and the Hill Tracts in politics remains marginal. By means of community policing, they are either excluded from or unwillingly included in village councils; their wisdom is considered not worthy of taking into serious account. There is pressure at home to disengage her from the public domain and confine her activities within the family circuit. Even tribal organisations identified by governments as separatist or insurgent groups are structured on the male bias, which, like the age-sets of former times, foster gendered spaces to keep the women out of their 'socialising' activities, arguing that it is an unsafe game of physical strain and mental endurance. Sadly enough, the excluded highland women are forced into the unsafe game. The men escape into the safety of the jungles, to carry out guerrilla warfare and to either die 'honourably' or make political and economic gains through negotiations with the government. But the women who are left behind in the villages to look after the house and the children, suffer isolation, aggression, torture as well as rape during military operations against their guerrilla 'warriors.' In times of compromised peace, they must live with old scars of violence and haunting memories of brutal ravishment.

8

Society and Transition

Traditionally, tribal societies of the Northeast functioned as independent village-based organisations under the domain of Chiefs who shared kinship ties with their village communities. In size, structure and function, the formations allowed internal variations. In one extreme was the Bru with their acephalous structure; in the other was the Bawm having a rigid polity and a stratified village with hierarchical value systems. The Lushais too were very strongly organised and had powerful Chiefs and military age-sets. In between the two extremes were the 'big man' societies of Mru and Khyang. Nevertheless, societal changes occurring along the line of historical progression steadily percolated corrective elements in existing socio-political constructs of the region, even replaced the traditional highland 'tribe' structures with new configurations of social control.

Pre-Colonial Communities

It is difficult to say when the Halam tribes achieved socio-political integration but if one went by their extant traditions, community management had emerged among them before they came under Tippera domination in the 14th century. As part of a cooperative community, different clans did their assigned work. In the archetypal Hrangkhwal village, the *Saitwal panchi* controlled the distribution of rice, the *Rwipu* found settlement sites for periodically shifting settlements and selected suitable hill slopes for swidden-farming, while the *Chawnbak* monitored the supply of cotton, the *Laktangya* gave clientele service to the *Saitwal*, and so on.

In ceremonies such as the annual gayal sacrifice of the Ranglong, an inner circle of five pure clans were involved. With the majority of tribe converted to Christianity, the gayal sacrifice has now become rare. The last one was held in 2007. Among the chief requirements of the ritual is the *Narengphang*, a tropical tree which is cut down, brought to the place of worship, usually in the centre of the village, and planted upright. A gayal is tied to it. The ceremony is preceded by a community discussion in the house of the *Tara* clan. Once the time for ritual is settled, none other than a *Vangru* gets the privilege to be the first man to touch the tree; also, the *Narengphang* cannot be felled until a member of the same clan makes an incision on its trunk. When that formality is over, preparations begin for sacrificing the gayal. For the prosperity of individual houses, family heads may also bring goats. Shortly before the *Tansurai* beheads the gayal, the priest from the *Sanghuipu* clan sprinkles *laisamti* or holy water on the animal and makes incantations. Later, the *laisamti* is passed on to the *Achep* who in his turn as *kanta* ('junior in worship') purifies the goats and gives them to the *Tansurai*; the heads of the goats are left at the place of worship but the bodies taken home by their owners. Should the *Tansurai* be temporarily indisposed, his aide from the *Tankar* lineage is authorised to behead the gayal.

Clan based social and ritual functions existed in former times but there is no evidence to show that any of the Halam tribes favoured any class distinction in terms of aristocratic and commoner clans; also there is no tradition whatsoever to indicate exclusion of a clan from participation in socio-religious ceremonies. The Ranglong practice can be explained as an instance wherein the original clans forming the group persisted with the old rituals long after disintegrated sections of other tribes got absorbed into them. Otherwise, all clans within the tribe are of the same rank, none is superior to the others.

The Lushai clans often refer to the Old Kukis as *Hnamchawm*, which connotes acephalous peoples with no Chiefs. The oral tradition of the Bru states that when they lived in Maini-tlang (in the northern parts of CHT close to the source of the Maini river), they had rulers who used the title *Pha*. Interestingly, the title *Pha* was used by Tippera kings before they became Hindus. In the 15th century, the Bru was subjugated by the Tippera (Debnath *Ibid*.:21). Prior to that, they lived in band societies, de-emphasising on centralised control except in crises, when by some form of consensus a 'big man' type leader emerged briefly. That leader was called *Kachkao*. Every Halam tribe had a *Kamchikao* who performed judicial as well as socio-religious functions. Among the Molsom, he collected subscriptions from the villagers for the annual worship of *Seng-krak*, the village deity. Another function of the Kamchikao was to ensure that the different clans of the tribe worked as a cooperative community. The Halams were not *Hnamchawms*. After months of investigation on the old ways, I discovered that they who identify themselves as *Hriam* had Chiefs who sat at the head of the village council. They called him *Ulien* (also pronounced *Ulyin*). The oldest tradition of origin of the *Hriam* from *Khurpuitabum* is attributed to the pluck and acumen of an *Ulien*. In some old tales he is also referred to as *Hriam-reng* or *Hriam raja*. Specifically, the tribal Chief was the *Nam-Ulien* while the heads of clans were designated as *Panchi-Ulien*. An old Ranglong song, as I have already noted, tells that the last Hriam *Ulien* committed suicide by jumping into the Tuivai.

The *Ulien* did not derive any revenue from his people but he was a 'thigh-eating' Chief who got the hind leg of every animal the villagers hunted. By itself, the tribute had little economic value but it symbolised the Chief's right to everything in his village. The Kachin *Duwa* was a 'thigh-eating chief' and the animal thigh he got as tribute from the villagers was in recognition of claims to other socio-economic rights (Leech 1954: 155). But the *Ulien* may have differed from the Kachin chief and also from the *Lal* of the Lushai in one respect– the right to make sacrificial offerings for the welfare of villagers. As already indicated, the Halam traditions associate all ritual functions with the *Kamchikao*. During the bitter ethnic feuds of the late 18th and the early 19th century, the *Lal* grew powerful, authoritarian; he secured uncontested right not only to decide on strategies of defence and aggression but also to make offerings for community wellbeing and organise feasts of merit for himself.

Subjugation of the Hriams by the Tippera altered the former's socio-political configurations. Fated thenceforth to be known as the 'Halam' or the people who followed the hill path, their internal governance saw the creation of the office of the *Kalim* over each tribe for a tenure of allegiance. Over the entire group, at the apex of the new structure was placed the *Halamsa;* he regulated the activities of the Kalims and through them collected house-tax for the *Raja* from highland villages. The post of the *Halamsa* was not hereditary, and he remained in office so long as the council of elders had confidence on him. During his tenure, he had access to the *Hasam Bhojan*, an annual feast at the Tippera darbar. It was a sort of community feast, royally laid out on *Vijaya Dashami*, the day Hindus submerge Goddess Durga in the river. The Halamsa did not keep any part of the revenue he collected from the tribes. For his allegiance, he got from the Tippera *Raja* a coat of arms, a medallion with the king's name inscribed on it, a spear, a shield, a pair of fetters, an iron chopper, and, in later times, a muzzle-loader. To keep the activities of the Halamsa under some check, the *Raja* appointed a *Laskar* who resided for short periods in the same village where the Halamsa lived.

Though the Halamsa could be appointed from any of the twelve tribes that originally formed the *Baro Halam* community, it was usually from the *Alian* or the four major tribes – Molsom, Kaipeng, Hrangkhawl and Ranglong – that he used to be chosen; in addition, each tribe had its own Kalim and other village officials. The *Kalim* ('*Khuolam*' in

Molsom) was the village chief, who regulated all socio-economic and political activities of the village or villages under him and he also adjudicated disputes through the village social council. In the past, the *Kamchikao* ruled hereditarily; under an altered administrative set-up, the Kalim was selected by communal consent and he remained in office with reference to the village council. As for the *Asin* tribes (Korbong, Bongcher, Mawrsephang, Langkhai, Chorei, Koloi, Rupini, and Dap) of the *Baro Halam*, each had a Kalim and a village council. Sometime in the late 18th century the Ranglong social council got divided into the three zonal units– Khawpui, Khawzawbak and Sakawrnal – following dispersion of the tribe from Ruongle-vai-shua (Tipaimukh). From native accounts, I learnt that the dispersion came with the outbreak of hostilities between 'Khosak' and 'Khongzai,' i.e., Lushai and Thado respectively. After the division, each zonal unit got its own *Kalim*. The three zonal *Kalims* coordinated the activities of the tribe with reference to the *Sadar Kalim* who sat at the head of the '*Chubai*' or unified village council of the Ranglong. There were other officers like *Kabur*, *Muktear*, *Suktear* and *Arawksenga*, who performed various social and judicial functions. At this point, it would be worth mentioning that the Khawpui unit is associated those who after leaving Ruongle-vai-shua settled in the northern parts of Tripura while the Khawzawbak migrated to Sylhet at the close of the 18th century. The Sakawrnal emerged at a later time, when disintegrated sections of other tribes assimilated into the Ranglong. In the time of Krishnakishore Manikya (1830-1849), the system of single Halamsa was abolished. My Ranglong informants remember one Zwapor of the Khawklapu clan of their tribe as the last of the Halamsas.

The Khyangs of CHT say that their ancestors originally lived in small village communities, comprising a number of clans. At a later time, security concern led to the emergence of the '*mat*,' a type of local military leader acting as chieftain. In the 18th century, a group of Khyangs came to CHT from

Arakan led by Thou, a military-general of the Bohmong. At the level of village administration, I came across the use of two terms, *goungsa* and *lenchaw*. The first term is Marma for 'the village headman,' while *lenchaw* connotes 'chief' in Khyang language. Probably, the *lenchaw* functioned like the 'big man' among the Mru (Brauns and Löffler 1990:169), ensuring correct social behaviour and penalising wrongdoers. There were several *lenchaws* within the tribe, and the jurisdiction of each did not extend beyond the village of which he was the headman.

Among the Aphya Khumi, on the contrary, there existed distinct chiefly clans which gave hereditary *Ahraings* to the villages. The *Ahraing* derived no revenue from the village but got from each family a yearly basket of rice, a bottle of rice-beer and the thigh of a hunted animal. On his part, he organised feasts and fortune war parties; in addition to that, he performed such essential tasks as selecting suitable sites for frequently shifting Khumi villages, securing provisions for his people in times of crises, etc. But the Awa Khumis, like the Brus (Riangs) were egalitarians among whom brief leadership emerged in crisis. In times of peace, they managed themselves on the lines of democracy. Each village formed a distinct socio-political entity, and there was no distinction among the clans in social ranking or privilege. If two persons became involved in a dispute, it was disposed by a social council consisting of three elderly men called *Lugyi* who as judges handed out a test of endurance to both parties in the belief that the man who spoke the truth would show greater endurance than he who lied.

In contrast to the Bru and the Khumi, the Lushai were highly organised, with powerful hereditary Chiefs who mitigated civil and criminal justice, organised raids, and allocated land for swidden-farming. Most significantly, they regulated the distribution of salt. If brine wells ('*chikur*') were discovered, the Chief was entitled to collect for himself as much salt as he required, giving a portion to the party that discovered the brine well. Other families got their allotted ration with the express consent of the Chief.

The plains' system of land rights was not familiar to the early Lushai but they sought to control extensive areas of tropical rainforest by dispersing other tribes from the neighbourhood. Within a village, individual families did not pay any tax to the Chief but offered him a yearly bottle of rice-beer, the hind leg of a hunted animal, etc. As already stated, this tribute of meat betokened his prerogative as Chief and his natural right to everything in the village. Lewin (1869: 100) wrote, 'all that is in his village belongs to the Chief; he can and does call upon his to furnish him with everything that he requires.' If his house needed repairs, villagers gave their voluntary service, and in a gesture of good will, the Chief entertained them to a feast. On the occasion of marriage in his family, the village community often shared the expenses and in return they partook of the marriage feast. In dispensing justice, the Chief's word was final, and every order passed by him was meant to be obeyed. Generally though, he consulted his *Upas* or advisors. Among most clans of the Lushai existed a curious practice that betokened the high social status of the *Lal*. If an ailing Chief failed to participate in a war campaign, the young warriors of his *Zawlbuk* always brought for him a living captive, so that he could strike off the head and give legitimacy to the expedition. A practical consideration that prevented the Lushai Chief from being tyrannical towards his people was that if families became unhappy with a certain Chief, they could always abandon him and go over to a different Chief.

The Lushai Chiefs maintained extended families – children, dependents and clientele; strategically, large families not only ensured economic surplus but also helped them effectively exert social control. Mature sons and male siblings of the Chiefs could set up separate villages but blood ties kept them united. In their resistance to British expansion, some Lushai Chiefs helped their kinsmen in other villages by sending young warriors from their own *Zawlbuks*. The Darlongs too had a strong military organisation. In times of war or at the outbreak of hostilities with other tribes, the *Lal* relied upon the young warriors of the *Bukpui* to fight for him and bring victory to the people. With regard to their political institution, the Darlongs had *Khawnbawls* who, like the Lushai *Upas*, advised the *Lal*. The *Lal* was the head of the village council. If there were several villages under a Chief, then each had its own *Khawnbawl*, who performed the additional charge of the village headman. Towards the close of the 19th century, the post of the *Khawpa* or village secretary was created to keep records of the proceedings of the social council.

The Bawm who were the last to arrive in the Chittagong Hill Tracts imbibed the societal traits of the *Lai-zo* or Shendu who subdued them. In the early 18th century, a hierarchical social-system emerged among them having two distinct categories of people – the high-ranking *Sunthlas* and the low-ranking *Panghawis*. Before Christianity gave to the Bawm a classless social fulcrum, the Sunthla exerted social control and the Bawm Chief always hailed from one of the Sunthla clans, while the Panghawis served the high-ranking masters as clients. The Bawm Chief wielded great authority on the tribe; like the Lushai *Lal*, he arbitrated civil and criminal cases, allocated land for swidden-cultivation and controlled the ration of salt. He was a thigh-eating Chief, who in addition to a token gift of the hind leg of every hunted animal got a yearly basket of *jum* produce and a bottle of rice-beer from each family.

Socio-political Transforms in the Colonial Period

In 1761, as the consequence of a quarrel between the Tippera *Raja*, Krishna Manikya, and the Fauzdar of Chakla Roshnabad, the British first interfered in the internal matter of the kingdom and fixed an annual revenue on the *Raja*'s estate in the plains of Comilla. Thereafter, it took the Company more than half a century to realise that the *zamindar* of Chakla Roshnabad was also an independent king of Hill Tripura. But by that time, the British had annexed large areas of cultivable land of the *Raja's* kingdom into the newly created Sylhet District, making the Kushiara River the limit of the British territory. For the *Raja*, it was a ground for grievance but he avoided confrontation with the British. The Company took little interest in the internal matters of the Hill Tripura so long as the frontier was peaceful. When the Puitu Kukis rebelled against Krishnakishore Manikya in 1842 and their leader Sibbuta refused to pay the family tax the *Raja* had fixed on them, the British let the Tippera king deal with the rebels in ways he considered befitting, as it was part of the internal matters of the hill kingdom.

Earlier, in 1822, the Sylhet-Tippera border was formally demarcated. Not far away from that border, in the Lushai Hills, ethnic rivalry and internecine feuds among different Kuki-Chin tribes caused ethnic dispersions and social changes. As already mentioned in an earlier chapter, from the close of the 18th century, the Lushai clans began to arrive in Mizoram; their arrival not only led to the dispersal of earlier groups but also saw much infighting among the clans themselves in unpredictable alliances. Between 1840 and 1890, a series of raids were made inside the British territory, especially in the tea-estates on the Cachar frontier. Initially, the British suspected that some connection existed between the raiders and the Raja of Tippera. But the Tippera kings themselves had problems in dealing with the Kukis. When there were many claimants to the Tippera throne, which situation occurred on the death of a ruler, dissentious members of the royal family used the independent Kukis to rebel against the newly installed king. One Sambhucharan Thakur tried to incite them against the British who had helped Ramganga Manikya (1815-26) ascend the Tippera throne. Sometimes even the tribute-paying Halams took the side of the rebels. Perhaps, their involvement with the rebels had compelled Krishnakishore Manikya to abolish the old system of a single Halamsa over the entire Halam group.

With the subjugation of the Lushai by the British, their powerful Chiefs were divested of traditional prerogatives and made to function as mere village-level functionaries. In former times, the Chiefs depended on their indigenous military organisation, the *Zawlbuk*. Strong Chiefs maintained very large *Zawlbuks*, which supplied them with young warriors trained in the Lushai way. The destruction of that age-set organisation after the British occupation of the Lushai Hill marked not only the end of the Lushai's military organisation but also symbolised decay in the power of the Chiefs. Chiefship was not abolished straightaway; the British did not fail to realise that the success of the Sailo's economic system was due mainly to a great social cohesion the Chiefs had achieved through long warfare and the politics of domination. In the new system introduced shortly after the creation of the unified Lushai Hills District under a single charge in 1898, the continuance of hereditary charges became subject to the good conduct of the Chiefs and their efficiency in levying tribute from the people. Control on the activities of the Chiefs was achieved through the Circle system in which a number of villages were grouped and placed under a Circle Interpreter who was aided by a Chaprasi. Over the Circle Interpreters was the Lushai Clerk who was responsible for all supplies required by Government officers.

As for the Chittagong Hill Tracts, the dominant Chakmas and Marmas, both valley-dwelling tribes, had entered into politically beneficial relations with the plains. In 1713, Jalal Khan, a Chakma Chief, acquired monopoly in trade between the hills and the plains on payment of an annual tribute in cotton bales to the Mughal governor of Bengal. Sometime between 1774 and 1788, Bohmong Kaung-hla-pru obtained settlement for the Marma in the southern part of the Hill Tracts (which subsequently became the Bohmong Circle) against revenue payable in cotton. Earlier, in 1760, with the Mughal power waning in Bengal, the District of Chittagong was ceded to the East India Company but it was not until 1860 that the British interfered with the internal matters of the two hill Chiefs, Chakma and Bohmong. In 1874, the Chakma Circle was divided and the new Mong Circle created with the head of the Palaingsa Marmas as the Circle Chief. The three Chiefs were invested with authority to collect annual revenue from all villages under their jurisdiction. In the traditional set up, villagers were bound by kinship ties to the tribal Chieftain and they recognised no authority above him. The new arrangement destroyed the traditional structure of the hills, making all independent Chieftains tax collectors with limited judicial powers. It also allowed the Circle Chiefs 'to dismiss the traditionally elected village heads and install loyal followers of their own in all villages' (Mey 1984: 92) and, in much contradiction to the hill custom, the elected headmen were empowered to collect house tax from all families, irrespective of their ethnic affiliations.

The independent tribes of the Hill Tracts, especially the Bawm, persisted for some time with their traditional ways; the Bohmong had no control over them. But by the close of the 19th century, they too felt the impact of socio-political changes occurring in the Hill Tracts. With the end of inter-ethnic feuds, the traditional military organisation of the independent tribes fell into disuse and powerful tribal chiefs lost their legitimacy in office; the old clientele system too was prohibited, thus causing the high-ranking clans loose their means to secure economic surplus (Mey *Ibid.*: 94).

The territory of Hill Tripura was never annexed by the British. But from 1871, a Political Agent was appointed for the hill kingdom to report, nayo put curb on the activities of native raja, who he held *zamindaries* in South-East Bengal under the British and maintained the Sovereign State of Hill Tripura. Within the hill territory, he was free to regulate the activities of the highland communities. Interestingly, soon after the British take-over of the Lushai Hills, the Tippera king too imposed annual revenue on the highland groups, including the Lushai Chiefs of the Jampui Hills. The Darlong society too felt the repercussions of the change. With the cessation of ethnic rivalry and abolishment of the *Bukpui* system, the power of the *Lal* gradually weakened; on the contrary, the *Khawnbawls*, who advised the *Lal* and performed, when required, the additional duty of village haedaman, began to exert greater social control than they formerly did in the time of the powerful *Lals*. Christian missionaries who come from Aizwal to preach the gospel to the Darlong in the 1920s also played a significant part in bringing about social transforms mainly through the instrument of education. The *Bukpui* was dismantled.

We have already seen that the system of single *Halamsa* was abolished in the early 19th century. The change was occasioned by two factors – the complicity of the Halam in Kuki uprisings and the dispersion of the tribes following the advent of Lushai and the outbreak of ethnic hostilities in the Lushai Hills. Most *Alian* tribes were strongly organised and showed greater cohesion than the *Asins* in the face of disintegration among the Old Kukis. A section of the Ranglongs of Ruongle-vai-shua settled in North Tripura while another moved to eastern Sylhet, where yet another ethno-demographic division occurred within the group; nevertheless, they continued to endorse to a unified social council that monitored the activities of the three zonal units. By contrast, the Karbong, the Langkhai and the Mawrsephang disintegrated and sections of their people assimilated into the other tribes of the Halam group. In the new administrative structure imposed on the Halam in the 19th century, the Tippera king installed his loyal highland followers as *Rai* over each Halam tribe. The post was not hereditary but once an individual was appointed as *Rai*, he held the post as long as the social council of elders, usually the heads of the *panchis* ('clans') within the tribe, vested their confidence on him. For a long time after the abolition of the Halamsa, the Ranglongs of North Tripura continued to designate the nominated chief of their tribe as *Halamsa*, though he was actually a *Rai* in function and his jurisdiction did not extend beyond the tribe he headed. At the end of the Rai's tenure or on his removal, the *Kalim* of that tribe succeeded him. Next to the Kalim was the *Kabur* who acted as assistant to the former and was in charge of carrying out all public duties at the village level. In the older order, the social status of the *Kamchikao* was high; but in the new order, he was put between the *Kalim* and the *Kabur* – an indication of the village headmen gradually gaining in power. At the base of a vertically-structured social council were the *Yaksum* ('*Jaksum*' in Koloi) and the *Khuksum* who did regular errands for higher officials and rendered peonage services, while the *Senga* (called *Arawksenga* in Ranglong) acted as law enforcer with the power to use force if necessary to bring defaulters before the village council.

In an early chapter, a reference was made to the Murasing's ethnic system. Their socio-administrative set-up was similar to that of the other highland tribes of Tripura in the 19th century, with the *Rai* at the apex of their social council. The post was not enjoyed as a hereditary charge. Down the hierarchy, the *Sanuwan* performed administrative functions similar to that of the Halam *Kalim* while a *Kachkao* was in charge of levying revenue from villages under the jurisdiction of the Rai. All activities of the social council was put under the supervision of the *Misip* who was a member of the Tippera royal family and bound to the Tippera *Raja* by dual ties of kinship and loyalty. The system of *Rai*-ship was abandoned when the princely state of Tripura merged with India in 1949.

Ethnicity and Nationalism in Post-Colonial Period

Numerous dimensions of socio-cultural transforms in the highland societies of Tripura and the Chittagong Hill Tracts have led to the surfacing of ethnic claims that verily contradict the nationalist presumptions of the governments of India and Bangladesh. The cultural matrix of the Indian Sub-Continent has seldom appealed to the eastern tribes. Most Kuki-Chins today aspire for self determination with reference to not only near-at-home Mizoram but also across

India's territorial border to the Chin State of Myanmar. The Kuki-Chin tribes of Tripura, North Cachar Hills, Manipur, Mizoram and Chittagong Hill Tracts share common ethnic ties with the Chin tribes of Myanmar– ties that existed before the birth of modern nation states and the demarcation of territorial boundaries.

The so-called 'Halam' tribes came under Tippera domination in the 14th century AD and within a short time, the people who had followed the hill path were socially mobilised into a centralised system that cut across their old ethnic identities and primitive autonomies. Assimilative cementing of small sections of the two tribes led to the emergence of the ethnic system of the Rupini who are Halam in their material cultures but close to the Tippera in language. As for the other Halam tribes, they retained the original language, but their own community-based independent organisations underwent radical change, and instead of tribe-based affiliation to hereditary chiefs, collective allegiance of these tribes toward a centralised authority was generated through nominated representatives. Several groups that lived on the frontiers of the Tippera kingdom or further east within the hilly terrain of the Lushai Hills persisted with their tribal ways. Some like the Rivung and the Darlong entered into politically beneficial alliance with the Tippera. They helped the Tippera king suppress revolts or oppositions from the groups the latter had subjugated and, in return, enjoyed exemption from taxation and also the legitimacy to tribal chieftainship.

The economic and political systems of the hills were different from those of the plains, and when the British government perpetrated a policy of isolating the hills, as in the case of the Chittagong Hill Tracts, it seemed that there was some concern for preserving the indigenous systems of the eastern tribes. To some extent, the influx of Bengalis was checked. But the same policy also excluded the hill tribes from participation in the collective identity that the Indian Nationalist Movement progressively fostered against the British Raj in the early 20th century. With Christian missionaries active in the highlands, some developments not favourable to Indian nationalism took place. Political centralisation among the valley-dwelling tribes (Tippera, Chakma and Marma) had begun long before the advent of the British rule; later, under the British Raj the territorial jurisdiction of the native rajas was extended and their participation in local governments as tax-collectors with some judicial powers encouraged. With the subjugation of the Lushai, the highland resistance to external socio-political forces crumbled. Christianity provided a common fulcrum to the eastern tribes by reintegrating them into ethnic blocks but, at the same time, missionary activities alienated the highlanders from the mainstream Hindu ethos of India. Educationally, the Kuki-Chins had been backward before the missionaries arrived; with education, political consciousness dawned on them and they increasingly realised that they differed from the mainstream people of India on ethnic, linguistic and religious grounds.

In 1947, political power was transferred to the people of Sub-Continent India, which got religiously divided into India and Pakistan. In the case of CHT, there was no referendum to the three Circles Chiefs – Mong, Chakma and Bohmong – and the tribes living therein were herded into a type of nationhood they would not have opted for if free choice was given. The princely state of Hill Tripura joined the Indian Union in 1949. But the Mizo Union, a socio-political organisation formed under the dominant Lushai clans, sought secession of the Lushai Hills (Mizoram) from India. A parallel northern unit of Kuki-Chins, the Kuki Nationalist Assembly, too had adopted a secessionist stand in the early part of its movement. When the Government of India introduced the Scheduled Tribes category to promote the uplift of all tribal and backward peoples, a step towards reconciliation of discontented section of the population was apparently made but within a few decades, the same policy saw increased segmentation in the highland communities of the Northeast. Regional ethno-politics perpetrated by the dominant groups within the existing ethnic blocks caused schismogenesis. The small groups, which found themselves steadily pushed into areas that excluded them from educational attainments, decent livelihood and the right to preserve their distinct sub-cultures, soon stirred to break away from the ethnic blocks and assert independent identities on old tribe-based allegiances. British missionaries had fostered a consensus mechanism through the institution of the Christian Church; today the highland Church is itself divided on the lines of ethnicity. The Tripura Baptist Mission Union (TBSU) is largely controlled by the Darlong while the Ranglong and the Chorei have their separate churches. In the Hill Tracts too, the Bawm and the Lushai have their own churches.

Counter-nationalism on ethnic and linguistic lines has been at the root of the tribal resistance to Bengali expansion in CHT. Yet the major contending parties are Bengalis and Chakmas, the latter an Indic-speaking Tibeto-Burman group. The chief opposition to Bangladesh nationalism came from the Shanti Bahini, a Chakma dominated organisation that has always placed Chakma interests above those of the other tribes living in the Hill Tracts and succeeded in drawing much international attention against violation of the indigenous rights of the Chakmas. Participation of the other groups is minimal and there is some resentment against the Shanti Bahini. In the early 1980s, the Mru had even set up their own military organisation to counter the Shanti Bahini. This was despite the fact that the Mru, like the Chakma, resented the presence of Bengalis in the Hills Tracts, including the latter's notion of linguistic nationalism that led to the creation of Bangladesh out of East Pakistan in 1971.

Ideologically, a uniform language cutting across ethnic boundaries is essential to nationhood but in places where diverse cultures exist, the attempt to suppress the vernaculars may not be conducive to a long-lasting national identity.

Bengali is endorsed to as national language by millions of Bengladeshis but for the tribal peoples of the Hill Tracts, the same language is a symbol of suppression; it is the language of the people who infiltrated into their territory and forcibly occupied their lands. There is little respect for Bengali and literally none for the people who speak it. In the British period, English was the administratively sanctioned language of India. Especially for all highland tribes of Northeast India, it was the language of those who brought to them education and enlightenment. The Roman script was used to write the tribal vernaculars. Hindi, which combines several dozens of dialects of North-Central India and uses Devanagari script is not acceptable to the Christianised sections of Kuki-Chins for its Hindu bias. In Tripura, Bengali has prevailed over the other tribal languages as the chief mode of instruction and communication, and, in the 19th century under the patronage of Tippera kings, it had even gained the status of official language. The Hinduisation process under the Tippera kings made the Halams familiar with Bengali and formal education was received through that language. But their indigenous myths and long-standing traditions suffered much owing to the language and culture gaps that the nation state agencies steadily perpetrated. The Mru of the Chittagong Hill Tracts evolved their own script. A steady bonding of language with ethnicity continues to create new tensions, and unless genuine efforts are made to amicably reconcile the opposed claims of mother-tongue vernaculars and state approved languages, participation of the highland tribes in the national governments of India and Bangladesh will remain uninsured, challenged.

The instituting of regional autonomies and sub-autonomies to preserve ethnic identities and to integrate different cultures and sub-cultures within the nation state is a probable means to reconciling the claims of ethnicity and nationalism. Ideologically, at least, India as a nation fosters diversity within a unified federal frame.

Bibliography

ARHT. (1879). Administration Report of the Political Agency, Hill Tipperah, 1878-79.

__________ (1880). Administration Report of the Political Agency, Hill Tipperah, 1879-80.

__________ (1883). Administration Report of the Political Agency, Hill Tipperah, 1882-83.

__________ 1885). Administration Report of the Political Agency, Hill Tipperah, 1873-84.

Ascoli, F.D. (1918). *Report on the Administration of the Chittagong Hill Tracts*. Calcutta: Bengal Secretariat Press.

Ba Thin, U. (1931). The Awa Khamis, Ahraing Khamis, and Mros in the Chin Hill Area (Saingdin), Buthidaung Township. *Census of India 1931*, 11, 248–56.

Bhattacharya, S. (1980). *The Kaipengs*. Agartala: Tribal Research Institute.

__________ (2004). *The Halams of Tripura*. Kolkata: Kreativmind.

Bernot, L. (1964). Ethnic Groups of Chittagong Hill Tracts. In P. Bessaignet (ed), *Social Research in East Pakistan* (pp. 137–70). Dacca: Asiatic Society of Pakistan.

Brauns, C. and L.G. Löffler. (1990). *Mru – Hill People on the Border of Bangladesh*. Boston: Birkhäuer Verlag.

Butler, J. (1990). *Gender Trouble: Feminism and subversion of identity*. New York: Routledge.

Carey, B.S. & H.N. Tuck (1896). *The Chin Hills: a history of the people, British dealings with them, their customs and manners, and a gazetteer of their country*. Rangoon: Superintendent, Government Printing.

Chakraborty, B.C. (1964). *British Relations with the Hill Tribes of Assam since 1858*. Calcutta: Firma KLM.

Chatterjee, S. (1995). *Mizo Chief and Chiefdom*. New Delhi: MD Publications Pvt. Ltd.

Chorei, D. (2004). *Christianity and the Choreis*. Damcherra: Chorei National Union.

Dalton, E.T. (1872). *Descriptive Ethnology of Bengal*. Calcutta: Superintendent of Government Printing.

Davis, A.W. (1891). Naga Tribes. *Assam Census Report* 1891, I, 237-51.

Debbarma, S. (ed) (1931). *Census of Tripura* (1934. *Tripura Rajyer Census Vivarani*). Agartala: Census Office.

Debnath, R. (ed.) (2008a). *McCabe's Report on Eastern Lushai Rising 1892*. Kolkata: Kreativmind.

__________ (2008b). *Ethnographic Study of Tanchangya of CHT, CADC, Sittwe and South Tripura*. Kolkata: Kreativmind.

Dena, L. (2008). *In Search of Identity: Hmars of North-East India*. New Delhi: Akansha Publishing House.

Darlong, L. (1995). *The Darlongs of Tripura.* Agartala: Tribal Research Institute.

Gait, E. (1963) (Revised 3rd edn.). *A History of Assam.* Calcutta: Thacker Spink & Co. (1933) P. Ltd.

Gan Choudhury, J. (1983). *The Riangs of Tripura.* Agartala: Tribal Research Institute.

Gangte, T.S. (1993). *The Kukis of Manipur.* New Delhi: Gyan Publishing House.

Grierson, G.A. (1904). *Linguistic Survey of Bengal,* 3.3 (Tibeto-Burman Family – Specimens of Kuki-Chin and Burma Groups). Calcutta: Superintendent, Government Printing

Guthrie, D. and J.A. Motyer (1970). (3rd Edn.) *New Bible Commentary.* Leicester: Inter-varsity Press.

Hodgson, B.H. (1853). On the Indo-Chinese Borderers and their connexion with the Himalayans and Tibetans. *Journal of the Asiatic Society of Bengal,* 58 (New Series 22.1), 1–25.

Hutchinson, R.H.S. (1906). *An Account of the Chittagong Hill Tracts.* Calcutta: Bengal Secretariat Press.

__________ (1909). Chittagong Hill Tracts. (*Eastern Bengal and Assam District Gazetteers*). Allahabad: Pioneer Press.

Hutton, J.H. (1921a) *The Angami Nagas with some notes on the neighbouring tribes.* London: Macmillan & Co. Ltd.

__________ (1921b) *The Sema Nagas.* London: Macmillan & Co. Ltd.

Kerkhoff, E. and E. Sharma. (2006). *Debating Shifting Cultivation in the Eastern Himalayas.* Kathmandu: ICIMOD.

Kipgen, M. (1997). *Christianity and the Mizo-Culture.* Aizwal: Mizo Theological Conference.

Leech, E.R. (1954). *Political Systems in Highland Burma.* Massachusetts: Harvard University Press.

Lehmann, F.K. (1963). *The Structure of Chin Society.* Urbana: Illinois Studies in Anthropology.

Lewin, T.H. (1869). *The Hill Tracts of Chittagong and the Dwellers Therein.* Calcutta: Bengal Publishing Company.

___________ (1870). *Wild Races of South-Eastern Asia.* London: Allen.

Luce, G.H. (1931). Notes on the Peoples of Burma in the 12th-13th Century AD. *Census of India 1931*, 11, 296-302.

___________ (1959). Chin Hills – Linguistic Tour. *Journal of Burma Research Society*, 42.1, 19–31.

___________ (1985). *Phases of Pre-Pagan Burma: Languages and History.* London: Oxford University Press.

Mason, F. (1843). *The Karen Apostle: or Memoir of Ka Thah-Byu.* Boston: Drew Kendall and Longchamps.

McCall, A.G. (1949). *The Lushai Chrysalis.* London: Luzac & Co.

Menon, K.D. (1975). *Tripura District Gazetteers.* Agartala: Department of Education, Govt. of Tripura.

Mey, W. (1980). *Politische Systeme in den Chittagong Hill Tracts, Bangladesh.* Bremen: Ubersee-Museum.

___________ (1984). *Genocide in the Chittagong Hill Tracts, Bangladesh.* Copenhagen: IWGIA.

Mills, J.P. (1931). Notes on a Tour in the Chittagong Hill Tracts in 1926. *Census of India* ***1931***, 5, 514–521.

Moore, H.L. (1988). *Feminism and Anthropology*. Cambridge: Polity Press.

Ohn Pe, U. (1931). The Awa Khamis, Ahraing Khamis, and Mros in the Ponnagyun Chin Hills, Ponnagyun Township. *Census of India* ***1931***, 11, 257–64.

OPHRA. (1966). *Outlays and Programmes for the Hill Region of Assam for the Fourth Plan (proposals of the Joint Centre-State Study Team – May* ***1966***). Annexure IV: 'Tentative suggestions for further work on development plans of the Hill Districts of Assam.' Planning Commission, Government of India.

Parry, N.E. (1928). *A Monograph on the Lushai Customs and Ceremonies*. Shillong: Assam Government Press.

__________ (1932). *The Lakhers*. London: Macmillan & Co.

Phayre, A.P.P. (1841). An Account of Arakan. *Journal of the Asiatic Society of Bengal*, 117 (New Series 33), 679–712.

__________ (1844). On the History of Arakan. *Journal of the Asiatic Society of Bengal*, 13.1, 23–52.

__________ (1883). *History of Burma including Burma Proper, Pegu, Taungu, Tenasserim, and Arakan from the Earliest Time to the End of the First War with British India*. London: Trübner.

Ping, H. (2006). Rise and fall of Kantu: A historical study of an ancient Tibeto-Burmese speaking group. *Frontier History China*, 4, 535–543.

Pollak, M. (1980). *Mandarins, Jews, and Missionaries*. Philadelphia: Jewish Publication Society.

Rawlins, J. (1792). On the Mountaineers of Tipra. In W. Jones, et. al (ed.), *Dissertations and Miscellaneous Pieces relating to the History and Antiques of the Arts, Sciences, and Literature of Asia*, pp. 156-65. London: G. Nicol, J. Walter & J. Sewell.

Rengsi, V. (2004). Mizo Tribe in Tansition. In Momin, M and Cecile A. Mawlong (eds.) *Society and Economy in North-East India*, Vol.-I, pp.88-104. New Delhi: Regency Publications.

Rigby, G.C. (2000 Reprint; 1897). *History of Operations in Northern Arakan and the Yawdwin Chin Hills*. Aizwal: Tribal Research Institute.

Risley, H.H. (1891). *Tribes and Castes of Bengal*. Calcutta: Bengal Secretariat Press.

Sailo, S. (1992). *The Bongchers*. Agartala: Tribal Research Institute.

Shafer, R. (1955). Classification of the Sino-Tibetan Languages. *Word*, April 1955, 101.

Shakespear, J. (1912). *The Lushei Kuki Clans*. London: MacMillan.

Sinha, K.C. (1985). *Rajmala*. Agartala: Barnamala Prakashani.

Songate, H. (1956). *Hmar Chanchin*. Pherzawl: Mao Press

Spielmann, H.J (1968). *Die Bawm-zo, Eine Chin-Gruppe in den Chittagong Hill Tracts*. Heidelberg: Südasieu-Institut.

Soppitt, C.A. (1893) *A Short Account of the Kuki-Lushai Tribes on the North-East Frontier*. Shillong: Assam Government Press.

Spearman, H.R. (1880a). *British Burma Gazetteer*, I. Rangoon: Government Press.

__________ (1880b). *British Burma Gazetteer*, II. Rangoon: Government Press.

Stevenson, H.N.C. (1943). *The Economics of the Central Chin Tribes*. Bombay: Times of India Press.

Trant, T.A. (1828). Notice of the Khyen tribe inhabiting the Yuma Mountains between Ava and Aracan. *Asiatic Researches* 16, 261-69.

Van Dung, N., T. D. Vien and N.T. Lam. (2006). Impact of Upstream Soil Nutrient Losses on Soil Fertility in Paddy Fields. (Paper in Conference Booklet for the International Conference on 'Sustainable Sloping Lands and Watershed Management: Linking research to strengthen upland policies and practices,' December 12-15, 2006.)

van Schendel, W. (ed) (1992). *Francis Buchanan in Southeast Bengal (1798). His journey to Chittagong, the Chittagong Hill Tracts, Noakhali and Comilla*. Dhaka: University Press Limited.

Watson, B. (1961). *Records of the Grand Historian of China (Shiji)*. New York: Columbia University Press.

Vumson (1986). *Zo History*. Aizwal: NT Thawagn.

Zawla, K. (1976). *Pipute leh An Thlahte Chanchin*. Aizwal: self-printed edn.

Zhou, X. (2005). The Kaifeng Jew Hoax: Constructing the Chinese Jews. In Kalmar, I.D. and D. Pensler (eds.) *Orientalism and the Jews*, pp. 68-79. Lebanon: University Press of New England.

Index

***

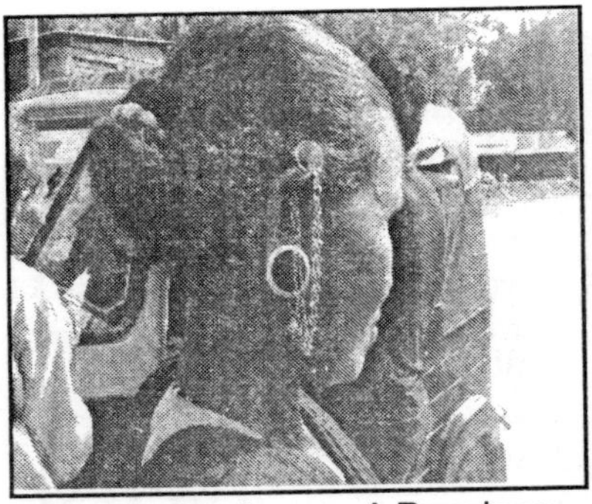

Decorating the ear, A Ranglong female in Bagbasa, North Tripura

A Molsom female sitting on the door of her bamboo house

Like her Ranglong counterpart above, this Marsephang woman of Naitungul Para, Longtrai Hills, too has extended earlobes

Khumi boys posing for a photograph

Bamboo raft on the Sangu for transportation of commodities

The Voga Kain which swallowed a Khumi village

A Marsephang woman with grandchildren

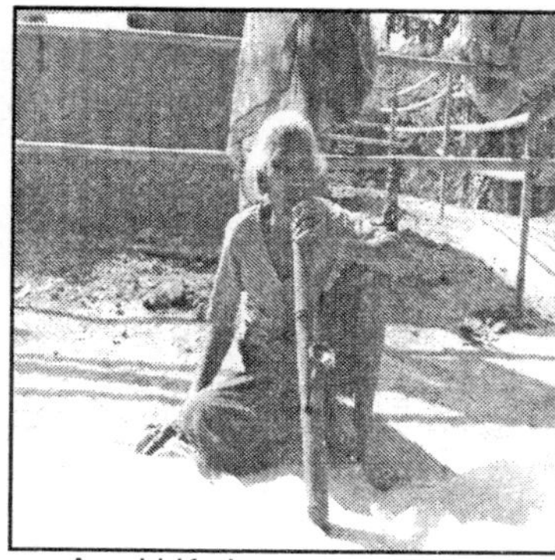

An old Korbong woman smoking the daba

Betu boys repairing a wooden bridge in Hawabari

Rumber Khama, Baramura, a Rupini Village

A jum plot in the Longtrai Hills, Tripura

In Zoitang, North Tripura, Ranglongs now produce large quantities of betelnut

A Korbong returning home after sacrificing a duck on a river bank in Champabari Korbong Para

An old Uchai female getting ready to go out

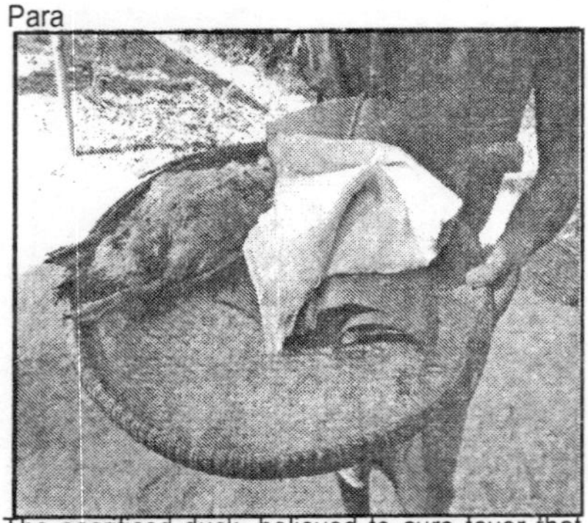

The sacrificed duck, believed to cure fever that some evil spirit has induced

In a market at Thanchi

Khumi girls on their way to the market

Gowing down to the river to clean utensils

Left: Father of my Khyang friend, Thoesafru.
Right: Dead man's hut of the Mru with provisions

Mru Women in domestic chores

Bru (Riang) bottle dance

The common granary is now absent in highland villages. This picture is of a storeroom in an individual's house in a Bru hamlet in Chelagang, South Tripura.

Timber is still used for house posts

PEOPLE'S MOVEMENTS IN THE PRINCELY STATES

People's Movements in the Princely States

Edited by

Y. VAIKUNTHAM

MANOHAR
2004

First published 2004

ISBN 81-7304-528-3

Published by

Ajay Kumar Jain for
Manohar Publishers & Distributors
4753/23, Ansari Road, Daryaganj
Delhi 110 002

Printed at
Lordson Publishers Pvt. Ltd.
Delhi 110 007

Contents

Preface

Princely States which form 45 per cent of the land and 24 per cent of the population of India occupies an important place in modern India. The growth of nationalism in those autocratic Princely States was rather slow and painstaking when compared to British India. People's movements against the princes was an absorbing encounter. They used different strategies to retain power but the people were for change in governance and demanded a responsible government. The British who were firmly entrenched here by the first quarter of the twentieth century, lost its power by 1947 through fascinating saga of India's independence. Similarly about 563 states which believed in their continuance under the umbrella and protection of the British even till 1940s suddenly became extinct and joined the Indian Union by 1947-8, which was again an incredible story. Thus the People's movements in the Princely States is an illustration of the growth of the national consciousness and fight for their rights and ultimately forcing the princes to join Indian Union.

This book is an outcome of the National Seminar entitled 'People's Movements in the Princely States' funded by the Indian Council of Historical Research, New Delhi, in 1994.

I take this opportunity to thank late Prof. Ravindra Kumar, former Chairman, ICHR. Also I would like to thank all the paper contributors in the seminar. They were Sarvasri V.H. Desai, Mohd. Ishaq Khan, R.L. Hangloo, S. Chandrashekar, K.K. Kusuman, K.A. Mani Kumar, V.K. Bawa, V.R.K. Reddy, S. Bhanumathi Ranga Rao and A.C. Pradhan. Four papers have been invited from Mayank Kumar, E. Sudha Rani, M. Jamuna, and K. Maddaiah to make the book more representative and I acknowledge and thank them.

Thanks are due to the authorities of Osmania University, staff of ICHR, my colleagues in the Department of History who helped me in making the seminar a success. I would like to thank K. Veeresha, who has typed all the papers and for his computer assistance. Finally I would like to thank Sri Ramesh Jain of Manohar Publishers & Distributors, New Delhi for neatly bringing out this book.

Y. VAIKUNTHAM

Contributors

Y. Vaikuntham, Professor of History, Osmania University, Hyderabad.

V.H. Desai, Hon Director, Bharatiya Vidya Bhavan, Hyderabad.

V. Ramakrishna Reddy, Professor of History (Retd.), Dr. B.R. Ambedkar Open University, Hyderabad.

S. Bhanumathi Ranga Rao, Professor of History, Osmania University, Hyderabad.

E. Sudha Rani, Associate Professor of History, Dr. B.R. Ambedkar Open University, Hyderabad.

V. K. Bawa, Senior IAS Officer (Retd.), Hyderabad.

S. Chandrashekar, Professor of History, Bangalore University, Bangalore.

M. Jamuna, Reader in History, Bangalore University, Bangalore.

K.A. Mani Kumar, Professor of History, M.S. University, Tirunelveli, Tamil Nadu.

K.K. Kusuman, Professor of History, Kerala University, Trivandrum.

R.L. Hangloo, Professor of History, University of Hyderabad, Hyderabad.

Mohammed Ishaq Khan, Professor of History, P.G. Department of History, University of Kashmir, Srinagar.

Mayank Kumar, Senior Lecturer in History, University of Delhi, Delhi.

A.C. Pradhan, Professor of History, Utkal University, Bhubaneshwar.

K. Maddaiah, Lecturer in History, Govt. Degree College for Men, Kurnool, Andhra Pradesh.

Introduction

Y. VAIKUNTHAM

Nations do not make States and Nationalisms but other way round

E.J. HOBSBAWM

The study and research on modern India and the Freedom movement would be incomplete if we fail to critically assess the attitude of the people of the Princely States towards their rulers and against the increasing link between the colonial state and the Paramountcy and above all the relation between the people of the Princely States and that of British India. The Princely States by and large appear to be less progressive, medieval in social and political outlook, and failed to involve the people in the governance of the state. In some states like Baroda, Mysore, and to some extent Travancore there was a different picture where the rulers tried to emulate the British in socio-economic and political reforms. In those states progress was visible. But in the rest people suffered under dictatorial and autocratic governments. Therefore critical understanding of various movements in the Princely States are not only essential but also relevant to understand modern India; specially the colonial period.

Lee-Warner argued that there was a coherent British policy towards the states between 1820-57, which he characterized as a policy of 'subordinate isolation'.[1] However, throughout the colonial period if we seriously examine their policies there was 'no coherent place for the princess in their (British) imperial ideology . . . they were to form a constituency frozen in time and space integrated into the larger imperial system only through the ritual acts of subordination'.[2] Therefore, the states were treated as 'ring fence' 'protected', 'subordinate alliances', and a paramountcy was imposed which affected the absolute form of sovereignty of the local rulers. In other words a limited sovereignty was permitted with a right to intervene whenever the time demanded in the administration of the Princely States. Different strategies have been employed by the British, one among them was to give the princes protection from any threat from other political powers. This assurance of the British made the princes autocratic and many of them did not bother about even the internal development. Anti-colonial struggles in British India naturally influenced the people in the states against the autocratic rule of the princes. After the Indian States Commission Report (Butler Commission Report) was published and the Govt. of India Act of 1935 was passed, the possibility of the federal government at the Centre made the issue of sending the state's representatives to the federal government instrumental in the demand for responsible governments in the Princely States. Further the working of the provincial autonomy and Congress ministries in British India also influenced the Praja Mandal movements for democratic institutions in the states. These brought about psychological changes making the people in the states demand for representative and responsible governments. The princes, consequently, never showed any active interest in improving the governance or involving the people in responsible governments or bringing about an enlightened rule except a very few rulers. For example Sayaji Rao of Baroda and Krishnaraja Wodeyar of Mysore had began to experiment with new, Westernized forms of governance (legislative council, representative assembly, public services board, board of competitive exams), others such as the Nizam remained firmly wedded to traditional notions of benevolent autocracy. This form of rule (Osman Ali told Reading) suited the genius and temperament of Hyderabadee people and has resulted in peaceful progress and prosperity.[3] Hence they were happy and contented. The division among the princes was not only on ideology but also owing to race, religion, and upbringing. The efforts and steps taken by the princes to concede representative and responsible government varied from state to state.

The existing socio-economic and political studies on the Princely States need a critical conceptual understanding and analysis. The centralization of power in the hands of rulers, merciless repressive policy in many states, lack of participation of the subjects in the governance of the state, increasing aspirations of the people both in socio-economic transformation and political developments became the cry of the people. It was said that:

> The Princes (Rulers) were ruthlessly suppressing the exposition of public opinion. Not a day passed without hearing the news of some Maharaja or other using letters [*sic*] de cachet' to prohibit public meetings, summarily arresting . . . respectable citizens (and engaging in) wholesale confiscation of property and banishment of people from their native land.[4]

In reality both the economic system and the political policy in the states was directed by the colonial rulers. The disciplined bureaucracy of the British was also fresh with new policies and was strict in their enforcement to consolidate the British power and to expand its trade monopoly, markets, and political hegemony.

The British colonized and exploited the whole India through direct and indirect rule. By 1919, the rulers were arguably at the peak of their power—safe under the military umbrella of the British Raj imbued with the 'illusion of permanence' venerated by the overwhelming majority of their subjects, admired even by many nationalists and yet in about thirty years they were extinct.[5] About 563 Princely States holding 45 per cent of the territory and 24 per cent of the population have been integrated into India and submerged into the body politic of Indian Union in quick pace.[6] The story of the integration of the states indeed was a phenomena contradicting the long term existence of those states. However, the story of the days of the Princely Rule will sound incredible and amusing to many as to how they have been integrated into the Indian Union.

I

From the middle of eighteenth century the Indian states slowly played into the diplomatic manouvers of the British. The British with no certain ideological move to colonize the native states, pretended friendship, supported them, and created a ringfence as a security to their conquered territories. They also treated them as subordinate states after the subsidiary alliance, ultimately establishing the political hegemony of the British over the Indian states and firmly establishing paramountcy from the time of Lord Hastings. Any policy of expansion subsequently never visualized that it would lead to a revolt as could be seen in 1857-8. Therefore the policy of expansion proved to be counter productive by the middle of nineteenth century.

The end of the 1857-8 Revolt and the subsequent Queen's Proclamation of 1858 gave some confidence to the princes regarding their authority, dignity, titles, status, etc. The colonial government also tried to involve the Indian people in the administration and tried particularly to bridge the gap between the ruler and the ruled and the colonial government and the princes.

In the Princely States, the popular representatives had no say in the administration. The political structure in British India was gradually getting changed and parliamentary or representative institutions were slowly established to contain and satisfy the emerging forces in the national movement. The administrative structure in the states continued to be traditional and autocratic denying 'good government'. Several Viceroys suggested socio-economic and constitutional improvements in the states.[7] Industrialization, commercialization of agriculture, communications, education, social life, and also political and constitutional reforms including local self-government were also given emphasis. The socio-political policies of the British had some useful results since they generated new ideas, critical and scientific thinking and outlook. Therefore the first generation of people became loyalists though the subsequent generations got disappointed with the colonial mode of the British administration, its racial supremacy, exploitation, etc., and became anti-British demanding self-governing institutions and constitutional reforms and ultimately organized the national movement to fight for freedom from the alien rule. Therefore the anti-colonial struggles in British India and people's struggles in the Princely States against the autocratic regimes needed a distinct as well as complimentary nature to unite India into a democratic fabric. The triangular structure in the struggles has been given some focus in this study. The forces that operated the political chess board in India were:

The peoples aspirations, the means to achieve them, and the ultimate

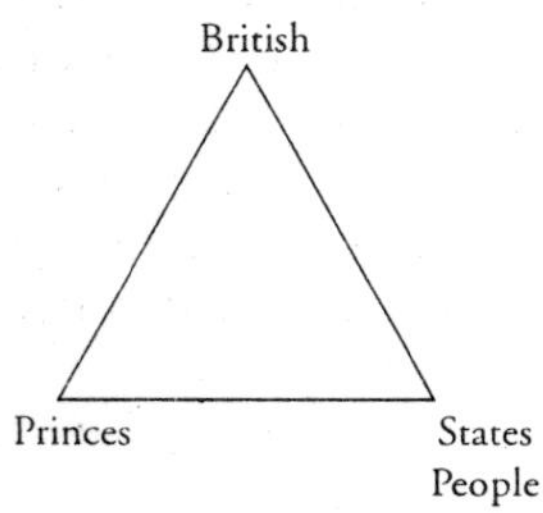

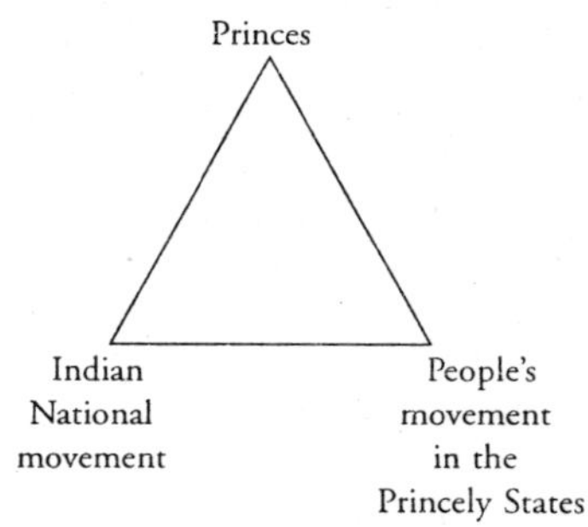

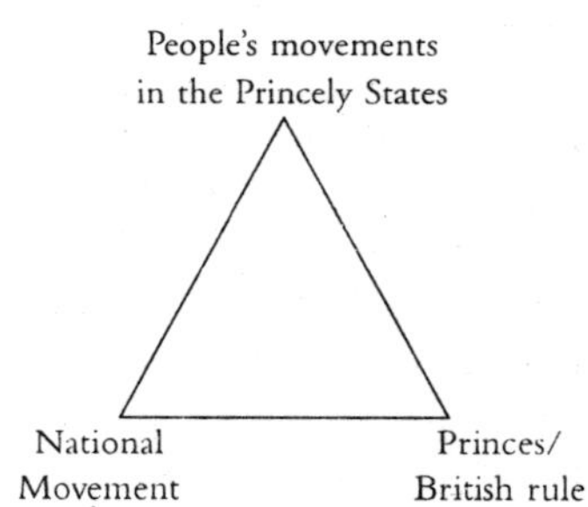

endgame was to eliminate the autocratic rule of the princes by demanding a responsible government in the states initially and forcing them to ultimately join the Indian Union. On the other hand, the people's movements in the Princely States and their leaders not only directly or indirectly supported the national movement but also took support from it in the process. Finally, the people from Princely States also strengthened the national movement by forcing the princes to realize the changing scenario either to strengthen the national movement or join India to establish a united India.

It is also essential to study the British policies and the way they controlled the Princely States from the nineteenth century. On the eve of India's Independence the princes insisted on the obligation of the Britisher's treaty rights and the intervention syndrome for the retrocession of their territories to transfer power to the princes ultimately to support the rule of the princes in the states. The British never tried to jeopardize its own interests in dealing with the princes. This whole process was to consolidate the British power in India. Therefore the purpose of the national movement was to eliminate the colonial rule and also to fight for the integration of India. The federation issue was used by the British Conservatives, specially Churchill, provoking the princes as instruments for failure of the federation at the Centre enabling the centralized power of the British at the Centre to continue. These princes and Narendra Mandal (Chamber of Princes) was seen as a powerful third force to suppress the national movement, and even serve as supporters in the penultimate stage or after Independence. On the other hand, many princes tried to remain independent till the last. Either diplomacy or military intervention or serious reaction of the people against Independence of the Princely States, were ultimately responsible for the merger of the states in Indian Union. The nature of the struggles differed. The national movement basically was an anti-colonial struggle in British India and in the Princely States it was against the feudal and autocratic rule of the princes.

Civil liberties and democratic principles dominated the anti-colonial struggles as well as those against the autocratic rule of the princes. The nature of the administration in the Princely States varied from state to state. Some were more modern and democratic called the 'model states' and others still backward and feudal. Many states were too small to be counted as states. However, the study reflects and represents some states receiving twenty-one gun salute status and nineteen gun salute while others much less signifying the nature of these states.

II

Hyderabad State, receiving twenty-one gun salute status, occupies an important position not only because of its territory, population, and resources but also because of the nature of the socio-political movements, geographical situation, and the consequent police action and merger with the Indian Union. There are five papers on the Hyderabad State.

Not many research works have come out on this movement for responsible government in Hyderabad State. Lucien Benichou in his work *From Autocracy to Integration: Political Developments in Hyderabad State (1938-1948)*, examined the nature of the political rule, the efforts of the intelligentsia to bring about political consciousness through socio-cultural organizations, and the ultimate effort for the establishment of a responsible government. It was, however, never implemented till 1948. Achoyut Khodwe's work, *People's Movement in Hyderabad* though a pioneering work is only a descriptive one. Sarojini Regani's *Highlights of Freedom Movement in Andhra Pradesh*, a publication of the State Archives, covers Hyderabad in a section. Therefore Vaikuntham's paper is a critical analysis of the nature of the Nizam's rule, administration by using notorious *gastis* to throttle the political activity including the freedom of the press, agitations, writings, political meetings, etc. He has also examined how ideology played a role, though slowly, in nurturing public consciousness. The efforts of the state in the establishment of the Constitutional Reforms Committee under Aravamudu Aiyangar to analyse how to modernize the state by introducing constitutional reforms which were initiated in the form of Qanoon-cha-Mubarak in 1893 are also studied. The various committees appointed during the last Nizam's period to suggest constitutional reforms between 1920-46 never could be implemented as the Nizam was not serious to implement those reports. The reforms committee under the chairmanship of eminent jurists like Balmukund in 1920-1, Aravamudu Aiyangar in 1937 and 1946 were only some attempts of the government to bring about constitutional changes to establish responsible government, but it was argued that those reforms could not see the light of the day except few notional changes in the composition of the legislative bodies and the ministry of the Nizam.

The impact of the Indian national movement on the Hyderabad elite, the work of the Hyderabad State Congress, Arya Samaj, Hindu Civil Liberties Union, and the Communist Party has also been examined. The whole process of transformation from medievalism to modernism and from autocracy to democracy and the various stages in which the attempts were made for constitutional transformation in the state has been explained. However, the sufferings of the people after 1944 under the growing communal forces and the deliberate suppression of the political ambitions of the people and the repressive policies of the state and the denial of responsible government till it joined the Indian Union is the thrust of his paper, 'Ideology, Political Consciousness and Movement for Responsible Government in the Hyderabad State'.

V.H. Desai being a participant in the later part of the movement after 1938, in his paper 'People's Movement in the Hyderabad State', vividly explains the nature of the state, the impact of national movement, the student movement on the campus of Osmania University, and Gandhian influence on the nature of people's movement. The participation of important leaders in the movements cutting across religion and caste was a significant aspect in this study. In the process of his discussion he tried to give his nostalgic memories of the movement, important incidents, and personalities that he came across.

Finally in an annexure he has discussed about his journalistic outlook, starting of *The Democrat* as a jail journal, how it influenced the jail inmates and settled the ideological differences and quarrels among them. This was also called *Bandal Gazette* (nonsense gazette) by him but it actually instilled nationalism and a sense of patriotism. The mock-parliaments he conducted called the 'Bandinagar Republic, I and II' really had full of insights into the movements. This was also called *The Jail Journal Calling* which takes the readers to the struggles and its reminiscences. It is a paper from the pen of a freedom fighter and participant.

Two papers have been included in this volume on land distribution and peasant movements which cover an important aspect of the peoples movements on land and exploitation.

V.R.K. Reddy in his paper 'Land Distribution, Utilization and Peasant Movement in the Hyderabad State, 1724-1950' examined the pattern of land distribution, the nature of revenue collection, size of the holdings, nature of holdings, etc. In his book entitled *Economic History of Warangal Suba 1900-1956*, he had examined these issues but in this paper he has tried to put it in the larger context of the state and how the Nizam's government policies were leading to land concentration and monopolization. The changing scenario, increasing exploitation led to peasant unrest and resistance movements ultimately culminating in the Telangana Armed Struggle. Anwar Iqbal Qureshi in his book, *The Economic Development of Hyderabad State* examined the revenue and economic policies, including trade and commerce. B.K. Narain in his *Agricultural*

Development . . . and *Industrial Development in Hyderabad State* examined the state policy and lack of dynamism to create capital and modern economy. However, V.R.K. Reddy in his paper has tried to examine how the state policy towards land distribution and utilization led to absentee landlordism and concentration of land in the hand of a few. Barry Pavier in his *Telangana Movement* and Ian Bedford in his *Telangana Insurrection*, tried to examine the socio-economic policies and changes, how they were responsible for the Telangana Armed Struggle. P. Sundarayya, Chandra Rajeswar Rao, T. Nagi Reddy, D.V. Rao and many other activists in the Armed Struggle left their records as participants. Ashok Rudra, Dhanagare, A.R. Desai, Sunil Sen, etc., also critically analysed the nature of the Armed Struggle. V.R.K. Reddy in his paper tries to provide a backdrop for those later movements by examining the land distribution and utilization that led to the peasant movements in the Hyderabad State.

S. Bhanumathi Ranga Rao in her paper entitled 'Historical Background of Peasant Movement in Telangana' narrated how the revenue system was in diwani, jagir, inam, and paigah lands. The exploitation of the peasants in those lands led to peasant discontentment. The primitive method of revenue collection, illegal exactions led to illegal occupation of land and naturally rising land concentration and absentee landlordism in Hyderabad State. As explained earlier Barry Pavier, Bedford, Dhanagare, etc., examined these issues in the light of the Armed Struggle.

She also examined how the Salar Jung's Reforms attracted the wrath of the vested interests in the state. These issues have been also discussed in Chirag Ali's work (3 vols.), Sarojini Regani's *Nizam-British Relations* and V.K. Bawa's *The Last Nizam*, and *The Nizam between the Mughals and the British*, etc. Bhanumathi has tried to explain how land revenue policies led to or provided the background for peasant movements in Telangana.

One paper has been included in this volume on women's consciousness in the Hyderabad State. E. Sudha Rani in her paper 'Consciousness and Participation of Telangana Women in the People's Movement in Hyderabad State, 1901-1951' discusses feminist consciousness in the people's movement in Hyderabad. The writer has divided this movement into three phases: a reformist, women's participation in anti-colonial nationalist struggle, and women's movement as parallel movements, to the national movement in tribal, peasant, and left movements in addition to freedom struggle leading to mass movement of women. Women suffered in many ways in a feudal society. Lack of education, denial of access to jobs, and social evils kept them to the homes. *Jogins*, enforced widowhood, *adapapas*, etc., were humiliating social practices. The scholar argues that the library movement, social conferences, Andhra movement, and the efforts of the reformers were responsible for the women's awakening in the Hyderabad State. Number of journals had been started which took up the cause of women. Sudha Rani also highlighted about the work of women's associations like Bharata Mahila Samajam, Yuvati Sharanalayam, Hyderabad Women's Education and Social Development Association, Andhra Mahila Sabha, etc. The women took active part in socio-political movements after 1920. In the Telangana movement women, particularly from the rural areas participated in a big way. Atrocities were resisted but however they still continued unabated in the feudal system including the atrocities of the Razakars. The local socio-political movements and the changing political scenario at the national level, the writer argued, were mainly responsible for not only the rise of social consciousness but also their participation in the people's movements against the state and the feudal institutions.

Mysore, another large state getting a twenty-one gun salute status, was transformed on the modern lines in the twentieth century. The works of Hayavadan Rao, *Freedom Struggle in Mysore State*, deserves mention as the first work on the subject. Vanaja Rangaswami's *The Story of Integration: A New Interpretation* is a good analytical work. S. Chandrashekar and M. Jamuna presented two interesting papers on Mysore dealing with the two facets of the people's movement which are included in this volume.

Chandrashekar in his paper 'The Struggle for Liberation from Double Slavery: The Princely Mysore, 1881-1947' has highlighted how the people suffered under the dictates of the Maharaja and his Diwan and that of the Paramount power, i.e. the British. Mysore was both under the direct rule of the British as well as their nominee Wodayar as independent rulers. Though Mysore was called a model state, people at large felt that they were denied a responsible government, the assembly being only a nominal body. Unlike in Hyderabad land concentration was very limited here. The impact of the Indian National Congress on Mysore leaders, Brahmin and non-Brahmin confrontation, the work of the Praja Mandals have been discussed to show how the state neglected the issues at the grass root level. However, 1938-9 was a remarkable period in the growth of nationalism among masses specially rural people in the Mysore State as an aftermath of Vidhuraswatha satyagraha. The róle of the Mysore State Congress and other facets of the people's movement were responsible for relieving the people of Mysore from the slavery of both the princely rule and that of the colonial masters.

Jamuna in her paper 'Women and Freedom Movement in Princely Mysore' stressed about the contribution of the various schools of reformers for the uplift of women including production relations, status, and reforms. Though there are very few works on women's role in the Freedom movement, specially in the Princely States, Gandhi's emergence heralded mass movements and women were brought into the mainstream. She observed that though the awakening was slow, in the Dhvaja satyagraha at Shivapur, and in the Viduraswatha satyagraha women participated in a big way and was a landmark in women's political consciousness. Jamuna in her paper clearly demonstrated how women's progress and role in the Freedom movement in the Princely State slowly got strengthened and obtained a mass character.

V.K. Bawa who has extensively worked on the history of the Hyderabad State including his books, *The Nizam between the Mughals and the British*; *The Last Nizam: The Life and Times of Mir Osman Ali Khan* has also tried in his paper to examine the 'Regional Identities and the National Movement in Hyderabad and Mysore'. He tried to explore how the French initially tried to dominate both in Mysore and Hyderabad and later gave way to the English East India Company. Regarding the developments it was Mysore which showed better performance in industrialization, constitutional reforms and general administration. He has closed the paper with some tentative findings on their relations with the British, the support of the princes to the Indian National Congress and Muslim League, and finally the emergence of linguistic states and how the Hyderabad and Mysore people reacted.

Travancore, which received a nineteen gun salute status, has also played a very important role among the Princely States. Many works have been published on the modern Travancore State. The papers of K.A. Mani Kumar titled 'Peasant Resistance in the Princely State of Travancor, 1850-1939' and K.K. Kusuman, 'The Struggle for a Responsible Government in Travancore, 1938-1947' are included in this volume.

Mani Kumar tries to examine the payment of the annual grant for the subsidiary forces, the emergence of *jenmis*, and holding 80 per cent of the cultivated land and their exploitation of the tenants. The agrarian revolts of Velu Thampi and the Mappalas was against the enhancement of rent by *jenmis*, the revolts were against the agrarian policies and the land revenue system in the state. Governments efforts to protect peasants from evictions like proclamation of the 1929 and protection to tenants and *kanamdars* have been examined. In fact K.N. Panikkar in his work *Against the Lord and the State* critically examined these issues. Even P. Radhakrishna in his book *Peasant Struggles, Land Reforms and Social Change: Malabar* demonstrated the situation in Travancore. The emergence of caste associations to resist the *jenmis*, to demand equal treatment became an important facet of the peasant uprisings. In this paper the writer argues how the peasants got protection in the collection of rent as a result of the peasant movements.

K.K. Kusuman in his paper 'The Struggle for a Responsible Government in Travancore' maintains that the Indian National Congress supported the State Congress in the Princely States after the Haripura session. Freedom of press and associations, promotion of communal harmony, economic prosperity of the state, etc., were the demands of the State Congress. They wanted even the Diwan, an autocrat, be removed. Pro-Diwan groups protested against this. The State Congress mainly tried for the establishment of a responsible government but mixed with the demand for the removal of the Diwan. Gandhi asked for the withdrawal of the memorial against Diwan. The writer argues that the agitation and satyagraha of the State Congress was against the situation in 1938-9. The Diwan C.P. Ramaswamy Aiyar using the Cabinet Mission provision tried to keep the state independent but State Congress opposed it. It is argued in this paper that the movement for responsible government and civil liberties took violent turn, consequently the Diwan became more authoritarian. Instead of conceding the demands and joining the Indian Union, he wanted the independence of the state. The central theme of this paper is to highlight this struggle. The work of the State Congress was not only in forcing the state to join Indian Union but also in establishing responsible government in Travancore.

There are two papers on Jammu and Kashmir in this volume by Ratanlal Hangloo and Mohammed Ishaq Khan. R.L. Hangloo in his paper 'Agrarian Conditions and Peasant Protests in the Princely State of Kashmir, 1846-1931' argued that the overwhelming majority of the people laboured in agriculture. The mountainous nature of the region, snow-bound climate made the Dogra chiefs to allow semi-autonomous chiefs to consolidate; who collected 50 to 66 per cent of the produce as revenue leaving peasants to all problems and misery. Batai, kardari, chakladari, ijara systems, village cash assessment system, etc., were in vogue. Fluctuating harvests, heavy assessments led to corruption and graft. *Vetti* was also common. Hangloo argues that peasants protested against this system by abandoning cultivation, migrating to Punjab and neighbouring places, and submitting petitions, etc. Impoverishment of shawl weavers also affected the Kashmiris. Under the circumstances Kashmir leaders organized Muslim Conference, and mobilized masses to put pressure on the government for changes in the laws and assessment. In this paper it is also argued that Dogra Rajas hardly had any control on the jagirdars and chiefs, therefore the exploitation continued and mass protests against the state went on unabated.

Mohammed Ishaq Khan in his paper 'The Social Background of People's Movement in the Jammu and Kashmir State, 1846-1931' is on the Kashmir State, which receives twenty-one gun salute status, argued that the establishment of the Dogra Raj in 1846 brought unity in Jammu and Kashmir. The assertion of the Raja was that all lands were purchased by him and belonged to him, the whole state was his personal property. The Dogra chiefs created a class of landed aristocracy with Rajputs and Pandits who settled in the cities. Ishaq Khan argued that the growth of a closed village economy was a new feature. Feudal restrictions, monopolies, political and economic controls became common even among the artisan labour and the shawl industry. However, social awareness was not absent among the Muslims of Kashmir, Ishaq Khan argued that they had appealed to the Dogra Raja, Viceroy, Resident and Settlement Officers, etc., which slowly led to social tensions. Sheikh Abdullah started the Muslim Conference in 1932 to demand a responsible government. Ishaq Khan argues that though Sheikh Abdullah used mosques and shrines to mobilize the masses, there was no religious conflict. Press played a divided role both in support of the ruler and the National Conference. However, these writings created a national consciousness and the concept of responsible government gained significance. Ishaq Khan raised some broad issues but left them without specific answers. The writer examines the changing nature of the national consciousness in the state specially against the authoritarianism of Dogras and demand for responsible government by the peasants, masses, and the National Conference.

In central India a number of Princely States existed. Even in the 1857 revolt, Lord Canning made it public that 'if the Sindhias joins the Mutiny, I shall have to pack off tomorrow'. Gwalior under the Sindhias was very loyal to the British till the last. Mayank Kumar in his paper 'People's Movement in the Princely State of Gwalior' tries to show how the state was backward and supported the British. Though people's awakening was slow, they responded to all the phases of the Freedom movement in India. This paper, though based on the secondary sources presents a 'liberal state' scenario. If the state was to play a more nationalistic role and help the Indian princes, the fate of India would have been different and the Britishers would have been driven out and the hopes of paramountcy would have been shattered. Mayank Kumar tries to demonstrate this point in his article.

Atul Chandra Pradhan in his paper 'People Movement in the Princely

States of Orissa in the Wider Context of Nationalist Movement: A Case Study of the Nilgiri State' discussed about disparities in the growth of nationalism in those states. This was a small state having 75,000 people and 281 sq. miles of an area in Orissa. Education was backward and public awakening was slow. The state was under incompetent rulers, suffered with number of handicaps including no rule of law or fundamental rights. Peasants had no rights on agricultural land. Forced labour (*bethi*), peasant exploitation, etc., was common. Though this state adjoins Balasore and Bengal nationalism influenced the people slowly. Harikrishna Mehtab and Banamali Das took keen interest in the public awakening and forced the ruler to respond to the developments in British India. The Praja Mandals became powerful tools to ventilate the grievances. A popular ministry was formed in November 1947. The outbreaks of the aboriginals in this area were stalled and the state was merged with the Indian Union in December 1947. The writer emphasized that in a feudal state, though small, democratic rights were suppressed and not only public awakening was delayed but also its joining Indian Union. Though it was close to Bengal and Orissa province was created in 1936.

K. Maddaiah in his paper 'Freedom Struggle in the Banaganapalle State' gave a chronological and descriptive account of this small state, and how it joined Indian Union. The political awakening was not only slow but late and the Banaganapalle State Congress was established in 1947 to force the Nawab to join the Indian Union. The writer deliberated on the various factors responsible for the political awakening through the Indian National Congress and other movements in the Madras Presidency. Kurnool District Congress and its leaders like Nivarthi Venkatasubbaiah, Pendekanti Venkatasubbaiah, and Swami Hamsananda, took active interest in the public awakening here. The people of the state responded to all the important activities in the national movement. It was only in February 1948 that this state joined the Indian Union. This paper is a micro level study on a small state receiving a ninegun salute status having 64 villages and 74,000 population. This paper helps in understanding the role of the small states in the national movement, specially how the Princely States and their leaders reacted to the ongoing movements in British India and how nationalism can be understood in the twentieth century.

NOTES

1. Quoted in Robin Jaffery, ed., *People, Princes and Paramount Power: Society and Politics in the Indian Princely States*, New Delhi, 1978, p. 9.

2. Thomas R. Metcalf, *Ideologies of the Raj: The New Cambridge History of India*, vol. III, 4, CUP, New Delhi, 1996.
3. Readings collections 23, Hyderabad to Lord Reading, 7 July 1921, Quoted in Ian Copland, *The Princes of India in the Endgame of Empire: 1917-1944*, CUP, Cambridge, 1997, pp. 9-10.
4. S.K.P. Singh, *The Indian Ruling Princes and the National Movement*, New Delhi, 1991, pp. 14-15..
5. Ian Cupland, *The Princes of India in the Endgame of Empire*, p. 2.
6. The number of states depends on how they were defined. Rajas or princes, jagirdars, taluqdars, etc., were also called as princes. Though more than 600 Princely States are listed but while considering privy purses the number of states listed are about 563.
7. Lord Ripin, Lord Curzon, Lord Hardinge, Lord Chelmsford, Lord Reading, Lord Irwin suggested to the princes that their governments in regarding education, health, welfare and above all the interests of the subjects should be protected. See for details Urmila Phadnis, *Towards the Integration of Indian States*, Asia Publishing House, New Delhi, 1968, pp. 81-3.

Ideology, Political Consciousness and Movement for Responsible Government in the Hyderabad State

Y. VAIKUNTHAM

> Alas! Democracy has to be taken to Hyderabad on a gun carriage
>
> D.F. KARAKA

The achievements of the anti-colonial struggle and the 'nation-making' in India will be better appreciated if we can critically look into the political process in the Princely States. Suppression of peoples' movements in the states as well as the anti-British struggles in India became the designs of the colonial policy. Princes were the collaborators and the local allies and played the role of 'breakwaters', 'bulwarks of reaction', 'buffers', etc.[1] The paramount power used the princes to suppress any challenge to their political and economic hegemony and therefore the princes were guaranteed of their autocratic powers, personalized, backward, medieval rule. The Princely States were only 'dependent states' since the creative forces in the state—human and natural resources—were subordinated to the colonial paradigm. The Hyderabad State provides a unique case in this direction. The purpose of this paper is to examine the ideology, the political process as a part of the peoples struggle for responsible government in Hyderabad.

Political awakening was a complex and slow process, but in the Nizam's Dominions it was much more difficult due to autocracy, feudalism, and illiteracy. Let us look into the social base of the Princely State. The ministers were used by the Raj as constitutional counterweights to the royal autocracy. But the ministers never tried to share power with the people nor was the Raj interested. According to Galleghar and Robinson's 'formal and informal', 'direct or indirect' rule was to strengthen the cause of the Raj rather than bring out any social policy or political freedom in the princelydoms. The growing middle class and mass resistance after 1857 made the Raj evolve a policy of building up the princes and feudal gentry as subordinate partners (instead of annexation and expansion of territories). Even the commercial interests of the Raj and international commercial forces weakened the Indian rulers and distorted the society and destablized the political fabric.

I

Established in 1724, on the Deccan Suba of the Mughals, Hyderabad under Asaf Jahis was an autocratic state, representing medieval feudal institutions. Power was centralized in the hands of the Nizam and his Diwan. In the nineteenth century it was one of the biggest and most populous Princely States.[2] The rule was mainly based on *gastis* or circulars or *firmans* issued by the Nizam regulating the state administration both in political, economic, and socio-religious matters. In fact, the concept of paramountcy has been slowly but systematically applied to the states in the broader political design of the colonial rulers.

It was from the time of Lord Wellesley that the principle of paramountcy and subordinating the collaborating rulers became the state policy of the Raj. In reality, the indirect rule of the British increased through the Resident and the Political Department, thus, replacing the personal rule of the princes whom they considered as 'feudal and autocratic'. Peoples' involvement in the administration was conspicuous by its absence in Hyderabad.[3] There were neither civil liberties nor any growth of political consciousness or responsible government in the Nizam's state. There was discontentment and backwardness in the state. Syed Abid Hasan while writing on the situation in Hyderabad points out:

> Outwardly it presents a picture of peace and contentment. But if you scratch the surface you will begin to see the sore of discontentment that is robbing every Hyderabadi of happiness.[4]

The process of the peoples' struggle in Hyderabad was painful and was delayed since the administration suppressed every effort of the subjects in this direction. Law and order situation was also bad and corruption was rampant. Before the Prime Ministership of Salar Jung-I (1853-83), John Kaye pointed out:

> The whole administration was rotten to the very core. It was a congeries of diseases. Nothing seemed to flourish except corruption. . . . No one cared for the people, no one cared for the state. . . . Every public office, in every department of the state was accessible to a bribe. There was nothing left indeed but the name of the Government, all the rest was lawlessness and confusion.[5]

Moulvi Chirag Ali pointed out:

> Before the administration of . . . Salar Jung-I, there was no regular or systematic form of government, nor were there any separate departments of administration. Everything was in the hands of the Diwan or Ministers without any regular form of administration. It was altogether a new idea, an element foreign . . . to have anything like an organised system of government. . . .[6]

Bureaucracy and the muslim nobility dominated the administration.

Agriculture was the mainstay of the population. Salar Jung-I introduced some changes in the revenue administration including the form of collection. Instead of revenue farming, collection through taluqdars and their assistants had been introduced. Diwani and jagirdari systems could be seen in the Hyderabad State on the model of ryotwari and zamindari systems in British India.

The land was divided broadly into khalsa, sarf-i-khas, and jagir areas. In this, approximately 60 per cent of the land was under diwani, 30 per cent jagirdari, and 10 per cent sarf-i-khas. The survey and settlement was started in khalsa or diwani areas, though in a limited way in a slow process, but in the jagirs the people were left to the mercy and caprice of the jagirdars and their agents. The Nizam himself with 10 per cent of the land under his private control was the biggest jagirdar.[7] However, Salar Jung introduced monthly revenue statements and proper accounting to streamline the economy of the state.

TABLE 1: REVENUE AND EXPENDITURE IN HYDERABAD

(in thousands of rupees)

	1853	1883	1900	1910-11	1920-1	1930-1	1940-1	1947-8	1950-1
Revenue	8,00	3,11,00	4,31,94	5,22,36	6,48,17	7,62,32	10,88,90	20,99,38	29,89,03
Expenditure	N.A.	N.A.	4,27,90	3,94,76	6,40,14	8,29,64	10,37,84	34,72,41	30,00,44

SOURCE: *A Review of Hyderabad Finances*, pp. 36, 38, 67, 74, 76, 81.

TABLE 2: LAND REVENUE

(in thousands of rupees)

	1910-11	1922-3	1930-1	1940-1	1947-8
Revenue	2,66,65	2,72,84	3,00,35	3,30,18	3,41,87
Expenditure	32,93	62,90	68,66	69,11	83,12

SOURCE: *A Review of Hyderabad Finance.*, pp. 36, 38, 67, 74, 76, 81.

Education was very backward. In 1898, only 5.8 per cent of the boys and 0.51 per cent of girls of school going age were in schools. There were 13 high schools, 49 middle schools, 707 primary schools for boys, 67 schools for girls with 3,425, 8,635, 46,581 and 3,812 pupils respectively.[8] Whereas in British India, the literacy was 10 per cent among boys, 7 per cent among the girls in 1901-2. The foregoing shows the educational backwardness in the Nizam's Dominions, the government's failure to provide specific encouragement to educate their subjects like in the British India which was responsible to restrict the free flow of rational and progressive ideas and democratic institutions. The staggering illiteracy was slowly transformed by inviting non-*mulkis*, i.e. educated people from outside, which slowly brought about intellectual awakening in the state. The establishment of the Osmania University in 1917-18 and many other colleges, gave fillip to the educational development as well as political consciousness among the people in Hyderabad.

Even by 1951, literacy varied from 5.9 to 7.2 per cent in the countryside though in the city of Hyderabad, the literacy was about 25.2 per cent.[9] The educational backwardness was responsible for the lack of political consciousness as well as socio-cultural backwardness. In fact, the literacy per thousand in comparison to few other states was as follows:[10]

Hyderabad	50
Travancore	289
Mysore	106
Baroda	209
Jammu & Kashmir	40

Higher Education was totally neglected, except the Nizam College (1886), Aurangabad Second Grade College (1892-3), opening of civil service classes in Madrasa-e-Aliah (1884-5).[11] In this situation non-*mulkis*, especially from Aligarh were invited to occupy important positions in the administration. This process in a way led for *mulki* and non-*mulki* conflict calling the pro-British Indians as '*Mulki Namak Haram*'. Lack of education hampered political consciousness in the State. However, the non-*mulkis* and the movements in the British India could influence the Hyderabadees.

The pro-British policy of the government, surrender of Berar, Osmanabad, Raichur in 1853, the disturbances in Hyderabad during the 1857 revolt, tribal revolts in the second half of the nineteenth century show that the anti-British feelings and anti-Nizam's struggle gained momentum in Hyderabad, though the Nizam's administration, in collaboration with or under the guidance of the Resident had been suppressing them. Anti-British feelings triggered in the agitation of the anti-Chanda railway scheme. The attendance of the Hyderabad elite in the sessions of Indian National Congress (INC) was another factor that contributed to the political awakening in the state after 1885. The 1891 regulation of the Nizam's government to gag and control the press was very critically responded. The editors of the vernacular papers had to submit papers regularly or show cause for unwillingness to do so imposing number of restrictions on the press. The circular no. 4956 enabled the state to take action on those who, 'threaten an injury to a Government servant or tend to prejudice the mind of the people against the Nizam's Government or any of its officer'. *The Deccan Times* called this policy as indecent, ridiculous and 'hectoring or terrorising policy and lacked the modicum of self-respect'.[12]

One of the reasons for the state's backwardness was the continuance of Persian as the court official language till 1884. However, it was replaced by Urdu, extending the same to the administration from 1886. However, these were not the languages of the people and profoundly affected the progress of education as well as the growth of western ideas, scientific outlook, and political consciousness.

The communication policy of raising 'Nizam's guaranteed railway', connecting the Madras-Bombay line through Sholapur, linking Hyderabad with this line at Wadi called the Chanda Guaranteed Railway Scheme of 1883-6 led to public resentment. The state policy of guaranteeing British lines, helping the policy of economic exploitation, subordinating the state's interests to that of the paramountcy of the Raj, led to public protest from Aghornath Chattopadhyaya, Abdul Qayyum, etc. These agitations helped in moulding the public opinion against 'The Nizam and The Raj Nexus' ignoring the interests of the state and its subjects.

A decade after the death of Salar Jung-I, the famous Prime Minister of Hyderabad, the Nizam promulgated what was popularly known as 'Qanoon-cha-Mubarak'; and the Cabinet Council with a President and a 6 member Legislative Council in 1893 came into existence without any non-official members. The Legislative Council was to frame the rules, whereas the Cabinet Council was to implement them. This was mainly to take the help of experienced officials, to determine the functioning and powers of the ministers and secretaries of the departments.[13] Thus, began the modernization of administration by constituting a Legislative Council rather than democratization of the Councils to progressively involve the people in the governance of the state. However, the appointment of Maharaja Krishna Pershad as the President in 1901, marked a liberal attitude in the Nizam's administration.

The first two decades of the twentieth century were the beginning of the political movements in British India. Beginning with the imperialistic policies of Curzon, partition of Bengal, Vandemataram, Home Rule movements, etc., there was a change in the nature of anti-colonial struggles from a moderate approach to extremist activities. These developments did influence the intellectuals in the Hyderabad State also.

The Library movement[14] was launched by the establishment of Sri Krishnadevaraya Andhra Bhasha Nilayam in 1901, Vignana Chandrika Granda Mandali, and number of other public libraries all over the state in general and Telangana in particular from 1901 onwards helping the growth of mother tongue, moulding public opinion on the dissemination, and imparting knowledge about the movements in British India. Madapati Hanumanth Rao, Kommaraju Lakshamana Rao, Gadicharla Hari-sarvothama Rao, mostly from the Andhra region could influence them. This led to socio-cultural changes followed by public awakening and political consciousness in the state.

The socio-religious movements to promote widow re-marriages, Harijan uplift, and against the *devadasi* system, etc., attracted the attention of the intellectuals and the government. Not only did it lead to cultural revival but it also brought about a certain renaissance in the state which gained momentum after the establishment of Andhra Mahasabha and its women's wing. Establishment of the Vivekavardhani Educational Society and the genesis of the Swadeshi movement in early twentieth century Hyderabad was responsible for the new spirit in the state.

Hyderabad leaders and intellectuals like Waman Naik, Kesava Rao Koratkar, and many others attended the All India Congress Conferences at various parts of British India and got the inspiration for political activities. The ideas and thoughts of Ghokhale, Tilak, and other leaders from Maharashtra also influenced the Hyderabad leaders.[15] The First World War, the Nizam's support to the British, the Khilafat issue, the Montagu-Chelmsford reforms too had major impact on the Hyderabad people. A branch of INC was started in Hyderabad in 1920 after the Nagpur session of the INC.

Maharaja Kishan Pershad who succeeded Vicar-ul-Umra as the President of the Council not only tried to define the work of ministers and the Council, but was also soft towards the socio-cultural activities in the state, and was responsible for the growth of the libraries and literary activities.

Osman Ali Khan Bahadur, the VII Nizam was not in favour of sharing power with people. He became his own Prime Minister in 1914. Neither reforms nor democratic ideals have been accepted even on the recommendations of the Balmukund's Committee. Even they went to the extent of issuing *gasti* no. 52 of 1921 which banned any political activity in the state. It is more relevant to look into the attitude of the Nizam who consented to this *gasti*. It throttled the democratic aspirations of the people and the civil liberties like freedom of expression and writing. The typical feudalistic nature of the state did not create the objective conditions requisite for the growth and development of democratic ideas.[16] However, it remains as a very crucial period in the political activity of the state.

Gandhi's influence was increasing. Same was the case with the influence of the Congress and the Muslim League in the state by 1920. National leaders visited the state, leaders from Maharashtra like Maharshi Karve addressed Hyderabadees. The trend was set for social and constitutional reforms.

Through the 1920 reforms, the Nizam had tried for some elective element in the Legislative Assembly by giving representation to 'Important Classes' and educated people, but the implementation of the scheme was not envisaged immediately. But these efforts were in the process of a modernization of Hyderabad, which created, or provoked enthusiastic public reaction in Hyderabad, even thanked the Nizam for the constitutional reforms.

II

The period between 1921-38 was crucial in the history of the Hyderabad State in many respects. Not only the Nizam's efforts to introduce constitutional reforms were initiated, but political activity in the state itself increased. This period also witnessed the strengthening of the communal forces, changing attitude of the Nizam towards communal forces, suppression of all political organizations by using the draconian *gastis* became another characteristic of this period. [17]

During this phase, the Nizam's government tried to be more autocratic by ruling the state with the support of *gasti* no. 52 of 1921, *gasti* no. 53 of 1929, etc. The powers of the state came to be centralized and the communal forces were encouraged. The *gasti* no. 52 published in the Gazette extraordinary no. 52 of 1921, dt. 9 Aben, 1330 F. ruled:[18]

> Any political or social meeting creating political issues should not be held without permission of the Chief Secretary and the Chief Secretary will first seek my (the Nizam) permission for it. Failing this, the Convenors of such meetings will be solely responsible for the consequences. Besides this, the Agenda of such meetings should be submitted to the Chief Secretariat before-hand for information. Until

the Agenda of the meeting is sanctioned by the Chief Secretariat no action should be taken by the Convenors of the meeting.

In fact, this circular was criticized as draconian which tried to suppress the democratic aspirations of the people in convening social or political meetings. The government made it clear that 'any person whether a resident of this place or an outsider, would be permitted to take part in such political meetings that may not invoke revolutionary spirit in the minds of the common people or disturb peace of the country only with the written permission of the magistrates'.[19] Any defaulter was to be punished under the Hyderabad penal code no. 164 with an imprisonment for one month or Rs. 200 or both. All meetings—political, social, religious—were brought under its scope. People agitated against this *gasti* and got it amended in 1929 without even withdrawing *gasti* no. 52. It resulted in the issue of *gasti* no. 53 which was much more autocratic and notorious than the *gasti* no. 52 of 1921. *Gasti* no. 53 was published in *Zarida* in Khardad 1342 F which prohibited any meeting 'which creates suspicion, provokes religious rivalry or antagonism or anti-government feelings and working against the Nizam or the British rule or creating disaffection against any institution or employees, those associations would be called political associations and would be banned'.[20] In fact the press and public criticized them and pointed out 'trust begets trust' but not suspicion and repression.[21] Therefore, it can be understood that the government was more concerned to centralize the powers and administer the state with the 'Iron Hand' than introducing constitutional reforms.

During this period, on the advice of the Viceroys, an Executive Council was constituted in 1919. A committee was constituted to discuss the powers of the Councils under Rai Balmukund. But due to the retirement of Ali Imam, the President of the Executive Council, these reforms could not see the light of the day. However, to advice Rai Balmukund Committee, Hyderabad Political Reforms Association (HPRA) was established in 1921 as a political organ of the citizens of the Hyderabad State under Waman Naik as President and Raghavendra Sarma as Secretary; but the government took serious note of this. This association was never allowed to meet in the state by the raising of some objection or the other.

Due to the absence of the effective educated middle class, the demand for political rights was in the formative stage. Political activity was also quite dormant. There was hardly any resistance against government actions. The Political Reforms Association, however, met in British India—since it was not allowed to function in the state—in Kakinada (1923), Bombay (1926), Pune (1928), and Akola (1931) during the sessions of the

INC with an intention of getting wider sympathy for their problems. This Association demanded constitutional reforms, responsible government, removal of the draconian restrictions on political meetings, press, etc.[22] In these conferences, the growth of healthy public opinion for political reforms was ventilated. This was also indicative of the growing political unrest. But, these meetings did not have substantial results as the public was not very responsive to the political demands as could be seen in British India.

During this period, the state witnessed communalism rather than politicization. It became an important point and a real source of agitation and conflict in the state. However, before the public was mobilized politically, a number of social organizations came to the forefront in the state influenced largely by the social movements in Maharashtra.

In fact the struggle during this period was between the Nizam, his Council and the British rather than the political organizations in the state. However, during this period, Hindu-Muslim antagonism also increased. Though the British considered the princes as the source of their strength, they directed them to introduce reforms in tune with liberty, democracy, nationality, and self-government to contain people's movements in the States.

The period between 1921-38 was crucial in the sense the Ittehad-ul-Musalmeen party was established in 1927, which slowly but steadily grew from its cultural and secular origins into a communal organization trying to interfere in the day-to-day affairs of the state. Between 1935 and 1938 organizations like the Nizam's Subjects League, established in 1935 by Nizamat Jung Bahadur, ex-political member, tried to take up the cause of responsible government and politicization and democratization of the state. In fact in 1938, Hyderabad State Congress was established as a political, and secular organization to fight for a responsible government under the aegis of the Nizam. This was crucial in the sense, the ideological formulations of the state on one side, and people's aspirations and movements on the other to become part of the state administration had ultimately got locked in a deadly struggle for the autonomy and the supremacy of the state. The following discussion will explain this phenomena.

The paramount power, i.e. the British, its Viceroys and the Executive Council, had started realizing that in the states, participation of the people in the administration was necessary and they periodically advised the rulers slowly to make it both representative and responsible to the people. On the other, the Chamber of Princes, which was established in 1919, tried to uphold the authority of the princes. However, the Nizam was always questioning the concept of equality among the princes and maintained his identity by being aloof from the Chamber of Princes.

Culturally the people were looking for reforms. The Social Reforms Conference of the Marathas which met in Hyderabad did not allow the other linguistic groups specially Telugus to discuss their problems in their mother tongue which led to the establishment of Nizam Andhra Kendra Jana Sangam under the leadership of Madapati Hanumantha Rao. It became the forerunner for the political movements, in the state. Subsequently it enlarged the scope of its activities including socio-economic and cultural activities and called itself as Andhra Mahasabha from 1930, the State Congress from 1938, and the Communist Party from 1940 to achieve demands both on ideological grounds as well as in the interests of the people and the state. Except the Communist Party, moderate methods dominated their struggle. These movements were not only united but also projected the consciousness of the people of Hyderabad State. The political agitations in British India, and Constitutional reforms in Mysore and Baroda made the Hyderabad elite conscious of their political status in Hyderabad State.

Let us look into the work of Andhra Kendra Jana Sangam in bringing about the socio-political consciousness in the state. On 27 April 1922, it was decided to establish libraries and reading rooms to encourage education and scholars and procure manuscripts and conduct research to spread knowledge through handbills, booklets, and public speeches to propagate Telugu language and culture.[23] As a part of its programme about 12 booklets were published of them 4 were very significant, viz., *Vettichakiri*, *Vartaka Swatantram*, *Nazrana*, *Mahatarfa Maggapu Pannu*, etc., in Telugu to educate the people on the prevalence of bonded labour and exploitation of merchants and weavers. The Sangam also translated the *firmans* into Telugu and explained its impact on the spread of social, cultural, and political movements in the state. Though the Sangam was not against any community or language they were primarily to work for the popularization of Telugu culture and incidentally to generate cultural and political consciousness about their problems.

Meanwhile the Khilafat and Non-Cooperation movements in British India had their impact on Hyderabad. Number of moderate leaders like Madapati Hanumanth Rao, Burugula Ramakrishna Rao, Mundumula Narasinga Rao and Sarojini Naidu (daughter of Aghornath Chattopadhyay), took active part in those activities. The Congress and the HPRA in their meeting at Kakinada demanded responsible government and removal of restrictions on the political meetings as well as ban on newspapers in the State. The social movements among the Marathi people and the cultural movements of Kendra Jana Sangam of Telugu people certainly influenced broad but moderate elite consciousness akin to INC in its early phase. At this stage, the Ittehad-ul-Musalmeen party was established in 1927 under Salar Yar Jung; and in 1928 it came under Bahadur Yar Jung to promote national and cultural consciousness among the Muslims. In this phase, Nizam made some attempts for the retrocession of Berar, involvement of non-Muslims in the administration, as well as attempts to contain the spread of political consciousness among the people. But the Nizam also tried to uphold paramountcy of the British in this state. In fact on 21 December 1926 the Nizam issued a *firman* with the concurrence of the Resident enunciating the general principles, viz., abolition of existing abuses, restricting the practice of *nazars*, avoiding any disregard to the British. The message was that any deviation would compel the Nizam's government to take repressive measures as per the regulations.

Political ambitions among all organizations was on the increase. The Ittehad-ul-Musalmeen party worked for the following aims and objectives, viz.[24]

a. To oppose British paramountcy;
b. To fight for the independence of the state;
c. To oppose responsible government;
d. To obtain political dominion for the Muslims;
e. To unite various Islamic sects and also to protect their socio-economic and educational interests.

This party gained the status of a political party and subsequently fought vigorously to uphold the 'Anal Malik' concept—opposing any responsible government in the state.

The All India State Peoples Conference, established in 1928, was to play the role of a National Congress in the Princely States. The grievances of the states people, liaisoned with National Congress and fight against the rulers and their exploitation were its main objectives. It certainly had its impact on the conditions in the Hyderabad State.

Hyderabad Political Reforms Association under the leadership of Raghavendra Sharma submitted a representation to Indian States Commission, popularly known as the Butler Commission on 16 March 1928. It could not evoke any response from the Commission. Butler Commission though had sympathy for the princes but could not give any concessions to the princes. The administration run by the draconian circulars in controlling the freedom of the press, speech, and political meetings had been questioned. These contradictions ultimately culminated in the establishment of the Andhra Mahasabha in 1930. Meanwhile the Nizam's representatives participated in the Round Table Conferences ignoring the demand of the people for a responsible government.

From 1930 to 1948 a number of developments took place in the state both to alleviate the problems of the ryots and their debts and also to mobilize the public on political issues. The feudal ideology of the Nizam on one hand and people's growing democratic aspirations on the other and the following movements amply emphasized the situation and the outcome.

The paramountcy in this period got consolidated. The Nizam further centralized his authority during this period. The influence of the Majlees and their leader Bahadur Yar Jung on the administration increased. Andhra Mahasabha, the Arya Samaj, the State Congress, and the communists, etc., took up agitational approach against the Nizam's rule and to achieve demands such as religious freedom, civil liberties, responsible government as well as for the eradication of *vetti* and feudal institutions. This period saw some political activity but those organizations largely remained moderate, politically unmobilized and unorganized. Lucian Benichou rightly argued that communalism rather than politicalization emerges as the real source of agitation and conflict in Hyderabad.[25]

Achyut Kowde argued that the Nizam's state was under the 'Imperial tutelage' and was kept as an Islamic cultural centre in India. Muslims were treated as a protected class thus creating a cleavage between the ruler and the ruled and the Muslims and the Hindus.[26] The *mulki* and non-*mulki* struggle strained Shia and Sunni relations, all affected the political system in the state specially the deprival of the subjects in sharing the power in the state. Initially the movements were started on social issues, ultimately paving the way for political movements.

The Andhra Mahasabha established in 1930 as a social organization, started annual conferences every year and took up the issues of peasants, merchants, and all-sided development of the state. On political issues though it restrained for long but in its sixth session held at Nizamabad in 1937, a resolution was passed demanding a responsible government.[27] But the autocratic Nizam's state did not permit political resolutions and forced it to be withdrawn. Meanwhile Hyderabad State Congress was floated in 1938 but the same was banned on 7 September 1938, before it was inaugurated. After 1938, members of the Andhra Mahasabha joined the State Congress till the Mahasabha was revived on a strong footing in 1940. During this period the people of Maharashtra and the general Marathi speaking people started Maharashtra Parishad in 1937. In its third session held at Umri, Nanded district in May 1941, it discussed, debated, and resolved on responsible government in the Nizam's state under the presidentship of K.S. Vaidya. This, they demanded, should come into force immediately so that the popular representatives could frame the laws and establish a responsible government under the rule of HEH the Nizam.[28] The Kannadigas started Karnataka Parishad in 1937 but its work wa limited and not very effective.

The world economic depression and its impact on the British Empi.e naturally affected India including Hyderabad State. The price fall and inflation affected the peasantry. To curb the problems, number of irrigational projects including Wyra, Palair, Nizamsagar, Singabhoopalam, Pocharam, Dindi reservoir, etc., were constructed between 1929-42. The Barucha's Commission was appointed in 1937 to go into the issue of debt and suggest remedial measures. Further, the Tenancy Committee was appointed in 1940 to study and suggest measures to improve the lot of the tenants and agricultural labourers having small holdings and inams. However, these reports were never implemented, thus leaving the people to their fate and the feudal and exploitative tendencies continued as before.

Under the circumstances the establishment of Nizam's Subjects League by the ex-political member of the Nizam, viz., Nizamat Jung Bahadur, along with Padmaja Naidu, Mir Akbar Ali Khan, K.S. Vaidya as other members was started in 1935. However, the clause 7 of its constitution which speaks of responsible government in the state made the Nizam's government to impose all types of restrictions till the regulation was withdrawn. However, in the process this organization could not function properly. All this indicates that the Nizam never allowed any organization to start with political ideas to emerge.

The appointment of the Aravamudu Aiyangar Committee in 1937[29] to suggest constitutional reforms in the state provided an opportunity for the state elite to organize like-minded political leaders, viz., Madapati Hanumanth Rao, Burugula Ramakrishna Rao, K.S. Vaidya, R.K. Dhoot, Janardhan Rao Desai, etc., to come together and start the Hyderabad National Conference, subsequently called the Hyderabad State Congress to advice the Commission about the constitutional reforms. This was the first political organization with a specific agenda but yet this was banned before its first session on 7 September 1938. In fact the Haripura session of the INC in 1938 recognized the rights of the people in the states and promised to support their movements in the princely states for obtaining political reforms in their respective states. In fact this strengthened the political consciousness of the people in this state and also motivated to start the State Congress.

Between 1938-48 ideology was slowly dominating the activities of the intelligent to shape the movements in the state. The Hyderabad State Congress, the Arya Samaj and the Communist Party with different ideological framework worked against the Nizam and his feudal institutions. The objectives of the Hyderabad State Congress were:[30]

a. To attain responsible government under the aegis of the Nizam;
b. To attain fundamental rights and civil liberties;
c. Reservation for minorities for not more than 10 years;
d. Public Service Commission to fill up vacancies;
e. To guarantee cultural, religious, and educational rights.

The effort to develop nationalism, intellectual, moral, economic, and industrial development was undone by the imposition of a ban on the Congress on 7 September 1938 two days before its general session. The firm commitment of the State Congress to attain responsible government could be seen in their discussions, constitution, and subsequent correspondence with the government.[31]

The ban was seriously challenged by the State Congress by starting a Satyagraha movement from 24 October 1938 demanding the withdrawal of the ban order. Eighteen batches of satyagrahis defied the law, courted arrest. The students boycotted the classes.[32] The ideology of the National Congress formed the main basis in launching the State Congress activities. The Congress leaders felt disadvantaged by the ban and the declaration of the state that the State Congress was a communal organization. When the satyagraha was in progress, the Congress represented by Mundumula Narsing Rao and Muslims represented by Bahadur Yar Jung of Ittehad held Hindu-Muslim unity talks from November 1938 till the middle of 1941 but without reaching any tangible consequences. The representatives of the State Congress and the press criticized the government's repressive and humiliating measure to collect the taxes 'to fill the government coffers'. Removal of the restrictions on civil liberties, political and administrative reforms, they argued, would develop mutual trust in the constitutional advancement and it was resolved in the talks 'that the legislature be so constituted that no community or class be in a position to transgress the legitimate rights of other communities'. Bahadur Yar Jung did not accept the ideal of responsible government as an advancement in constitutional development or lifting ban on the State Congress.[33] Urdu press, especially *Rahbar-e-Deccan* and *Anjuman-e-Ittehadul* opposed the constitutional reforms. Anti-reform demonstrations were held to show the strength of the Muslims. Even Bahadur Yar Jung said that 'Muslims would never accept it'.[34] While anti-reform agitations from Muslims were in progress, Gandhiji advised Narsing Rao not to weaken on 'responsible government' and the State Congress members and Narsing Rao pointed out that the responsible government scheme would never encroach into the Royal prerogatives and rights.[35] During this period Hindu Civil Liberties Union and the Arya Samaj started the satyagraha on the issue of freedom of worship and religious liberties. After 1938 Hindu-Muslim antagonism clouded all political issues in the state. In fact all organizations, while criticizing the government, also rejected the reforms since they were not aimed at a responsible government.

The Hyderabad State Congress started the satyagraha on 24 October and continued it up to 24 December 1938 not only for the ban to be lifted but also for the demand of constitutional reforms in the state. The leaders of the movement were Ramananda Tirtha, Govinda Rao Nanal, Ravi Narayan Reddy, etc. The moderates still kept themselves away from the satyagraha.

Gandhi who was closely watching the developments in the state advised the State Congress to withdraw the agitation since it was likely to be branded as a communal organization along with the Hindu Civil Liberties Union and the Arya Samaj satyagraha. Even the students of Osmania University started the Vandemataram movement in the campus on the freedom of worship.[36] It is pertinent to mention here that the government was committed not to allow any political organization to work in the state as well as to introduce any constitutional reforms worth mentioning. The satyagraha had only a limited impact though public consciousness got a fillip due to these programmes. To quote the confidential report, 'the performance of this programme was nowhere completely achieved and varied from being a total failure in several districts to partial success in a few. . . . Nowhere did the police find it necessary to use force in effecting arrests or dispersing crowds.'[37] The state authorities were vigilant and the agitation was under control.

III

The state, being feudal in nature, never gave powers to the people to participate in the administration. If one closely examines the type of constitutional powers given to the people or the constitutional reforms intended to introduce in the state, the character of the state would become obvious. The Muslims always worked under the notion of 'Anal Malik' concept, i.e. as a ruling class having perpetual rights.

The first Legislative Council was created on 20 February 1893 as per the Qanoon-cha-Mubarak issued by the Sixth Nizam to reduce the burden of Madar-ul-Moham (Diwan) with an advisory committee of Assistant Ministers (Moin-ul-Maham). The members of the council were 6 and all were officials. They included the chief justice, one judge of high court, one inspector of revenue, DPI, IGP, and the finance secretary. The very concept of the legislative body and the powers entrusted defeated the purpose for which it was created. Knowing the inadequacies in the council the membership was increased to 15 on 18 January 1894. They included the ex-officio: chief justice, the judicial secretary, legal advisors (3); government nominated members (6); elected non-officials: Jagirdars (2), vakils (2); non-official nominated members (2)—total 15.[38] The membership of the council was increased to 17 by 1900. These reforms were only to discuss the issues but not to reject or amend in any case and not to impinge on 'Royal Prerogatives'. However non-official element was inducted into the council in 1894, but only by government nomination.

The foregoing again clearly shows that majority were government servants. The elected non-official element again was from jagirdars and vakils. It is clear that the Nizam was not contemplating to introduce popular franchise or at least a broad based electoral college.

Till 1919 periodically the composition of the council was being enhanced. In 1899-1900, a paigah and a shahukar was added. In 1905-9, 2 retiring officials, in 1911-12 three members, one from Hyderabad municipality, 2 local boards, and in 1913, one member from the sarf-i-khas was added, thus making the council membership 23. Again if one examines the composition, it was neither broad based nor it represented election based on franchise.

The council had only limited powers to introduce bills and all the powers were rested in the hands of the ruler. The composition of the Council further strengthened the opinion that various vested interest groups—both official and non-official—were made to fill in this council enabling to get their concurrence for all the activities of the state. During this period Minto-Morley Reforms of 1909, Montagu-Chelmsford Reforms of 1919 in British India slowly extended the franchise to various groups and also partially transferred the responsibilities of governing the state to its subjects. In other words, Diarchy was introduced in the provinces as per the Government of India Act of 1919 and provincial ministries were formed having full control on the transferred subjects. However, in the princely states, specially Hyderabad, no such attempt was made to progressively involve the people in the state administration.

During Ali Imam's presidentship the Executive Council was constituted for the first time in 1919.[39] As a result of the Viceroy's advice and ongoing constitutional reforms in British India, a committee under the chairmanship of Rai Balmukund was constituted on 24 February 1920 and it submitted the report in September 1921. It basically recommended bicameral legislature entrusting some additional responsibilities. Also it recommended 21 member assembly with 15 officials, 6 non-officials. However, the report could not see the light of the day as Ali Imam resigned the presidentship in 1921. It, however, accentuated political activity in the state.

To advise the Rai Balmukund Committee, HPRA was established in 1921, however, the association was not allowed to meet in the state, as discussed earlier, by the various circulars of the Nizam's government. Hence this exercise almost ended without any positive results on the establishment of the responsible government in the state except popularizing the cause of the people's movement in the Hyderabad State when they met outside the state in the INC pandals. Committees and sub-committees were formed in 1924 and 1927 to suggest various steps in the constitutional reform' but to no avail.

Balmukund Committee recommended seats with an intention of healthy development of non-political people to contribute for political and moral strength of the state, though, it was a serious hindrance for self government principle. This was done keeping the special conditions of Muslims in Hyderabad State though in British India Viceroy and Secretary of State was against communal represenation.[40]

The composition of the Legislative Council before the appointment of Aravamudu Aiyangar Committee was[41]

	Total Members	:	20
(a)	Ordinary members	:	18
	i. Officials (ex-officio: 3, others: 9)		12
	ii. Non-officials (elected: 4, nominated: 2)		6
(b)	Extraordinary members		2

The Government of India Act of 1935, and as a prelude to it the discussions both by the Indian Statutory Commission (Simon Commission) and the Indian States Committee under Butler, Round Table Conferences, all resulted in more popular awakening on the necessity of responsible government in the states. An important step in this direction in the Nizam's state was the establishment of the Diwan Bahadur Aravamudu Aiyangar Committee with four members on 22 September 1937.[42] The preamble of the committee said:

> Keeping in view the conditions in and the requirements and circumstances of the state to investigate and report on all suitable alternatives for the more effective association of the different interests in the state with the government whereby the later may be placed in continuous possession of their needs and desires.

There were 22 representations to the Aiyangar Committee and most of them advocated 'no reforms' on the ground that only a handful of outsiders wanted reforms for their selfish ends. They said that even democracy was a failure. These representations were mainly from linguistic, religious minorities and vested interest groups. However, the committee submitted its report on 21 August 1938, and the notification to that extent was issued on 17 July 1939. The main recommendations were:[43]

a. Effective association of the people with the government for internal and external security;
b. Freedom of association, speech and writing should be granted within legitimate bounds;
c. The present Legislative Council can not adequately meet the needs of the time, therefore it should be reconstituted so that a non-official majority could be provided for effective representation of the different interests of the people.

The legislature was to be composed of 70 members including the President. It would enjoy powers of legislation, interpretation and discussion with regard to all subjects except specified subjects. It would have rights to discuss budget (majority members felt) and minority members referred that the rights to pass or reject the budget and the term of legislature should be of 5 years. However, regarding its implementation the public and the press had doubts and apprehensions about the government's intentions on responsible government.[44]

The government claimed that the representation in the legislature was neither communal nor of a territorial nature but based on economic

TABLE 3: THE STRENGTH AND COMPOSITION OF THE PROPOSED LEGISLATIVE COUNCIL

Nominated	37
i. Officials	18
ii. Non-officials	19
(a) Ilaqas	8
i. Sarf-i-khas	2
ii. Paigahs	3
iii. Peshkari	1
iv. Salar Jung	1
v. Samsthans	1
(b) Others	11
i. Rural Arts and Crafts	1
ii. Backward Classes	1
iii Minor Unrepresented Classes	3
iv. Others	6
Elected	33
a. Agriculture (pattadars 8, tenants 4)	12
b. Graduates	1
c. University	1
d. Jagirdars	2
e. Mashdars	1
f. Legal	2
g. Medical	2
h. Teaching	1
i. Commerce	1
j. Industry	2
k. Banking	2
l. Organized Labour	1
m. Harijan	1
n. Rural Boards	1
o. Municipalities	2
p. Women	1

SOURCE: Report of the Reforms Committee, 1938, chart opposite p. 66.

interests which alone can satisfy the different interest in the state, i.e. ethnic, linguistic and religious interests.[45]

The reforms suggested by the Aiyangar committee were never taken seriously by the Nizam, therefore nothing emerged. Since the Aiyangar committee could not be implemented there was continuous pressure from the organizations or associations for progressive participation of the people in the government. As a result of the growing pressure the constitutional reforms were announced in 1946 to broaden the Legislative Council which included:

TABLE 4: COMPOSITION OF THE PROPOSED LEGISLATIVE ASSEMBLY, 1946

I. Elected	
Samsthans	6
Agriculture	32
Labour	4
Industries	2
Commerce	2
Banking	2
Law	2
Medicine	2
Graduates	2
Local Bodies	2
Contonment Boards	16
Owners & Tenants of Hyd & Sec'bad	4
Total	*76*
II. Nominated	
Ilaqadars	5
Others	38
Total	*43*
III. Appointed	
Sarf-i-khas	3
Executive Council	10
Total	*13*
Grand Total	132

SOURCE: V.B. Raju, *Legislative Reforms*, 1946, pp. 5-6.

The foregoing clearly indicates the creation of professional constituencies rather than territorial constituencies. It was to associate different interests in the state with the government than the establishment of a responsible government.

The Assembly was to be presided over by the President. The Assembly had powers only to debate and recommend but no rights to enact. One Muslim and one Hindu were to be nominated to the Council by the government. The nature of the electorate was more or less like what was suggested in the Minto-Morley Reforms in 1909.

There was to be a joint-electorate of the Hindus and Muslims and whoever could secure 51 per cent of his community vote or polled higher were declared elected. In other words it was nothing but communal electorate. The qualifications for franchise were linked with property rights, i.e. those who paid revenue or a rent of Rs. 100 or occupied Rs. 5 rented value buildings. Of the 1.633 crores population only about 1.5 lakh, i.e. less than 1 per cent of the population were voters. Every voter had to vote for one Hindu and one Muslim and if he voted for either only one or two candidates for the same community the vote would be invalidated. Proceedings of the council were in Urdu, the official language of the state. Table 5 indicates the religious overtones of the proposed assembly.

The foregoing representation was based on the 86.1 per cent of Hindu, 12.7 per cent of the Muslim and 1.4 per cent of the Christian population in the state. As V.B. Raju pointed out it was not a political reform but a communal uniform, oversize for the Muslims and tightfit for the Hindus.[46] Under those circumstances and on the eve of India's independence, Hyderabad was under great pressure to introduce constitutional reforms, mainly to usher a responsible government in the state, which was eluding the people all through.

Lord Mountbattan in his letter sent to the Nizam through Sir Walter Monckton on 8 April 1948 pointed out that with the exception of the Nizam, the rulers of every state in India had introduced or declared their intentions of introducing responsible government and as a well-wisher of the Indian state, he emphasized the imperative of the desires and aspirations of the people of Hyderabad as a whole.[47] In fact Nehru in his discussion with Sir Walter Monckton pointed out 'that in all the acceded states, the rulers had either introduced responsible government, or declared their intention of doing so in the very near future; Hyderabad was the solitary exception'.[48] Lord Mountbattan said that the Nizam seemed to fear that the introduction of responsible government in his state would result in accession to India.[49] On the advise of Mountbattan, Nehru assured Sir Walter Monckton of his intentions neither to invade nor to impose economic boycott of Hyderabad but to recommend drastic action on Kasim Razvi and to introduce responsible government in the state. In reality Razvi continued his provocative speeches, e.g. 'the waves of Bay of

TABLE 5: COMPOSITION OF THE PROPOSED LEGISLATIVE ASSEMBLY: RELIGION-WISE 1946

Assembly	Muslims	Hindus	Christian	Paigah	Non-Hindus	Total
Elected	38	38	-	-	-	76
Nominated	20	20	2	1	-	43
Appointed	11	1	1	-	-	13
Total	69	59	3	1	-	132

SOURCE: V.B. Raju, *Legislative Reforms*, Hyderabad (Deccan), 1946, p. 10.

Bengal will wash the feet of our sovereign'. 'We would plant the Asaf Jahi flag on the Red Fort in Delhi', etc. Nehru warned them and in reality it was the conflict between the authoritarian or autocratic state and the democratic urges of the people and Nehru insisted on a full responsible government.[50] Patel told Laik Ali that the Hyderabad problem had to be solved as in the case of other states and under no circumstances independent status could be maintained. Laik Ali was given the alternatives between accession and the grant of responsible government. Laik Ali felt it was difficult for the Nizam to accede but also felt that the grant of responsible government meant accession, so it was rather preferable to grant a responsible government. If it was in his interest to protect the legitimate rights of the Muslims, it was suggested to concede the responsible government and call constituent assembly wherein the Nizam can fix the legitimate rights of the Muslims. Laik Ali's interpretation of responsible government was something more than it in real sense.[51] Meanwhile after tentative discussions with Monckton, Nehru, Mountbattan, and V.P. Menon a tentative programme was drawn up, i.e.

i. To put controls on Razakars;
ii. To release the Congress detenues;
iii. To reconstitute the cabinet with all communities;
iv. Formation of a Constituent Assembly to introduce responsible government.

V.P. Menon gave Laik Ali the clear choice: either accession or grant of responsible government. On 22 April the Nizam wrote to Mountbattan stating that these were internal matters, between the ruler and the people. On 23 April a *firman* was issued asking the non-represented political parties to join the interim government in Hyderabad. Alan Campbell Johnson, Mountbattan's press attache after discussion with the Nizam, Laik Ali, Nawab Moin Nawab Jung, Kasim Razvi, El Edroos, and K.M. Munshi in May 1948 felt that the Nizam was the ultimate decision maker and he was in the mood of 'aggressive fatalism'.[52] There were problems in the borders while internally the state faced communist armed struggle from 1946. Nehru made it clear on 17 June, that there was no point in continuing these protracted negotiations, and leave the draft standstill agreement to the Nizam, and till such time open door policy was to continue towards Hyderabad. Nothing worthwhile emerged.

On the eve of India's independence, on 11 June 1947 the Nizam announced that Hyderabad would join neither India nor Pakistan. This increased tensions in the state. Communal forces under Razakars whipped up activities. The State Congress, after lifting the ban in 1946, held its open conference in July 1947 and demanded Hyderabad to join Indian Union as well as the introduction of responsible government with full powers including law and order.[53] A plan of action was decided and a 'Committee of Action' was formed for agitation in the state under the State Congress. Tirtha said, 'we shall break but not bend' till they achieved responsible government, Hyderabad joining Indian Union, and the sovereignty of the people was recognized.[54] Border camps were organized to defend the Union from Razakars and state forces. Simultaneously the Communist Party started its armed struggle in July 1946 and continued against the feudal autocratic government. After prolonged negotiations between August-November 1947, the Nizam's government signed the standstill agreement on 29 November 1947.

While the Congress and Communist Parties were continuing their struggle, the Nizam asked the State Congress to participate in the new government admitting the principle of responsible government provided it was accepted that 'Hyderabad will be for Hyderabadees' and parity between Hindus and Muslims maintained in the executive and Legislatures of the new constitution [Nizam suggested 4 Majlees, 4 Hindus (3 Congress + 1 SC), 4 nominated by the Nizam of them 1 Hindu].[55] The efforts to woo and induct State Congress could not materialize and Tirtha declared that there will be no compromise except responsible government and an interim government by the State Congress. The united front of the State Congress and communists continued. The atmosphere vitiated due to the activities of Razakars. The efforts of Mountbattan could not get any positive result.

Razakars intensified their activities and the atmosphere in the state was communalized. Under the circumstances on 9 September, the Government of India decided to ask the Southern Command to march into Hyderabad on the morning of 13 September under Maj. Gen. J.N. Choudhari and Rajendra Singhji. The entire exercise was called 'operation polo' by the Army Headquarters. On 17 September evening the Hyderabad Army surrendered, on 18 September morning Indian Army under J.N. Choudhari entered the Hyderabad city after 108 hours of operation. On 17 September, Laik Ali's cabinet had resigned and Military Commander J.N. Choudhari was made in charge of its administration.[56] Razakars were banned and Razvi was arrested on 19 September, on 23 September the Nizam withdrew the case from the Security Council of UNO.

It is sad to note that not only was responsible government denied but communal forces were strengthened in the state. It was only in 1950, four Congress ministers were appointed in Vellodi's ministry. Though some Hindus were included in the ministry during the Nizam's period that was only for participation and not to introduce a responsible government. Though the movement for responsible government could not achieve the desired goal it could instil political consciousness and waged ideological struggle for democratic rights, against feudal institutions and ultimately for the accession of the state into the Indian Union.

When the groundwork was going on in moulding public opinion on political and economic ideology, socialist ideology under the communists slowly but strongly emerged by 1940's. The Comrades Association (1939), and the establishment of Communist Party (1940) the left wingers in Andhra Mahasabha, responsible for its split in 1944 slowly paved the way for armed struggle from July 1946. The main issues were:[57]

a. Against *begari* and *bhagela* (forced labour);
b. Feudal exploitation including that of deshmukhs and jagirdars;
c. Lack of civil liberties;
d. Against autocratic state, i.e. the Nizam's state;
e. Return of illegally 'seized lands' (for debt and manipulation of land records).

The Communist Party gave a left direction to the movements in Hyderabad State and led the armed struggle from 1946 against the exploitative feudal set-up on one hand and the autocratic government on the other. The armed struggle continued in two phases 1946-8 and 1948-51. During the first phase communists and the State Congress formed the united front and fought against the Nizam resulting in Hyderabad joining the Indian Union in September 1948. This resulted in a section of liberal, moderate communist leadership under Ravi Narayana Reddy and Baddam Yella Reddy to withdraw the struggle but another group under extremist ideology of Sundarayya continued the struggle though it was suppressed and withdrawn by 1951. The work and the sacrifices of the communists in the Hyderabad State strengthened the progressive elements in the state thus upholding the necessity of people's participation in the government.

The Second World War was instrumental in the collapse of the British colonialism in India. In fact the imperial forces tried to reinforce their presence, but the constitutional changes and people's mood were responsible for rapid changes in the colonial outlook. Though princes were benefited by the War, the people's movements against their rulers started liberalizing their administration. But the Nizam's darbar could neither reasonably be liberalised the government nor preferred to join Indian Union. Akbar Hydari retired in 1941 and the leadership including the Nizam slowly moved towards hardliners under the influence of Ittehad-ul-Musalmeen and its leadership. But the collaboration between the British Indian Empire and the princes collapsed in 1947. Though the British thought Hyderabad would be 'a distinct imperial asset', it became harder for the darbars to face up to the threatening reality of a fast changing order in India.[58] Some of the members of the Chamber of Princes realized that the responsible government in the states could not be delayed indefinitely and attempted a pre-emptive strategy. The princes lacked any political commitment towards the responsible government or to understand people's aspirations and worked without any commitment for the welfare and involvement of the people in the administration. Thus in Hyderabad the Nizam and his coterie never worked with an accountability except under the notion of 'Anal Malik'. It was ultimately responsible for liberal, nationalist as well as Communist movements which worked from different directions and the ideological background, ultimately leading to the decolonizing and dethroning of the feudal rule of the Nizam in 1948 and the establishment of the responsible government after the general elections in 1952.

NOTES

1. Urmila Phadnis, *Towards the Integration of Indian States 1919-1947*, New Delhi, 1968, pp. 1-20; also see Bharati Ray, *Hyderabad and British Paramountcy, 1858-1883*, OUP, 1988, pp. 32-6.
2. An area of about 98,000 sq. miles with Berar and excluding it, i.e. after 1860 it had 82,698 sq. miles. It had 1.61 crore population in 1941, had only around a crore population in the nineteenth century.
3. Mir Laik Ali, *Tragedy of Hyderabad*, Karachi, 1962, pp. 30-7.
4. Syed Abid Hasan, *Whither Hyderabad*, 1935, Preface.
5. Sir John Kaye, *Life of Lord Metcalfe*, quoted in John Law, *Modern Hyderabad (Deccan)*, Calcutta, 1914, p. 32.
6. See for details, Moulvi Chirag Ali, *Hyderabad (Deccan) under Sir Salar Jung*, vol. I, Bombay, 1884, p. 111.
7. *A Review of Hyderabad Finance* (Introduction by C.V.S. Rao), Hyderabad, 1951, pp. 26, 32, 36, 39, 45, 68, 73, 75, 83, 87 (1950-1).
8. Report on the Administration of the HEH the Nizam's Dominions for four years 8-10-1894 to 7-10-1898, vol. I, pp. 228-42, also see Mazar Hussain,

Census of India, HEH the Nizam's Dominions (Hyderabad State), vol. XXI, Part I, pp. 237-41.

9. Abul Khasem, Md. Shamsul Alam, 'Education in Hyderabad State: 1853-1948' (unpublished Ph.D. thesis of O.U.), 1983, p. 300.
10. *Census of India*, Hyderabad State, 1951, p. 458.
11. In 1897-8, there were three colleges with 153 students, 13 high schools with 3,425 students in the Dominions. See Report on the Administration of HEH the Nizam's Dominions 1894-5 to 1897-8, p. 228.
12. Circular no. 4956, of Home Secretary the letter no. 183 dt. 25 Shawel. Quoted in *Freedom Struggle in Hyderabad*, vol. III, pp. 40-2.
13. Report of the Reforms Committee 1938 (1347 F) (Aravamudu Aiyangar Committee), Hyderabad, 1938, pp. 5-6.
14. Sri Krishnadevaraya Andhra Bhasha Nilayam in Sultan Bazar, Hyderabad was established in 1901. Subsequently number of libraries were started in the state specially in Telangana at Secunderabad, Warangal, Suryapet, etc. See for details; Madapati Hanumantha Rao, *Telangana Andhrodyamamu*, vol. I, Hyderabad, 1949, pp. 52-67.
15. *Freedom Struggle in Hyderabad*, vol. III, p. 162.
16. *Feudal Oppression in Hyderabad (Deccan)*, A Survey of the Conditions of the Paigah Jagirs of HEH the Nizam, 25 May 1939, British Library, London, p. 5.
17. *Gasti* no. 52 of 1921, no. 53 of 1929. The *gashtis* throlled the public opinion and suppressed democratic political movements including civil liberties, etc.
18. *The Freedom Struggle in Hyderabad*, vol. IV, pp. 26-7.
19. Ibid., p. 27.
20. *Golkonda Patrika* (editorial), 3-6-1933; also see for more details, Y. Vaikuntham, 'Notorious Gasties and Public Reaction in Hyderabad State', *Proceedings of South Indian History Congress* (21st Session), Madurai, 2001, pp. 89-92.
21. *Golkonda Patrika* (editorial), 20-12-1930 and 20-5-1933.
22. K.S. Vaidya, *Hyderabad State Congress*, pp. 2-3.
23. Madapati Hanumantha Rao, *Telangana Andhdrodyamamu*, vol. I, Hyderabad, 1949, pp. 87-98.
24. R. Khan, 'Muslim Leadership and Electoral Politics in Hyderabad: A pattern of Minority Articulation', *Economic and Political Weekly*, vol.VI, nos.15 and 16 (10-17 April 1971), p. 786.
25. Lucian Benichou, 'From Autocracy to Integration, Political Developments in Hyderabad' (unpublished Ph.D. thesis), Western Australia, p. iii.
26. Achyut Kowde, *The Peoples Movement in Hyderabad*, 1947, pp. 2-10.
27. 'Badyatayuta Prabhutvamavasaramu' (Telugu), *Golkonda Patrika*, 13-12-1937. Also see the resolution numbers 2a, 2b of Andhra Mahasabha in its sixth session at Nizamabad. For more details see, Madapati Hanumantha Rao, *Telangana Andhrodyamamu*, vol. II, Hyderabad, rpt. 1995, pp. 137-41.
28. *The Freedom Struggle in Hyderabad*, vol. IV, pp. 121-4.

29. The members includes Aravamudu Aiyangar as Chairman, Gulam Mahmood Qureshi, Qadir Hussain Khan, K.S. Vaidya, Mir Akbar Ali Khan and Yusuf Ali as Secretary.
30. K.S. Vaidya, *The Hyderabad State Congress*, pp. 1-13, Rama Chari, *Hyderabad State Congress*, 1948, pp. 13-15; also see, Y. Vaikuntham, 'Genesis of Hyderabad State Congress', *Osmania Journal of Social Sciences*, vol. I, 1986, pp. 42-3.
31. See for more details, 'Congress and Hyderabad', File no. 613, vol. VI s. no. 1081, Constitutional Affairs Secretariat, HEH the Nizam's Government.
32. *The Freedom Struggle in Hyderabad*, vol. IV, pp. 149-58.
33. For further details see 'Hindu-Muslim Unity Talks'; Instalment no. 47, Lists 10, serial no.1197, File 18/51 (R), Constitutional Affairs Secretariat, HEH the Nizam's Government.
34. File no. 18/51 (R), vol. II, Press Section, vol.V, s. no. 1148, Hyderabad State, Also see *Report on the Anti-Reform Demonstrations of Shehrewar 12, 1348,* File no. 26/51 (R), Anti-Reform Agitation.
35. File no. 18/51 (R), vol. II Confidential, 19-1-1941, Dr Vaidya to the Nizam.
36. Y. Vaikuntham, 'Vandemataram Movement in Hyderabad State', *Journal of Indian History*, vol. LIX, 1981, pp. 335-45.
37. FR1/11/38, p. 2, India Office Library.
38. V.B. Raju, *Legislative Reforms*, Hyderabad, 1948, pp. 4-5.
39. Sir Ali Imam before joining as the President of the Executive Council of the Nizam Government was working as the member of the Executive Council of Bihar and Orissa. His rank was next to peshkar but above all the nobles and Sadar-ul-Mahams. He has resigned in 2 years, could not rise to that occasion in the implementation of constitutional reforms. Also he failed in dealing with the freedom struggle and the aspirations of the people. For more details see; N. Ramesan (ed), *The Freedom Struggle in Hyderabad*, vol. IV, Hyderabad, 1966, pp. 1-6.
40. *Report of the Reforms Committee*, 1938 (1347 F), Govt. Central Press, Hyderabad, pp. 39-43.
41. Ibid., p. 66.
42. The four members were K.S. Vaidya, Akbar Ali Khan, G.M. Qureshi and Prof. Qadir Hussain, see *Report of the Reforms Committee*, 1938 (1317 F), p. ii.
43. See *Report of the Reforms Committee*, 1938, pp. 21-84.
44. See 'Mana Nutana Rajakeeya Samskaranalu' (Telugu), *Golkonda Patrika*, (editorial), dt. 27-9-1937. See for more details *Golkonda Patrika* (editorial), dt. 23-9-1937, 13-9-1937, 13-12-1937.
45. *Census of India*, Hyderabad, 1941, vol. XXI, p. 31.
46. V.B. Raju, *Legislative Reforms*, p. 20.
47. V.P. Menon, *Integration of the Indian States*, Orient Longman, rpt., 1998, p. 352.

48. Ibid., p. 351.
49. Ibid.
50. Ibid., pp. 351-3.
51. He wanted 50:50 for the Hindus and Muslims in the ministry and some proportion for various other communities.
52. See for more details, V.P. Menon, *Integration of the Indian State*, pp. 353-8.
53. Ramananda Tirtha, *Memoirs of Hyderabad Freedom Struggle*, Bombay, 1967, p. 175.
54. *The Nizam Defied (An Account of the Glorious Struggle of the People of Hyderabad)*, 7 August to 16 September 1947, Bulletin no. 2, Hyderabad State Congress, Bombay.
55. Lucian Benichou, 'From Autocracy to Integration', pp. 299-301.
56. J.N. Choudhari continued till December 1949 and M.K. Vellodi was installed as civilian administration, and in general elections Congress ministry under B. Ramakrishna Rao was installed in March 1952.
57. Against three leeches (landlords, moneylenders, profiteers) see *People's Age*, 13.1.1946 in Barry Pavier, *The Telangana Movement, 1944-51*, New Delhi, 1981, p. 97.
58. Ian Copland, *The Princes of India in the Endgame of Empire 1917-1947*, Cambridge, 1997, p. 276.

People's Movement in the Hyderabad State

V.H. DESAI

'Bliss was in that dawn to be alive but be young was very Heaven', said the bard. Those immortal words come to my mind whenever I think of the days, the hectic and memorable days, when I was at the centre of maelstrom that shook Hyderabad during the most eventful chapter in its chequered history; the last phase in the story of the fabulous Nizams. Even today the thrill and the bliss I experienced in those days inspire me. I am here attempting to recapture the historic moments of the Hyderabad freedom struggle for the edification of the present generation and inspiration of the future.

The last Nizam, Mir Osman Ali Khan, was wholly responsible for the collapse of the Dominions of Hyderabad over which he had presided for a long span because of his lust for power, hunger for riches and weakness for women. His unwillingness to share power even with the elite was his undoing. Perhaps, 'Destiny' had a bearing in whatever he did; as if to confirm an old Hyderabad story.

It is said Nizam-ul-Mulk Asaf Jah, when in north India, was on a hunting spree in the jungles far from his headquarters. He felt so hungry that anything offered would be a boon from the almighty. While going around in search of something to eat, his eyes fell on a holy man who gave him *kulchas* (backed bread) to eat. When he ate seven *kulchas*, it is said, he told the holy man that he had enough of it and wanted nothing more. This was taken as a sign that the family of Nizam-ul-Mulk would rule the Deccan for seven generations only; as the holy man blessed him as such.

Nizam-ul-Mulk adopted yellow colour for his flag, the colour of the *kulchas* which the holy man offered him when he was in dire need of food. From then onwords the round-shaped *destar* (turban) became the official head-dress. The flag and the *destar* became the national emblem of the state, when the Dominions of Hyderabad joined the main stream in 1948. Nawab Mir Osman Ali Khan was the seventh ruler in the line from Nizam-ul-Mulk. The dynasty which had lasted a little over two centuries, thus passed into history, fulfilling the prophecy.

If objectivity of the history of Hyderabad has to be observed from AD 1800 onwards till the disintegration of the erstwhile Nizam's Dominions in 1956; indeed, volumes could be written; if only one makes an honest attempt to unfold the events in all their dimensions without distorting facts.

Distortion of facts is no history. There were many salient features peculiar to erstwhile Hyderabad State, under His Exalted Highness, Nizam the VII. Nawab Mir Osman Ali Khan Bahadur, whose reign from 1911 to 1948 had its none-too-happy backdrop. The Nizam was 'an enigma wrapped in mystery inside a riddle', to subjects who took his sweet poetic language without doubting his bona fides, till the Razakars came on the final scene.

Consequently, the Freedom movement did not receive the attention it deserves due to the kaleidoscopic changes in hundreds of native states—big and small on the eve of the transfer of power.

The most intensive phase of the Hyderabad freedom struggle, however, was enacted immediately after the transfer of power to the Indian hands in 1947. As such, the freedom struggle assumed both the characteristics of liberation and problem of India's unity, integrity and security, thereby providing a wider canvas. However, the struggle in Hyderabad was ever shadowed due to the euphoria that immediately followed the dawn of independence on 15 August 1947.

In such a context the standard-bearers of the Hyderabad freedom struggle, led by Swami Ramanada Tirtha have to come out with their heart-rendering stories of sacrifice, the inter-linkages, the political cross currents through which the struggle had to pass, the important and imaginative turn it took, leading to a successful culmination of achieving democratic freedom of the people and strengthening in a larger sense the integrity and unity of India.

For a fuller understanding of the freedom struggle waged in Hyderabad, there is a need for backward linkages besides the last phase of the struggle. As such, the history of freedom struggle in Hyderabad may have to go beyond the historic police action (1948) up to the re-organization of the states (1956), when the disintegration of the erstwhile Hyderabad State become complete, paving the way for the emergence of an united Indian polity.

Further, an integrated view of the three constituents of Telangana, Marathwada, and Karnataka has to be taken. For they formed part of the then Hyderabad State, and owed their political awakening to different organizations and different schools of thought.

Our long story starts with 'Vandemataram' and ends with 'Jana-Gana-Mana' following the Hyderabad State joining the mainstream on 18 September 1948. Looking back, I feel myself lost in an ocean of thoughts.

The year, 1938 was an year of great significance for the people, because it marked the beginnings of an open popular political upsurge in the Dominions of the Nizams. The 1938 satyagraha was of a unique nature; several organizations like the Arya Samaj, the Hindu Mahasabha, Praja Mandals, under the Hindu Civil Liberties Union and the Hyderabad State Congress undertook the satyagraha from their respective platforms and carried on the struggle for the basic civil rights. The Vandemataram movement of the students also served as the basis for political awakening and political unrest.

Simultaneously the historic struggle of the students of the Osmania University began following their decision to sing Vandemataram in the university campus specially in hostels, despite prohibitory orders by HEH the Nizam's government. This heralded the beginning of a deep-rooted crisis in the state, closely following the Silver Jubilee of the ascendancy to the Asafia throne by Nawab Mir Osman Ali Khan Bahadur, HEH the Nizam VII of Hyderabad in the grace year of 1937.

The saga of the Vandemataram movement in Hyderabad State took a queer turn, following the Nizam's government giving it a communal colour. The spread of the Swadeshi movement was carried on through institutions like the Arya Samaj and the Ganesh Utsav celebrations. Apart from Arya Samaj, lectures on swadeshi were arranged in the house of Aghornath Chattopadhyaya, where leaders like Keshavarao Koratkar, Damodar Setwalekar, Vaman Naik, Appaji Tuljapurkar and others used to discuss the pros and cons of the Swadeshi and Boycott movements.

The restless students of the Osmania University who were forbidden to sing the Vandemataram song in the prayer halls in university hostels on the eve of the Dussehra celebrations in 1938, spontaneously rose in revolt. The hostel authorities, on instructions from the British Resident, issued prohibitory orders and closed down the prayer halls. The students took it as a challenge and started singing Vandemataram in the corridors of prayer halls. Upon this, the university authorities issued a circular, prohibiting the singing of Vandemataram in the university precincts. The students appealed to the university to withdraw the ban on the singing of the Vandemataram song. Their pleas fell on deaf ears. The Pro-Chancellor on 29 November 1938 asked all the Hindu students to vacate their rooms by the evening and suspended all of them from the college. Harsh methods were employed. This had a chain-reaction. The students refused to give up their agitation. They actually intensified their struggle by openly selling buttons inscribed with 'Vandemataram' in defiance of the prohibitory orders.

The Osmania University Students' strike continued from the 29 November till 10 December 1938. The strike was so spontaneous that even students from other districts joined the agitation and the university authorities on 10 December 1938, announced that the striking students should appologise and return to their colleges least their names would be struck off from the rolls of the university. The student refused to obey the orders. Following this 70 students from the city college, 310 from the Gulbarga Collge (including high school), and 120 from Mahaboobnagar High School were removed from the rolls. During this period, there was continuous strike in Aurangabad, Bidar, Nanded, and Parbhani districts. The Osmania University also took care to see that the 'dismissed students' were not given seats in any other University in India, then under the British Government, by appealing to the Inter-University Board. But the Nagpur University came to the rescue of these students and admitted them. The former Prime Minister P.V. Narasimha Rao was one among the few living beneficiaries of the gesture shown by the Nagpur University. Prominent among others expelled from the Osmania University Colleges was former minister late K. Achyuta Reddy, who was the leader of Osmania University students. Altogether 350 students were rusticated from the university.

The Nizam's government was shy with the nomenclature of 'Congress'. The Hyderabad State Congress was banned even before it was launched in 1938. Some moderates, however, were having negotiations with the government to find a solution. Finding that the Nizam's government was pre-determined to suppress people's urge, the Hyderabad State Congress decided to offer satyagraha, with Govind Rao Nanal, as the President and Ramakishen Dhoot as the General Secretary from different parts of the state.

The government declared the State Congress and its Council of Action as unlawful bodies on 24 October 1938. Altogether there were 18 batches comprising 400 satyagrahis. Simultaneously with the State Congress, the Arya Samaj, the Vishwa Hindu Parished, and the Hindu Civil Liberties Union continued the Satyagraha.

The All-India States' People's Conference had, by then become a strong body welding together the progressive elements in the Indian states for a common purpose. As a result of the Quit India movement, it came to be converted into a wing of the Indian National Congress for all practical purposes though constitutionally it was an autonomous body. When the members of the Congress Committee were realized it was decided that a meeting of the Standing Committee of the AISPC should also be convened. Sheikh Mohammed Abdullah, then the veteran leader of the Kashmiri people invited the Committee to meet at Srinagar at the residence of Mohammed Afzal. Pandit Nehru was the President, Swami Ramananda Tirtha attended the meeting as a special invitee.

Sheikh Abdullah, the 'Sher-e-Kashmir' had organized the people of Jammu and Kashmir under the banner of National Conference. Though he began with a communal outlook, later on realizing the true nature of the issues, had become a confirmed and committed nationalist.

The situation in Kashmir and Hyderabad was almost identical. It was the Hindu Maharaja who ruled over the people of Kashmir, the large majority of subjects being Muslims. The Hindus there enjoyed the privileges. In Hyderabad, it was a Muslim ruler who governed the people, the Hindus forming an overwhelming majority, but the Muslim being the privileged class. Naturally when the freedom struggle came to be launched in Hyderabad, it evoked the sympathies of Sheikh Abdullah and his colleagues. In 1940, he toured Hyderabad State for over a week and gave the Freedom movement a new fillip, especially in what followed during the historic 'Quit India movement'.

National Conference workers took keen interest in the struggle for freedom in Hyderabad. They felt that the people's movement in these two states would have to develop on similar lines. They often used to say that they considered the Hyderabad struggle as their own. Do not slacken, thereby we will suffer, they used to urge the people of Hyderabad.

The British imperialism, with 'divide and rule' as its sheet anchor to perpetuate its rule over the vast Indian subcontinent had at last found a match in Mahatma Gandhi. One of the greatest achievements of Gandhi's stewardship of the Non-Cooperation movement in the cause of freedom was, perhaps his call for 'Do or Die', sequel to the 'Quit India' resolution adopted by the Working Committee of the All India Congress Committee held at Bombay. As soon as the AICC resolution was passed, the British struck. The AICC meeting terminated on the night of 8 August 1942. Before the next day dawned, the police in swift action arrested all leaders, including Gandhi, Nehru, Patel, Azad, and all members of the Working Committee.

The 'Quit India call given by Mahatma Gandhi was mischievously misrepresented that with the British withdrawal from India, the Dominions of Hyderabad, under the aegis of HEH the Nizam, would remain 'Independent' of India. To give a fillip to the ulterior motives, the reactionary-cum-communal forces raised as new slogan 'Azad Hyderabad Zindabad'. Thus, the issue took a new dangerous turn.

However, the State Congress was undeterred. Following the mass arrests in British India, the Nizam's government too followed suit and arrested Pandit Narendraji, Dr G.S. Malkote and his wife Vimalabai Melkote, H.C. Heda and his wife Gyankumari Heda, Padmaja Naidu, Smt and Sri Ramaswamy, B.Ramakrishan Rao, G. Ramachari, Krishna Dube, M.S. Rajalingam, Vandemataram Ramachandra Rao, Kaloji Narayan Rao, Komaragiri Narayana Rao, Ravi Narayana Reddy, Govinda Rao Shroof, S.K. Vaishampayan, Baba Saheb Paranjipe, A.K.Waghmare and his wife, K.S. Vaidya, Sirajul Hussan Tirmizi, Janardhan Rao Desai, Hanumantha Rao Kakkeri, Fatullah Khan, Vinayaka Rao Vidyalankar, Jaffer Hussain, Akbar Hussain, and thousands of leaders in all the 9 districts of Telangana, 5 districts of Marathwada, and 3 districts of Hyderabad-Karnatak, which constituted the Hyderabad State. With the arrest of most of the leaders in the Hyderabad State Congress, the students abstained from the schools and colleges and came out in processions. The police brutally lathi-charged them, I was one of those who was caught in the procession and was rusticated for a full one year for having protested against the arrest of our national leaders. That was the turning point in my life.

Sensing the demand for the restoration of civil liberties and responsible government getting popular support even at the grass-root level, the Nizam's government engaged the services of a BBC correspondent on a princely salary of 200 pounds per annum to carry on propaganda in support of HEH the Nizam's claim that once the British paramountcy lapsed in British India, he had the right to proclaim himself as an independent monarch of this state.

In the wake of the 1942 movement in Hyderabad, late Col. Abed Hassan Safrani and Prof. Suresh Chandra joined Netaji's Indian National Army after crossing India.

With the lapse of British paramountcy from the 15 August 1947, the rulers of Indian states realized that it was better for both the provinces and the states to make laws sitting together as friends than to make treaties as aliens and they acceded to the Dominion of India, barring HEH the Nizam and HH the Maharaja of Jammu and Kashmir. The Hyderabad State had its own civil service, police, and an army.

A number of other states had also maintained armed forces. The

Hyderabad State had a currency. It survived only because it was linked with Indian currency at a fixed rate of exchange. The state had a postal system of its own, railways, etc.

On the strength of the above, with the honorific title of 'Faithful Ally' accorded to the Nizam by the paramount power, the Nizam made an astounding assertion on the eve of transfer of power from the British crown to the Indian representatives that 'Hyderabad, in fact is a country and is organized as a country'. In one of the brochures issued by the Nizam's government it said:

> The Nizam bound to maintain individual entity of Hyderabad with its special problem, history and traditions.
>
> Among the 600 Dominions it is largest and are larger than the United Kingdom and about half the size of France. His subjects number seventeen millions, more than twice the population of any other Indian State and more than Canada, Austria and many services: its own modern army, its own police, University, railways and industries. Its finances are organized on modern lines with budget and the budget is surplus.

It is well-known that the history of Hyderabad was linked with British rule in India. The paramount power operated as a standing check on the misrule of Hyderabad. The paramount power's intervention in state affairs had been practically continuous since 1800.

Logically speaking, the Freedom movement in Hyderabad was a fight against the feudal-reactionary regime which was out to destroy the unity and integrity of free India with the active connivance of British imperialism.

The approach of the Government of India to the problem of Hyderabad was understandably their general policy towards other Indian states. India is not a mere geographical expression but an economic and political entity. The states were an integral part of that India. The economic and political unity of India was maintained till the lapse of paramountcy by the Crown, which operating through the political officers, provided the nexus between the Indian states and the central and provincial governments. The pivot of this arrangement was the Viceroy, who represented to the Indian states the sovereignty of the British Crown, while at the same time, he was, in relation to the British India, the head of the government. The Indian Independence Act relieved the states from all their obligations to the Crown and in consequence India's unity was seriously threatened with disintegration. The Government of India sought to avert this grave threat, their accession to the Dominion of India on the three subjects of defence, foreign affairs and communications. This was neither an emotional approach, nor an expansionist policy, or power politics. Highly practical reasons of geography, all compelling defence and internal security requirements and other equally strong considerations rendered India's organic unification imperative. The following quotation from Sir Raginald Coupland showed very clearly how vital this unity was to the very existence of the Dominion of India:

> An India deprived of the States would have lost all coherence. For they form a great cruciform barrier separate among all four quarters of the country. If no more than the Central Indian States and Hyderabad and Mysore were excluded from the Union, the United Provinces would be almost completely out of from Bombay, and Bombay completely from Sind. The strategic and economic implications are obvious enough. The practicability of Pakistan must be admitted, but the more the separation of the States from British India is considered, the more impracticable it seems. India could live if its Moslem limbs in the North, and North-East were amputed but could it live without its heart?

It may not be out of place to mention here that HEH the Nizam's government at this crucial phase declared that the Arya Samaj was a 'non-communal political' body, while the State Congress was 'communal', despite the fact that stalwarts like Syed Sirajul Hussan Tirmizi, Abul Hassan and a host of other nationalist Muslims were with the Congress' struggle for independence. By declaring Arya Samaj as a 'non-communal political' organization, the Nizam's government was justifying the existence of Majlis-e-Ittehad-ul-Musalmeen and its wing, the Razakar organization and saw no taint of communalism in its open support to the emergence of a fascist organization, headed by Syed Kasim Razvi.

On 22 August 1948, the young editor of *Imroze*, Shoebullah Khan was murdered. *Imroze* was his lifebreath. The news of his death appeared in *Imroze* without being submitted to the censure. That was Shoebullah's last defiance. His martyrdom was ennobling and inspiring.

Under the conditions prevalent then the Government of India could not have afforded to be a helpless spectator of the misrule in Hyderabad. If the law and order situation there, which were already showing signs of collapse, further deteriorated it would have led to the imperilling of peace and order in India. In the age of bullock-carts when small states lived in isolation and feudalism flourished, Hyderabad was either a *satrapy* or a military protectorate in India. Not only did the state have any external affairs relations independently, even its internal sovereignty was ever-borne and blunted by the over-riding British authority.

With the martyrdom of Shoebullah Khan, the brave pathan editor of *Imroze*, a nationalist Urdu daily, the Government of India published 'White

Paper on Hyderabad'. It was the beginning of the end of the Asaf Jahi rule in Hyderabad State. Every aspect of Hyderabad problem has had its own dimension. The story of the 'Last Days of Asaf Jahi Rule' cannot be told straight away. There are many characters, episodes galore, and contradictions too numerous to be unfolded in this short story. To understand the many-faceted face of Hyderabad, one will have to know not only the 'Real Rule' in Hyderabad but also how 'freedom' could be dawn on this soil as late as 13 months after the mainland woke up to greet the 'Tryst with Destiny' on the midnight of 14-15 August 1947, when the world was fast asleep, while India was awake—(as Jawaharlal Nehru described the historic event while proudly unfurling tricolour flag on the Red Fort on 15 August 1947).

The entire population, barring the Ittehads and a few other renegades, in one voice opposed the Nizam in his bid to carve out yet another Pakistan in the heart of India. Even sensible Muslim leaders like Nawab Manzoor June, Abdul Ghani, Nawab of Rampur, Raja of Mahamoodabad, Sir Sultan Ahmed, and several others condemned Nizam's claim for independence as preposterous. Sir Mirza Ismail called Nizam's game as an exercise in futility. The situation was becoming grim and on 14 December 1947, the Council of Action of the Hyderabad State Congress decided on launching a no-tax campaign. Revolution cries girded up their loins to pay the Nizam in his own coin, when the life of women belonging to the majority community was becoming too miserable; with rape, arson, looting, and burning becoming the order of the day.

The Nizam realized that the defensive measures taken by the Government of India were only a prelude to a far stronger action against him. All his efforts to mould world opinion in his favour had failed. He had estranged the sympathies of the progressive elements in the sub-continent of India. Barring the British conservatives and a few reactionaries in Hyderabad itself, nobody else supported him. The Government of England had made its position crystal clear—that of absolute non-intervention in the Indo-Hyderabad tangle.

So, as a drowning man who would rush up even to catch a straw to save himself, the Nizam decided to take up his case to UNO to seek according to Laik Ali, 'their good offices for a peaceful and enduring settlement'. His government informed the authorities at New Delhi of his above intention and also applied for passport facilities to send his delegation headed by Nawab Moin Nawaz Jung. The Government of India in their reply to him observed:

The Government of India regard the difference between them and Hyderabad as a purely domestic issue and cannot admit that Hyderabad considering its historic as well as its present position in relation to India, has any right to international law to seek the intervention of that or any other outside body for a settlement of the issue.

Paying little heed to this and to the last-minute appeals of several of his well-wishers, the Nizam tried to play upon the sentiments of some of the Islamic countries to help him in bringing his case for discussion in the Security Council. It was reported that Syria had agreed to help him. But this never materialized because of an unexpected change of government in Syria.

At last the Nizam invoking nobody's help, himself addressed the following letter to the President of the Council of UNO.

It is understood that the submission of the present complaint to the Security Council does not prejudice the submission of the dispute to the General Assembly.

On 25 August 1948, Dr Pillai, India's permanent representative to the United Nations, in a press statement observed:

As during the days when Britain was in control the present arrangement is that the Indian Union continues to be in charge of the external relations and the defence of Indian States including Hyderabad. Hyderabad therefore, is disqualified from pledging and complaint of this kind.

Representatives of India and Hyderabad, Sir Ramaswamy Mudaliar and Moin Nawaz Jung respectively placed their view-points before the UNO each justifying their stand, the Hyderabad delegate pleading for a hearing of his case and Ramaswamy advancing his arguments criticizing the former's stand.

The final scene left nothing to be desired. All was set for action. The police action, master-minded by India's 'strong-man' Sardar Vallabhbhai Patel, has no parallel in history.

For the present generation it may read as a fiction.

JAIL JOURNAL CALLING REQUIEM FOR THE DEMOCRAT

When I cast a longing, lingering look back, the vicissitudes of my career, full of hills and dales, make a strange spectacle. But all the while the head that shaped my ultimate destiny remained discernible. It consider this as may greatest good fortune.

In the year of Grade 1947, when I was imprisoned for my political activities by the HEH the Nizam's government, little did I expect that my career would undergo such a dramatic metamorphosis.

During the last phase of the freedom struggle in the erstwhile Nizam's State of Hyderabad—perhaps its most crucial phase—I was an Hyderabad based correspondent, representing curiously enough, almost all the dailies banned by the Nizam's Government, namely *Free Press Journal. The Forum, Blitz, Tej* and *Samyukta Karnataka.* Even in the inner most recess of my heart, I did not harbour any qualms that by serving these front-rank nationalist newspapers and periodicals. I was perpetrating a 'crime' against the Nizam's government. On the other hand, I had the feeling that I was serving in my own small way, a people's cause as a journalist, good and true. In those turbulent days, this realization gave me the most profound self-satisfaction of having done one's job for a cause for which we were all put behind the bars. In the wake of the historic Bombay meet of the All India Congress Committee (AICC) and the Quit India resolution of 9 August 1942, I founded a small organization known as the 'Karnataka Mitra Mandali' in the heart of the Hyderabad city. This proved to be the beginning of my political career.

I was hardly 16. With my like-minded friends such as Sitaram Pisolkar, Narahari, Tunga, and a host of others who were itching for some kind of secret underground activity to fight the autocratic rule of the Nizam, I found myself in the vortex of secret political conclaves. Thus the small room housing the Mandali became the nerve centre of our activities, mostly distribution of pamphlets, circulars, etc., issued by the State Congress from time to time. This was our contribution—a contribution of the youth to the freedom struggle.

The other facet of my activity, purely professional in character, came in for close surveillance of the Nizam's government. My news coverage sent through mail was not affected though, but my telegraphic despatches were censored heavily. One of my family friends who served the Intelligence Department of the government dished out a veiled threat to my elder brother that I should be warned and if possible restrained. Ironically enough, my two elder brothers—one in the army (Ranga Rao Desai) and the other in government service (Dharma Rao Desai) did not discourage me in any manner. Verily, nationalism was in our family blood.

One incident that occurred against this backdrop still lingers in my mind—my encounter with the Director of Information who was then known as Nizam-e-Ittelat. The Director was Mohammed Taquiuddin, a gentle and a kind looking person. One fine morning I was summoned to his office and was received like a VIP. I was ushered into his presence and offered a cushioned chair. The Director did all the talking. He politely prefaced the sermon with a brief observation that I was still young with a bright future, which he felt would become a reality if only I gave up my 'anti-social activities' and turned over a new leaf.

After a cup of tea, he went on. He even offered me a job in his own department because of my journalistic background. All the while I listened to him with respect and some amusement. Then he proceeded to give a graphic picture—almost a blow to blow account—of my underground activities to my utter surprise and shock, because it was all very correct. All kudos to the Nizam's Intelligence Department and its lynx-eyed sleuth-hounds. This interesting encounter with the Nazam-e-Ittelat turned out to be but a prelude to a new phase of my career, a more exciting one.

Before long, the police swooped on to our rented house as well as the office of the Karnataka Mitra Mandali, seizing all newspapers and correspondence. I was arrested in the premises of the Mandali when the whole populace of the Esamia Bazar witnessed the climax. Nearly two dozen police officers and constables headed by a Deputy Commissioner did the job. Of this unique honour I felt proud.

II

The birth pangs of *The Democrat* within the four walls of the prison cell and the jubilation that followed are not known to the outside world. I was initially lodged in the lock-up of the office of the Police Commissioner for a week and then sent to the Chanchalguda Central Jail in a special police van. Here, the venue of my future activities and greater excitement awaited me.

I was lodged in the European ward of the jail, a preferential treatment. All the members of the Working Committee of the Hyderabad State Congress, leaders of the Arya Samaj and the Communist Party of India were already there. I felt proud to be in their midst and share the honour of rubbing shoulders with front-ranking politicians of the day. The galaxy included: Swami Ramananda Tirtha, B. Ramakrishna Rao, K.S. Vaidya, H.C. Heda, Maqdoom Mohiuddin, B.S. Mahadev Singh, A.R.V. Chary, Dr. G.S. Melkote, Pandit Narendraji, Konda Venkata Ranga Reddy, Dr. M. Channa Reddy, S. Alwar Swamy, Dattatreya Awaradhi, S. Hanumantha Rao, M. Jaigopal Naidu, Sitaram Pisolkar, Krishnamacharya Joshi, Birdhichand Choudhary, Dattatreya Pershad, Boijjam Narsimlu, D.V. Pangrekar, and a host of others.

In their company I thought life would be quite smooth and eventful. This was, however, not to be. Politics would undoubtedly rear its ugly head where politicians are. The Chanchalguda Central Jail was no exception. Even before the last phase of the freedom struggle was launched in Hyderabad, the State Congress was split vertically by the 'Desai' and 'Gosai' (the 'real' Congress factions). The former group was headed by Janardhan Rao Desai with Burugula Ramakrishna Rao, Dr M. Channa Reddy, K.S.Vaidya, H.C. Heda in tow. The latter group was spearheaded by Swami Ramananda Tirtha, Dr G.S. Melkote, Krishnacharya Joshi and others. Some of these top-notch Congress leaders were not on talking terms even in detention.

In great contrast, the Communist Party of India and the Arya Samaj leaders held regular afternoon classes for political re-education and exchange of views in an orderly fashion. The State Congress leaders, on the other hand, remained enigmatically uncommunicative and took pride in their splendid isolation. Swami Ramananda Tirtha was rooted to his solitary room, spending most of his time in reading and writing. But he was available for consultations with one and all. We, the members of the younger generation, could not relish this picture of disunity and disarray at a time when they all should be in a conclave to chalk out a brave new future for the state. Therefore, we felt that the widening gulf between them should be cemented and a fruitful cohesion brought about for the sake of the country.

My detenu-friends like Dattatreya Awaradhi, S. Hanumantha Rao, M. Jaigopala Naidu, A.R.V. Chari and others conferred among ourselves as to how best we could bring about the much needed cohesion among the leaders, and open first a channel of communication that could ensure a 'thaw'. Behind the bars we were awake till 2 a.m. anyway. It occurred to us that why not produce daily a 'wall journal'—that will educate, enthuse and satanise men and matters and paste it at the main entrance of the dining hall where everyone could read it? The idea immediately 'clicked'.

In Jaigopal Naidu we had a fine artist, while Hanumantha Rao could write in a beautiful hand. And as a journalist, I could provide political themes, captions, news stories and format. All this went into the columns of the wall journal that came out as '*Bandal Gazette*' (non-sense Gazette!). When the first issue of the '*Gazette*' was pasted at the main entrance of the dinning hall, many eye-brows were raised, mostly in admiration and partly in consternation. The '*Gazette*' did not fail to make many digs at the detained leaders especially at their irresponsible stances. This did make an impact on them. Slowly but steadily they changed their attitude. They became more and more alive to the challenges ahead. This change of heart was exactly what we belonging to the younger generation desired and yearned for.

Spurred by the initial success of the wall journal, we raised our sights. We decided to launch a manuscript jail journal, *The Democrat*, for the political re-education of the detenus of all shades of opinion and schools of thought. Now the million dollar question was the basic raw materials—pen, paper, and ink.

A kind soul (may his tribe increase) appeared on the scene and rose to the occasion. The jail official (daroga) incharge of our ward was a Muslim from Uttar Pradesh, a nationalist at heart. He used to discuss with us the burning problems of the day including the reckless autocratic rule of the Nizam and his satellites. At a person-to-person level, we used to exchange views freely and frankly, thus establishing a rapport. Encouraged by this, we slowly broached the idea of a manuscript journal and sought his help in the procurement of paper and ink. Enthused by the idea, the official smuggled in regularly government stationery under cover of darkness after 9 p.m. Thus was born '*The Democrat*'.

The editorial staff comprising four political detenues Jaigopal Naidu, Dattatreya Awaradhi, S. Hanumantha Rao, and myself went into action one night when all were fast asleep. We wrote in long hand the first issue of 'The Democrat'. This took place every fortnight. By clapping of hands or beating of the *thali* some one would announce the reading session of the jail journal. They used to assemble in large numbers and listen in pin-drop silence. Those who could not follow English used to have the benefit of free translation in Hindi, Urdu, or Telugu, as the case may be. These early issues cannot be traced now. Most of them were destroyed in the course of investigations launched by the jail superintendent who could not stomach these developments under his very nose.

The wall journal *Bandal Gazette* and *The Democrat* brought about a sea-change in the attitude of the inmates in the European ward. While the Congress leaders were not able to find a meeting ground amongst themselves even in the jail, the Communist front-rankers were religiously conducting regular classes on Marxism. This attracted me towards, them, and, I joined their ranks. My joining the Communist-rank became an instant controversy. However, I continued to attend the classes organized by the Communist Party leaders and also tried to strengthen my personal relationship with all other irrespective of close affiliations in the jail. This enabled me to study closely and intimately the working of the mind of the leaders lodged in the European ward. This gave me a new sensation of understanding the political overtones in the respective parties' role in the freedom struggle vis-à-vis the future of the native states, especially the Nizam's Dominions of Hyderabad.

My liaison with the detenu-leaders more especially with Pandit Narendraji exercised a healthy impact on me and widened my political horizon. I became more mature. Along with my friends drawn from my generation felt—and they shared my thought currents—that there was an imperative need for discipline among the elder-detenus at least inside the prison walls, for the common good of all. This paved the way for the preparation of a draft constitution and declaration of the European ward as 'Bandinagar Republic'. Its first President was Amrut Reddy, while K.S. Vaidya was elected the Speaker. (K.S. Vaidya was the Speaker of the Hyderabad State Legislative Assembly for four years between 1952 and 1956, till the disintegration of Hyderabad State as on 1 November 1956.) Shri Birdhichand Choudhary became the Prime Minister of the Republic. So, with a constitution and a republic, the day-to-day life inside the jail became more orderly and the elder-detenus more disciplined. Armed with *The Democrat* we the youngsters were in a position to dictate our terms.

The jail superintendent eyed these none-too-encouraging developments with indignation and contempt. To restrain our activities he made the first move by shifting Swami Ramananda Tirtha from the Chanchalguda jail, to the Sangareddi jail. Then came my turn, before long, I was also shifted with eight others.

I had spent over six months in the Chanchalguda jail. On the eve of my transfer I left the copies of *The Democrat* with my friend Jaigopal Naidu. A few copies are intact now, the rest being lost or misplaced. These issues, now in my custody, speak volumes.

Here I may narrate briefly the story of my transfer to another central jail. We were put in a police van and driven to the Nampalli station to entrain the Bombay Express. Now our destination became clear. We were being shifted to the Gulbarga jail. The train reached Gulbarga around 2 a.m. Since there was no transport to take us straight to the jail, the police constables—more than a dozen—escorted us. They showed great respect and even talked politics. They understood us and did not, therefore, fear my escape bid. We proved we were all good Gandhian satyagrahis which was jocularly termed as 'Seetagrahi' in a corrupted form.

We reached the Gulbarga jail next morning. This was a big one. When I went in, I saw more than five hundred political detenus there. The first thought that struck me was: *The Democrat* has a bright future indeed, from the point of view of target audience. Here I came into close contact with that fiery revolutionary poet, Kaloji Narayana Rao and Babulal Verma of Kanpur. We made a splendid team on the intellectual plane. When I unfolded my plan to restart *The Democrat*, response was one of the universal acclaim. However, we could smuggle paper, ink and pen with great difficulty. Our main source of inspiration remained cigarettes and they were rationed.

In the new avenue, the first issue of *The Democrat* was ready, as a result of our usual nocturnal exercise. I requested Jagannath Rao Chandriki (who was with us for a few days before he was sentenced to 7 years' rigorous imprisonment) to release the issue. Though Chandriki felt rather reluctant to take the honour, I insisted that he should. He had all the potentialities of leadership ingrained in him for he was in the limelight after our Independence. B. Ashwath Rao presided. *The Democrat* was released in an open ground in the presence of about 500 political detenus.

It turned out to be a gala function that could even today be the envy of any organizer. In the new environs it became increasingly difficult to bring out the issues regularly, all because paper and ink could not be smuggled in easily. The police officials took serious view and concern; and consequently harsh treatment was meted out to the detenus. Still, *The Democrat* came out with gaps in between; but its editorial quality did not suffer, adopting the previous Constitution we declared the Gulbarga Central Jail as 'Bandinagar Republic II'.

Fortunately, during this period, Swami Ramananda Tirtha was shifted to the neighbouring ward of the Camp jail of Gulbarga Central Jail from the Sangareddy jail. Frequent messages used to be exchanged between myself and Swamiji, especially for use in *The Democrat*. It became the organ voice of one struggle. Our long ordeal was coming to an end. Four days after the historic 'Police Action' we were all released on 22 September 1948. The curtain fell on a most memorable phase of my life. The story of the 13 long months life of *The Democrat* will be incomplete, if I fail to record the names of all my colleagues whose names appeared in the columns in the *Jail Journal Calling* both from Hyderabad and Gulbarga Central Jails. The *Jail Journal Calling* has been published. Yet, this will not be the complete list of the detenus of the two Bandinagar Republics.

Land Distribution, Utilization and Peasant Movement in the Hyderabad State, 1724-1950

V. RAMAKRISHNA REDDY

Hyderabad, was one of the largest Princely States in India, with its own flag, currency and coins, postal system, railway, airline, and even its own radio. It remained a unique state in which the ruler received the allegiance of families holding estates, which in size, population, and richness, surpassed the territories of several other Indian states.[1] Just as in the country over 68 per cent of the total population, in the Hyderabad State was principally dependent on agricultural occupations for its livelihood.[2] In other words, out of 1,86,55,108, as many as 1,27,14,824 came under this category.[3] Further, just as in all feudal societies, ownership of land had become a symbol of social eminence. A man's importance in the society was measured, among other things, by the extent of land he happened to own.[4] Land revenue (in the year 1933-4) formed as much as 50.29 per cent of the total tax revenue in the state.[5] But, an intensive and critical examination and study of the agrarian conditions in the Hyderabad State during the Asaf Jahi reign (AD 1724-1948) would reveal that glaring inequalities, inconsistencies, and imbalances existed in the vital sectors of land distribution and utilization. This has been overwhelmingly responsible for the mass and violent peasant upsurge that manifested itself during 1946-51. The fact that the number of agriculturists having little or no land of their own worked out to nearly one-third of the number of pattadars,[6] and they being virtually held in feudal serfdom or bondage.[7] It did not augur well for the economy, and the conditions in miniature—the 'privileged' and the 'unprivileged'; the 'haves' and the 'have nots'—very much and strikingly reminded and resembled those of the Pre-revolutionary France of 1789.[8] The earlier writers on the subject,[9] in their overall depiction of the general economic or agrarian scenario, appear to have failed to give sufficient or due focus to these vital aspects. Hence, an attempt is made in this direction through this study.

SYSTEM OR PATTERN OF LAND DISTRIBUTION AND ITS IMPACT ON THE PEASANT MOVEMENT

An idea about the pattern of land distribution that obtained in the former Hyderabad State, could be had from Table 1.

From the table, some glaring and vital trends relating to land distribution that have an immediate and important bearing on the outbreak of the Peasants movement in Hyderabad State, are available. The most visible fact is that, small pattadars with meagre holdings of 5 acres and 5 to 10 acres, accounted for more than one-third of the total number of

TABLE 1: STATEMENT SHOWING THE NUMBER OF PATTADARS AND THE SIZE OF THEIR HOLDINGS IN 1354 F. (1945) IN HYDERABAD STATE

Sl. No.	Size of the holding (in acres)	Number of pattadars	Their percentage (%) out of the total no. of pattadars*	Extent of the acreage of land held (maximum size of the holding was taken for computation)*	Percentage (%) of the acreage of land held out of the total cultivated and uncultivated land of 1934-5, i.e. 3,89,35,251 acres*
1.	5	2,13,515	22.87	10,67,575	2.74
2.	5 to 10	1,24,481	13.33	12,44,810	3.19
3.	10 to 15	1,07,036	10.14	16,05,540	4.12
4.	15 to 20	96, 543	10.03	19,30,860	4,95
5.	20 to 25	84,101	9.00	21,02,525	5.40
6.	25 to 50	1,61,646	17.31	78,52,341 #	20.16
7.	50 to 100	89,029	9.05	89,02,900	22.86
8.	100 to 150	29,113	3.11	43,66,950	11.21
9.	150 to 200	13,100	1.40	26,20,000	6.72
10.	200 to 250	8,011	0.85	20,02,750	5.14
11.	250 to 500	4,974	0.53	24,87,000	6.38
12.	500 to 1000	1,509	0.16	15,09,000	3.87
13.	1000 to 2000	444	0.04	8,88,000	2.28
14.	2000 to 5000	49	0.005	2,45,000	0.62
15.	Above 5000**	11	0.001	1,10,000	0.28

NOTES: * own calculations.

** Maximum size of 10,000 acres is taken.

Out of the maximum computed figure of 2,29,959 acres have been deducted to bring the total acreage figure to the level of AD 1934-5.

SOURCE: Compiled from *HEH the Nizam's Govt: Agricultural Statistics (Quinquennial) from 1350 to 1354 Fasli (AD 1940-41 to AD 1944-45)*, 1949, p. 39.

pattadars in the state. But, it is of greater significance to note that, this huge number of Pattadars who solely depended on their own cultivation for their livelihood, could possess only less than 6 per cent of the total land that was available. This is the crux of the problem of masses being deprived of land. The slogan 'land to the tiller' and consequent land hunger of the landless that was widely prevalent during the pre-struggle days is thus noteworthy. Again, within the Hyderabad State, the number of these small holders was more than double in Warangal suba[10] than in Aurangabad suba,[11] and was more by 50 per cent in Warangal suba[12] than in the other subas of Gulbarga and Medak.[13] This shows that Telangana,[14] more than Marathwada,[15] was the land of small pattadars.[16] Again in Telangana, it was the Warangal suba that accounted for most of them. This development, consequentially, has direct relation to the fact that, peasants movement broke out in Telangana and was more widely and virulently prevalent in the Warangal suba than in the Medak suba, excepting of course, Nalgonda district of the latter.

Another striking phenomena that is visible from Table 1 in respect of land distribution in the state is that big pattadars who owned holdings of sizes of 25 to 50 acres, 50 to 100 acres and 100 to 150 acres, even though they accounted for less than 30 per cent of the total number of pattadars, they were in possession of more than 50 per cent of the total land that was available. It was a clear case of land monopolization and concentration, in contrast to the situation of utter scarcity and starvation that was present, as we have seen above, in the case of small pattadars. Again, regional and individual variations in this regard, within the state, would be, to note, still more striking, alarming, and appropriate. As a result of the Economic Survey that was carried out in 1929-30 in 12 villages of Warangal district, it came out that 1.7 per cent of the occupants held more than 3 per cent of the total dry land and 2.5 per cent of the occupants held more than 50 per cent of the total wet area.[17] To cite two individual cases of highest concentration of landed power in the diwani[18] areas of the state, Jannareddy Pratap Reddy owned 1,50,000 acres in Suryapet taluq of Nalgonda district[19] and the deshmukh[20] of Kallur in Madhira taluq of Warangal district owned 1,00,000 acres.[21]

It is significant to note that, land concentration and monopolization in an extreme degree was not confined to the diwani areas of the state. It was equally and ominously prevalent in non-diwani[22] or jagir[23] areas which accounted for 35.7 per cent of the total state area and 34 per cent of the total villages in the state.[24] Jagirdars, especially of the 'exempted type,[25] enjoyed vast landed, administrative, judicial, and police powers over several villages that were spread over several districts of the state. For an idea of the enormity of the situation, two striking instances could be noted. Raja Dharam Karan Bahadur had 186 jagir villages in different parts of the state, including 40 such villages in the Sultanabad taluq of Karimnagar district, with an annual income of Rs.13,51,333.[26] Raja Shivraj Dharmvanth Bahadur's jagir estate was spread over 12 districts of the state with a total number of 222 villages, and an annual income of Rs. 7,00,000.[27] As a further and dangerous consequence, the state or the government was so much drained and depleted of its tax revenues that merely nineteen jagirdars, netted more than Rs. 5,00,00,000 in taxes, when the entire land revenue of the state total up to not more than Rs. 8,00,00,000.[28]

It is again significant to note that the peasant movement raised its ugly head in those taluqs and districts of Telangana where there was heavy land concentration and monopolization. These could be identified as the taluqs of Khammam, Mahboobabad, Madhira, Palvancha, and Warangal in Warangal district; Mahadevpur, Jagtiyal, Huzurabad, and Sirsilla in Karimnagar district; Adilabad, Sirpur, Rajura, Chinnur, and Luxettipet in Adilabad district; and Suryapet, Huzurnagar, Miryalagudem, Nalgonda, Ramannapet, and Devarkonda in Nalgonda district. To be more specific and pointed in illustration, in Mahboobabad taluq where there was the highest degree of land monopolization among diwani as well as non-diwani feudal lords, 96 out of 147 landlord killings that occurred in Warangal district between the police action[29] and the middle of 1949 (roughly one year) had been reported from this taluq only, amounting to 65.3 per cent of the district total.[30]

LAND UTILIZATION PATTERN AND ITS INCIDENCE ON THE PEASANT MOVEMENT

Under normal conditions, the volume or quantum of agricultural production of a country or state to a large extent gets influenced or determined by the pattern of land utilization of that place. Hyderabad was no exception. Let us have a glance from the Table 2, about the way the available land has been put to use for agricultural production in this premier Princely State.

Though the data furnished in Table 2 is not adequate in all respects, the basic trend of the State in respect of land utilization could be noticed. First of all, the state being primarily agriculturally-based, it is significant to note that the percentages of cultivated area to total area, and in turn,

TABLE 2: PATTERN OF LAND UTILIZATION IN THE HYDERABAD STATE
1902-3 TO 1949-50

(Acres in lakhs)

S. No.	Particulars of the Item	YEARS OF INFORMATION								
		1902-3	1912-13	1920-1	1922-6	1927-31	1932-6	1937-41	1942-6	1947-51
1.	Total Area of the State	525.87	525.87	525.87	525.87	525.87	525.87	525.87	525.87	525.87
2.	Cultivated Area	176.8	205.16	213.68	256.96	277.31	291.41	272.96	264.91	237.49
3.	Percentage (%) of Cultivated Area to Total Area	33.52*	39.04*	40.57*	50.44	52.39	55.05	52.14	50.05	44.87
4.	Total Cultivable Area	204.07	227.95	239.55	...	...	...	...	...	...
5.	Percentage (%) of Cultivated Area to Cultivable Area	86	90	89	...	...	...	...	...	...
6.	Per Capita Cultivated Area	...	...	...	2.14	...	2.01	...	1.59	...
7.	Irrigated Area	10.43	12.39	12.87	10.48	10.85	12.65	10.80	13.48	14.05
8.	Percentage (%) of Irrigated Area to Area Cultivated	4.90*	6.0	6.0	3.92	3.91	4.34	3.91	5.08	5.91
9.	Per Capita Irrigated Area	...	...	...	0.08	...	0.08	...	0.08	...
10.	Government Area	258.44	285.42	297.02	299.22+	...	...	...	...	...
11.	Parampoke or Unassessed Waste	64.33	58.20	62.30	63.28+	39.75	49.02	72.60	99.35	85.72
12.	Percentage of Parampoke to Government Area	24.8*	20.4	21.0	21.15+	...	...	...	...	...

(contd.)

TABLE 2 (contd.)

S. No.	Particulars of the Item	YEARS OF INFORMATION								
		1902-3	1912-13	1920-1	1922-6	1927-31	1932-6	1937-41	1942-6	1947-51
13.	Current Fallows	...	...	...	...	20.25	34.22	35.40	61.25	65.92
14.	Forest Area	...	...	...	...	61.56	63.20	63.38	61.74	61.87
15.	Cultivable Waste other than Current Fallows	...	22.05	22.36	18.78+	13.05	16.84	22.2	35.75	9.85

NOTES: ... Details not available.

* Self-calculated.

\+ Refers to only the figure of 1926-7.

= Refers to only the figure of 1949-50.

SOURCES: Compiled from: Administrative Reports and Statistical Abstracts of Hyderabad Govt. As quoted in B.K. Narayana, *Agricultural Development*, pp. 27 & 32; File no.157 of 1903 of *HEH* the Nizam's Govt., Finance Dept; *Decennial Report 1912-1922 of HEH the Nizam's Govt.*, pp. 82-3 & 85; *HEH the Nizam's Govt. Agricultural Statistics, 1925-26 to 1934-5,* pp. 2-3; 1935-36 to 1939-40, pp. 8-9; 1940-41 to 1944-45, pp. 55 & 70; *HEH the Nizam's Govt. Industrial Statistics, 1935-45,* p. 567; *HEH the Nizam's Govt.*, Report on the Working of the Dept. under the Secretary & Director General of Revenue, 1926-7, pp. 7-8 & 11, and S. Kesava Iyengar, *Rural Economic Enquiries in the Hyderabad State, 1949-51*, Hyd.-Dn., 1951, pp. 24 & 107.

that of irrigated area to total area cultivated, throughout the present century, do not at all seem encouraging. The percentage of the former never rose above 56 per cent and that of the latter never came up above 6 per cent, whereas the figure for Part 'A' States in India stood three times higher at above 18 per cent.[31] More alarming is the fact that the cultivated area went on sliding down appreciably from 1937-41 to 1949-50. The situation was equally bad, even worse with regard to irrigated areas. It started falling down steeply right from 1922-6, and could never touch the 6 per cent mark throughout the rest of the period.

It is equally interesting to notice from Table 2 that, the per capita cultivated and irrigated area were abysmally poor, sliding, and stationary. The former, which stood at 2.14 acres during 1922-6, went on sliding to 2.01 during 1932-6 and to 1.59 during 1942-6. Per capita irrigated area, still more pitiably and contrastingly, stood stationary at 0.08 acre from 1922-6 to 1942-6, for which the figures are available. For a state whose forest area formed only 11.6 per cent of the total area as against 15.5 per cent for Part 'A' States of India,[32] and which was endowed with varied and rich soils in abundance, and ever-full irrigational projects such as Ramappa, Pakhal, Laknavaram, Ghanpur, Palair, Nizamsagar,[33] etc., these per capita poor and stunted figures are highly amazing and perplexing.

Causes for Meagre and Under-Utilization of Land

These are not far to seek. They could be analysed and briefly discussed under the following heads.

Cultivable Waste other than Current Fallows

From item no. 15 in Table 2, it is evident that huge acres of cultivable land had been left uncultivated. It ranged from 22.05 lakh acres in 1912-13 to 35.75 lakh acres during 1942-6. It is really a paradoxical and traumatic situation that, when 3,28,000 small pattadars with meagre holdings of 5 acres and 5 to 10 acres were craving and straining every nerve to enlarge their holdings and make them a bit viable and sustainable, lakhs of acres of cultivable land have been, due to the faulty and careless system of land allotment by the government to some vested agencies, and individuals, allowed to remain fallow. Some examples would make this point very clear.

The government under the colonization schemes,[34] in 1924 granted 1,31,000 acres to Sir Fazalbhoy, a Bombay capitalist entrepreneur, in the

Rajura and Sirpur taluqs of the Adilabad district, and 10,500 acres in 1925 to Sir Amin Jung, a high dignitary in the Sarf-i-Khas Department[35] in the Pakhal and Mahaboobabad taluqs of Warangal district.[36] These huge grants were made at the nominal payment of Rs. 4 per acre.[37] But, the most unfortunate thing that turned out to be was that the former turned over the lands back to government after only two years of actual possession, but with payment from the government three times of what he paid with practically nil development of the lands, and the latter after 15 years of possession, and consequently payment from the government amounting to seven times of what he paid, with of course, marginal development of one-third of the land received by him.[38] Sifatul-Islam[39] a Islamic organization that was started in 1933 with service motto, and banned by high government officials both in and out of service, was allowed by means of patta, huge land donations from War returned soldiers and others that amounted to 11,000 acres of lands, out of which, 3,000 acres were there in the Banki village of Sirpur taluq, and the rest of 8,000 acres in Pakhal taluq.[40] Apart from the fact agriculture suffers on account of large-scale absenteeism, this organization, in spite of announcing an ambitious programme of starting factories, providing electricity, railway, etc., did nothing in practice.[41] To add to these layers of governmental wasteful munificence, the government after the last Great War, made it a policy to allot cultivable lands, even sometimes at the risk of evicting the existing cultivators, to those soldiers who distinguished themselves in the War, at the rate of 60 acres each.[42] These soldiers, most of whom still continued in service and were consequently away from these lands that required development, never showed any interest towards this, and either allowed the lands to remain fallow, or as in most of the cases, sold them away for little price to the local landlords who took full advantage of the situation to further augment their land monopolization.[43] Restriction of the powers of the suba revenue officials in allotting *laoni*[44] lands,[45] and the lack of coordination between Forest and Settlement Departments in removing timber and carrying on *phodi*[46] of the lands allotted, further resulted in unwanted and undue delay in bringing fresh lands under cultivation.[47]

Parampoke or Unassessed Waste

This category of land, which also could not be brought under cultivation, appeared, as evident from Table 2, on the average, not less than one-fifth of the government or diwani area in the state. Further, since 1937-41 its increase in area was considerably high. It rose from 72.60 lakh acres in

1937-41 to 99.35 lakh acres during 1942-6. This development, in other words, is an indicator of the fact that the efforts that have been made, or the encouragement that has been given by the government for bringing fresh, virgin, or unexploited lands under the plough, have been dismal or discouraging. This, in turn, could be traced from the fact that the state government had, by failing to realize the importance of the Department of Agriculture, spent low and meagre amounts on it, which ranged from 5 lakhs in 1911-12 to 9.65 lakhs in 1943-4.[48] Throughout this long period of 33 years, the government spending on the Agriculture Department never touched the figure of 10 lakhs.[49]

Current Fallows: Incidence and Impact

Current fallows refers to the cultivable area that had been, due to one reason or the other, kept deliberately uncultivated. This might have been due to unwieldy size of the holdings, or unfavourable crop conditions or rainfall rigours of wet cultivation, etc. Its dimension, incidence, and impact, however, appeared to be very much serious and debilitating for agricultural development in the state as a whole, as well as in individual or particular districts. From the figures that are available for the quinquennial periods ranging from 1927-31 to 1947-51 in Table 2, it is startlingly clear that the current fallows were not only on the constant rise, but it got itself more than tripled during this quarter century.

If we examine the percentage of fallow land to occupied land, the situation was equally disturbing. Whereas it was 26.9 in the state,[50] it was as high as 55.2 in Nalgonda district[51] and 53.8 in Warangal district.[52] Strangely, these were the two districts in which there was fierce peasant outburst during 1946-51, as against a situation of lull and calm in the other districts of the state, excepting to a moderate extent in parts of Karimnagar and Adilabad districts. In other words, this prevalence of and abnormal growth in fallow lands appear to be more due to unprecedented extent of absentee landlordism that was in vogue in these four Telangana districts, rather than other factors like leaving huge grazing lands, unfavourable crop conditions, lack of financial strength for agricultural investment, agricultural costs over running agricultural prices, etc. The contrasting situation and equation that loomed large was that, whereas a poor and small peasant, with his meagre and uneconomical holding of 5-10 acres, found it extremely difficult to make both ends meet and craved for a few more acres of land, the rich and absentee landlords, on the other hand, whose holdings ranged from 1,000 acres to 1,00,000 acres, did not mind at all to leave hundreds of acres of land for their cattle grazing, or for the grass to grow.

LAND DISTRIBUTION AND UTILIZATION: RELEVANCE TO PEASANT MOVEMENT

The Telangana peasant movement, thus appears to be strongly connected with the pattern of land distribution and utilization, and more so, the ills that arose out of this in the state. Warangal and Nalgonda districts, which became notorious or pronounced for the vile of greater land monopolization, excessive absentee landlordism, increasing landlessness among the tenancy, rack-renting, huge fallow lands, severe landlord oppression, etc., naturally became the key areas of the movement. The intensity of the struggle was witnessed in areas where these features or factors had been strong and pronounced. In a small measure, the seizure of lands from deshmukhs and their redistribution among the smaller and poor peasants, had also been resorted to, in consequence. In Madhira taluq of Warangal district, 20,500 acres have been seized, out of which, 20,000 acres were stated to have been permanently seized from the deshmukh of Kallur alone.[53] This programme, of course, has been spearheaded by the Left-wing Communist leaders, whose influence had got spread or confined to Nalgonda district, and a few adjacent taluqs of Warangal district, such as Madhira.

Further, in the same sequence, it could also be seen that landlords, deshmukhs, and jagirdars who had subjected the agricultural and general population of their villages to severe injustices and atrocities, had in turn, and proportionately, got subjected, during the struggle, to severe reprisals. These were witnessed in Mahaboobabad and Warangal taluqs of Warangal district, where landlord oppression was pronounced. Some such landlords, instead of falling into the hands of insurgents, took their lives themselves.[54]

CONCLUSION

It thus becomes clear that though other factors like the ills of procurement and levy, collection of feudal levies, practicing of the hated *vetti*[55] or *begari*[56] frequent evictions of the tenants, rack-renting, etc., had also aided in the outbreak of the Telangana peasant movement in 1946; it could not have taken shape or effect, but for the serious deficiencies and shortcoming that had crept into the system or pattern of land distribution and utilization that was there in vogue in the former Hyderabad State under the Asaf

Jahis. There was serious hunger for land among the tenants, small and middle peasants. In a state where more than 68 per cent of the total population depended for their livelihood on agricultural occupations and whose local industries got stunted due to stoppage from British imports, such a situation appears quite natural and inevitable. The tenant or the peasant, whether under a deshmukh or a jagirdar, had fallen prey to unrelenting and unending exploitation. When the cup was full to the brim, the volcano was ignited by the Communists. Masters and lords fell and their fort-like mansions were razed to the ground.[57] Jagirdari abolition, Tenancy and Agricultural Lands Act, followed in suit.

NOTES

1. Raza Ali Khan, *Hyderabad: 400 Years (1591-1991)*, Secunderabad, 1990, p. 8.
2. *Census of India, 1951*, vol. IX, *Hyderabad Part-I-A*, Report, Hyderabad-Dn, p. 120.
3. Ibid.
4. H. Rajendra Prasad, *Asif Jahs of Hyderabad: Their Rise and Decline*, New Delhi, 1984, p. 16.
5. Govt. of Hyderabad, *Memoranda Submitted to the Taxation Enquiry Committee*, 1953, p. 56.
6. S.M. Bharucha, *Agricultural Indebtedness in HEH the Nizam's Dominions*, 1937, p. 5.
7. Swami Ramananda Tirtha, *Memoirs of Hyderabad Freedom Struggle*, Bombay, 1967, p. 208.
8. V. Ramakrishna Reddy, *Economic History of Hyderabad State (Warangal Suba), 1911-1950*, New Delhi, 1987, p. 129.
9. A.I. Qureshi, *The Economic Development of Hyderabad*, vol. I, Madras, 1941; B.K. Narayan, *Agricultural Development in Hyderabad State, 1900-1956*, Secunderabad, 1960; Ian Bedford; 'Telangana Insurrection: A Study in the Cause and Development of Communist Insurrection in Rural India'; Barry Pavier, *Telangana Movement, 1944-51*, etc.
10. It consisted of the three eastern districts of Warangal, Karimnagar, and Adilabad, with suba headquarters at Warangal. These were Telugu-speaking districts.
11. It consisted of the Marathi-speaking districts of Aurangabad, Parbhani, Nander, and Bir, with suba headquarters at Aurangabad.
12. It comprised the four districts, of them three Kannada-speaking districts of Gulbarga, Raichur (Osmanabad was Marathi-speaking district), Bidar, and with suba headquarters at Gulbarga.
13. It consisted of the Telugu-speaking districts of Atraf-i-Balda, Nizamabad, Medak, Baghat, Mahboobnagar, and Nalgonda, with Medak as suba headquarters.

14. It was a division or region, consisting of the eight Telugu-speaking districts of Warangal and Medak subas.
15. It was another or second division or region in the state, comprising the Marathi and Kannada-speaking districts of Aurangabad and Gulbarga subas respectively.
16. Bharucha, *Agricultural Indebtedness*, p.12.
17. S. Kesava Iyengar, *Economic Investigations in the Hyderabad State, 1929-30*, vol. III, Warangal district, p. 4.
18. Areas directly administered by the state or the government.
19. P. Sundarayya, *Veera Telangana Viplava Poratam-Gunapatalu*, Vijayawada, 1973, p.19.
20. Village headman who enjoyed and exercised feudal status and power.
21. P. Sundarayya, *Veera Telangana Viplava Poratam*, p. 19.
22. Non-diwani lands included paigah or estates given to court and military nobles; sarf-i-khas or crown lands; jagirs or estates given for a specific purpose, service, or recognition, or none; and inams or lands, mainly allotted for religious service, or for the village watchman, waterman, and artisans, besides others who gained state favour.
23. Refers to those assigned villages or tracts over which the powers of revenue collection and administration have been granted to a person by the state, either for a conditional service or none at all.
24. A.M. Khusro, *Economic and Social Effects of Jagirdari Abolition and Land Reforms in Hyderabad*, Hyderabad, 1958, p. 2.
25. In this type, the jagirdars practically functioned as independent princes with little state control over them.
26. Khusro, *Economic and Social Effects of Jagirdari Abolition*, p. 7.
27. *Golkonda Patrika* (bi-weekly), 13 August 1936.
28. Rajendra Prasad, *Asif Jahs of Hyderabad*, p. 295.
29. Culminated on 18 September 1948, in the state acceding to the Indian Union.
30. *The Deccan Chronicle*, 8 July 1949; *The Golkonda Patrika*, 9 July 1949; Reddy, *Economic History of Hyderabad State*, Table IX in Chapter IV (percentage is calculated).
31. *Rural Economic Enquiries in Hyderabad State*, 1949-51, p. 23.
32. Ibid.
33. Ramappa, Pakhal, Laknavaram, and Ghanpur had been projects constructed over tanks that have been originally dug under the Kakatiyas, whereas Palair and Nizamsagar had been projects constructed during a later time over the rivers Palair and Manjera. All these projects, excepting Nizamsagar, had been located in the Warangal district, as against the later being located in Nizamabad district.
34. Scheme that was aimed at populating the villages and getting the lands cultivated.

35. Refer to note 23 of this paper.
36. Warangal Subedari (hereinafter referred to as W.S.), File no. 48 of 1351 Fasli (1942) and Record no. (hereinafter referred as R. no.) 1827 of 1354 Fasli (1945).
37. Ibid.
38. Ibid.
39. Means 'Grace of Islam' in Urdu.
40. W.S. File no. 4 of 1353 Fasli (1944) & R. no. 1946 of 1355 Fasli (1946).
41. Ibid.
42. W.S. File no. 3 of 1350 Fasli (1941) and R. no. 1365 of 1351 Fasli (1942).
43. There had been a good number of such sales. They averaged roughly 1/3 of the total number of land sale transactions effected in an year in the later forties, and the price for 60 acres ranged from Rs.1,000 to 2,000 only—W.S. File nos. 87 of 1353 Fasli (1944) and R. no. 1441 of 1353 Fasli (1944); no. 123 of 1354 Fasli (1945) and R. no. 619 of 1355 Fasli (1946), and no. 49 of 1355 Fasli (1946) and R. no. 654 of 1355 Fasli.
44. Allotment of land to needy and people of weaker sections and thereby get them developed.
45. Officials even up to the rank of subedar did not enjoy the power of allotting lands that remained uncultivated for less than 10 years — W.S. File no. 103 of 1338 Fasli (1929) and R. no. 3100 of 1329 Fasli (1930).
46. Demarcation of lands.
47. W.S. File no. 15 of 1356 Fasli (1947) and R. no. 14 of 1356 Fasli.
48. *A Review of Hyderabad Finance*, 1951, pp. 249-51.
49. Ibid.
50. *Rural Economy Enquiries*, p. 106.
51. Ibid., p. 107.
52. Ibid.
53. Sundarayya, *Veera Telangana Viplava Poratam*, pp. 91-2.
54. Edumanddula Sesha Reddy, '*Deshmukh* of Tatikonda in Warangal Taluq, was stated to have commited suicide—Sundarayya', *Veera Telangana*, p. 187.
55. Forced and unpaid labour or service that was extracted by the feudal lords from the agricultural as well as general population.
56. Forced and free labour that was extracted by officials and *watandars* from the village craftsmen or servants.
57. They got characteristically called as 'Gadis' and looked as impregnable and majestic as the Nizam's palaces in miniature.

Historical Background of Peasant Movement in Telangana

S. BHANUMATHI RANGA RAO

India with its agro-based economy is often described as a country of villages, more so during pre-Independent times. Even today, more than 70 per cent of the country's population lives on agriculture and allied sectors. No wonder land holds the key to the socio-politico-economic life of India. Even after 50 years of freedom and continued attempts at industrialization and socio-economic development, the situation has not substantially improved. It is precisely on account of this political and socio-economic background that several areas in the rural Telangana are currently witnessing acute unrest where a number of peasant movements were witnessed since the last quarter of the nineteenth century. They basically involved landownership and the relief measures, if any, not reaching the ryots who actually tilled the land.

An attempt is made in this paper to highlight the various problems of the peasants of the erstwhile Hyderabad State by tracing a brief historical evolution of the landownership and concentration of land in the hands of few which finally culminated in the peasant movements and consequent unrest that survive even today. In spite of the efforts of the government to ease the situation, the unrest had manifested itself in one way or the other. The problem defied a solution and the deplorable state of affairs continued until the merger of the territories with the Indian Union in 1948.

I

There is an interesting historical background to this state of affairs in the Princely State of Hyderabad, known as the Nizam's Dominions. Paradoxically enough the Nizam was supposed to be one of the richest persons in the world at one time while his subjects were the poorest. The government of the Nizam totally neglected the development of the rural areas with its peasant population which remained backward, while in the city of Hyderabad, the capital of the Dominions, attempts were made to industrialize, modernize and develop it as one of the finest cities of India. But in reality development could be witnessed only in the city and its surrounding called Atraf-i-Balda.

The independent state of the Nizam was established in 1724. That was the period of transition from medieval to modern times. There was political instability in the region until the beginning of the nineteenth century. The state was caught in wars with the Marathas as well as in the midst of the political struggle between the French and the English. This was followed by treaties and alliances signed by the Nizam and the British as a result of which he not only lost vast territories in the form of Northern Circars and Ceded Districts, but also had to maintain a heavy strain on his exchequer.[1] Thus on account of his involvement in wars, the Nizam's government was interested only in the collection of land revenue as it was the main source of income and he did not pay any attention to the problems of land management.

In the Princely State of Hyderabad, theoretically the state was the owner of the entire land in the state. It collected a share in the produce as revenue from the ryot. The peasant was allowed to till the land as long as he paid the revenue regularly. But in the Nizam's Dominions the land was in the hands of both the peasants and non-peasants.

The Diwani land came under the first category of ownership and the jagir, paigah, inam, ijara, etc., lands came under the second category. The diwani lands or crown lands or khalsa lands were directly managed by the state through a department where a crude form of ryotwari system existed. As mentioned earlier adequate attention was not paid to this category of land tenure until the advent of Sir Salar Jung-I in 1853. Very primitive methods of revenue collection were in vogue and there was neither survey of land nor any record of rights. Revenue collection in the diwani lands was entrusted to either revenue contractors known as big farmers or to the taluqdars, appointed by the state on commission basis. Such taluqdars or contractors were invariably either members of noble families or influential urban rich, who stayed in the capital and enjoyed the fruits of the revenue collected through naibs or deputies appointed by them. None of them were sure about their tenure and hence they collected as much money as possible in the shortest possible time. Consequently the peasants were exploited as the revenue to be collected from the individual ryot was not stipulated by the state. In the absence of survey and records indicating individual ownership precisely several of the ryots were also deceiving the state by cultivating a larger area than the one for which he paid land revenue.[2] The diwani land thus managed were of the order of 20 million acres constituting a little over 56 per cent of the total area of the Dominions.[3]

The other category of land tenure was in the possession of the jagirdars (inclusive of paigah, inam, and ijara lands). They were granted these lands in lieu of their services to the state and they were supposed to pay quit rent to the state, besides maintaining the stipulated number of soldiers. One interesting feature of this category was that the jagirs and inams, etc., were given lands indiscriminately not only by the rulers but even by the ministers and revenue officials in the nineteenth century.[4] The Nizam practically had neither control over them nor any independent machinery to regulate their internal affairs. Hence, the Nizam could not derive any benefit out of these lands which formed around 30 per cent of the area of the state.[5] Finally, the sarf-i-khas lands were held by the Nizam himself, the revenue of which went to the Nizam's personal account.

As mentioned earlier, due to political disturbances and preoccupation with wars for a long time, until the beginning of the nineteenth century the State could not bring forth any reforms nor it felt the need for them. Its main concern was only to obtain as much of revenue as possible. However the feudal nature of the state could never initiate reforms in revenue collection till the middle of the nineteenth century.

Thus, as far as the exploitation of the peasants cultivating the diwani and jagir areas was concerned, the difference was one of the degree rather than of kind, those living in the latter category of jurisdiction suffering the most. While there was no attempt to impose and collect land revenue on a rational basis, indiscriminate methods were adopted in collecting as much revenue as possible particularly from the poor peasants.

1. Even after the payment of the stipulated revenue by the ryots, collecting illegal exaction's continued throughout the year in one form or the other. On occasions of celebrations of various kinds in the houses of not only the nobles but even petty revenue persons, the peasants were made to contribute.
2. Even the slightest sign of prosperity like the possession of a couple of silver ornaments attracted the attention of the revenue people who forcibly collected revenue.[6]
3. On several occasions poor peasants were subjected to forced labour or *vetti* and there was no escaping from such free forced labour.
4. Where the peasants were unable to meet the ever increasing demands of revenue collected by the adoption of severe coercive measures by village officials, peasants abandoned their lands and ran away.

In most of the cases they were traced and forced to come back to cultivate the lands. Unfortunately the money collected by such dubious methods was misappropriated by middlemen and never reached the government's treasury. Consequently while the peasants suffered contributing even beyond their capacity, the government could not really benefit as the middlemen, jagirdars, contractors pocketed most of it, therefore the government was fast becoming bankrupt by the middle of the nineteenth century.

II

It was under such circumstances that Salar Jung appeared on the scene to save the government from total bankruptcy. His reform measures were primarily directed to reorganize the revenue set-up, while incidentally providing relief to the poor peasants to a limited extent. Salar Jung realized that in the absence of a survey of land on a scientific basis, it was not possible to know how much of land was possessed by each peasant or landowner so as to make it possible to impose and collect revenue.[7]

He initiated measures to eliminate nominated middlemen like contractors and taluqdars and provided for direct contact between the government and the peasants through the appointment of permanent officials.[8] However, these reforms mainly involved the diwani lands which constituted about 60 per cent of the Nizams territories while the peasants continued to suffer under the old system of assessment elsewhere in the dominions.

The survey revealed for the first time that large tracts of land were illegally held by many inams or jagirs, through forged documents. In fact it was noticed that such illegal lands were held for generations. Hence the reforms involved the creation of the Department of Atiyat or the Inam Commission,[9] which went into such illegal possessions. In practice the government of the Nizam allowed the jagirs or inams held through illegal means for generations to be regularized while others were resumed. The process, however, involved considerable litigation which continued right up to the time of the merger of the territories to the Indian Union.

Another distinguishing feature relating to the ownership of land involved the simultaneous claims of several inamdars and jagirdars over the same area. The Atiyat Department had to undertake an exhaustive examination of the issue of boundaries between the diwani lands on the one hand and jagirs and inams on the other also assumed special significance. It was partly due to the fact that survey of diwani lands alone was undertaken and not a comprehensive survey of the entire territory. The survey operations were incomplete till 1948. However, revision work could not be undertaken immediately due to administrative lapses and lack of awareness on the part of the peasants. It was revealed during the process of land survey and settlement that most of the lands of the villages were shown against the names of the villages officers or deshmukhs or deshpandyas which originally were tilled by the peasants.[10] Due to their ignorance the peasants were not aware of this sort of transfer. Consequent to the conduct of survey there was also an increase in the value of land and the peasants were tempted to mortgage their land and borrow money.[11] There were also several incidences where the deshmukhs and deshpandyas as well as the moneylenders advanced loans to the peasants, during times of calamity or even social occasions like marriages, etc., at high rates of interest besides mortgages of lands. In almost all such instances since the peasants could not repay the debts the moneylenders got the land transferred to them.[12]

Unfortunately, the survey operations were not immediately followed by the preparation of Record of Rights. Thus ownerships, if any, established during survey was not properly recorded. Consequently there were many difficulties involved in the assessment and collection of land revenue from the owners and tillers of the land, besides the innumerable sufferings involving the peasants.

It was only in the year 1937 when the Department of Record of Rights was established that the situation improved and the peasants came to know for the first time whether the land they tilled were legally against their names or not.[13]

The peasants of the Nizam's dominions were actually faced with a fresh problem as a result of Salar Jung's reforms. Earlier, under the *battai* system the peasants were parting with a portion of their produce towards the payment of revenue to the state. But after the reforms they were required to pay land revenue in cash. Consequently, they were required to sell the produce sometimes at a cheaper rate after the harvest to pay their taxes. This situation assumed a dangerous dimension during and after the depression period of 1929-30. The ryots faced terrible hardships as they had to sell a large portion of their crops in order to pay the land revenue. Even commercialization of agriculture could help only a few during this period.

The acute social and economic backwardness of the peasants in the Telangana areas was largely responsible for their suffering in silence without protest. Moreover, such coercive and cruel methods were used by the government and revenue officials that the poor peasants did not dare to raise their voice against the government. It was only after the Left ideologists and Andhra Mahasabha took up the cause of the peasants and protested against their inhuman exploitation that there was some awakening among the rural population. It was the Communist Party which organized the peasants during the 1940s which took up arms against the government and thereafter leading to greater awakening among the peasants of Telangana. By that time there were swift political developments in the state such as the armed struggle and the Razakar movement and hence the government could not pay sufficient attention to the redressal of the grievances of the peasants. The methods of suppression resorted to by the government further aggravated the situation resulting in untold sufferings of the peasants.

III

Under the feudal set-up in the Nizam's Dominions the peasants suffered from both exploitation and suppression. Moreover, favours were liberally bestowed by the Nizam on those who helped him in wars, by granting them large tracts of land as jagirs. Not only the Nizam but his ministers and even revenue officials were granted jagirs, inams, etc., as favours.[14] The jagirdars who maintained the soldiers did not bother to pay quit rent regularly as stipulated. Taking advantage of the confusion several unscrupulous people managed to forge documents to obtain grant of land. The deplorable state of affairs could be understood by the fact that such illegal possessions could not be detected for generations. Even after investigation through the Atiyat department, what all they could do was to regularize such illegal possessions in many cases while the lands resumed were too few.

Leaving aside jagirs, inams, and sarf-i-khas the personal lands of the Nizams, etc., the entire income of the government was derived from the diwani land which accounted for roughtly 60 per cent of the Nizam's territories. Until the middle of the nineteenth century when the coffers of the Nizam's government almost became empty, they never bothered about the assessment and collection of land revenue by the taluqdars and revenue contractors, most of whom were either nobles or rich and influential citizens who never cared to move out of the capital. Instead they appointed naibs and others to collect revenue on their behalf. There were also the deshmukhs and deshpandyas and patwaris who hereditarily were bestowed with the rights to collect revenue. The government had neither the means nor the will to know how much of money was collected by the middlemen and how much of it actually was remitted to the treasury.

Assessment of revenue was arbitrary and its collection was outrageous for a long time. The village officers or their counterparts visited the field and estimated the crops as 8 *annas* or 10 *annas* in a rupee, etc., and imposed the land revenue. Those who paid bribes were spared and the deficit was collected from other peasants. Such proposals were automatically confirmed by the naibs and revenue was collected accordingly. In addition to the regular land revenue, the peasants were made to contribute towards the expenditure on festivities and marriages in the families of the nobles and the revenue officials.

While all this was happening to the poor peasants, the Nizam preferred to look the other way. It is difficult to say at this point of time, whether such attitude on the part of the Nizam was due to his weakness for the nobles who exploited the rural poor and enjoyed life in the capital or his lack of sufficient love for his subjects. But ample evidence is available concerning the utter disregard for the people and callous indifference on the part of the government when the subjects who supported the government were subjected to untold misery. It was only when the treasury was empty that they started paying attention to land management.

In pursuit of his reforms Salar Jung had to face the wrath of the vested interests which even threatened his life. To begin with a survey of diwani lands was undertaken as it was found to be essential for the management of the ryotwari system. In the absence of such a survey several people possessed more lands than the ones for which they paid revenue. The boundaries between different kinds of lands were vague. Jagirdars and inamdars encroached on diwani lands. This litigation involving boundaries went on until the abolition of jagirs in 1949.

The survey of lands was not immediately followed by Record of Rights. Hence the peasants continued to be unaware of their ownership rights. For instance it was noticed that lands which actually belonged to the tiller were shown in the name of village officers or deshpandyas or deshmukhs. The fact was that peasants were not aware of the records, if any, and were manipulated without their knowledge. There is no doubt that remissions of various kinds were given to the peasants even before the advent of Salar Jung. But often bribes had to be paid to obtain such remissions.[15] In fact the assistance provided by the government by way of remissions was negative in nature. In the absence of financial assistance and interest free or low interest loans from the government the peasants had to maintain themselves until the next season when resources were required for raising fresh crops. Consequently with every bad season there was an increase in rural indebtedness. Moneylenders and the local rich advanced money at exorbitant rates of interest by mortgaging their lands. In most of the cases, unable to repay the debts, the peasants had to transfer their lands to the moneylenders or jagirdars or local officials. Unfortunately these happenings were particularly noticed after the survey when there was an increase in the value of lands. The suffering of the peasants reached the climax during the depression of 1929-31 when they were made to pay the land revenue in cash in spite of the sale of their huge produce at very low rate.

The reform, no doubt provided for the appointment of permanent officers in place of the nominated ones. But even under the new set-up it was only the urban rich and the influential families from which the officials were drawn. Further, there was widespread corruption and hence the peasants could not derive the benefits of the reforms.

Thus to conclude, the ignorant, illiterate peasants of Telangana could not even protest against blatant exploitation. Any sign of revolt was severely dealt with by the government through brute force. There was no attempt to organize them until the Communist Party and the Leftist elements of the Andhra Mahasabha entered the scene. The innocent peasants suffered too much for too long and hence the response to the call of the Communists was total, resulting in an armed revolt against the feudal system and the Nizams' government. Attempts at suppressing the revolts were unsuccessful, as it became virtually a people's movement. The half-hearted measures to appease the peasants taken up by the government came too late and were too insignificant to thwart the movement.

NOTES

1. Sarojini Regani, *Nizam-British Relations, 1724-1857*, Concept Pub., New Delhi, 1963, p. 219.
2. *Report on the Administration of Revenue and Allied Departments during 1324 F (1914-15 A.D.)*, p. 48.
3. Moulavi Chirag Ali, *Hyderabad under Sir Salar Jung*, vol. I, Bombay, 1885, p.14.
4. Ibid., p. 253.
5. Ibid., also see *Report on the Administration of Revenue and Allied Departments*, p. 65.
6. *Walker's Report 1848*, quoted in *Administrative Report, HEH the Nizam's Dominions for 1294 Fasli*, p. 257.
7. *Report on the Administration of Revenue and Allied Departments*, p. 48.

8. *Zarida*, dated 10th Rabi-ul-Aval, 1299 H.
9. For details see Bhanumathi Ranga Rao, *Land Revenue Administration in the Nizam's Dominions, 1853-1948*, Hyderabad, 1992, pp. 119-20.
10. P. Sundarayya, *Telangana People's Struggle and its Lessons*, National Book Centre, Calcutta, 1972, p. 11.
11. S.M. Barucha, *Agricultural Indebtedness in HEH, the Nizam's Dominions*, Hyderabad Deccan, Government Central Press, 1937, p. 15.
12. Ibid., p. 5.
13. It was originally established in the year 1935 under the Additional Revenue Secretary.
14. *Englishman*, 6 January 1865, *Hyderabad Affairs*, vol. 5, p. 251.
15. *Report on the Administration of HEH* the *Nizam's Dominions for four years, 1308-1312 Fasli*, para 48.

Consciousness and Participation of Telangana Women in the People's Movement in Hyderabad State, 1901-1951

E. SUDHA RANI

INTRODUCTION

The revival of the women's movement from the late seventies brought new dimensions and directions to women's studies. They have been used to raise women's consciousness. The courses of study are assessed not on the grounds of how efficiently they gather information but on how they can be located in building a feminist consciousness and playing a role in liberation. The structural integration of this movement into the nationalist revolutionary movement whereby feminism became linked to a socio-political alternative, marked the turning point in the history of women's movement.

The women's movement in India was at a slow pace being largely an appendage to other political movements. The status of women in India had varied in different historical periods, and in different regions of the country. There were also numerous variations depending on class, caste, religion, and ethnicity.

The women's movement in India can be divided into three phases. The first phase is the Reformist stage which began in mid-nineteenth century, initiated largely by male reformers such as Raja Rammohun Roy, Jotiba Phule, Ishwarachandra Vidyasagar, Keshav Chandra Sen, Kandukuri Veerasalingam, etc. They voiced opinions against various social evils such as *sati*, widowhood, child marriage, and polygamy. To bring about awareness among women they incessantly worked for widow remarriage, women's education, etc. The early women's organizations established their own associations and journals, making demands for changes in their position within the family and society.

The second phase of the women's movement can be seen in the participation in the national movement. During the colonial period it was linked with liberal and conservative currents of opinion and expressed in the challenge and resistance to imperialism.[1] It was in the political struggle against imperialism that Indian women began actively participating in life outside the home, and in this they had support of several leaders.[2]

The third phase of women's movement was parallel to the national movement and the people's struggle carried out by peasant and tribal women in different regions of India. Towards the end of the nineteenth century and the beginning of the twentieth century, women began to play an active role in Indian politics by taking part in various peasant, tribal, and labour movements. Struggles such as the Telangana people's armed struggle, the Tehbhaga movement in Bengal, the Worli tribal struggle in Maharashtra and the Punnapra Vayalar struggle in the Travancore State of Kerala are important landmarks. These struggles in the different regions of the country were waged on local and particular issues but they succeeded in raising the social consciousness of the people and also their responsiveness to the countrywide political struggle.

Women's movement cannot be judged by contemporary, universally validated feminist standards, but has to be examined in the context of women's status, political power, and ability to take independent decisions. Though in the beginning their struggle was slow it gradually gained momentum and resulted in the emergence of a mass movement. Along with the conscious, enlightened, educated, and advanced sections of women, vast masses of women played an active part in the people's struggle.

This study shall concern itself with the significance of women's participation in the people's struggle in the Hyderabad State. The main focus is on the period 1900-51. The perspective adopted in the study is to focus primarily on the repertoire of women's activities, their consciousness, perception, and experiences and on aspects of women's emancipation struggles.

STATUS OF WOMEN IN THE SOCIO-ECONOMIC AND POLITICAL CONTEXT

Any attempt to understand the nature of women's participation in the people's struggle of the Hyderabad State is to be necessarily preceded by an analysis of the status of women in the social, economic, and political context of the state. The basic feature that dominated the socio-economic life of the people of Hyderabad, especially Telangana, was the unbridled feudal exploitation that persisted well into the beginning of the Telangana armed peasants struggle.[3]

ECONOMIC CONTEXT

The main source of income for the state was land revenue. The territory of the state was divided into khalsa or diwani lands, sarf-i-khas, paigah, jagirs, and samsthans. Conditions in jagir areas were far more oppressive than in the sarf-i-khas lands. The imposition of a variety of illegal taxes reduced the peasants to penury.

The *bhagela* system was prevalent in Warangal and Nalgonda districts. The Bhagela was typically a landless member of one of the lower castes or from an aboriginal tribe. She would be obliged to offer her/his labour as a collateral for debts incurred, and work for the creditor as a domestic or menial labourer until the latter were repaid. This continued for generations together. When a man married, incurring expenses by taking a loan he would become a Bhagela and his wife would become a labourer in the house of the creditor.

The *vetti* system was a forced labour system that prevailed all over Hyderabad State. In Telangana the *vetti* system was an all pervasive social phenomenon affecting all classes of people in varying degrees, but affecting Harijans and Backward Castes the most.[4] There was no security for a farmer's crops. Harsh punishments were meted out by the landlords in order to exercise full control over the villagers. If the call came from the landlord or his wife they had to simply run and obey the commands even if they had just started to have food. Women could not breast-feed their babies while working in the fields of the landlords. The landlord not only had full rights over the land, but also exercised authority over every man and woman who were dependent on these lands for their livelihood. The *doras* considered them as part of their properties. Women suffered a great deal more than men in this dispensation. If the *dora* took fancy to any woman, she had to immediately surrender to him. If a woman got married she had to spend her first night with the landlord. The cruelty and notoriety of landlords, their methods of exploitation and the sad plight of bonded labour were graphically depicted in the Telugu novels on Telangana such as Vattikota Alwar Swamy's *Prajala Manishi* and *Gangu*, Dasarathi Rangacharaya's *Chillara Devullu*, Bollimuntha Sivarama Krishna's *Mrityuvu Needallo*, etc.

According to the 1901 census, 46 per cent of the people in the state were dependent on agriculture for their livelihood.[5] The oppressive land systems that prevailed in the state caused misery for agricultural labourers, both men and women. Women were employed in larger numbers as agricultural labourers. According to the 1931 census, in cultivation, there were 68 women for every hundred men, but as agricultural labourers they outnumbered men, being seven for every six males. Females also took large share in the market—gardening and growing flower and fruit.[6] Given the considerations of high social and ritual status, purity and pollution, the female labour recruited from the Dwija castes was negligible. The women among the upper castes, Reddys (Moṭati, Pakanati, etc.) and Racha Velamas observed *gosha* (purdah) and did not participate in manual work. But on the other hand, Kapu/Telaga women were actively engaged in field labour and other related activities.[7]

Social Context

Under the Nizam's rule the social conditions of the women and the common people were extremely painful. Linguistic or cultural rights were non-existent. There was little scope for education, as the medium of instruction was Urdu in middle and high schools. People who did not possess any knowledge of Urdu were barred from entering them. When education as a whole was in such a condition, women's education was obviously very backward. There were three major obstacles in the way of the progress of women's education. The first was the reluctance of the Muslims to teach their daughters anything beyond their scriptures. The other was early marriages among the Hindus. The greatest difficulty, however, was the absence of trained school mistresses.

The study of the social conditions in the Hyderabad State shows that there was a universal prevalènce of child marriage. Polygamy did not exist. A large number of widows seem to live there, which indicates the strong prejudice against widow remarriages. In Hyderabad city alone, the number of unmarried males was 45 and females 30; married males 52 and females 53, and widowers 4 and widows 18, respectively, of various ages per thousand in the year 1911.[8]

During the decade 1901-11, the number of widows under the age of 10 was 6,792 and the age of 15, 17,979.[9] The practice of child marriage, which was a social evil was prevalent all over Telangana in the twentieth century. In most cases the age of the bridegroom was around 10 and that of the bride ranged from 6-7 years. In one marriage the bridegroom was 8 years old and the bride was in the lap of the mother and the wedding was performed like a child's play, and was attended by great scholars and advocates.[10]

Another social evil was purdah; an age old custom prevalent in Hindu and Muslim societies. Deshmukhs and Deshpandes, Reddys and Velamas followed purdah in their households. Gradually, it entered into the middle class homes as well. Purdah hampered the free movement of women and consequently, their participation in various socio-political activities. Other social evils that led to the low status of women in India (and Telangana, in particular) were the bride-price and dowry systems. These are the two major modes of transfer of wealth accompanying a marriage. In both the customs, the consent of the girls was never a criteria. Rather, it was largely a market transaction. The dowry system was more prevalent among the Reddy and Velama castes, as compared to others.

The worst feudal exaction was the keeping of girls who were called *adapapas*, as slaves in the landlord's houses. The *adapapas* are mostly from the lower castes. The *adapapa* system was the evil attendant of the *vetti* system, the women from lower castes such as Kapu, Telaga, and Chakali, mostly from bonded labour families, were drawn into it. The Reddy, Velama, Deshmukh, and Deshpande families used to keep *adapapas* as slaves in their households before they attained puberty When the landlords gave their daughters in marriage, they presented these slave girls and sent them along with their married daughters to serve the latter in their new homes. These slave girls were used by landlords as concubines.[11] The *adapapas* were never allowed to get married. Even if anybody wanted to get married they had to invariably marry another bonded slave. The *adapapas* were never given any economic security. The lords would swallow the youths of these girls but often leave them without food to eat or a shelter to live in.

Another peculiar social evil that was confined to Telangana region was the prevalence of *jogins*. They are still seen in significant numbers in Karimnagar, Medak, and Nizamabad districts. These girls who were usually from the lower castes were drawn to become *jogins* under the pretext of pleasing the local deities into safeguarding the welfare of the village and preventing natural calamities and epidemics. This belief forced the women to marry the local deity. Typically, the priests and rich men of the village sexually exploited the *jogins*. Thus the *jogin* was forced to lead the life of a prostitute.

The evil of prostitution also prevailed in the Hyderabad State in the form of *nautch* system. Patronized by the Nizam and his nawabs and jagirdars, these dancing girls whose initial profession was dance, were used sexually and invariably took to prostitution.[12]

Political Context

There were no political activities in the Hyderabad State during the early years of the twentieth century. This left the political field free for the Arya Samajists to come forward as the champions of the struggle against autocracy, and enabled them to divert the democratic awakening of the people to a considerable rule as there was no question of civil liberties. Even for literary associations and for holding public meetings prior permission from the local official was required. To quote Pandit Jawaharlal Nehru, 'Political meetings are unknown in Hyderabad and even social and religious gatherings are looked upon with suspicion and special permission has to be taken.'[13]

There were no hard and fast rules regarding the holding of public meetings till the beginning of twentieth century. Subsequently the situation was changed by the *firman* of the Nizam-VII, i.e. *gashti* no. 52 of 8 September 1921 which stated that 'Political meetings or any meetings calculated to bring about political results should not be held without the permission of Executive Council, otherwise the convenors of the meeting will be held responsible in every way'.[14]

Similarly, an executive order called *gashti* no. 53 was promulgated on 21 November 1929. According to it 'every person desirous of holding a public meeting shall in writing intimate his intention, if the meeting is to be held in city of Hyderabad, to the commissioner of police and in other case, to the collector concerned, at least 10 days to the date of meeting. . . . If the government thinks it proper to demand security in any particular case, then the steps would be taken accordingly.'[15]

However, meetings which were purely of social, educational, literary or charitable nature were exempted from these rules. This paved the way for the Arya Samaj, the Andhra Kendra Jana Sangam, Andhra Mahasabha, Maharashtra Parishad, Karnataka Parishad, and other associations to project social issues and becoming platforms for political conscientization. But political organizations like the Hyderabad Political Reforms Association, Nizams Subjects League, Hyderabad State Congress were either not allowed to function or were banned.

Thus it is observed that a feudal socio-economic structure which was much oppressive, an education system which denied opportunity to majority of people, and a princely autocracy of the Nizam which was blatantly communal, caused discontentment among men and women of Telangana. Various protest movements were carried on against this system, and women took an active part in them.

FIRST STIRRINGS OF WOMEN'S CONSCIOUSNESS AND AWAKENING

In Hyderabad, a socio-political and cultural awakening started with the Library movement, in spite of the restrictions imposed by the government. A number of libraries were established in Telangana largely due to the efforts of Madapati Hanumantha Rao and Suravaram Pratap Reddy.

The first library which started in 1901 was the Sri Krishnadevaraya Andhra Bhasha Nilayam. The same year Komarraju Laxman Rao started the Andhra Chandrika Parishodhaka Mandali at Hyderabad. This was followed by Raja Raja Narendra Andhra Bhasha Nilayam in 1904 at Hanumakonda. These libraries became prominent institutions in the state and developed a kind of renaissance in Telangana.[16]

Due to the efforts of Madapati Hanumantha Rao and Ravichettu Ranga Rao women were included as members of Sri Krishnadevaraya Andhra Bhasha Nilayam and allowed to listen to the lectures. This was the first effort to bring women into the limelight in Telangana.[17]

EFFORTS OF THE REFORMERS

The beginning of the twentieth century witnessed the irresistible forces of nationalism, liberalism, and egalitarianism and imposed an outlook on the people. Several forces emerged to carry on the reform work in social fields. This period is of a great significance in Telangana history. Educated and enlightened men and women started questioning the deep-rooted social evils of society and attacked them with vigour and sustained energy. The centre of the focus of social reform activities in India, as well as in the Hyderabad State, was women.

Various efforts were carried out by prominent men who worked for the advancement of women. As early as 1878 Aghornath Chattopadhyaya started the 'Young Men's Improvement Association' to discuss social and political issues.[18]

Raja Murali Manohar, another prominent man, started the Hindu social club which worked for the eradication of superstitious customs that prevailed in Hindu Society.[19] Mullah Abdul Quayyum started a women's organization called Iqwasunnisa to promote women's education and to discuss various social reform activities.[20]

Amidst this growing awareness among intellectuals there emerged various organizations to fight for liberation from the Nizam. Pioneering among them was the Arya Samaj, which was established in Hyderabad in 1892. The notable schools started by the Arya Samaj were Viveka Vardhini Patashala, Bala Saraswati Patashala, Sharada Kanya Patashala, Savitri Kanya Patashala, Gajanan Kanya Patashala, etc. These worked for women's education, facing restrictions imposed by the government for being *khangi* (non-government) schools.[21]

Besides formal education, the Arya Samaj encouraged physical education for girls along with boys, through gymnasiums and *akhadas*.[22] Uma Bai

Aurangabadkar, Palsikar, Smt Kasinath Rao Vaidya, Susheela Pathak, Leela Laxmi Bai, and Kalavathi were the prominent women educationists.

ROLE OF WOMEN'S JOURNALS AND WOMEN WRITERS

The Nizam's government enforced a number of restrictions on the freedom of the associations and expression. The Samsthanams of Telangana played the harbinger role in establishing a press and publishing books.

In the twentieth century, Telugu journals such as *Hitabodhini*, *Andhra Mata*, *Nilagiri Patrika*, *Telugu Patrika*, *Golkonda Patrika*, *Andhraabhyudayam*, *Deshabandhu*, *Sujata*, *Divya Vani*, *Shobha*, etc., were started, focusing attention on various social issues.

There were only a handful of journals edited by women. Mention must be made of *Telugu Thalli* started by Rachamalla Sathya Devi from Secunderabad in 1939. Suravaram Pratap Reddy, P.V. Subba Rayudu, Yellapragada Sitakumari, Illendula Saraswati, Nandagiri Indira Devi, and Sangam Laxmi Bai contributed articles to it. This, however, gave a greater importance to literary activities. Another journal, *Mathru Bharati* started by the students of Andhra Balika Patashala, Hyderabad, strove to conscientize Telangana women on matters of reforms and the efforts of the national leaders towards the freedom struggle in the state. It also acquainted the women with socio-educational developments and trained them to serve the nation. Another important women's journal was the *Bharat Mahila* started and edited by Suryadevara Rajyalaxmi in 1948.

The Muslim women in Hyderabad started a number of journals for women. Among them *Ishmat*, *Tahazeeb*, and *Nisa* were popular. Suogra Humayun Mirza was the editor of *Nisa*. It continued up to 1931 in Hyderabad and later shifted to Lahore. Syeda Begum started another magazine, *Humjoli*, which was followed by *Safena Niswas* started by Siddique Qureshi. In 1944, *Kheyaban-e-Deccan* was published. Another magazine which continue to be published till today is *Sher-e-Niswan*.

The women writers of the twentieth century gave an impetus to the women's movement by portraying social reforms and developments. The important women writers in Telugu were Rupkhanpet, Rattamma, Yellapragada Sita Kumari, Nandagiri Indira Devi, Parsa Janaki Devi, Pakala Yasoda Reddy. The significant aspect of the writing of Yasoda Reddy is the use of the Telangana dialect.

The prominent Muslim women writers in Telangana were Afzal Unnisa Begum, Kismath Unnisa Begum, Thyaba Begum, Suogra Humayun Mirza,

Begum Amina Hussain, Kaisari Begum, Jamal Salma, Sakina Begum, Jahabana Naqvi, Dr. Rafia Sultana, Dr. Zeenath Sagera, etc.[23]

ROLE OF WOMEN'S ASSOCIATIONS

As the movement for the uplift of women in several fields was spreading through various conferences, educational and cultural activities, associations at several places in the region, the impact of these activities was clearly visible in women's associations.

The earliest known women's association in Hyderabad State was Bharata Mahila Samajam started by Sita Bai in 1907.

In 1916, Margaret Cousins visited Hyderabad. She, along with Sarojini Naidu, Amina Hyderi, and Rustomji Fardun started the Hyderabad Women's Education and Social Development Association. The association acted as the Hyderabad wing of the All India Women's Conference.[24]

In 1925, the Andhra Sodari Samajam was started with Nadimpalli Sundaramma, Pandita Veera Raghavamma, Lokanandi Janakamma, and Puram Rukminamma at Hyderabad.

Yamini Purnatilakam started another women's association, Yuvati Sharanalayam in 1922 at Secunderabad. The basic aim of Sharanalayam was to work towards the eradication of prostitution. It also worked in helping prostitutes seek other forms of livelihood and reportedly, helped some of them marry and lead a normal life.

These early associations, though shortlived, were a clear indication of the growing awareness among women. Women's movement gained a new momentum with the establishment of the Andhra Mahasabha (1930). One of the special features of the Andhra Mahasabha was that women's conferences called the Andhra Mahila Sabhas were simultaneously held along with their meetings.

The feature of holding both Sabhas simultaneously continued till 1942. During the ninth Sabha at Dharmavaram, Warangal district, in 1942, the women members felt strong and confident enough to hold independent and separate conferences. The Andhra Mahila Sabha had the privilege of having prominent women such as Nadimpalli Sundaramma, Tanguturi Varalaxmamma, Yellapragada Sitakumari, Madapati Manikyamma, Burgula Ananta Laxmi Devi, Nandagiri Indira Devi, R. Yogya Sheela Devi, Rangamma Obul Reddy, Gundigunta Lalita Devi, and Nimmagadda Satyavathi Devi leading its conferences at various places. Chronologically they included Jogipet, Medak district (1930), Devarakonda, Nalgonda district (1931), Khammammet, Khammam district (1934), Siricilla,

Karimnagar district (1935), Shadnagar, Mahaboobnagar district (1936), Nizamabad (1937), Malkapuram, Hyderabad district (1940), Chilkur, Nalgonda district (1941), Dharmavaram, Warangal district (1942), Hyderabad (1943), Bhongir, Nalgonda district (1944), Madikonda, Warangal district (1945), and Kandi, Medak district (1946). The scope of Andhra Mahasabha activities were extensive and contributions it made towards the women's movement were high.

By the third decade of twentieth century, the women's movement in Telangana gained momentum with the efforts of educated and enthusiastic young women. Number of Muslim and non-Muslim associations such as Andhra Yuvati Mandali (1935), Mahila Navajeevan Mandali (1935), Anjuman-e-Khavatin-e-Deccan (1895), ladies recreation clubs namely Lady Burton's Club and Lady Hyderi Club came into existence. Though some of the associations were limited in the scope of their activities, they contributed to and mirrored the rising awareness of the women in Telangana.

PARTICIPATION OF TELANGANA WOMEN IN POLITICAL MOVEMENTS

The twentieth century saw the emergence of women going beyond the bounds of home and family and actively participating in movements. For the early pioneers of social and religious reforms, women were at first objects of their emancipating efforts, but during the course of the nineteenth and twentieth centuries they increasingly became subjects in the political and social spheres.[25]

The propagation of swadeshi caught the imagination of the people and soon they took to spinning khadi. Wearing khadi became common among men and women. During Gandhi and Kasturba's visit (1912), a special meeting with women was arranged at the Prem theatre. An association under the chairmanship of Padmaja Naidu, started immediately after the visit of Gandhi, to propagate the use of khadi and swadeshi goods. More and more women, mostly from the backward communities started working in the charkha factories. Along with the local leaders, women like Gyan Kumari Heda and others started working actively to propagate satyagraha. They tried to awaken the women of the state through Charkha Sangham. The political activity among women which was ignited through the Satyagraha movement, gained momentum in the Quit India, and join India, and Telangana Armed struggles.

The year 1942 witnessed the upsurge of the Quit India movement.

Educated urban women such as Padmaja Naidu, Gyan Kumari Heda, Mrs Ramaswamy, Vimala Bai Melkote, and others took the lead. Meetings were convened in all districts of Telangana. In a meeting at the Victoria playground, convened against the ban on Gandhi Jayanti celebrations, Padmaja Naidu was arrested. But Mrs and Mr T. Ramaswamy, Gyan Kumari Heda, Vimala Bai Melkote continued the meeting. Gyan Kumari Heda made a speech and Mrs A. Ramaswamy held the Congress flag. Later, they were all arrested.[26] The Congress bulletin, *Azad Hind*, published the news of the arrest of Sarojini Naidu and Padmaja Naidu.[27]

The Nizam resorted to brutal suppression and banned the hoisting of the Union flag in the state. Big demonstrations were held on 15 August 1947. The orders of the Nizam's government were strongly resented by the people and they resisted the efforts of the police by openly hoisting the Indian National Flag in public places and ceremoniously organizing processions and meetings.

Women also took a leading part in this. Yashodha Bai and Brij Rani Goud were arrested on the 15 and 16 August 1947, for hoisting the Indian flag. After this, three or four batches of women followed and led the campaign. Vimala Bai Melkote, Gyan Kumari Heda, along with Usha Pangrekar and Ahalya Bai broke the curfew and faced a lathi charge and tear gas. Laxmi and Radhabai Deshmukh hoisted the Indian flag at Itakalamandi. The struggle continued till a 'Standstill Agreement' was signed and some prominent leaders were released on 30 November 1947.

Subsequent to the police action in the Hyderabad, the Union Government after observing the political conditions in the state, decided to keep it under military rule rather than to leave it to people's representatives. The feudal oppression over the peasants continued. People rallied around the Communists in strengthening the armed struggle.

WOMEN'S PARTICIPATION IN THE TELANGANA MOVEMENT

Women played a remarkable role in the anti-feudal, anti-Nizam, and Left movement known as the Telangana movement. In the Telangana struggle, there were women of all kinds from different backgrounds and with different experiences. Some from peasant and middle class families, some even from landlords' families, some from orphanages, some from the families of *devadasis*, some who had walked out of violent and disastrous marriages, and others from traditional Brahmin families who had been married since age of five. Many women were from the middle class, who were forced to observe one form or the other of purdah, women whose lives were circumscribed by the kitchen and the household.[28]

Some of the women leaders were educated and relatively privileged such as Pramila Tai, Achamamba, K. Koteshwaramma, Arutla Kamala Devi, and others. Some like Mallu Swarajyam and Pramila Bai had already taken active lead in the organizations such as the Andhra Mahasabha, Andhra Mahila Sabha, and Mahila Navjeevan Mandali, etc. There were also tribal women such as Mangili Poolamma, who joined the struggle. Some Muslim women such as Jamalunnisa Begum (Baji) and her sister Razia Begum participated in the struggle and made their house, the centre of party activities. Thus it is an interesting feature that women from different backgrounds joined the struggle. There were various reasons which accentuated their participation; whether it was an educated middle class women, elite urban women, or peasant women who were conscious of their natural rights and opted for the armed struggle.

Their participation was not an immediate reaction to the existing conditions. This is evident in Puchalapalli Sundarayya's observation that during the initial stage of the movement, many women did not join. They were watching their husbands and brothers join the Sangham and fight against the landlords.[29]

Women were drawn into the struggle in large numbers partly out of conviction that they had a role to play being half the human race and partly out of necessity. Priyamvada, Kamalamma, Pramila Tai, Rajamma, Moturu Udayam, and Mallu Swarajyam entered the struggle with the inspiration of their brothers.

The feeling of equality between men and women, the possibility of a better life where men and women would work freely together, and the promise of a different experience evidently brought the women folk into the struggle.

The Communist Party captured their dissent and gave encouragement to their involvement. There can be no question of the fact that their involvement with the party provided a significant growth in consciousness of the women. Reading, writing, discussing political questions, attending classes, addressing public meetings, and organizing women gave them a very positive idea of their role. Many women such as Priyamvada, Swarajyam, and Kamalamma joined the struggle through the party. Priyamvada said: 'We gained the confidence to speak at public meetings.'

WOMEN'S PARTICIPATION AND RESISTANCE

Women in Telangana actively participated in the land movement, in the agricultural labour wage struggles, in the seizure of landlords grain, and against the 'Briggs' plan of evacuating of Koya, Chenchu, and Lambadi people from their hamlets in forest areas or from their scattered hamlets in the plains. They were with their husbands and brothers, fighting the Razakars and the Nizam's police and later the Indian army. They joined the military and political squads and underwent all the difficulties and joys of life in the forests and hills and in the fields, in rain and in sun. They acted as couriers, as political agitators, and as organizers of people's movements and mass organizations.[30]

During the early phase of the struggle women's contribution to the movement was limited. But in later years, they rose to great heights of heroism and sacrifice. First, they moved in groups realizing that their strength lay in numbers. They drew on the skills they had and the objects around them, such as chilli powder, *vodiselu* (slings), and pistols to defend themselves.[31] They threw chilli powder in the eyes of the enemy and brought household utensils to beat out the Razakars, and these weapons some times proved effective, because the women formed united groups.[32]

Many women worked in the dens. Women in large numbers worked as copyists of thousands of pages of reports, circulars, documents, correspondences patiently day and night. Women played a crucial role as couriers, distributing letters from one Dalam to another sometimes concealing their identities and many times escaping narrowly from the attacks of the Razakars.

Educated women from towns and cities helped by holding classes for rural women by writing circulars, making copies of important letters, and by working as nurses.[33] In Hyderabad, many women rendered their help to the struggle and women's organizations such as the Navjeevan Mandali, did splendid work in helping the Communists. The Communists carried on their activities through the Mandali. They also helped in fund raising in many ways. Women activists such as Pramila Mahindra, Sarojini, Yashodha Bai, Jamalunnisa Begum, and many others joined the struggle through the Mandali. Chakali Ailamma of Palakurti village, Jangaon taluq, who was initially with the Andhra Mahasabha and later the Communist Party, bitterly fought to retain her land and crop from being seized by the Visnur Deshmukh.[34]

Ordinary women in the villages heroically defended their land and it is an undoubted fact that tens and thousands of women stood along with their men folk in the struggle for land.[35] As women formed a large percentage of the agricultnral labour, they participated in all the agricultural labour strikes. In demonstrations women brandishing red flags came in large numbers. They participated in seizing grain from the landlords who were thereby forced to concede their demands for 4 *seers* of grain as daily wages, raising the quota from the prevailing 2 or 3 *seers*.[36]

In the Godavari forest belt struggle to increase wages for plucking of *bidi* leaves, an occupation in which tens of thousands of women were employed, they were at the forefront.[37] In the centres of Pindiprolu and Yellandu, women from ninety villages participated in the strikes and struggles that took place. In twenty of these villages women were in the forefront.[38]

The Telangana women's participation in guerrilla warfare was one of the significant facets of Indian history. After the Telangana struggle adopted guerrilla warfare, it became more vigorous and intense. The guerrilla squads were started to assess the implementation of the programmes of the Communist Party, such as abolition of forced labour, re-occupation of lands grabbed by the deshmukhs, jagirdars, and other landlords and the distribution of government land among agricultural workers, enforcement of fair rents and wages for poor peasants and workers, and the abolition of exorbitant interest rates imposed by the landlords. According to Sundarayya, many women demanded to be taken into guerrilla squads in forest areas, maybe partly in order to escape enemy attacks.

ATROCITIES AGAINST WOMEN

The Razakars (the para military wing of the Ittehad-ul-Musalmeen), combined with the landlords resorted to mass rapes in the villages of Akunuru, Machireddipalli, and Akkirajupalli. When the peasants of Akunuru and Machireddipalli resisted police and revenue officials who had come to collect the grain levy, the police retaliated with torture, looting, and rape.[39] When the district committee of the Communist Party sent an organizer to enquire into the atrocities, he found that at Akunuru, nearly 77 women were raped. The majority of them were agricultural labourers and poor women.[40] At Machireddipalli women tried to defend their paddy by revolting against revenue officials. The officers brought the special police, ransacked the village and perpetrated a mass rape.[41] These incidents were publicized by the Free Press journal at Bombay and attracted nationwide attention. An enquiry committee was sent by Gandhi through

Padmaja Naidu, Mrs Hussain Ali Khan, and Gyan Kumari Heda.[42] The committee gave the evidence in court and on the advice of Gandhi, the Prime Minister constituted a judicial enquiry headed by a High Court judge.[43] At Akkirajupalli, when the Communists offered resistance to the Razakars, the latter resorted to rape on women.[44]

During the armed struggle the Razakars ransacked 70 villages and killed thousands of people, raped, and abducted a number of women. The worst affected villages in this respect were Talkat, Ameerpet, Punjagutta, Asrafpet.[45]

According to the reports of the Communist Party, fifty women in the Munagala paragana, two in Nilayagudem, fifteen in Balpala (Manukota), seventy in Chimalpadu (Yellandu taluq), and eighty in Narmetta and Nanganur (Jangoan taluq) were raped.[46] Mass rapes also took place at Ghanapuram, Ragipadu, Bairanpalli, and many other places.

As per the underground reports, during the days of terror, more than a hundred women died from being raped brutally.[47] In the year 1946 alone more than a thousand women were raped, and wherever police and military camps were established, mass rape and forced prostitution were a common feature.[48]

Women waged a bitter fight against these attacks, by beating the police and saving themselves and other women from torture and brutality. At Nawabpet, Mallela, Medarigudem, Jallalapuram, Bathu Venkanna Bavi Thanda, Tirumalgiri, Koyagudem, Nerjerla, Chetlamupparam, Pammi, and many other places, women chased the military away by putting up a fierce resistance. At Chetlamupparam, when twenty-three women were caught by the army, 'all the women folk of village surrounded them and forced them to be let off.

The party trained women volunteers to save themselves from these attacks and posted two or three volunteers in each village.[49] Women in groups of fifteen or twenty used to sleep together in the village so that they could protect their honour.[50]

JAILS AND CONFINEMENTS

In Telangana, military and police carried out any number of raids and arrested people en-masse. Anyone who was suspected of being an Andhra Mahasabha worker or sympathizer was arrested and tortured.[51] The women captives were put in various jails at Hyderabad, Rajahmundry, Rayavellore, and sometimes outside the state and most often ill-treated and not provided with minimum facilities. At times women protested against bad conditions in jails. Manikonda Suryavathi and others went on a hunger strike for 17 days in Rayavellore jail for improving the conditions.[52] The union army set up concentration camps at various places for detaining women and subjected them to innumerable indignities.

There were many instances where women prisoners were lathi-charged in jail. In Warangal Central Jail when rations for women detenues were stopped 50 of them went on a hunger strike, lasting for 3 days. The superintendent directed a lathi-charge on these women as a result of which, 8 women were seriously injured. Among them, was Annapurnamma of Govindapuram, Tumma Narasamma of Sankesa, P. Narasamma of Munagala, and Kanthamma of Velidanda village. Ramabayamma of Pindiprolu died in the lathi-charge. All the political prisoners went on a hunger strike protesting against the brutal lathi charges, the Warangal Trade Union Congress appealed to democrats to condemn this bestial action and demanded a public enquiry to identify and punish the guilty.[53] There were several instances where a number of innocent women, some of them quite old, who were relatives of Andhra Mahila Sabha workers were put into jails.[54]

IMPACT OF THE PEOPLE'S STRUGGLE ON WOMEN

We have observed that women's participation in the struggle was expressed in terms of joining political demonstrations and processions, working as couriers and food suppliers, looking after the health of the squads, etc., and taking up guns against the Razakars, police, and Indian army. Viewing that participation within the socio-economic structure of the society, historians today admit that it was no mean an achievement.

According to Renu Chakravarthi, the militant participation of women in the Freedom movement as a whole indirectly enabled Indian women to attain their civic rights within the constitution of India after 1947, without their having to struggle for them separately.[55] Though it is difficult to draw such qualitative conclusions regarding the Telangana armed struggle, the movement did bring about a qualitative change in the lives of the women, by bringing about a cultural and ideological change in them. In fact, the movement had a greater impact on the lives of the women than men. Humanist organizations came into being to look after the specific problems of the women. The party tried to seek solutions to the women's problem in the broader context of the struggle and failed to evolve a separate policy towards the women's issues.

For those who came from the middle classes, the gains were perhaps less tangible but the struggle brought them out of the four walls of their homes. Vempati Kausalya says that 'We did not know what was behind this wall. We could never go out of the house, but now we go out to look after agricultural work.'[56] Renu Chakravarthy goes further in assessing the impact of the struggle on women: 'in this great struggle women showed great fortitude and in the process liberated themselves from feudal chains that had bound them down for centuries'.[57]

Despite the socio-cultural inequalities in the existing social order, with its 'prescribed' class structure and the ambiguity of its leadership, it is evident that the participation of women in the people's struggle was in a large-scale, especially from the peasantry and landless labourer.[58]

There is no doubt that the Telangana struggle proved very beneficial to the peasantry, men and women distributing land to the farmers guaranteeing their rights. It can also be said that the progressive laws like the Kowludari Act (1950) was achieved tangibly in this struggle. The qualitative changes in the society achieved with the abolition of *vetti* and jagirdari system. It did give women a new consciousness about and a perspective of the world. It not only affected the lives of the women participants, but also influenced and gave new hopes to the successive generations. The struggle also brought into, limelight, the inner strengths and bravery of the Telangana women who questioned the oppression and sought liberation through their participation in the struggle.

CONCLUSION

Women's participation in the people's struggle is moulded or preceded by the consciousness which in turn was historically and culturally conditioned. In Telangana, the spread of education and social reform movements brought about consciousness among the women. Step by step this flowered into the movement of all round social, cultural, economic change and finally developed into a people's struggle. The national movement created conditions where women were called upon to move outside their customary domestic spheres and enable the middle and upper class educated women to actively participate in the movements. It is only when the nationalist movement became people's movement, the mass participation of women became possible. Every advancement in the movement towards a people's struggle brought women several steps further in their own struggle for emancipation.

NOTES

1. Kumari Jayawardena, *Feminism and Nationalism in the Third World in the 19th and 20th Centuries*, Institute of Social Studies, The Hague, 1982, p. 77.
2. Ibid., p. 97.
3. P. Sundarayya, *Telangana People's Struggle and its Lessons*, Calcutta, 1972, p. 9.
4. Ibid., p. 12.
5. *Census of India*, 1901, vol. XXII, Part I, Hyderabad Deccan, 1903, p. 23.
6. *Census of India*, 1931, vol. XXIII, Part I, Report, Hyderabad, 1933, p. 162.
7. A. Satyanarayana, 'Land, Caste and Dominance in Telangana', Research in Progress, *History and Society*, 2nd Series, no. LXXVIII, New Delhi, 1993, p. 23.
8. *Census of India*, 1911, vol. XIX, Hyderabad State, Part I, Bombay, 1913, p. 86.
9. Ibid.
10. *Golkonda Patrika*, dated 28 November 1938, p. 1.
11. Sundarayya, *Telangana People's Struggle*, p. 14.
12. K. Chandraiah, *Hyderabad 400 Glorious Years*, Hyderabad, 1996, p. 266.
13. Jawaharlal Nehru, *An Autobiography*, New Delhi, 1962, p. 274.
14. Balwantrai Mehta, *A Peep into Hyderabad Deccan*, Bombay, 1938, p. 32.
15. *Hyderabad District Gazetteer*, Nizam Government Publications, 1922-9, State Archives, Hyderabad, p. 1.
16. N. Ramesan, *The Freedom Struggle in Hyderabad*, vol. II, *1885-1920*, 1957, p. 152.
17. *Vignana Sarvaswam (Encyclopaedia)*, vol. I, Madras, 1959, p. 975.
18. Veldurthi Manikya Rao, *History of Hyderabad Freedom Struggle*, Gandhi Bhavan, Hyderabad, 1984, p. 73.
19. Ibid., p. 74
20. Ibid., p. 77.
21. *Vignana Sarvaswam*, vol. I, Madras, 1959, p. 974.
22. Sarojini Regani, *Highlights of Freedom Movement in Andhra Pradesh*, Hyderabad, 1972, p. 172.
23. Nasiruddin Hashmi, *Anjuman-e-Kavatin-e-Deccan* (Women Writers and Poetess of Hyderabad), Hyderabad, 1940, p. 26.
24. *Vignana Sarvaswam*, p. 974.
25. Maria Mies, *Indian Women and Patriarchy*, New Delhi, 1979, p. 117.
26. N. Ramesan, *The Freedom Struggle in Hyderabad,* vol. IV, Hyderabad, 1966, p. 240.
27. Ibid., p. 242.
28. K. Lalitha, *We Were Making History*, New Delhi, 1989, pp. 258-9.
29. Sundarayya, *Telangana People's Struggle*, p. 329.
30. Ibid., p. 328.
31. *Political Organisational Report of CPI*, CC no. 6, P.C. Joshi Archives, New Delhi, p. 260.

32. *People's Age*, 11 April 1947.
33. Sundarayya, *Telangana People's Struggle*, p. 3.
34. Ibid., p. 239.
35. Renu Chakravarthy, *Communists in Indian Women's Movement*, New Delhi, 1980, p. 127.
36. Ibid.
37. Ibid.
38. Ibid.
39. Barry Pavier, *The Telangana Movement 1944-1951*, New Delhi, 1981, p. 3.
40. Devulapalli Venkateshwar Rao, *Telangana Prajala Sayudha Porata Charitra (1946-51)*, vol. I, Hyderabad, 1988, pp. 340-1.
41. Ibid.
42. *Meejan*, 18 September, 1946, p. 3.
43. Venkateshwar Rao, *Telangana Prajala Sayudha*, p. 343.
44. Lalitha, *We Were Making History*, pp. 55-64.
45. Kashi Reddy, *Niyanta Nizam Nizarupam*, Hyderabad, 1992, p. 23.
46. Sundarayya, *Telangana Peoples Struggle*, p. 341.
47. *Prajashakti*, dated 9 August 1947.
48. *Janmabhoomi*, 4 September 1947.
49. Venkateshwar Rao, *Telangana Prajala Sayudha*, p. 357.
50. Renu Chakravarthy, *Communist in Indian Women's Movement*, p. 125.
51. *Communist Party Document, PQM Open Forum*, no.10, dated 2 October 1950, P.C. Joshi Archives, New Delhi, p. 1.
52. Ibid., pp. 156-7.
53. Sundarayya, *Telangana People's Struggle*, p. 320.
54. *Document of Communist Party of India*, pp. 1-6.
55. Malini Battacharya, 'Communist Party and Indian Women's Movement', Book Review of Renu Chakravarthy's *Communists in Indian Women's Movement, Economic and Political Weekly*, 2-9 January 1982, pp. 22-3.
56. Lalitha, *We Were Making History*, p. 16.
57. Chakravarthy, *Communists in Indian Women's Movement*, p. 135.
58. *Document of Communist Party of India, Political Thesis of Social Congress of C.P.I.* held during 28 February to 6 March 1948, Calcutta, p. 656.

The Struggle for Liberation from Double Slavery: The Princely Mysore, 1881-1947

S. CHANDRASHEKAR

Princely Mysore was the second largest state in colonial India. The state was carved out of the dominions of Tipu Sultan after he was defeated and slain in 1799 in the battle of Srirangapatnam. The former ruling dynasty of the Wodeyars which had been displaced for four decades and sent to political oblivion was reinstated by the colonial rulers under the dictates of the Subsidiary Treaty. What the British overlords bestowed on the princely house could also be taken over under some pretext. This happened in 1831, after a bloody revolt by the oppressed peasantry.

For fifty years Mysore was under the direct colonial rule. In 1881 the Wodeyar family was restored again and this time the restrictions on their rule were increased. While, as per the Subsidiary Treaty of 1799 apart from the other conditions, Mysore was to pay an annual subsidy of Rs. 24 lakhs, in 1881 it was raised to Rs. 35 lakhs. Thus on both occasions it were the imperialists who 'restored' the Wodeyars and thus Mysore became a 'Child of Imperialism' more than any other state in the country. And it is against this background that Mysore's revenue was drained out in the form of subsidy and other levies for 150 years. Any discussion of the levy and its impact on the state was forbidden by treaties.

The British Commission laid the foundations of the administrative system and handed it over to the native rulers. It was after fifty years of relentless petitioning and lobbying that the native men of public opinion were successful in getting the throne restored to the Wodeyars. Even the public associations such as the Madras Native Association had campaigned for the restoration of the Raja. As such, the rulers of Mysore could not ignore public opinion either in their own state or in British India. Similarly they could not displease the British for that could cost them their throne itself. They adopted such a strategy that their moves evoked least resistance from all concerned.

This they continued till they were ultimately overthrown after independence. The first such act was the establishment of a powerless assembly. This assembly was to consist of nominated ryots and merchants from all the taluqs of the state. It was to meet during the annual Dussehra festival and besides participating in the colourful festivities at the cost of the state they could also have a *darshan* of their Maharaja. Moreover, they could also petition the Diwan about grievances if any![1]

What is to be noted here is that the princely authorities in Mysore in a way sealed the attempts of the early nationalists to have a political association by establishing the assembly. This assembly which preceded the Indian National Congress (INC) by five years was a great obstacle, in a way to people to mobilize public opinion in Mysore to complain against the autocracy. For, such men in British India, the press and the nationalists wanted that 'the government of India should carry on the administration by learning the real wishes of the people through the medium of such Representative Assemblies (to obtain) for greater peace and contentment'.[2]

This assembly was proudly referred to as one which embodied the 'Oriental concept of Democracy' and the Legislative Council of the 'occidental'.[3]

The socio-religious reform organizations and their activities which were not directly political, found a ready response from the ruling princes. They took up the programmes of the Indian Social Conference and in fact, Mysore by passing some social legislations in the forefront of the Infant Marriage Regulation or the opening of girl schools.[4] The reform activists in British India were overwhelmed and wrote 'Mysore was often the first to adopt a measure which was only under discussion in the presidencies'.[5]

The Mysoreans also could not raise the bogey of equality with the Europeans when their counterparts in British India did in asking for simultaneous examinations to Indian Civil Service and an opening for the natives on the executive. This prima facie had already been in their hands. From the ruler and the Diwan to the ruled they were all natives though they were all subject to the colonial control. The nationalists of British India and later the INC never took the problems of the subjects of native states seriously. They saw native rule and everything Indian especially in a state like Mysore. The opinion of the nationalists about Mysore was so high that they did not make an issue of the suppression of a newspaper by the state as early as 1894. The Mysore ruler on his part had been in the good books of Congressmen and he had in fact contributed Rs.1,000 to the Madras Congress in 1887 and even allowed his officials to attend its sessions.[6] The next Maharaja Krishnaraja Wodeyar was invited to inaugurate the industrial exhibition of the Congress at Madras in 1903.

The colonialists had no axe to grind against the Mysore regime. Everything they wanted was complied with. Europeans and their interests were zealously safeguarded.[7] The 'one man rule' in Mysore was supported by them. All this could go on in the name of 'administrative efficiency and good government', which the paramountcy was harping on in India and advanced the lack of it as the reason why Indians could not be considered for responsible positions in British India. The Indian nationalists for a similar reason were supporting the 'native rule' and showed Mysore as an example of how best the Indians could manage the show all by themselves.

Thus under the cover of a 'Model Indian State' Mysore's treatment of all sorts of dissension with contempt and ruthlessness could go on. The attempts of the Mysoreans to resist the autocracy and galvanize public opinion were declared 'dead' and 'buried' openly by Seshadri Iyer the autocratic Diwan.[8]

It was under these heavy odds that the early nationalists of Mysore had to train their guns against autocracy. They were at a loss to see that the nationalists outside Mysore at least up to 1937 behaving more or less like the Mysore rulers rather than the supporters of the demands of their people, the 'double slaves'. In fact the nationalists in Mysore were very unhappy with their attitude. It is an irony that the Anglo-Indian Press which was so much opposed to Indian nationalism, occasionally took up the cause of the state's subjects. One liberal nationalist journalist of Mysore was so desperately provoked by the attitude of the Congress towards the people of state that he wrote:

> . . . we have no hope that *Madras Mails*' (An English daily edited by a European from Madras which when suited the colonial interests spoke about problems of the people of the native states) appeal—to recognise the problems of the States' people by Congress men will bear any fruit. We have had the pleasure of speaking to a few of them and the pain of finding them reluctant to recognise the problem at all. . . .'[9]

The rural society of Mysore, essentially a peasant society could not play a prominent part in the changes taking place in early colonial India. This is more true of areas that were under the ryotwari system. Further, colonial penetration in Mysore was rather slow and the absence of any urban rich—both business and service—elite in the rural agricultural economy impeded their participation. Added to this was the absence of a large group of zamindars in the state. The number of families who had around 500 acres of land were only 89 and this was also due to the break up of the joint family system. While it is true that Bombay and Madras presidencies were also governed by ryotwari, there was a recognizable class of zamindars who played a significant role in the political developments. In Mysore, 'we can not speak of a class of big landlords', observes Lala Dushkin.[10]

The urbanites, since they had no stakes in the rural agricultural economy, did not try to intrude upon and influence the rural parts. This void also contributed to the slow penetration of the nationalist ideas in the countryside. It is true that the peasant society was squeezed beyond its capacity. But so long as it was not properly organized it reacted by migrating to neighbouring district towns or cities. It was a silent majority, and though unorganized discontent flowed in an undercurrent and found violent expression in times of distress, famine, and drought.[11] But this discontent could not be properly channellized into the nationalist mainstream because of the inadequacies of the nationalist leader.

The urban centres in Mysore were very few and were only marginally affected by industrialization. It was only after 1915 that Mysore saw the growth of industries and the emergence of a working class. Thus initially there emerged towns which hardly were cosmopolitan in nature. The social composition of the middle class which played a crucial role in the movements against the princely autocracy and colonialism was seriously circumscribed in Mysore for various reasons. Mysore was a landlocked state and there could not emerge a prosperous business and industrial elite and capital formation itself was seriously hampered.

But south India in general and Mysore in particular had made rapid progress in acquiring a knowledge of English language and higher learning. Despite drawbacks like the absence of riches, the Brahmins who migrated to the urban centres in the later half of the nineteenth century were quick in taking advantage of the educational opportunity in many cases selling their lands to educate their children. By 1891 literacy among Brahmins in Mysore was 63.8 per cent of its total population and this was the third highest average among the Brahmins of all states including the presidencies.[12] In fact the presence of Brahmins was so overwhelming that in the towns of Mysore half their total population consisted of Brahmins.[13] After 1885 about 20 per cent of the students in Madras law schools and other courses which were not available within Mysore were from Mysore.[14]

As such the middle class in Mysore consisted mainly of Brahmins. Conditioned by these factors Mysoreans had to give consent to their aspirations. While in British India the nationalists of different hues wanted preference to be given to Indians as against the Europeans, in Mysore and other native states like Travancore and Cochin it was for subjects of their own states against the 'foreign Madrasis'. In Mysore the fight of early public men, against what they called 'alien domination' spread over four decades from 1870-1910. They did not differentiate between Europeans and non-Mysoreans as far as enjoying state patronage was concerned.[15]

The crucial issues taken up by public men in British India were drain of wealth, simultaneous Civil Service examination, and equal treatment of Indians. Mysoreans dictated by circumstances reacted to these in their own ways. They, besides protesting against the ill-treatment of the Indians by the Europeans, spoke of the dominance of 'foreign Madrasis' and regarding the drain of wealth by Britain they complained of the complicity of 'foreign Diwans in plundering Mysores' wealth by Britain.[16] Not that the public men in Mysore were not concerned about other issues. They spoke and resented the ill-treatment of the Indians by Europeans, the plight of the Indian emigrants, supported the Congress, and deplored the arrests and imprisonment of nationalist leaders.[17] But the burden that they were smarting on in various occasions placed them in peculiar spots and so we find them at variance with nationalists outside Mysore. The entry into Civil Services of British India and the Imperial Legislative Council were such issues. The British Indian nationalists were opposed to the entry of native state subjects, in such services.[18]

Public men in Mysore were primarily concerned with official power and patronage and seats of learning as they had no stakes in land and elective offices. There was hardly any reference to land taxes either in the newspapers edited and owned by them or in the assembly which had been functioning since 1881. It was only in the closing years of the nineteenth century that the English educated, forced by circumstances, had to turn their attention towards the ryots in a bid to enlist their support against the dominant 'foreign Madrasis'.[19] But it proved to be shortlived. It snapped when the rural landholders, again smarting under similar burden realized that it was the so-called 'public men' and nationalists who were opposed to the ambitious rural people who were attempting to share the spoils available within the state which had become the near monopoly of the former class and not the 'foreign Madrasis'. The Mysore autocracy played its own part, just as the imperialists did, and manipulated these developments to their own advantage. In fact the most influential factor was the autocracy itself which controlled state power. This was more pronounced in Mysore because it was a native state and the contending parties opposed to each other had to inevitably accept the arbitration of the government.

The emergence of the conflicting groups with different social background resulted in the growth of a new liberal democratic movement which is variously known as the Non-Brahmin movement, Backward Class movement, anti-Brahmin movement, etc.

The Non-Brahmin movement, which manifested itself in the 1910s, rocked the state politics from 1915 to 1930. The major achievements of the Non-Brahmin movement was to end the monopoly of one community over the power wielding bureaucracy and the institutions of higher learning. The state also so long as the movement did not threaten their authority was liberal enough to concede the demands. The Congress committee that came to be established after the Nagpur Congress in 1920 was on the defensive so far as the non-Brahmin demands were concerned. It could make no headway as only a few youths and retired officials were associated with it. In fact the opposition of the INC to allow state's people from carrying on any agitational work in their States was a blessing in disguise for Congressmen in Mysore. For, there were neither men nor materials with them. Thus politics in Mysore between 1915-30 was centred round the palace and the secretariat in Mysore and Bangalore.[20]

But the rising tide of Gandhian nationalism and his struggles largely contributed to the new shift in Mysore politics. Despite the fact that the Mysore government was sympathetic to the demands of the ambitious political men, they were totally opposed to all political dissent and ruthlessly suppressed all those who questioned their authority and demanded a share in the state power. But the suppression of political dissent was accompanied by the acceptance and implementation of the Gandhian constructive programme. Much to the chagrin of the colonial government, the state even took to teaching of Hindi and promotion of khadi. What more, the state even opened a khadi centre at Badanval.

Gandhi was invited as a State guest and when Gandhi visited him, the Maharaja appeared in khadi cloths and was seen spinning which was most dear to Gandhi.[21] Mirza Ismail, the Diwan of Mysore between 1926-41 went to the extent of claiming himself as a 'better Congressman than any one' he could see, openly in the assembly. He paid encomiums to Gandhi and his swadeshi gospel only to be firmly admonished by the Viceroy.[22]

While the Congressmen within Mysore fretted and fumed at the attitude of both the INC and the Mysore administration, the non-Brahmin party was at a loss to know the distrust of the state in parting with any real power. Both the groups realized in time that it was only a united challenge of the people that could really force the autocracy to mend its ways. The growth of the Left wing in the INC and Nehru becoming the Congress president helped alter the situation in Mysore. Nehru in the Lahore Congress appealed to the states and declared that 'the Indian States could not live apart from the rest of India. The only people who had a right to determine the future of the States must be the people of those States.'[23]

The Belgaum Congress over which the Mahatma presided in 1924, the Civil Disobedience movement and Salt satyagraha had an electrifying effect on the situation in Mysore. The countryside was stirred into action. A returning educated youth in the country could carry the message of the Congress and the Mahatma. The ruthlessness with which the state dealt with the dissenters had also been brought home convincingly to all politically conscious people. The labour strikes in the late 1920s, which were a result of the great depression, were answered by ruthless suppression. The student demonstrations were equally severely dealt with.[24] The hollowness of the civil rights and 'Model State' image stood exposed.

The first to realize the importance of mobilizing the rural masses was the non-Brahmin party, the Prajapaksha. They started organizing ryot conferences at the taluq level. But the state was ruthless enough to ban them. Similarly the satyagrahis who were heading towards the British Indian parts to participate in the Civil Disobedience movement were ruthlessly dealt with. Even the entry of a liberal labour leader like V.V. Giri was banned.[25] The ruthlessness of Mysore towards political dissent increased in proportion to the increase in political awareness among its people. What served to drive every one against the government was the latter's intolerance of growing anti-colonial national consciousness.

The Government of India Act of 1935 with provincial autonomy and the proposed Federation made it inevitable for all concerned to change their strategy. In the federal scheme the states were allotted an imposing 1/3 of the seats, all of which were to be nominated by the princes. These members were certain to prove a stumbling block in the way of the freedom struggle. It was to avoid this that the states' peoples movements were to be strengthened to fight for and wrest responsible governments. Thus the National Congress had to change their strategy towards states.

For public men in Mysore, be they of the Congress or of the non-Brahmin party, the formation of popular ministries in presidencies was a great lesson. Compared to the British provinces and their constitutional advancement they felt that they were left far behind. That had become possible there largely because of their struggle through the INC. Mysoreans realized that without the support of the masses, they could not hope to force the autocracy to part with the executive powers.

The autocracy of the state reached its zenith during the election of March 1937. Meetings, processions, and hoisting of the national flag were banned. Whatever rights and privileges the legislators, district board presidents, and members and councillors enjoyed were curtailed.[26] Both the Congress and the Praja Samyukta Paksha (The non-Brahmin party) were enraged. Authorized to violate all bans by Jawaharlal Nehru, the Congress president, Congressmen in Mysore declared that they would do so and formed a 'Council of Action'. The government resorted to pre-emptive strikes, arrested leaders of the Council of Action and raided the Congress office.

K.T. Bhashyam, the 'Dictator' of the Council of Action, who was in Mysore to attend the Legislative Assembly session, was arrested from his hotel at midnight. The newly elected legislators who had all converged at Mysore to attend the session were shocked at Bhashyam's arrest. The leaders of the Praja Samyukta Paksha realized the gravity of the situation and the next day, i.e. the morning of 15 October 1937, it was announced from Mysore that the two parties had merged.

Thus came into being the Mysore Congress. Soon followed the Nariman episode in which a 5,000 strong crowd that had gathered to listen to the Bombay Congress leader was fired upon killing six, wounding several, and the 'speaker being arrested'.[27] These incidents were condemned by the AICC in a resolution at Calcutta, though Gandhi was not happy with it. Nevertheless the Congress was seized of the matter.[28]

The Haripura Congress session in February 1938, while supporting the state's peoples movements forbade the state's Congressmen from using Congress name in undertaking any political struggles. But most of the people's movements in the states including the Mysore Congress men unmindful of this resolution launched the Mysore Congress in March 1938 and went on to organize its first session. This was at Shivapura in April 1938. The government again by banning the hoisting of the flag demonstrated its hostility. This provoked the Congressmen to continue the Flag satyagraha against the ban orders.

The most remarkable incident that demonstrates at once the popularity of the nationalist movement and the ruthlessness of the government occurred at Viduraswatha on 25 April 1939. The village where a *jatra* (fair) was in progress also became a scene of a ghastly tragedy when a Congress meeting was fired upon and several innocents were killed.[29] This tragedy is remembered as the Jallianwala Bagh of Karnataka. The government tried to cover up and belittle its significance, though it was stunned to see the awakening among the rural masses.

These developments in Mysore seem to have served as an eye-opener to the National Congress and particularly to Gandhi. Two years before Gandhi had remarked that Mysore and its Maharaja nearly approximated to his utopia of 'Ram Rajya' and 'Rajarshi'.[30] Mysore thus led the leaders to define the Congress policy towards the states. Gandhi admitted of his ignorance of the situation in Mysore. He cabled Mirza Ismail, the Diwan that 'there was unprecedented awakening . . . the only remedy is immediate transfer of responsibility to the people . . . delay was dangerous'. He deputed Patel and Kripalani to Mysore. Patel before coming to Mysore reiterated Gandhi's words and advised Mirza that 'the honour and interest of the state could be preserved by complete endorsement of Gandhi's views'.[31]

The outcome of the Patel-Kripalani visit was the Patel-Mirza agreement. The Diwan agreed to recognize Congress and allow 3 Congress members to be on the Constitutional Reforms Committee. In return the Congress agreed to withdraw the Flag satyagraha.

But the government continued to suppress the nationalist agitational activity in the state. The Viduraswatha Enquiry Committee as expected exonerated the government. The Constitutional Reforms Committee did not fulfil any demands of the Congress. The political prisoners after release stood debarred from contesting the elections. The Mysore Congress renewed its agitational activity fully backed by the National Congress.[32] Explaining the changed attitude of the National Congress Gandhi said, 'the policy of non-intervention by Congress was in my opinion, a perfect piece of statesmanship when the people of the states were not awakened. The policy would be cowardice when there is all round awakening among the people of the states and determination to go through a long course of suffering for the vindication of their just rights. The moment they became ready, the legal, constitutional and artificial boundary was destroyed.[33]

It is remarkable that it was against this background of developments in Mysore that the Tripura session met in March 1939 and announced its new policy towards the states. The Congress removed all restrictions and pledged its support to political activity including direct action and called upon the princes to establish responsible governments in their states. This served as a background for the launching of the massive Quit India movement.

There was no distinction so far as Congress activity was concerned between British Indian and Princely States after Tripura. However, it was not the Congress leadership that was responsible for the momentous happenings during the Quit India movement in Mysore. It were the students and labourers who were in the forefront and formed the pith and marrow of the struggle. By 10 August 1942 the students from every town and city had forced the government to close the educational institutions. Such was the rising tide of nationalism that even the children of the ministers in Mysore joined the movement and led it.[34] The combined might of the students and labourers was such that despite indiscriminate firing and arrests they did not relent and the government panicked.[35]

One of the greatest centres of the 1942 struggle in the whole country which of course has not been recognized as such so far was Isur, a village in the Shimoga district. The villagers established a parallel government for some time in September. Daily meetings were held in the village temple and decisions were reiterated to disregard the authority. The village Patel, Shanubogue, the symbols of state authority, were forced to wear khadi dress and resign their jobs. They were insulted for being in the services of an 'irresponsible government'.[36]

Police and revenue officials including the tahsildar and sub-inspector who visited the village to restore order were done to death. The whole incident took such a serious turn that the government was forced to send paramilitary forces to control the situation. Space forbids a detailed discussion of the historic event here. It would suffice to say that this was an incident, the like of which never happened in the history of the freedom struggle in Karnataka. The government let loose terror in the village and its surroundings. The whole village was looted and women were disgraced by the authorities. The government and the Congress leadership were stunned alike. A special trial was ordered and ultimately five were sent to gallows and about twenty others were sentenced to rigorous imprisonment varying from deportation for life to 10 years.[37]

Elsewhere in the state, sabotage activities went on in rotation to the high-handedness of the authorities. The Quit India struggle firmly entrenched the nationalist spirit among the people in the state. The Congress leaders were emboldened henceforth to dare the autocracy because they were confident of the resolve of the people for independence. In fact the Mysore State's capitulation into agreeing to accede to the Indian Union was no less dictated by the determination exhibited by the state's people during 1942.

The last phase of the struggle against the autocracy was not to stop it on the exit of the British from India but Mysoreans had to launch a struggle to liberate their state and themselves from the autocracy. No doubt they were emboldened by the formation of the interim government by Nehru. But they had to be on their guard. The hesitation by the Mysore ruler for one month regarding the installation of a popular ministry naturally made the people apprehensive. They spent anxious moments, particularly after the states ministry under Patel declared that the princes would be allowed internal control except foreign affairs, defence, etc.

The leaders started preparing the people for the last struggle. *Jathas* were planned from different parts of the state to converge at Mysore and the agitation was named 'Mysore Chalo'. The *jathas* were to start on 4 September and converge at Mysore on the thirteenth and start the picketing of the palace to force the Maharaja to grant the responsible government and become a constitutional ruler. The response to the *jatha* was widespread. All classes of people enthusiastically participated. An 'Azad Mysore Sarkar' was established at Hindupur, a border town in the then Madras province. The Mysore government issued shoot at sight orders against the members of the Azad Sarkar. Thousands of satyagrahis were arrested. But the enthusiasm of the people was unprecedented. The authority was totally set at naught. The impact of the struggle was such that the authorities could not even procure enough provisions to feed the inmates of the jails. Villages established parallel governments.[38]

With all options exhausted in the face of the determined struggle put up by people, the government had to bow. The arrested leaders were freed and negotiations started. The government at last gave in ending the movement of anxiety. Mysore shed its autocracy and became a part of the Indian Union with a responsible government.

Despite being a native state, and a subsidiary of the paramount power Mysore is an example of how the forms of struggle evolved for British India could be applied with the same force and validity. This was possible because the Mysore administration despite being 'personal' in theory, did not remain so in practice. There was Rule of Law, a Constitution especially after 1923, and the state remained responsive to popular pressures. Though anti-Congress and against sharing executive authority, the state and its administrators were not autocratic in the real sense of the term. In fact the Congressmen in Mysore found it very difficult to hurl such charges at the government. In fact the responsiveness of the government and the popularity of the princely house were great impediments in the way of the ambitious politicians in Mysore. But neither the responsiveness of the state, nor the difficulties of the Congressmen could endure for long. Once the state administration reached a stage of being responsible and beyond which they could not go without surrendering their own authority, the state Congressmen stood to gain. Once the rulers became ruthless to remain firm in the saddle, the other face of it was exposed to the people of the State and the latter rallied round the nationalist forces. Thus ended the rule of the Princely authority in Mysore.

NOTES

1. Mysore was generally acclaimed as a 'Model State'. See, e.g. *Nagai Neelalochini*, a weekly from Nagapattinam, 9 November 1891, in *Report on Native News Papers* (*RNNP*) hereafter, Tamilnadu Archives, Madras.
2. For details see S. Chandrashekar, 'Reforms and Reactions and the Regime in Mysore 1881-1910', in *QJMS*, no. 2, 1 February 1985, Bangalore, pp. 131-44.
3. Mysore was generally acclaimed as a 'Model State'. See, e.g. *Nagai Neelalochini*, 9 November 1891.
4. For details see Chandrashekar, 'Reforms and Reactions and the Regime in Mysore 1881-1910', in *QJMS*, no. 2, 1 February 1985, Bangalore, pp. 131-44.
5. Lalah Dushkin, 'Non Brahmin Movement in Princely Mysore', unpublished Ph.D. thesis, University of Pensylvania, 1974, p.75.
6. B. Hettne, *Political Economy of Indirect Rule, Mysore 1881-1947*, New Delhi, 1978, p. 179.
7. See for details, Chandrashekar, 'Reforms and Reactions', specially the Introduction.
8. In the early 1890's the more vocal of the assembly members constituted themselves into a Standing Committee to function as a forum when the assembly was not in session and enable the government to consult them in taking vital decisions. The Diwan Seshadri Iyer, who initially encouraged it, later when found them to be critical of him and the administration ignored it totally on enquiry by members as to what had happened to the committee, the Diwan gave this reply. See for details, *Proceedings of the Mysore Representative Assembly for the Years 1890, 1892 and 1893*, p. 1
9. *Karnataka*, an Anglo-Vernacular weekly from Bangalore, 6 January 1891. The editor was D.V. Gundappa, a follower of Gokhale and founder of the Gokhale Institute of Public Affairs at Bangalore.
10. *Census of India*, Mysore, 1921, Lalah Dushkin, 'Non Brahmin Movement', 1974, pp. 38-41. Also Gustafson, 'The Making of Model State, Mysore 1881-1902', unpublished Ph.D. thesis, University of Wisconsin, 1969.
11. Whenever severe 'calamities afflicted they resorted to looting of shops and such other acts which were put down ruthlessly as 'crime' for, e.g. see *RNNP* 1876-8 and 1918-19.

12. S. Sathianadhan, *History of Education in Madras Presidency*, Madras, 1894, p. 3.
13. Dushkin, 'Non-Brahmin Movement', 1974, p. 58.
14. *The Hindu*, 18 March 1887.
15. There is no exaggeration if it is said that no Mysorean paper of the period up to 1910 appeared without an attack on 'foreign Madrasi dominance'. For more bitter of such attacks see *Suryodaya*, 25 June 1897, *Karnataka Prakasika* of 1883-4. Also Gustafson, 'The Making of Model State', 1969, specially the chapter 'Madrasis versus Mysoreans'.
16. *Karnataka Prakasika*, 2 week of May 1886. For details see Chandrashekar, 'Emergence of Native Politics, Mysore 1918-20', *QJMS*, vol. LXXIV, nos. 2-4, April-June 1983, pp. 128-48.
17. *Karnataka Prakasika*, 4 January 1892, 25 July 1892, 12 Sept. 1892, 6 Sept. 1894, 22 June 1896, 30 Oct. 1898, 3 Oct. 1902 (*Vrittantachintamani*), 9 Oct. 1984, 4 Sept. 1995, 15 April 1903, 28 Oct. 1903, 24 and 28 Jan. 1903, *Mysore Vrittantabodhini*, 6 Jan. 1994, 30 June 1894, *Suryodaya Prakasika*, 7 Jan. 1903, 18 Feb. 1903, 24 Dec. 1903, *Suryodaya*, 23 May 1892, 25 June 1897. *Nadegannadi*, 2 May 1903, Nov.-Dec. 1907, etc.
18. *Swadesha Mitran*, 6 and 26 June 1916. *West Coast Spectator*, 22 Jan. 1913. There were two nationalist newspapers representing the extremist and moderate schools of nationalism respectively, opposed entry of native state subjects on the ground that the latter were opposed to the entry of the British India subjects into the state services.
19. For details see Chandrashekar, 'Reforms and Reactions', 1985, Chapter-Ī.
20. Ibid.
21. *Fortnightly Report*, 30 Jan. 1925.
22. Mirza Ismail, 1954, p. 27.
23. Jawaharlal Nehru, *Selected Works*, vol. 4, pp. 192-3.
24. For details see Chandrashekar, 'Reforms and Reactions', 1985, specially the chapter 'Labour Organisation and the State Policy'.
25. Ibid.
26. *The Hindu*, 28 and 31 July 1937.
27. *The Hindu*, 26 October 1937.
28. For details see H.S. Doreswamy, *Horatada Dutta Heijjegalu*, Bangalore, 1972, pp. 26-7.
29. For details of this incident see *F.R.I.*, May 1938, R/I/1670. National Archives of India. *The Hindu*, 29 April 1938. Also for disturbances at Viduraswatha, see *Report of the Committee of Enquiry*, Bangalore, 1938.
30. *The Hindu*, 1 June 1936.
31. For more on this issue see Ms. Eur, F 125/5, pp. 126-427, India Office Library, London.
32. Chandrashekar, 'Reforms and Reactions', 1985.
33. Gandhi, *Collected Works*, vol. 38, pp. 326-7.
34. *The Hindu*, 17 and 24 August 1942.

35. *Madras Mail*, 18 and 20 August 1942.
36. Confidential Records, Home Dept. C.C.115-142, CB. 160-47-2. Judgement delivered by the Special Judge in the Isur Murder Case, State Archives.
37. For details see K. Veerathappa, Isur episode in *QJMS*, vol. LXXIV; no. 3, July-Sept. 1983, Bangalore, pp. 209-20.
38. Doreswamy, *Horatada Dutta Heijjegalu*, pp. 100-10; *The Hindu*, 7 September 1947.

Women and Freedom Movement in Princely Mysore

M. JAMUNA

One of the most important movements for liberating humanity was the movement to free India from the colonial yoke. The movement, which was of epic dimensions, fought in a number of phases, involving various schools of thought, was in course of time able to bring into its vortex every section of the society including women. The extent of participation of this subaltern group in the anti-colonial struggle was indeed significant. Women of every region, presidencies or native states, contributed to the success of the movement. No less significant has been the role played by the women of Mysore, one of the premier states in southern India. The state had undergone a tumultuous experience. The fall of Tipu Sultan in 1799 was followed by the restoration of the state to the old ruling family, the Wodeyars. As in other Princely States, the Raja owed his position to the paramountcy; hence, the state was never independent of British control.

Within thirty years of the installation of Krishnaraja Wodeyar III as the ruler of the state, powers were snatched away, now by the British, on charges of mismanagement, misrule, and tyranny.[1] Hence from 1831 for a period of fifty years, the state fell under direct rule of the British colonialists. In 1881, native rule was once again established with the rendition of the state though indirect rule of the British continued.

Developments in British Indian provinces produced a peculiar effect upon the Princely State. The social reform as well as the political movements in the neighbouring presidency towns did not fail to impress the subjects in native Mysore. Western ideas of Liberalism, Conservatism, and Romanticism had created a ferment in the educated elite in the country. Sections among the English educated became self-conscious when the Christian missionaries attacked the existing social practices and called the Hindu form of worship 'licentious'.[2] Utilitarians like James Mill looked down upon the manners, customs, arts, and sciences of the people as inferior.[3] The new awareness made many of the reformist minded address the social ills prevalent in the society. In the efforts to reform the society the question of women became most central. In order to pacify the orthodox, and the conservatives including the educated among them, all arguments were based on Shastras. The efforts at reform launched in the early years of the nineteenth century continued in the twentieth century.

In making a perusal of the work of the various schools of reformers and thinkers who upheld the cause of women, one cannot fail to notice that no attempt was made to provide a space for her to emerge and carve out an identity for herself. The economic nationalists had exploitation of the country as the basis of their argument,[4] but that women were the 'exploited' in the male dominated society was not their concern, though there existed a close relationship between women and means of production.

With the rise and growth of nationalism in the nineteenth century, no attempt was made to involve them in the political movements. The Indian National Congress (INC) steered clear of any discussion on women and other social issues, as is evident in the speeches of the presidents at various Congress sessions.[5] Moreover, in the political embroil between the Moderates and the Extremists, women's issues got sidelined, though the debate over the betterment of women's position continued outside the portals of INC.

For the extremists political questions were more important than social issues. Not that Tilak was anti-reform per se, but he had his own compulsions. His reliance upon the middle class orthodoxy from whom he drew the greatest support came in the way of supporting women's cause. Therefore, if a few women were found in the sessions of the INC, their presence was merely ornamental. They were in most cases either wives, mothers, or daughters of the male leaders.

The usage of symbols, both historical and mythological like Shivaji, Ganapati, Shakti, Mother Earth, and Gomata in politics by the new ideology acted as a deterrent for the participation of women in the movement. Though many of the symbols were feminine in nature, there was no organic line established with the living mothers. With Ganapati, Shivaji, and Shakti becoming militant symbols, a 'Manly Revival' was generated. This is evidenced in Lajpat Rai saying 'We want our masses to grow in manliness, frankness and in power.'[6] Added to it was the Hindu concept of women and the militant psyche, which failed to accord a role to women. Militancy increased during this phase. Physical training and exercises became a feature. Societies were founded for imputing physical and military training for boys only.[7]

The revolutionaries had a handful of women participating in terrorist activities. Women remained a microscopic minority in the movement either as sympathizers in the early stages or as violent activists in the 1930s when the movement became highly militant.[8] As political issues occupied a centre stage women came to be marginalized and women's issues once again got sidelined. The aggressive revivalism was unable to accommodate and integrate women meaningfully into the movement.

The emergence of Mahatma Gandhi on the national scene made all the difference especially as far as women or other subaltern sections were concerned. The movement for the first time came out of its elitist confines. Gandhi being an objective student of reality felt that to accomplish the goal of freedom, with the participation of all sections of the society, the mode of fight itself had to be different, it had to be socially acceptable. Firstly, it was not to offend the Indian sentiment and secondly, it was to disarm the British colonialists to a state of sheer helplessness. Gandhi realized that fighting the imperialists, who were reputed for their military strength would be a physical impossibility, given the conditions in India. Hence weapons foreign to the imperialists had to be invented. He, thus evolved 'satyagraha', 'non-violence', 'constructive programme', and 'passive resistance'. Such weapons, given Gandhian strategy of struggle could successfully mobilize all sections, especially women for the national cause. It could at the same time bring women out of the sheltered life and they could identify themselves with the national movement. Gandhi was the first to evolve the technique of involving women in the movement.

Describing women as 'sacrifice personified' and 'incarnation of ahimsa' endowed with 'infinite love' and having 'infinite capacity' for sacrificing,[9] Gandhi exhorted them to extend these qualities to the warring world. Through spinning he aimed at instilling confidence, patriotism, and the spirit of freedom in women. Spinning, he said, would not only deliver the country from the imperial yoke, but would give women a 'special status'.[10] All these activities according to Gandhi could be carried out from within the 'domestic sphere'. Gandhi's mode of fight brought an immediate response, as he himself once described ... 'everywhere they have come out of their purdahs and given their blessings. They have instinctively understood the purity of the movement. and that the purity of the pure women in India is hidden in the music of the spinning wheel.'[11]

As his invention did not cut off women from domestic duties, it found acceptance in their male guardians as well. This facilitated the participation of women on a mass scale in the movements. With this the tide of political movement took a swift turn as scores of women became non-violent warriors in the fight for independence.

Speaking of the role of women in a movement as profound as that in Mysore, it may be said the absence of a free spatial mobility had hindered their emergence for years. But the 1920s saw an unprecedented response of women to the calls of the Mahatma. Women of all ages and of different backgrounds enthusiastically joined the anti-colonial movement.

For the study of the role of women of the Princely State of Mysore in the nationalist movement, one is confronted with the total absence of studies, focusing exclusively on women. In fact there are no works available even on the nationalist movement in the state as such. The few available studies have tended to focus broadly on the Freedom movement in Karnataka in general. But for some published papers and unpublished dissertations, there are no major works on the aspect. In the works on the movement in Karnataka, women have been marginalized as the studies have focused broadly on the movement in Karnataka. To mention a few of the well-known works, the earliest is G.S. Halappa, *History of Freedom Movement in Karnataka* in two volumes. Volume II is relevant in as far as the present paper is concerned.[12] Though comprehensive, the work has not attempted to analyse and critically expound the various schools of thought or the various phases of the movement. Women's role has been treated as the sub-topic in this large volume. It makes no attempt to understand the emergence of the various subaltern groups, including women in the fast changing socio-economic-political scenario during the period.

Quit India Movement in Karnataka by S.U. Kamath, is an exhaustive study of the last phase of the Freedom movement in the region.[13] This work also makes no attempt to study women's role exclusively, though women were a major section in the movement as such. The marginalization of their role to only references here and there are the hallmarks of most of the works. The same may be said of Kamath (ed.), *Swatantra Sangramada Smritigalu*[14] brought out in three volumes. They are memoirs and eyewitness accounts of the freedom fighters in Karnataka. All the three volumes put together have about 855 names, out of which only 29 are that of women. Names of some women appear in the narration of certain important events. Otherwise, the mass of women are pushed into invisibility.

The one work exclusively on women freedom fighters is *Women Freedom Fighters in Karnataka* by Sarojini Shintri and K. Raghavendra Rao.[15] It is a biographical sketch of some prominent women of Karnataka. The work classified Chand Bibi, Rani Chennamma and such other queens also as freedom fighters. Consequently, it is in line with contemporary history as only a few women are glorified ignoring the mass of women who were in actual fact the backbone of the movement.

Karnataka Charitre, vol. 7, edited by S. Chandrashekar, is one in the series of the 'Comprehensive History of Karantaka', brought by the Kannada University.[16] The work makes a departure from other studies in as far as adopting not only a wholistic and objective approach, but in treating every section, community, or a subaltern group in the movement by devoting separate chapters to each, including women. This work once again is not a study of the movement in Mysore, but examines it in the broader perspective of Karnataka,

Compared to the women in British India provinces, women of Mysore were rather slow to awaken to the situation. This is primarily because they did not have the kind of exposure women of British India provinces had. Societal restrictions contributed sufficiently to the non-emergence of women into public life. The educated elite of the state were all products of Madras educational institutions and therefore had a good exposure to the socio-political developments there. Yet they failed to create an awakening in the state. Strong conservatism came in the way of a reform movement taking shape in the state.

The growth of nationalism itself had been a slow process in the state. Tilakian influence had been quite profound upon the educated elite of Mysore. A number of newspapers[17] as well as individuals in the state were clearly Tilakite in their thinking, be it over social or political issues. But still a strong movement failed to emerge. This may be attributed to the fact that the rulership was native as well as the kind of progressive image in the state had been built up. The reputation of a 'Model State' had successfully extended beyond the state frontiers. The impression among the nationalists that the subjects in the state were unexploited, living in peace and contentment, also hampered the emergence of a strong movement. Added to these were certain internal political developments, first the 'Mysore for Mysoreans' and the 'Brahmin-non-Brahmin' controversies,[18] which engrossed the minds of a large number of people, in particular the early nationalists.

The state on its part had successfully created a favourable image for itself. Chamarajendra Wodeyar X, the first ruler of the restored state had contributed to the Congress fund. His son and successor, Krishnaraja Wodeyar IV had taken to spinning. A khadi experimental centre was opened by the government at Badavanala, which financed about three hundred weavers.[19] The state with a view to supplement the existing income of the servants at the Chamundi Hill Temple ordered 20 charkhas through the Maramath Department in 1925.[20] The charkhas were purchased from the Khadi Pratishthan at Calcutta, the state also evinced interest in the promotion of khadi, Hindi uplift of downtrodden, and so on. The princes encouraged these activities so long as the interests of the state and the paramountcy remained unaffected as it was to the paramountcy that they owed their existence. The nationalists looked upon the state appreciatively as a benignly administered state and felt no cause for complaints. Mahatma Gandhi went to the extent of calling it a 'Ram Rajya'.[21] But the actual conditions of the subjects behind such a facade was yet to be realized by the nationalist leadership. It was these factors which hindered the growth and emergence of a full-fledged movement in the state until the 1930s.

It was from within such environs that women emerged. Political activities came to be limited to propagating the Gandhian Constructive Programme which had been a decision of the INC. It had been as late as 1921 that the Mysore District Congress had been formed after the Nagpur session. For the women of Mysore, women leaders from British presidencies like Kamaladevi Chattopadhyay, Krishnabai Panjikar, Annie Besant, Sarojini Naidu, and Margret Cousins were of great inspiration. Kamaladevi Chattopadhyay and Krishnabai Panjikar conducted extensive tours in the state. The increased popularity of socialist ideas in the state may be attributed to Mrs Chattopadhyay. For her activities in the state, prohibitory orders had been served in a number of places.[22]

Initially the programme of work adopted by the women of Mysore state, was popularizing spinning, and picketing of foreign cloth stores. Exhibitions were held and lectures delivered to spread the message of khaddar. Gandhi's tours further helped in popularizing them. Gowramma, a noted freedom fighter, while delivering lectures at Mysore on the usefulness of khadi, spoke of the economic drain of the country.[23]

It was in the phase of the Civil Disobedience movement that women got activated. Satyagrahas became a regular feature. Women indeed did full justice to the confidence Gandhi reposed in them. The call of the Mahatma to overcome all fears, be it the bullets, military, police, magistracy or even loosing property, evoked a whole-hearted response. Satyagrahas were staged against confiscation and auctioning of properties of the people by the government. Women satyagrahis staged fast in front of the houses of those who purchased auctioned properties. A praiseworthy act was the efforts of Gowramma in mobilizing women for a satyagraha at Hecche, in Shimoga district, to protest against the Patels' purchase of vessels and a buffalo at the auction.[24] Women worked ceaselessly in the satyagrahas.

A fast unto death was launched by Gowramma, Kaveramma, Duggamma, and Bhagirathamma. This was also for the restoration of the auctioned buffaloes to the owners.[25] Another, well known event was the Tigane satyagraha, held in protest against purchase of three buffaloes. Though women satyagrahis led by Subbamma Jois, were terrorized and attacked by the henchmen of the village head, the women continued undeterred. Many of them—including Mrs Jois were arrested and put in the lockup.[26] Picketing of foreign cloth stores and liquor shops continued ceaselessly.

A new chapter in the history of the Freedom movement in the state began with the emergence of women during the Dhvaja satyagraha at Shivapur in 1938. It was an occasion for women to display their intrepidity. At a meeting of the Congressmen under the chairmanship of T. Siddalingaiah, a decision was taken to hold the first convention of the Mysore Congress on the banks of the Shimsha at Shivapura village near Maddur. Programmes were charted for the flaghoisting and flag salutation ceremony. Fearing disturbances and finding the Congress flag derogatory to the sovereignty of the Mysore State, the District Magistrate of Mysore district ordered imposition of prohibitory orders on the hoisting of the flag. It was also ordered that copies of the letter be served to about twenty-five Congress leaders.[27] Shivapura attracted huge crowds. Nearly twenty to thirty thousand people from different parts of the state gathered at the convention. On 10 April 1938, the Mysore Youth League Conference was held under the Presidentship of Tagadur Ramachandra Rao. It was scheduled to hoist the Congress flag on the next day. As soon as T. Siddalingaiah hoisted the flag and unfurled it he was arrested. H.C. Dasappa then took up the presidentship. This was followed by speeches by leading Congressmen. Subbamma Jois addressed the gathering. Messages of notable national leaders were presented. Two of the messages were from Kamaladevi Chattopadhyay and Umabai Kundapur. In her message Kamaladevi pleaded 'I make a special appeal to you to avoid all superfluous activities and sectarian tendencies but treat always yourself part and parcel of All India National Struggle for Freedom.'[28]

As all the male leaders were arrested one after the other for violating the order, it was women who came forward, occupied the frontline, and exhibited exemplary courage. The determination and fearlessness displayed by the women led by Yashodhamma Dasappa, Subbamma Jois, Bellary Siddamma, Venkamma, Kamalamma, Savithramma is indeed laudable. Bellary Siddamma who had been arrested along with the male leaders had on the previous day urged the youth to rise to the occasion but not to deviate from non-violence.[29] Attacking the repressive acts of the government, she had added, 'one should face situation as warriors. We should win our object or go to "Veera Swarga ...".'[30] Subbamma Jois pleaded with the women not to be disheartened by the arrests of the men instead prepare themselves for a greater sacrifice.[31] The satyagraha was indeed a milestone as far as women were concerned, as for the first time women of Mysore entered in a direct political action by defying the law.

One important event, which further prompted the subjects of Mysore to continue with the struggle, was the Vidhuraswatha tragedy. The meeting called by the Congress had been going on peacefully when all of a sudden bullets were sprayed indiscriminately by the police to disperse the crowd which had assembled. A large number of innocent lives were killed. Very heart-rending was the killing of Gowramma, a pregnant woman. The repressive measures of the state only strengthened the resolve of the people to intensify the struggle.

By now staging satyagraha had become a regular feature in which women played a very significant role. Another well known satyagraha was the Hamilton Building satyagraha. Protests were held against the name 'Hamilton' being given to a police station at Dodpet. Hamilton had been a I.G.P., whose name had become synonymous with cruelty. Responding to the criticism, the Diwan defended the decision to be his own.[32] Tagadur Ramachandra Rao attacking the decisions of the Diwan as unwise called for a satyagraha. As per the decisions of the Mysore Congress Working Committee, the satyagraha commenced on 15 February 1939.[33] Yashodamma Dasappa and T. Sunandainma were the chief organizers.

In April 1939, the second convention of the Mysore Congress began at Vidhuraswatha. Kamaladevi Chattopadhyay camped at Vidhumagar to participate in the All Karnataka Socialists Conference to be held there. On her arrival, orders were issued to her by the Deputy Commissioner to refrain from attending the meeting and delivering speeches.[34] Undeterred she attended the meeting and in a highly provocative speech, said 'the honour of the flag which meant the honour of the country should always be safeguarded'.[35] Next, she addressed the Mysore Socialist Conference and spelt out its aims and objects. The Ladies Conference at Vidhumagar was addressed by Yashodamma Dasappa and Annapurna Thimma Reddy, who urged women to continue the struggle paying no heed to the governmental measures. For the first time the women spoke of the need for a responsible government in the state.

An enthusiastic response was displayed by women in the Forest satyagrahas. The cutting of toddy trees was first launched in the Chitradurga district. The Thiruvennur satyagraha began on 18 September 1939. Bellary Siddamma and Nagarathnamma Hiremath joined in organizing the satyagraha. Women toiled equally with men in the felling of toddy trees. About 5,000 trees were cut in the district.[36] These acts were followed by large-scale arrests. Bellary Siddamma had to undergo imprisonment for 18 months.[37] The movement later spread to Davangere, Tumkur and Sira taluq, where similar responses were received from women.

The passing of the Quit India resolution in August 1942, saw the outbreak of a mass struggle throughout the country. This phase was marked by widespread agitations and violent disturbances. The call for 'Quit India' was soon followed by the arrests of all the leaders. News of the arrest of the Mahatma spread like wild fire. To prevent the movement becoming widespread, the All Mysore Congress Committee, the All Mysore Congress Working Committee and District and City Committees of the Mysore Congress were declared unlawful associations.[38] Hartals were observed almost throughout the state on 9 and 10 August. Students abstained from educational institutions. Demonstrations and *prabhat pheries* were a common site. Everywhere the precisionists shouted 'Quit India' slogans.[39] In a chaotic atmosphere such as this, indiscriminate firing was ordered by the authorities taking a heavy toll of life. Everywhere telephone and telegraph wires were cut, rails were removed, railway stations were attacked, and records were set on fire.

The slogan 'Do or Die' stirred the emotions of women who unhesistantly plunged into the movement. Some of the women leaders went underground. Girl students played a very significant role in helping those who had gone underground. Repressive activities only intensified the movement. Students braved lathi charges and arrests. Intensive campaign of picketing of educational institutions was carried out by them.[40] The students of Maharani's College played a very crucial role in all these activities. The warden of the hostel was asked by the authorities to inform the parents that the 'Girls were not behaving properly and that their wards should be taken back home.'[41] Following this the students resorted to a hunger strike. The strike intensified with the resignation of Kesari Keshavan from the post of lecturer of the college. Meenakshi, Pomiamma, Kamala Sethu Rao, and Komala remained active in picketing of schools and colleges. The message was also propagated in the rural areas.

The most memorable events during the Quit India struggle were those that broke out at Davangere, Shravanabelagola, and Isur. The struggle at

Isur in Shimoga district was the most violent and tragic. The movement began on a peaceful note. Students and children donning Gandhi caps, and dress made of khadi carried the tri-colour national flags. The activities took a violent turn on the visit of the Amildar. Resignations were demanded from him and the police sub-inspector. At the entrance to the village, people even put up a board 'Swatantrya Halli' (Independent village). When the mob forced the officials to remove their hats and wear Gandhi caps, the angered officials fired at the mob. Infuriated, people turned violent and killed both the officials. On hearing the news, the authorities dispatched the military and police to Isur. In order to escape from them people took cover in the forests. But the patrol caught the people and tortured them including the women and the children. Houses were looted and a number of girls were raped. A large number of people including women were arrested. Of the 41 arrested 11 were given death sentence and others were awarded life imprisonment. On appeals made to the High Court, death sentence given to people was reduced to 5, among whom were two girls, Salamma and Parvathamma, aged 14 years.[42]

The Isur episode, an unforgettable chapter in the history of the Freedom movement in Karnataka, remains a testimony to the depth of national consciousness among the rural people of Karnataka.

Women also joined hands with men in labour agitation. In the procession of the labourers organized at Bangalore on 6 September 1942 which carried the coffin of the effigy described as the Defense of India Rules, one of the coffin bearers was Bhagirathamma Chengalradhya. She was arrested and convicted. A number of young girls also participated in the struggle in the form of making arrangements for the striking labourers, providing relief to the families of the labourers.[43]

Many of the girl students responded to the call of the Student Federation to intensify their struggle. When a large procession was carried out in the city of Bangalore, the police detained the girls and took them to their respective homes and advised the parents not to allow their children to take part in such activities.[44] Defying Prohibitory orders, girls along with their classmates assembled at St. Joseph's College, carried broomsticks and buckets to clean the roads at Rissel Market Square.[45] Many of the girl students were also arrested for picketing District Courts in the city of Bangalore. Women at various headquarters committed such acts.

The participation of women in all aspects and phases of the national struggle had been most fascinating as the docile and shy Indian women was transformed into a force that counted in the struggle for freedom. The exemplary courage displayed in the staging of demonstrations, satyagrahas, processions, picketing, and stoically suffering the police excesses, which find no words for description, were beyond the comprehension of the male leaders.

Mahatma Gandhi made possible the coming together of all sections of women—the literate and the illiterate, the urban and rural, the rich and the poor, the old and the young, thus transforming it into a mass movement. Having deep faith in the 'shakti of women' Gandhiji invoked the concept of '*Ardhanari*' and '*Purusha Prakruti*'. 'Shakti' was the moral power, the inner strength of women. Women's physical weakness was transformed into strength. Satyagraha according to him was the weapon of the weak against the strong. He took up items which people were most sentimental about. The symbols were not religious, but found in everyday use salt, a most essential item in everyday life, was also a symbol of opposition of the British Government; cow, a means of livelihood; land, not only a means of living, but an essence of life, visualized as the 'mother' and 'sacred'. Moreover, calling non-violence as a 'moral substitute to war', Gandhi stressed that women had a greater role to play. He said, 'if non-violence is the law of our being, the future is with women'.[46]

Thus, unlike his predecessors when Gandhi accorded a special status to women in the movement, there was an overwhelming response. Every home became a law breaking one. Sacrificing the comforts of their homes women were found either in organizing political activities or behind bars. Many of them entered the prisons with infants in their arms. Those who had been widowed or orphaned felt that the only way to pay tribute to the deceased was by re-dedicating themselves to the movement. Their dedication gave the struggle a new meaning. The British imperialists were astounded by the sudden upsurge of women. They found the Gandhian mode of fight most foreign and it deified femininity. As a Secretary Gen. Smuts had once told Gandhi '. . . I often wish you took to violence like the English strikers and then we would know at once how to dispose of you. But you will not injure even the enemy. You desire victory by self-suffering alone and never transgress your self-imposed limits of courtesy and chivalry. And that is what reduces us to sheer helplessness.'[47] Similar was an impression shared by Gen. Smuts about the Gandhian mode of fight.[48]

The participation of women not only gave the movement a spiritual tone but accorded it a national character and the much needed femininity, for it the movement could really become natural, as nature consists of both *Purusha* and *Prakruti*. It was a combination of both that made the movement complete. There is no exaggeration if it is said that here the movement acquired its real strength. Shakti that is what Indian women are traditionally described as, could be realized only after women came into the struggle.

NOTES

1. *The Mysore Representative Assembly: Its History and Proceedings*, 1903, The Standard Press, Bangalore, 1904, p. xi.
2. *Missionary Records, India,* London, Religious Tract Society.
3. James Nfill, *History of British India,* University of Chicago Press, London, 1975, pp. 233-42.
4. For instance Dadabhai Naoroji as well as Romesh Chandra Dutt.
5. To mention a few:
   Budrudin Tyabji, at the Third Congress, Madras, 1887.
   W.C. Banerjee, speech at the Eighth Congress, Allahabad, 1892.
   Surendranath Banerjee, Eleventh Congress, Poona, 1895.
6. Vijay Chandra Joshi (ed.), *Lala Lajpat Rai: Writings and Speeches*, vol. II, 1920-8, University Publications, Delhi, 1966.
7. *Sedition Committee 1918*, Report submitted by S.A.T. Rowlait, New Age Publications, Calcutta, 1973, p. 2.
8. See for details I. Mallikarjuna Sharma, *The Role of Revolutionaries in the Freedom Struggle: A Critical History of the Indian Revolutionary Movements: 1918-1934,* Marxist Study Forum, Hyderabad, 1987.
9. For details, see M.K. Gandhi, *The Role of Women*, Bharatiya Vidya Bhavan, Bombay, 1964.
10. *Harijan,* 2 December 1939.
11. *Young India*, 22 December 1920.
12. G.S. Halappa, *History of Freedom Movement in Karnataka*, vol. II, Government of Mysore, 1964.
13. Suryanath U. Kamath, *Quit India Movement in Karnataka*, Lipi Prakashan, Bangalore, 1988.
14. Suryanath Kamath (ed.), *Swatantra Sangramada Smritigalu*, Directorate of Kannada and Culture, Bangalore, 1998.
15. Sarojini Shintri and K.Raghavendra Rao, *Women Freedom Fighters in Kamataka*, Karnatak University, Dharwad, 1983.
16. S. Chandrashekar (volume editor), B. Sheik Ali (chief editor), *Karnataka Charithre*, Kannada University, Hampi, 1997.
17. For instance *Sadhvi* and *Deshabhimani*.
18. For details, see Chapter 1, S. Chandrashekar, *Dimensions of Socio-Political Change in Mysore*, Ashish Publications, New Delhi, 1985.
19. Siddanavalli Krishna Sharma, *Gandhi Mathu Karnataka*, Gandhi Smarak Nidhi, Bangalore, 1970, p. 413.

20. Avasarada Hobli File. B II. 156, 1925-7, Karnataka State Archives (hereafter KSA).
21. *Collected Works of Mahathma Gandhi*, vol. 63, Publications Division, Ahmedabad, 1975, p. 468.
22. Secret Special Branch Abstract, 15/39, 22 April 1939 (KSA).
23. G.S. Halappa, vol. 11, p. 632.
24. Ibid., p. 204
25. Suryanath Kamath, *Swatantra Sangramada Smritigalu*, Mysore, 1977, p. 298.
26. Sarojini Shintri and K. Raghavendra Rao, *Women Freedom Fighters*, p. 58.
27. Congress Convention, Shivapura, 1938. In the Court of the District Magistrate, Mysore District, 9 April 1938 (KSA).
28. Ibid, p. 296,
29. *Proceedings of the Mysore Youth League Conference*, held under the auspices of the Mysore Congress Convention at Shivapur, 10 March 1938, Congress Convention, Shivapura, 1938, p. 5 (KSA).
30. Ibid.
31. Short Notes Regarding the Congress Convention, Shivapura, 1938 (KSA).
32. *Sadhvi*, 30 January 1939.
33. Ibid.
34. Congress Convention, Vidhurashwatha, 1939.
35. Ibid.
36. Mysore District, 13 October 1939, 13 January 1940.
37. Letter from the District Superintendent of Police to the District Magistrate, 29 September 1939. Chitradurga Satyagraha (KSA).
38. Review of the Political Situation since 1942, August Disturbances. Confidential, Year 1945-6. Confidential Branch File 12-45-82, no. 86, p. 8 (KSA).
39. Ibid.
40. C.B. File, p.10.
41. Suryanath U. Kamath, *Swatantra Sangramada*, 1988, p. 26.
42. Lakshmi Devi Kadidal in 'Isúru Duranta' (A booklet published by K. Srinivasa, 1946).
43. H.S. Doraswamy, *Horatada Dutta Hejjegalu*, Yodharamelada Prakatane, Bangalore, 1972, p. 81.
44. *The Hindu*, 17 September 1947.
45. Ibid., 25 September 1947.
46. M.K. Gandhi, *Satyagraha*, Navajivan, Ahmedabad, 1958, p. 325.
47. Gandhi, *Satyagraha in South Africa*, Navajivan, Ahmedabad, 1993, p. 295.
48. Ibid.

Regional Identities and the National Movement in Hyderabad and Mysore

VASANT K. BAWA

THE FREEDOM STRUGGLE IN THE STATE IN THE EIGHTEENTH AND NINETEENTH CENTURIES—SOME QUESTIONS

Historians of the freedom struggle writing after Independence tend to assume that most of the rulers who ruled the Indian states were collaborators of the British, and therefore anti-national. However, certain rulers have become heroes of the Freedom struggle, e.g. Tipu Sultan. But Tipu was allied to the French. Is French colonialism more acceptable than British?

The Nizam also employed French troops till just a few months before the battle of Srirangapatnam (1799) when Tipu was defeated and killed. Till the death of Raymond in 1798, the British Resident at Hyderabad was unable to reduce the French influence at the court. Raymond's death triggered off the Nizam's acceptance of alliance with the English East India Company on a permanent basis.

Sikandar Jah (1803-29), the third Nizam, continuously resisted the British pressures to treat him as a 'subordinate ally'. He wanted to appoint Raja Mahipat Ram, a close associate of Raymond as the Diwan, but was not allowed to do so. Instead he was forced to appoint, as de facto Diwan, Raja Chandulal, who had endeared himself to the British by supporting the continuance of the Hyderabad contingent, an armed force whose main virtue was that it gave employment to a large number of European officers. Under the treaty of 1853 the Nizam was forced to cede Berar to the British on account of the arrears of pay of the Hyderabad Contingent, which the Nizam allegedly owed to the East India Company. These dues were, however, questioned by Colonel Davidson, Assistant Resident in Hyderabad at the time, who also worked as Resident from 1857 to 1862.[1]

Meanwhile, Mysore State was going through a strange period of transformation. Purniah, the last Diwan of Tipu was brought back to office by the British and continued till 1812, when Krishnaraja Wodeyar III was invested with full ruling powers. During the two decades that the young Maharaja held power, he appears to have antagonized one of the Paleygars, who led a revolt in the Nagar province (now in Shimoga district). Hettne describes this as a 'peasant revolt'. Taking advantage of the unrest in the state and a provision in the treaty of 1799 permitting temporary takeover of the state in case of misgovernment, the East India Company decided to remove the Maharaja and take over the administration into their own hands.

Although Bentinck, the Governor-General seems to have regretted his decision and proposed to the Court of Directors the restoration of some districts in 1834, the proposal did not meet with the approval of the Home Government. Two successive British administrators Cubbon and Howring, played a major role in the restructuring of Mysore's administration between 1834 and 1870.

Krishnaraja Wodeyar, notwithstanding his ignominious removal from the *gaddi* in 1831, maintained good relations with officials and supported the British during the mutiny. In September 1835 he had been assured by the successor of Bentinck, Lord Auckland, that the British Government would continue in possession of the state of Mysore till some 'salutary rules and safeguards', were introduced to make for a permanent effective government. The matter was reopened by the Maharaja in 1844 but he got no reply to his representation. The invitation extended by the Maharaja to Lord Dalhousie to visit the state in 1848 only resulted in the latter's resolve being strengthened that the British would stick to Mysore, and not bring back the Maharaja.[2]

In spite of Lord Canning's refusal to concede the Maharaja's claim and the exclusion of the Maharaja from the Adoption Dispatch of April 1860 (which came as a great blow to him) the latter continued to press his case, and in April 1892 wrote to Canning's successor, Elgin, pointing out that the 'British rights of conquest (asserted by Canning as the source of their sovereignty over Mysore) are swallowed up in self-imposed obligations'. The creation of the Mysore dynasty was an act which the British themselves could not undo. He also argued for the first time that the Nizam was in fact a party to the treaty and shared the benefits of the right of conquest.

Following a vigorous campaign carried on by the Maharaja from 1844 onwards, the Secretary of State for India took a decision not to annex Mysore and to restore the state provided the adopted son of the Maharaja to the Wodeyar family proved to be capable of governing the country when he came of age. This decision was taken in February 1867 by the

Conservative Secretary of State Lord Cranborne (later Marquis of Salisbury).

The two major states of southern India influenced each other in several ways over two and a half centuries. The most remarkable example of this influence was in the restoration of the Maharaja of Mysore in 1881. We have seen that Cranborne took a decision in 1867 not to retain Mysore as a British colony. This decision was altered by the next Secretary of State Northcote who took a firm decision that the adopted son of Krishnaraja Wodeyar would become the Maharaja of Mysore on reaching his majority in 1881. This was done, subject to the signing of a new treaty by the young Maharaja, which made him and his state completely subordinate to the British Government of India.

The restoration of the Wodeyar dynasty after a gap of 50 years was a remarkable development which requires explanation. Cranborne overruled the powerful lobby of British job-hunters and annexationists (who wanted to convert Mysore into British territory) only on account of the claim put forth by Salar Jang, the Diwan of Hyderabad state in 1866.

Salar Jung's argument was that the Nizam had a rightful claim on the part of the Mysore territory under the partition Treaty of 1799. Therefore if the British proposed to absorb Mysore, the Nizam should be given an equal share in the revenues of Mysore, amounting to Rs. 41.5 lakhs per annum. Cranborne found this claim valid and could see no way of getting around it. In order to avoid increasing the power of the Nizam, he decided that Mysore should not be annexed to the British territories and the Wodeyar dynasty shall be given a chance to succeed.

Salar Jung's actual goal had been to use the claim on Mysore to get back Berar. He did not achieve his goal but his efforts led to the Wodeyars of Mysore being restored to the *gaddi* of that state. There was probably a close coordination between the Mysore and Hyderabad efforts in London in regard to this matter.

It is important to find out Hyderabad was playing a role in the Freedom struggle by challenging the British and seeking to get back Berar. Second, was the restoration of Mysore (a by-product of Salar Jung's policies and those of the Maharaja), a 'progressive' trend or was it a 'reactionary' move, by two antiquated feudal states?

DEVELOPMENTS IN HYDERABAD AND MYSORE: 1880s TO 1940s

The restoration of the Mysore dynasty in 1881 was considered an act of grace by the British Government. The British took advantage of the young

Maharaja's weak position by laying down restrictions which they could not do for other states which were covered by treaties entered into in the early 1800s. The Governor-General was to be the authority on all questions of succession to the throne. And the state was to 'remain faithful in allegiance and subordination, and perform all the duties which may be demanded of them' by virtue of such allegiance and subordination.

The government undertook to protect and defend the state, and the Maharaja to pay an annual revenue in return for being relieved of all military obligations. The Governor-General was to fix the strength of the military force required for internal order, or for the prince's personal dignity, and to direct its enlistment, organization, and equipment. Fortresses were not to be built, a common stipulation; and arms, munitions, or military stores were not to be manufactured or imported without permission.[3]

Moreover, the British administrative reforms were to be preserved by the Maharaja's administration without change. British Indian currency was to be used. The manufacture of salt and opium and the cultivation of poppy were to be prohibited or limited as required by the government of India. Lastly, the Maharaja was told that he should:

> be all times (to) conform to such advice as the Governor-General in Council may offer him with a view to the management of his finances, the settlement and collection of his revenues, the imposition of taxes, the administration of justice, the extension of commerce, the encouragement of trade, agriculture and industry, and any other object connected with the advancement of His Highness's interests, the happiness of his subjects, and his relations to the British Government.

It should be noted that Hyderabad also worked under considerable restrictions in practice, but this pattern was not in accordance with the 'Treaty of Perpetual and General Defensive Alliance' of 1800, which stated that the company's government would 'have no manner of concern with any of His Highness' children, relations, subjects or servants with respect to whom His Highness is absolute'. This provision had been violated at least from the year 1803 when Mir Alam and then Chandulal were first imposed on the Nizam. Thereafter almost every Diwan was appointed in consultation with the British.

Mysore thus emerged as a weak state by virtue of the treaty of 1881. But surprisingly it turned out to be a strong state in practice, in some ways stronger than the Hyederabad of the Nizam. How did this happen?

The first Diwan after the restoration was C. Rangacharlu (1881-3). He had published in England a critique of the 50 years of British rule in

Mysore with which he had been closely associated. This document indicates that he had a mind of his own and was no rubber stamp of the British. Secondly, far in advance of his times, he tried to introduce a representative assembly for Mysore which prepared the ground for an emerging public opinion though not for a popular government.

Rangacharlu served for only two years as the Diwan. His successors, especially Sir P. Seshadri Iyer (1883-1901) and Sir M.Visesvaraya (1912-18) were able to build on his achievements and Mysore came to be known as a 'model state'. Mahatma Gandhi once called it 'Ram Rajya' although he did not share Visvesvaraya's deep commitment to modern heavy industry (which Gandhi considered Satanic).

The next major Diwan was Sir Mirza Ismail (1926-40) who was cast in the same mould as Visvesvaraya—efficient, paternalistic, and committed to modernization and industrialization.

While Mysore was a leader among the Indian states in the twentieth century, Hyderabad had its ups and downs. The sixth Nizam Mahboob Ali Khan (1869-1911) was browbeaten by Curzon to hand over Berar on a permanent basis in 1902. The famine of 1899 and the loan of Rs. 2 crores they had given him enabled the British to assert their will over him and in administrative matters.

The seventh Nizam Mir Osman Ali Khan (1911-48) after an initial period of promise as an administrator, became known as a taker of bribes, and was accused, not without reason, of favouring the Majlis-e-Ittehad-ul-Musalmeen which sought to enforce Muslim rule in the state.

It was the British intervention of 1926 which brought the administration of Hyderabad to some level of stability. But the emerging struggle for political power after the expected withdrawal of the British, created a situation which brought the state to a serious crisis and led to the police action by India in September 1948.

SOME TENTATIVE FINDINGS

There are several propositions to be put forth, which can serve as hypotheses deserving further exploration by research scholars.

First although the treaties with Hyderabad and Mysore were entered into at the same time (1800), the British regarded the Nizams as theoretically on a footing of equality, whereas the Maharajas of Mysore were clearly subordinate, having been brought to power after the death of Tipu. Nevertheless, both the states were treated alike, as subordinates. In Hyderabad, not only the ruler, but the Diwan as well was appointed with

British consent. In Mysore, the Maharaja was deposed by the British in 1831 without a just cause.

Second, both Mysore and Hyderabad went through periods of strong British influence. In Mysore the 50 years direct British administration was followed by the administration of a series of competent Diwans under a benevolent Maharaja. From 1853 to 1883 including a long tenure as Regent (1869-83), Salar Jung-I, introduced a British India pattern of administration in the state. However, the sixth Nizam Mahboob Ali Khan's rule after he attained majority (1884-1911) proved disappointing. The paigah nobles and Maharaja Kishen Pershad (who succeded Salar Jung-I and -II as Diwan) lowered the standard of administration. Many thought the British were only waiting in the wings for the state to fall into their lap when the last Nizam came to the *gaddi* in 1911.

Third, the Maharajas of Mysore and his Diwans played a dual game of supporting the Congress at the all-India level but suppressing popular revolt at the local level in the state. This created a public opinion akin to that in British India which weakened the Maharaja's bid for independence in 1947. In Hyderabad on the other hand there was for a long time no cohesive policy on the part of the people of the state for self-government or for merger in India. Linguistic identities developed after the suppression of the Hyderabad political conferences in the early 1920s. A strong Mulki movement (partly based on anti-outsider feeling) was weakened. When the Nizam's Subjects League collapsed in the mid-1930s, all-India communal parties had a strong impact in the 1930s. The State Congress came too late (1938) and was too weak to make the kind of impact the Mysore State Congress did in Mysore.

Fourthly, the Nizam's government, unlike Mysore, was saddled with the albatross of All-India Muslim League's influence as well as the Majlis-e-Ittehad-ul-Musalmeen. Thus the communal issue weakened the cohesiveness of the state. The demand for linguistic states arose after the emergence of Hyderabad State in 1950.

NOTES

1. V.K. Bawa, *The Nizam between the Mughals and the British*, S. Chand, New Delhi, 1986, pp. 147-9.
2. M. Shama Rao, *Modern Mysore*, pp. 479-551.
3. *Scraps of Paper: India's Broken Treaties, Her Princes, and the Problem*, Ernest Benn, London, 1930, pp. 226ff.

Peasant Resistance in the Princely State of Travancore, 1850-1939

K.A. MANI KUMAR

By the middle of the nineteenth century the agrarian conditions in British provinces had undergone rapid changes leading to pauperization of the peasantry. In consequence, peasant struggle began to erupt in a number of regions that remained under British colonial rule. It was felt at that time that a nationalist government would have handled the situation differently, initiating some decisive steps in favour of the suffering peasantry. Therefore, one becomes curious to know the contemporary developments in the realm of agriculture in a Princely State. In this paper, the agrarian conditions and peasant resistances in the Princely State of Travancore is attempted in order to bring out the marked distinction between colonial and native rule.

Travancore was reckoned as the strongest ally of the British in the later part of the eighteenth century. In view of the ever threatening invasion of Tipu Sultan, the state had entered into an agreement with the East India Company in 1788. The agreement reached was formally confirmed in a treaty signed in 1795, by which the company agreed to protect Travancore from all foreign enemies. Later, based on another treaty concluded in 1805, Travancore made an annual payment of Rs. 8 lakhs for a British subsidiary force with a Resident.[1] Under the British tutelage, the Raja of Travancore subjugated all chieftains within the state and converted all the landed properties of the conquered chieftains into sircar (state owned) lands known as *pandarvaka* or the ruler's property.[2]

Following the revolt of Velu Thampi the Prime Minister of Travancore, against the British, the British Resident-cum-Diwan of Travancore, prompted by financial consideration, acquired the properties of 378 important and wealthy temples for the state in 1812 which amounted to 1,00,000 acres of private lands, a revenue of Rs. 4 lakhs, all of which became sircar lands. Thus, by the middle of the nineteenth century the state had become the chief *jenmi* (landlord) and possessed nearly 80 per cent of the cultivated land, in addition to waste and forest lands.[3] The remaining 20 per cent of the cultivated land was owned by a small number of landlords who enjoyed freehold or paid a nominal tax to the state called *rajabhogam*. These landlords were mainly Brahmins, attached to temples and descendants of local chieftains.[4] This was in contrast to Malabar, where there was no government land, where all the cultivable waste, fallow, and forest lands had been declared as private property.[5]

The first agrarian outbreak in Travancore can be traced back to 1809 when Velu Thampi mobilized the peasants for his anti-imperialist struggle. Though Velu Thampi represented the old feudal interests, though his was a pro-Maharaja revolt, in his effort to achieve a massive mobilization he involved the peasants in a big way. In his famous Kundara proclamation, he made a pointed reference to the interests of peasants that were at stake then. He said, '. . . if they [British] are allowed to use their traditional methods of trickery to bring our country into their hands, they will . . . measure every plot of land and every house site and levy excessive land tax, etc. . . .'[6] In his rebellion against the British, Velu Thampi commanded a following of 30,000 of his army men and even larger number of cultivators.[7]

Logan, the investigating officer into the Mopla ourbreaks of 1836, reported that indiscriminate eviction and enhancement of rent resorted to by the *jenmies* constituted the root cause of distubrances. Although the Travancore situation did not develop into an explosive one, there was certainly serious discontent among the agricultural class. The steady increase of population and the absence of any other profession excepting agriculture had led to pressure on land. The ever growing demand for cultivable lands prompted the *jenmies* to let their lands to the highest bidder. If a tenant failed to comply with the *jenmies*, demand for larger sum as advances or larger rents, he was promptly turned out of his holding.[8]

It was only under this distressing situation, that a royal edict was promulgated in 1829. According to it, courts were instructed to regulate the unreasonable evictions of tenants by *jenmies*. The relevant provision of the Act read: 'In all suits of this nature (for eviction) decided, filed or which may be hereafter be preferred, the courts maintain the established usage in the country, viz., that the tenant should pay the *jenmi* his usual, ordinary, extraordinary fees, and the *jenmi* receive the same and let the tenant remain in possession and enjoyment of the property'.[9] But the Travancore Courts did not act according to the royal instruction. The judiciary in Travancore represented the vested interest as its members were mostly drawn from landowning Brahmin class. Therefore, the *jenmies* could carry on their policy of harassment of their tenants.[10]

In the above backdrop, the movement for tenancy reforms started gaining ground. Those who showed the way in taking to a path of struggle were the *kanamdars* who were well-to-do peasants in the state. *Kanam* was the most common traditional tenure in Travancore in which the tenant (*kanamdar*) paid a fixed rent, about a third of the crop, to the landlord in addition to a cash renewal fee every twelve years.[11] The *jenmies* oppression and the judiciary's anti-tenant proclivity forced the *kanamdars* to adopt an agitational approach to get their grievances redressed. The *jenmies* were considered the oppressors of the peasantry and became the target of attack. The *kanamdars* formed associations, led deputations, held meetings, and conducted agitations. The government was finally moved and it issued first a Pattam proclamation on 2 June 1865, which conferred full ownership rights on the tenant cultivators of sircar lands. The notification issued by the Raja stated: 'The ryots holding these lands, may regard them fully as private, charitable, saleable and otherwise transferable property'.[12]

The state also conferred occupancy rights on *kanam* tenure by issuing another proclamation in 1867. But there were certain loopholes in the proclamation and hence it could not be implemented. The government, thereupon, appointed a commission to suggest measures to rectify the defects. On the basis of the recommendation of the commission, the Jenmi-Kudiyan Act was passed in 1896 that secured not only permanent occupancy rights for the *kanam kudiyans* but also provided other relief in the form of fixation of rents and fees.[13] The tenants of sircar lands and *kanamdars*, thus, gained some benefits as an outcome of their agitations. But those benefited were Nairs or other high caste Hindus and high ranking Christians and Muslims. The large mass of peasants, the *verumpattamdars*, tenants-at-will, and landless labourers were, however, kept out of their movement. *Verumpattam* was a common tenure, occupied mainly by the low ranking cultivating caste of Ezhavas. The lowest untouchable castes such as Pulayas and Parayas formed the landless labourers.[14]

Meanwhile, the impact of the policy of the colonial government was felt in Travancore. The Madras government had removed the duty on paddy in 1861 and consequently large quantities of rice from other colonial territories were imported into Travancore. On account of large-scale imports of rice, the prices fell sharply and in consequence paddy cultivation was seriously affected in the state. The government's encouragement for cultivation of cash crops around this time prompted the peasants to opt for coconut cultivation. As the Travancore State Manual pointed out, in 1936-7, the acreage under coconut came a close second, with its 5,77,418 acres, to paddy which covered 6,63,184 acres.[15] The state was also forced to promote plantation crops during this period. The government offered liberal tax concessions, provided forest and waste lands either as grants or at very low prices, one rupee per acre, and constructed roads connecting hill regions with trading centres. The export of coffee in 1853-4 was to the value of Rs. 6,553. It went up to Rs. 1,87,875 in the next 76 years. There was no export of rubber, tea, and cardamom in 1853-4. But by 1937-8, the value of exports of their commodities had increased to Rs. 74,89,464, Rs. 2,25,61,823 and Rs. 33,01,502 respectively.[16] The process of commercialization of agriculture that took place in Travancore facilitated the land changing hands from agriculturists to non-agriculturists. The non-cultivating proprietors who were rent receivers increased from 18,728 in 1923 to 23,519 in 1931 an increase of 26 per cent. The census report of 1931 observed that 20 per cent of the land transferred in a year from agriculturists to non-agriculturists.[17]

As we have seen, the tenants and the *kanamdars* who were protected by the state intervention belonged to the upper castes of Namboodris and Nairs. Therefore the agrarian poor drawn from lower castes like Ezhavas and Pulayas developed caste consciousness that resulted in their organizing themselves into caste organizations. The formation of the caste organizations of Ezhavas and other untouchables and the movement they conducted against caste discrimination laid the foundation for the future peasant movements in Travancore. On this E.M.S. Namboodiripad writes: 'It is a historical fact that one of the first forms in which the peasant masses rose in struggle against feudalism was in the form of caste organizations. In spite of the fact that they had no clear perspective of changing the social order, of breaking the backs of the landlord as a class, of ending the rent system and redistributing lands the Nair peasantry rose against the Brahmin *jenmies* and the Ezhava peasantry against their caste-Hindu oppressors including the Nairs. . . . The peasants who were rose by and organized in caste organization in the early years of the twentieth century were subsequently brought into the class organisation of the peasantry in the thirtees and the forties.'[18] This is very much true. The Pulayas, for instance, fought for eradication of untouchability under the auspices of their caste organization 'Sadhujana Paripalana Sangam'. When they struck work in 1907-8, their demands included increase in wages and job security, apart from seeking admission to their children in the existing schools.[19]

It is to be noted that the tendency to form caste associations was not confined to the Ezhavas and the Pulayas.[20] Even the Nairs and the Namboodris formed their respective caste associations. The caste organizations in Travancore, while struggling for equal treatment, also pressed for the reform of the family inheritance system. Travancore was first state to promulgate legislation on partition of joint families into different sub-families called *thai-vazhees* (matrilineal) or on an individual basis if any family or the majority members comprising a sub-family asked for it. The legislation was followed by the Travancore Ezhava Regulation of 1925, the Nanjalnad Vellala Regulation of 1926 and the Travancore Malayala Brahmin Regulation of 1931.[21] These enactments led to the partition of joint family properties.

The amendment to the Jenmi-Kudiyan Act effected in 1932 converting the *kanams* into peasant proprietors with the only obligation of paying *jenmikara*, the computed value of the rent due to the *jenmi*. Besides, the inflation of the post-War years and the great depression of 1930s began to seriously disrupt the joint family system. Because of commercialization of agriculture, land had already become a commodity. The changed land relations on account of legislation on *kanam* tenures and laws on joint family system, the post-War situation and the impact of the great depression, had created a condition in which anybody who had enough cash in his possession could become a landlord.[22] In Travancore Christians (mostly Ezhavas) and Muslims were engaged in trade and processing of local agricultural products. These communities took advantage of the transfer of land and the Christians in particular, acquired large acres of land in Travancore with their gains from the trade.[23] In view of all these developments, land ceased to be the preserve of a few feudal families and in the process the legitimacy of traditional caste discrimination was undermined.

In Travancore, to match the policy of the Congress, no interference of the nationalists in the internal affairs was permitted. The Congress had stated that the struggle was only against the Britain and not against the Indian rulers. In view of the decision that the national movement should not interfere in the internal affairs of the Indian states, the cultivating and landless peasants were not initially drawn into politics in Travancore. Politics in the Travancore state, therefore, revolved around castes.

Travancore politics of the twentieth century was a succession of struggles by a coalition of excluded communal groups. First, it was the coalition of Christians, Ezhavas, and Muslims against the Nairs. In the 1931 Legislative Assembly, of the 23 seats, the Nairs with a sixth of the population had 15 seats, Ezhavas with an equal population had none, Muslims none, Christians with double the Nair population had only 4 seats.[24] So, the Ezhavas, Muslims, Christians began to agitate by boycotting the next elections. They won some quotas of assembly seats and civil service positions. The Maharaja antagonized the Nairs by appointing an authoritarian Diwan C.P. Ramaswami Aiyar, whose high-handedness drove many Nairs into the opposition. The result was that Travancore State Congress was formed in 1937 to fight for civil rights and a responsible government. In this way, the Travancore peasants' plunge into politics occurred through the communal organizations. At this juncture, A.K. Gopalan and a few others mobilized the peasants in Alleppey that led to the formation of the Travancore Agricultural Labourers' Union in 1939. The history of the Travancore Agricultural Labourers' Union, to a great extent, is part of the history of Communist movement in Kerala.[25]

Three important points emerge out of the study. First, the peasants in the Princely State of Travancore gained protection and fixity of tenure much earlier than their counterparts in British provinces. Second, commercialization of agriculture attempted by the British turned out to be a great success, transforming thoroughly the land relations in the state. This had a definite bearing on social relations. Third, when deprived of their legitimate role in the political life of the state, in view of the Congress decision not to fight the native rulers, the peasants began to organize themselves prominently. This caste identity vitiated the political climate of the Kerala State in the post Independence period.

NOTES

1. *Travnacore Administration Report for 1933-34*, p. 4.
2. T.C. Varghese, *Agrarian Change and Economic Consequences: Land Tenures in Kerala, 1850-1960*, New Delhi, 1970, pp. 31-3.
3. Ibid., pp. 30-45.
4. T.K. Oommen, *From Mobilisation to Institutionalisation: The Dynamics of Agrarian Movement in 20th Century Kerala*, Bombay, 1985, p. 65.
5. E.M.S. Namboodiripad, *Kerala: Society and Politics—An Historical Survey*, New Delhi, 1984, p. 86.
6. Ibid.
7. Kathleen Gough, 'Indian Peasant Uprisings', in A.R. Desai (ed.), *Peasant Struggles in India*, p. 97.
8. T.K. Velu Pillai, *Travancore State Manual*, vol. III, p. 161.
9. Quoted in T.C. Varghese, *Agrarian Change and Economic Consequences*, pp. 31-2.
10. Ibid., pp. 65-6.
11. Kathleen Gough, 'Peasant Resistance and Revolt in South India', in A.R. Desai (ed.), *Peasant Struggles in India*, p. 719.

12. T.C. Varghese, *Agrarian Change and Economic Consequences*, pp. 64-5.
13. Ibid., pp. 56-7.
14. Kathleen Gough, *Peasant Resistance and Revolt in South India*, p. 719.
15. T.K. Velu Pillai, *Travancore State Manual*, vol. III, pp. 352-60.
16. B.A. Prakash, 'Agricultural Development of Kerala from 1800 A.D. to 1980 A.D.: A Survey of Studies', working paper no. 2 of Centre for Development Studies, Trivandrum, June, 1987, p. 14.
17. G.K. Lieten, 'Nature of Travancore's Economy Between the Two World Wars', *Journal of Kerala Studies*, vol. II, March 1975, pp. 107-11.
18. E.M.S. Namboodiripad, *Kerala: Society and Politics*, pp. 94-6.
19. T.K. Oomman, *From Mobilization to Institutionalisation*, pp. 62-3.
20. Ezhavas formed Sri Narayana Dharma Paripalana Yogam (SNDP) in 1903.
21. T.C. Varghese, *Agrarian Change and Economic Consequences*, pp. 100-1.
22. G. Parameswaran, *The Peasant Question in Kerala*, Bombay, 1951, pp. 11-12.
23. T.C. Varghese, *Agrarian Change and Economic Consequences*, p. 107.
24. Henry C. Hart & Ronald J. Herring, 'Political Conditions for Land Reform: Kerala and Maharashra', in Robert Eric Frykenburg (ed.), *Land Tenures, and Peasants in South Asia*, New Delhi, 1977, pp. 258-9.
25. K.C. Alexander, 'Emergence of Peasant Organisation in South India', in *Economic and Political Weekly*, vol. 15, no. 26, 28 June 1980, pp. 104-72.

The Struggle for a Responsible Government in Travancore, 1938–1947

K.K. KUSUMAN

The Haripura session of the Indian National Congress in 1938 was crucial for the native states; they had to search for a new organization and a flag to carry on the struggle for responsible government, delinking their activities with the Freedom movement in British India. It provided the backdrop for the genesis of state Congresses in the native states. The Princely State of Travancore too identified a name for its organization—the Travancore State Congress—with Pattom Thanu Pillai as president. Founded on 25 February 1938, the State Congress at the very outset, as a forum of popular will, demanded a new orientation in the administrative framework of the state, in which the Diwan's absolute executive right, under the bulwark of royalty, was trampling the political and civil rights of the people. The State Congress activists, assuming new vigour and strength, thanks to the merger of the Abstentionists[1] with the State Congress, pressed for restraining the absolute and autocratic powers of the Diwan. While the State Congress wanted to convert the legislature of the state as a forum for taking decisions on all important political and economic matters of the state, the Diwan Sir C.P. Ramaswamy Aiyar, preferred it to be a venue for discussions only; decision-making and its implementation, he thought, should be his prerogative. A determined State Congress and an adamant Diwan stood face to face—a show down could not be averted. The Congress, actually, had a comprehensive programme to achieve, viz.

(1) freedom of press and associations;
(2) promotion of communal harmony;
(3) protection of the industrial and agricultural workers;
(4) economic prosperity of the state;
(5) attainment of legitimate place for the state in the All India Constitutional Scheme, etc.

Soon after launching the State Congress, leaders indulged in a very effective propaganda work; meetings were held in various parts of the state. The political aims of the state virtually clashed with the office of the Diwan, where real powers had been concentrated. Hence political meetings and propaganda of the State Congress were viewed with due disregard by the Diwan.

The Working Committee of the State Congress on 25 February 1938, took the momentous decision of submitting a memorial to the Maharaja, Sri Chithira Thirunal, in which the administrative lapses, irregularities, etc., had been enumerated. This was not all—the Congress wanted to dispense with the service of the Diwan in Travancore and in his place a cabinet of ministers responsible to legislature must be formed.[2] The political overtone and implication of the memorial was well understood by the Diwan; he sensed danger lurking under his very nose. Also he was very much incensed at the personal allegations levelled against him. As a retaliation, it is said, pro-Diwan elements in the state caused disturbances in the meetings of the Congress and assaulted Congress activists and leaders.[3] Besides, the government machinery too turned against the State Congress and its supporters, the vernacular press, etc. Congress meetings were banned and licenses of certain papers were cancelled. The *Kaumudi*, edited by C. Kesavan, a Congress leader thus incurred the displeasure of the government—its license was cancelled and deposit forfeited. The *Malayala Manorama*, another daily which publicised Congress activities and criticized the government was warned. *Malayali*, *Malabar Advocate*, etc., were also unfavourably treated. But those papers which supported the Diwan and the government were properly pampered.

Simultaneous with repressive measures, the government was keen on creating a few puppet organizations which supported it and the Diwan. The origin of the State Peoples' League, Travancore National Congress, Loyalist Union, etc., have to be understood in this background. Thus, Congress and its leaders were systematically heckled by the Diwan and his henchmen. But these measures were inadequate to emasculate the Congress activities.

To press its demands, on 3 August 1938 the State Congress decided to launch a Civil Disobedience movement. A deputation of the State Congress leaders met Gandhi and sought his guidance for the proposed struggle and the latter advised for the observance of non-violence and discipline. He authorized Rajkumari Amrit Kaur to discuss the matter with the Diwan and patch up the differences between the Congress and the government, but the mission was a failure. The State Congress then took the decision of starting the Civil Disobedience movement on 26 August 1938.

On 25 August the government promulgated the Criminal Law Amendment Act I and X of 1938 by which Congress activities could be effectively curbed. Fundamental rights were abrogated and the Congress was banned. The Youth League, a radical forum of the youngsters in the State Congress, too was banned.

However, ban and restrictions could neither deter nor debilitate Congress activities. Leaders violated ban orders, addressed public meetings, and courted arrest. There were enough police excesses to weaken the morale of the leaders and frighten the people who were in sympathy with Congress propaganda. Protest meetings at Trivandrum and Neyyattinkara were followed by violent incidents—the handiwork of the police. Soon after the firing at Neyyattinkara, an attempt was made for an understanding between the State Congress leadership and the government, but it was in vain.

At this stage Gandhi intervened. He felt that the establishment of responsible government, the cause for which the State Congress was formed need not be mingled with the removal of the Diwan as a pre-condition. Hence he wanted the State Congress leadership to withdraw the memorial against the Diwan. But the Congress leaders in prison, after discussing the issue, decided otherwise; they were not convinced of the relevance of Gandhi's stand at that stage.

Bypassing the norms of non-violence irate mob in certain places indulged in damaging public properties and violently clashed with the police. At Chenganoor the mob turned violent, on hearing the arrest of the Congress leaders. This was the origin of the 'Chenganoor Waging War Case'.[4] Kadakkal-Kallara-Pangoda riots too were violent. Here the grievances of the local people, over the clandestine dealings in the collection of toll in the local markets of these places, between the contractors and the local government officials were taken up by local State Congress activists. While they effectively challenged the officials and the machinery of the government the latter could not submit meekly. Police and the military had to co-ordinate their effort in checking violent riots in these places. Though the State Congress leadership as such had not provided the necessary directive for these riots, individual Congressmen of the locality had come to the rescue of the local people and provided timely leadership. Kadakkal-Kallara-Pangoda riots are considered an important phase in the struggle for responsible government in the State. State Congress activities meanwhile caught the all India attention. The AICC and Subhas Chandra Bose congratulated the people of Travancore for braving the oppression of the government.[5] As a token of sympathy for the State Congress worker, and volunteers. *Jathas* started from various points of the Madras State.

Meanwhile, to seek the release of prisoners, it was decided to organize an All Travancore Volunteer Jatha on 23 October, the birthday of the Maharaja. However, some of the prisoners were released on the previous day. But as decided, the *jatha* of volunteers under the leadership of Akkamma Cheriyan, the twelfth 'dictator', made an unsuccessful attempt to meet the Maharaja on 24 October Pattom Thanu Pillai, the president, announced the suspension of the Civil Disobedience movement in view of the release of the prisoners.

However, the suspension of the Civil Disobedience movement, on the ground of releasing a few prisoners had not enough justification; even the ban on the Congress and the Youth League had not been lifted by the government. Hence the Working Committee of the Congress evaluated the situation and ventured for a 'direct action', before which necessary spadework had to be done. The president and other prominent leaders were to tour the state and communicate with the people on all outstanding political issues.

Gandhi, repeatedly pointed out to the State Congress leadership on the propriety of withdrawing the memorial of May 1938 in which the personal allegation against the Diwan had been levelled. The argument of the State Congress leaders against this did not convince him. Finally, to calm down the situation and sooth the wounded pride of the Diwan the State Congress decided to withdraw the personal allegation against the Diwan. But it had no effect on the government and this was evident when the Congress decided to hold its annual conference at Vattiyoorkkavu, a suburb of Trivandrum, on 22-3 December 1938.

The District Magistrate, Trivandrum issued a ban order against the proposed conference. However, the Congress decide to defy the ban order. Breaking the police cordon people managed to reach the venue, where the conference was held. Even though the meeting was not disturbed, many leaders of the State Congress were arrested on the next day. However, the conference had taken certain momentous decisions:

(1) holding of meetings, violating prohibitory orders;
(2) distribution of prohibited literature;
(3) picketing of liquor shops;
(4) withdrawal of deposits from the postal savings bank;

(5) offering satyagraha before the palace;
(6) non-payment of taxes.

The withdrawal of the memorial did not tally with the sentiment of the Youth League activists. They openly criticized the State Congress[6] leadership and submitted another memorial to the Maharaja in which the charges against the Diwan were repeated. Now the government turned towards the Youth League with further repressive measures. The State Congress leaders also were disappointed over the vindictive attitude of the government even after the withdrawal of the memorial. Meanwhile, to activate the people, R. Sankar, the acting president of the Congress, suggested the branch committees to concentrate on the temperance programme. Dissatisfied with the slow and sluggish policy of the Congress, the Youth League threatened a radical direct action, independent of the Congress. The threat of the Youth League and the no-change in policy of the government forced the Congress leadership to act. It held a session from 17-20 January 1938 and gave six weeks time to the government to mend its ways and meet some of the immediate demands of the Congress, the non-fulfilment of which, it was made clear, would lead to an open agitation.[7] It was subsequently decided that the 'direct action' would be commenced on 25 March 1939. But it never materialized owing to the intervention of Gandhi. The advice of Gandhi certainly demoralized the Congressmen and this was followed by a period of lull in the Congress activities.[8] Gandhi suggested that the State Congress leadership should enter into dialogue with the government. But the Diwan made it clear that the government was not prepared to talk on responsible government; also he expressed his disapproval of the State Congress seeking outside help and guidance. The State Congress obviously disagreed with this position of the Diwan.

The future of the State Congress to pursue a dynamic and consistent policy proved to be costly—enthusiasm of the people gradually dwindled. Meanwhile, some of the communities like the Ezhavas developed a feeling that their association with the State Congress activities has been viewed with enormous vengeance by the government and this had brought those communities to a standstill position so far as their progress was concerned. These communities slowly got alienated from the Congress and finally began to support the government.[9] Some of the State Congress leaders, were meanwhile, seduced by the government. Enamoured of offices, they left the Congress. The State Congress now faced an unprecedented crisis.

The setback to Congress activities provided the background for the rise of Leftist and Trade Union movements in the state. Workers of various trades formed unions under the leadership of the Communist Party.

The Quit India movement and the arrest of Gandhi had their reverberations in Travancore too. By organizing protest meetings against the arrest, the State Congress leadership thought of resuscitating political activities in the state. The students also reacted in a sensible and disciplined manner. But these efforts did not activate the rank and file of the party. However, the State Congress could not remain idle. Hence it harped on a 'constructive programme'. The ravages of the Second World War brought about an acute shortage of food. The party activists tried to provide succour to the poor by the distribution of rice and clothes. Propagation of khaddar was another item of the constructive programme.

The Second World War provided the Communist Party an opportunity to get rid of its stigma and to befriend the government—an aftermath of the joining of the Soviet Union on the side of the Allied Powers. Now it could function openly both in British India and in the native states. In Travancore, the party made much headway in the labour front. In the Alleppey-Shertallai belt it could command the support of the majority of the people and the workers. The unstinted loyalty of the workers and the tenants of these areas, who were victims of capitalists and landlords goaded the party to get embroiled in an adventure—an armed confrontation with the government.

The Alleppey-Shertallai area was known for its coir based industries and factories, where the labour was overwhelmingly dominated by the Ezhavas, who were then socially backward. The Palayas came next in manual labours of other kinds, especially the work in paddy fields. Hence these two caste groups mainly formed the class group in the region, and in Kerala in general. There were certainly a few members of the other socially backward Hindus and economically poor Christians too who worked in the coir factories. The factory workers were systematically exploited by the owners. Some of the landlords of the area were caste Hindus and they owing to casual reasons, trampled the Ezhavas and Palayas, in which the latter communities were seething with discontent. The social emancipation measures of Sree Narayana Guru and Ayyankali had imparted a new life to these sections of the society. Their outbursts against socio-economic exploitation found a confluence with Communist ideology. The Ezhavas who were already under the spell of the Sree Narayana movement found in Communism, a method of retaliating the caste Hindu landlords and other vested interests of the area. The Communist Party superbly exploited the situation and succeeded in organizing the workers of this region, as mentioned earlier, under the trade unions. The party thus assured an alarming strength, creating ill-will among the capitalists and landlords on the one hand and the oppressive government on the other.

The political situation of the state and of British India provided the scope to the Communist Party to take cudgels against the Diwan who remained obdurate in spite of the State Congress agitations for the past several years. The ravages of the Second World War and the concomitant scarcity of essential commodities, spiralling prices, etc., provided the party the necessary economic background to react and consolidate its position among the working class. It chalked out a two-faced programme, one having economic urgency as far as the workers were concerned, and the other, with political overtones. The various labour unions under the party were prepared to press their demands. The workers of the coir factories were the vanguards of the venture.

Punnapra, a coastal village, a few kilometres south of Alleppey town, was dominated by fisherman caste, mainly Latin Catholics, who were exploited by the Church and the rich owners of boats and nets. The hopeless fishermen too found an asylum in the Communist Party. Workers of other trades also were brought under the framework of trade unionism with affiliations to the Communist Party. Thus the party had a solid foundation in Alleppey-Shertallai region.

The formation of trade unions and the attempts of their leaders to bargain on wages and service conditions with factory owners and landlords irked the sentiments of the latter; they sought the assistance of the government, and its agency, the police, to tackle the situation. The collusion of the vested interests with the government goaded the workers to form volunteer camps, where they received training to evade bullets. The party mobilized the services of ex-servicemen in this connection.

Meanwhile, the workers listed some of the economic oriented demands along with certain political demands. Among the political demands the termination of Diwan's rule and monarchical system were also included. These radical demands were unacceptable to the Diwan and the government. However, the Diwan was prepared to concede all the economic demands of the workers.

On 24 October 1946, workers, tenants, and party sympathizers held a procession at Alleppey. This ended in shooting and mass killing of workers and volunteers of the workers' camps. More than two dozens of policemen were also killed. On 27 October it was staged once again at Vayalar, a place in Shertallai taluq, where a few volunteer camps had been formed.[10] Here the number of casualties on the side of the workers was alarmingly greater. Thus the move to dispense with Diwan's rule sustained a setback, but the party could cash out of it later on.

It was a fact that C.P. Ramaswamy Aiyar, with the approval and knowledge of the Maharaja, tried to avail a constitutional convenience or choice given by the British Government in India on the eve of Independence. When the British Paramountcy lapsed the Indian states were given the option either to join the Indian Union, or Pakistan, or to remain independent. It was this offer of the British which caught the imagination of the Diwan to think on the like of an 'Independent Travancore'. The Travancore State Congress, naturally opposed this move. On 27 January 1947, the proposed new constitution of Travancore, under the scheme of an 'Independent Travancore' was published. Under the new Constitution too the absolute powers of the Diwan, unrestricted by the legislature, continued as before. The State Congress had to step up its agitation in this background and it continued as before.

On 11 June 1947 C.P. Ramaswamy Aiyar made a formal announcement: 'Travancore would assume and maintain an independent status after the tranfer of power by the British Government and the lapse of paramountcy'.[11] In July, the Maharaja actually issued a proclamation creating an 'Independent Travancore'. The Diwan even met Jinnah and tried to establish diplomatic relations with the proposed Pakistan. Hyderabad, another important native state that was pursuing the line of Travancore, too was contacted by the latter. In this background while Travancore was invited to participate in the Constituent Assembly, the Diwan conveyed the inability of his state to respond favourably to the invitation.[12]

The move of Travancore and some other native states, was viewed with considerable seriousness by the All Indian Congress Committee. On 15 June 1947 it made it categorically clear that moves of this kind, by passing the known desire of the people of the concerned states, would not be favourably entertained by the Congress.[13] The Congress leaders like Jawaharlal Nehru, B.R. Ambedkar, Jayaprakash Narayan, etc., too came but with statements, condemning the move of these states.

The State Congress and the Communist Party now joined hands against the move of the Diwan. Meetings of the Congress to protest against the move of the Diwan and the government were banned. The Congress placed before the people an eight-point programme to challenge the government and win the goal. Defying the ban, meetings were conducted in certain places. Police excesses were reported from some of the places where meetings were held. On 13 July police opened fire at Pettah, near Trivandrum, in which a lad of twelve was killed.[14]

On 5 July 1947 the Parliament of Britain passed the Indian Independence Act. To decide the future of Travancore C.P. Ramaswamy Aiyar arrived at Delhi and exchanged ideas with Mountbatten, the Viceroy. In view of the strong feelings of the people of Travancore against the move for 'Independent Travancore', Sir C.P. Ramaswamy as a statesman, changed his mind and lent support to V.P. Menon who was negotiating with the rebellious states. However, C.P. Ramaswamy didn't divulge the modification of his earlier stand on the future of Travancore, neither to the press nor to the State Congress leadership.

The State Congress, therefore took certain important decisions on 22 July 1947. Establishment of responsible government, ending of the Diwan's rule, convening a Constituent Assembly on the basis of adult franchise to frame a constitution for Travancore, merger of Travancore with Indian Union, etc., were the major decisions. Pattom Thanu Pillai was made the 'Dictator' to campaign for direct action from 1 August onwards.

However, on 25 July 1947 there was a cowardly attack on the life of the Diwan. In connection with the death centenary of Maharaja Swati Tirunal, a music programme had been arranged at the Swati Tirunal Music Academy, Trivandrum, which was attended by the Diwan. As the government press note goes: '. . . The Diwan was leaving the *pandal* after music performance and when he neared the entrance where his car was waiting for him, one man rushed at him with a sword-stick and hit him on the neck three or four times. The blows fell on the cheeks and neck and the fingers of the hand, which was raised to ward off the blows causing some injuries.'[15] It was a pre-meditated attack and this was obvious from the temporary failure of electricity while the attack took place. The assailant thus, could manage to escape. This could have been certainly avoided if his consent was given to V.P. Menon and he had formally announced the same after his return to Travancore.

The Diwan advised the Maharaja to send a message to Mountbatten on the willingness of Travancore to accept the Instrument of Accession. In spite of this move of the Maharaja, the State Congress proceeded with a plan of agitation, which was actually superfluous. 1 August was to be observed as 'Travancore People's Day'. Meetings and processions went on without any untoward incidents.

Since Travancore was to merge with the Union of India, there was no point in the Diwan continuing in the office; he decided to step down on 19 August and left the state. This was followed by the appointment of P.G.N. Unnithan as the Acting Diwan. He entered into discussions with the State Congress leadership and explored the feasibility of a negotiated settlement of the political crisis. Subsequently he advised the Maharaja for issuing a proclamation granting responsible government to the state. Accordingly, the Maharaja issued a proclamation on 4 September 1947.

The State Congress activities from the start to finish, were subjected to trials, repression, betrayal of various sections of participants, etc. Caste groups in Travancore, at times gave priority to the interests of their communities than to the interest of the state. While certain castes thus left the State Congress, certain others very ardently participated in the political activities, owing to reasons other than political. Differences in the ideological outlook of the Congress leaders, the youth wing, etc., too contributed their share in debilitating Congress activities.

However, Sir C.P. Ramaswamy's vision as a statesman and his sharp intellect was a major factor in avoiding a clash with the State Congress and the government on the one hand, and the state government and the Congress government in the centre on the other. Though he was on a strong constitutional foundation so far as his move for 'Independent Travancore' was concerned, as a pragmatist he thought it wise to change his stand from the overall interest of the state as well as the general will of the people.

NOTES

1. The Abstention movement in Travancore (1932-7), in which the non-caste Hindus like the Ezhavas and the non-Hindus, Christians and Muslims mainly, got involved in a very active political agitation for securing their legitimate rights in the socio-political and economic fronts in the state was a major political movement in the state. Therefore, on the whole, they kept away from the Congress activities which were under the leadership of the caste Hindus. By 1937 all the major demands of the Abstentions were condemned by the government and then they put their heart and soul for the success of the struggle for responsible government. Boycott or abstention from election to the state legislature was a strategy of the aggrieved communities but later on the whole protests and agitations came to be known as Abstention movement. For details see K.K. Kusuman, *The Abstention Movement, Kerala Historical Society*, Trivandrum, 1976.
2. *English Records*, Govt. Secretariat, Trivandrum, D. Dis. 308/1948/CS.

3. C. Narayana Pillai, *Tiruvitankoor Swatantriya Samaram* (Malayalam), Karmabhoomi Press, Trivandrum, 1972, p. 201
4. *English Records*, D. Dis. 508/1939/CS. Also see K.K. Kusuman, *The Extremist Movement in Kerala*, Charitram Publications, Trivandrum, 1977.
5. *The Hindu,* 5 Oct. 1938.
6. *English Records*, D. Dis. 2724/1944/CS.
7. Ibid., D. Dis. 2923/1944/CS.
8. D. Daniel, *Struggle for Responsible Government in Travancore, 1938-1947*, Raj Publishers, Madurai, 1985, p. 113.
9. *English Records*, D. Dis. 64/1939/CS.
10. See *Extremist Movement in Kerala.*
11. *English Records*, D. Dis. 2688/1947/CS.
12. Ibid., D. Dis. 238/1947/CS.
13. *The Hindu*, 1 June 1947.
14. *English Records*, D. Dis. 508/1947/CS.
15. Ibid., D. Dis. 4944/1949/CS.

Agrarian Conditions and Peasant Protest in the Princely State of Kashmir, 1846–1931

R.L. HANGLOO

The examination of agrarian conditions is clearly seen as the first task in any attempt to comprehend the nature of peoples movement and its historical specificity in any Princely State of India where overwhelming majority laboured in agriculture.[1] For studying these aspects in the Princely State of Jammu and Kashmir, the appropriate starting point is provided from 1846.

The Princely States of India can be classified under different categories like the very old Hindu states such as Rajaputana, Central India, Kathiawar, Mysore, Travancore, and small Rajput states of Himalayas (which included the Dogra state of Jammu and Kashmir). The second category includes the fragments of Mughal Empire whose generals became independent and established small kingdoms such as Hyderabad, Rampur, Oudh, and Bengal the latter was annexed by the British at its earliest. The third group comprises Maratha states like Gwalior, Baroda, Indore, Kolhapur, and Bharatpur and Hindu, Sikh, and Muslim states of Bhopal, Tonk, and Bhavalpur. There were also the small states of Orissa and Central Provinces.

Of all these states it seems that serious legitimizational problems were faced by the Nizam of Hyderabad and the Dogra Maharaja of Jammu and Kashmir. In Kashmir proper the religio-cultural organization made it difficult for the Dogra Raj to exercise its hegemony over majority of Muslim population. I do not intend to suggest that the ideology of the ruling classes becomes the ruling ideology by the grace of God. But the popular religious beliefs do not stand in isolation, they together constitute complexes and it is the nature of these beliefs which stands together in some systematic way giving the legitimacy for ruling activity. In 1846 the Jammu and Kashmir state was founded under Maharaja Gulab Singh.[2] With the establishment of the Dogra Raj a semi-anarchical period commenced in Kashmir's history which saw an increasing neglect of the entire agrarian economic infrastructure, the transport, irrigation and flood control systems, tax remissions during the difficult years or during poor harvests, through corrupt and inept bureaucratic management.

Though owing to the mountainous character of the region and peculiar climate the land under cultivation in Kashmir has always been very small, the agrarian conditions have been a matter of comprehensive interest affecting all sections of Kashmiri society in a variety of ways.[3] For the Dogra Raj, too, land was the principal source of income and a means to obtain the civil and military services. In such a project the Dogras were helped by the semi-autonomous chiefs from Khatai, Dupatta, Muzaffarabad, Buniar, Chikar, Kotli, Dhana, and Uri.[4] The cooperation and help provided by the politico-military elements of the Dogra Rajputs and a very small section of urban Kashmiri Pandits and Sayyids was found so valuable that they were also awarded jagirs and *chaks* and made useful intermediaries between the state and people.[5] The term jagirdar refers to those semi-autonomous chiefs who held large number of villages and did not personally cultivate the land and subsisted instead on rental earnings from the tenants, revenues from peasants, and also the proceeds of cultivation by agricultural labourers.[6] The land revenue was realized in kind, theoretically at the rate of one-half of the produce but in actual practice the state took 66 per cent of the peasant's produce. It was out of the remaining 33 per cent that the peasant had to meet liabilities of family, social functions, and religion. There were also jagirdars who enjoyed jagirs below Rs. 3,000 worth of a revenue.[7] They were known as pattadars. Under this jagir system the peasant was not only exposed to the land revenue demand but was subjected to innumerable legal and illegal exactions as well.[8] There was hardly any item of the peasant's life and property which was not subjected to tax.

We can cite the examples of Satram a peasant of pargana Adwin to illustrate the system.[9]

Hardohisa of Satram (total produce)	90 *kharwars*
Sarkaree hissa (state demand)	45 *kharwars*
Trakee and *abwabs*	15 *kharwars*
The total state demand	60 *kharwars*

It is true that the state carried out a series of revenue assessments/settlements from the beginning till the end of the Raj. But all these were only aimed at the regularization of the extraction from agriculture which was by far the most important source of income to the state. The methods of assessment carried out were those of batai 1846, kardari 1857, chakladari 1873, ijara system 1876, village cash assessment system 1880, izadboli system

1882, regular settlement and cash/kind assessment of 1889.[10]

From the frequency of these assessments it becomes clear that the revenue system in Kashmir was based on the practice of fluctuating harvest by harvest assessment, a system which was highly inconvenient for the government for it required the surveillance of every harvest by a large assessing staff.[11] This not only entailed a great deal of work but also greatly increased the opportunities for graft and corruption by the subordinate staff. The situation led to bureaucratic complexities of which Mr Wingate wrote 'the patwaris carry three editions of their records and all on scraps of paper, one for himself, one for tehsildar and the one for peasant'.[12] The peasants always remained uncertain of their future liabilities. Although the crude system of fluctuating assessments, not regulated by any recognized theory or principle but mainly depending on the will of kardars, chakladars, and other officials, were in vogue to the great detriment of the peasantry.[13]

The land revenue demand and the taxes and cesses actually realized were far in excess of those that finally went to the treasury. Lawrence very rightly remarks, 'Only air and water were exempt from taxation.'[14] As a result of this heavy demand of revenue the peasants were often forced to give up cultivation and consequently payments fell in arrears. In 1851, Rs. 30,00,000 were in arrears because most of the peasants had left their lands despite the efforts of Ranbir Singh and Diwan Jawalasahai.[15] In 1852 the arrears amounted to Rs. 15,000 with a revenue deficit of Rs. 23,00,000. In 1857, Maharaja Ranbir Singh issued an order that all the arrears, if not paid by *Nauroz* (new year) day, may be charged interest at the rate of Rs. 2 in cash and 2 *kharwars* of rice for every hundred per month. Table 1 shows how the collections had fallen for the period from 1880 to 1887 owing to the contraction of the arable lands.[16]

In many villages the chakladars applied and got land which they

TABLE 1: DECLINE OF REVENUE COLLECTION FROM 1880-7

Year	Actual demand for 252 villages	Actual collection for 252 villages
1880	3,88,613	3,45,031
1881	3,96,274	3,51,547
1882	4,23,440	3,53,673
1883	4,64,200	20,44,389
1884	4,69,701	4,09,562
1885	4,36,872	1,97,841
1886	4,41,357	2,48,369
1887	4,41,404	2,48,369

SOURCE: W.R. Lawrence, *Assessment Report of the Ich Nagam Tahsil*, 1891, pp. 2-6.

afterwards abandoned. The villages in which the lands were situated were held responsible for payment of revenue assessed on them. The peasants neither took possession of land nor paid the revenues but it was entered against them as arrears. Often mustajirs made a bid for a village and offered a large increase on fixed revenue. They remained in a village for three to four years of good harvest, embezzled large sums of money out of the amount the peasants paid as revenue, and subsequently these were entered as arrears against the village.[17] The arrears outstanding against the peasants were also due to the fraudulent accounting by revenue officials whose records were seldom straight and reliable.[18]

The chakdars had turned the state of affairs even worse. In order to bring the waste land, i.e. navabadee under cultivation the state granted these to various officials in lieu of their services.[19] But these officials treated the orders of the Durbar as mere formalities. We have a number of cases in which the chakdars made the peasants to bring the waste lands under cultivation at a concessional revenue rates, evicted the peasants from cultivable holdings by forging records and also by purchasing peasant held villages for petty sums. We cite a few examples: Diwan Badrinath got a deserted government garden allotted as a *chak* and then with it was included the cultivatable land of some peasant family. On this Diwan was to pay Rs. 48 as revenue. A few years later he bought some more land for a hundred rupees and expanded his *chak* further. The whole area was 48 acres and before laying down the office of Diwan, Badrinath got the whole land converted into a muafi, i.e. charitable grant and made it exempt from the revenue.[20] Most of the chakdars soon after taking possession of the *chak* they immediately expelled all the peasants in order to destroy all the proof of this having been cultivated when they entered upon it.[21] The minor officials of the village struck to no scruples in exacting their respective shares which were always out of proportion to their legitimate share.

Besides all these problems, the state's demand for forced labour from the peasants resulted in periodic migration from Kashmir to other parts of India in search of living. Most of the *begar* (forced labour) was carried in summer when the peasants were needed in their fields. Every year thousands of peasants were taken for forced labour.

Sometimes the peasants would loose their lives during the course of service in *begar* and it was then that their families would permanently become victims of hunger and starvation. This oppressive practice also led to the de-population of some of the villages and consequently resulted in the transfer of land from actual owners of soil to the powerful bureaucracy.[22] There are reports of some of the villages being sold for petty sums in order to earn exemption from *begar*, i.e. forced labour. In one such instance three villages were sold for a miserable amount of Rs. 40 per village.[23]

As if this was not enough, the state also monopolized trade in agricultural produce. With the consequent depression of prices paid to the peasant brought them often to such levels where it was impossible for them to make a reasonable living.[24] Owing to the lack of credit facilities on the part of the state, the peasants were only at the mercy of the *wadhdar* (moneylender). Even as late as 1906, 60 per cent of the peasants were in debt and the average rate of annual interest was 81 per cent.[25]

However, the peasants protested against this excessive exploitation in their own way. From the last quarter of the nineteenth century the peasant protest manifested in several forms such as abandonment of cultivation, migration to various parts of Punjab, concealing their harvest, marches and procession to various shrines of Sufi saints and submitting of petitions to the Maharaja and his officials. The first petition to be submitted by the peasants to Maharaja Ranbir Singh was in 1877 during his visit to Achabal.[26] But despite the Maharaja's assurances nothing substantial was done to mitigate their problems. All these forms of protest were not in themselves effective enough to bring about a social change but they did reflect the undercurrents of stresses and strains in the Kashmir society, although building consensus on the need to protest collectively and the type of action to be taken was not that easy a task. But acting together as a group could give their demands a legitimacy that transcended prohibitions on united and concerted action. Groups of peasants tried to convince and instigate their members in other villages who had the same grievances and faced similar problems. Initially this was all done without making their own role so prominent as to attract undue attention of the state. Because they knew fully well that anyone caught organizing the peasants against the Dogra Raj for whatever reasons was liable for punishment. This attitude of state forced the peasants to be extremely circumspect in expressing their grievances. But someone had to organize the peasants, make plans, and ultimately take the responsibility for confronting the Raj.

From the last decades of the nineteenth century there appeared several factors which strengthened the movement at various levels. The decline in the shawl trade led to the total impoverishment of shawl weavers in Kashmir. This strengthened their resolve to overthrow the Dogra Raj and they joined the peasants. Secondly, the opening of the Jhelum valley road in 1890 brought Kashmir into direct contact with the rest of India. The popular organizations in the neighbouring region of Punjab influenced Kashmiris to start programmes for educating their masses to ameliorate their conditions. Gradually the growing public opinion also began to be expressed through literary and folk media. This task was accomplished by M.A. Fauq and the great poet Mehjoor through their poetry and journalistic efforts.

Khak Pakh Khatai Kashmir Hai Janat, Magar Khar Dozuk Ka
Nammona Hai rahan Begarbe Amlogun Ka rahan Kya Hal
Hoga Sonchlo. Khoof Hakim Se rahan Larzad ho Nambar
Dar be. Yeh Tashadud Kash Ponchuheye Koi Maharaj Tak
Be Khabar Hal-i-Rayat se Ho to Sarkar be . . . [27]

Fauq through his poetry and journalistic efforts exhorted Kashmiris to raise their voice against the tyranny.

Apni Shajahtoon Ka Charcha Tha Ekjahan moor Himat Karo to Ayo Phir roh Door
Dubara Ai Inkalab-i-Alam Gardish Idar be koi Kohna libar to ne har rom ka utara.[28]

It was a clear intention of the poet Mehjoor to inculcate qualities of courage, tenacity and strong resolve at popular levels.

Navou gul tai navou buulbul navou gulzar asan goch . . .
Navou qanoon, navou daftar, navour darbar asan goch . . .
Rathu ha bagrano navbaharich shan paida kar . . .
che Rahman Mir hue kandara naron kaptan parida ka . . . [29]

The services that *Akhbar-i-Kashmir*, Lahore, Jammu, Kashmir, and *Punch Gazette* of Fauq rendered to Kashmiris for more than three decades of the twentieth century have been highlighted by the president of Kashmiri Muslim Conference in their speeches. These efforts of Fauq projected the Dogra Raj as the principal enemy responsible for the conditions of Kashmiris. The famous Kashmiri poet Mehjoor also played a no less significant role in affecting the mobilization of mass support from both rural and urban areas through his folk songs, etc.

At this stage the direction of a satisfactory programme of action was planned by Qami Anjuaman at Lahore.[30] By this time, the wave of the nationalist movement had spread to the whole of India. In Kashmir the mobilization to a large extent depended on the availability of the leader within the subjugated group and the adoption of ideological mechanism.[31] In Kashmir, leaders emerged from the urban base and when they tried to look for the political ideology that would help them to fashion the people of various social profiles they found that religion was the only force through which individual interests were to be subsumed under a strong sense ot commonality. It is as a result of this that entire social milieu got tapped into the Muslim Conference.[32] Here it should not automatically lead us to the conclusion that the movement was communal or had a narrow outlook in the beginning. We should note that the supreme goal was to defend the material, moral and social interests of the Kashmiri masses (majority of whom were Muslims) and overthrow the Dogra Raj. Besides, when the political society was more fragmented and less controlled by its class consciousness, it became essential to pilot the struggle through the religious content of populism. However, it needs to be additionally stressed that the movement was a value oriented one (even before being renamed as National Conference) because it did not find accommodation for dissatisfied social groups within the existing structure of political institutions. Instead, identified the conditions as a source of evil and put forth a positive pressure for complete transformation of the system by resorting to mass protests.

NOTES

1. For details see Sir William Barton, *The Princes of India*, rpt., Delhi, 1989. Apart from the semi-independent Princely States which were allied to the British crown there were also directly ruled British Indian possessions. This type of situation was not only in India but two-fifths of entire South Asia were ruled by the semi-independent Princely States, Robin Jaffery, *People, Princes and Paramount Power*, OUP, New Delhi, 1978, p. 1.
2. In the first half of the nineteenth century British colonialism became more conscious of the mounting dangers of Russia from the north-western side to its Indian colony. As a result the British began to think in terms of the liquidation of the Sikh Empire which could not only transfer to them the material resources of the Punjab but also provide them with some of the important strategic possessions for safeguarding their interests in India. This was expressed by M.B. Bayley, Chairman of Board of Directors, in his letter dated January 1841 to John Hobhouse, the President of Company's Board of Control. The letter reads '. . . even if the holding of a force in Afghanistan should be necessary for their maintenance, we would find in the resources of Punjab. The resources necessary in difficulty and with Kashmir on our flank, the whole attacks whether from European or Asian enemies can be handled without problems', 'Home Miscellaneous Correspondences', Research Department (Manuscript), India Office Library, London, 184, 185 and 936. In course of time, the Sikh principalities between river Sutlej and Jammu passed under the protection and care of the British. The Anglo-Sikh wars followed in 1845-6 in which the British came out victorious and in the

process of setting the political future of occupied territories and their autonomous vassals, they handed over Jammu and Kashmir to Maharaja Gulab Singh in 1846, H.M. Lawrence, 'Transfer of Government to Maharaja Gulab Singh', secret correspondence, 28 January 1846, File nos. 33-44 (in Manuscript form), Jammu Archives. In fact Marx also mentions that when British army entered Lahore in triumph on 20 February 1846, it appears that there was no money in the treasury for payment of $ 150.000 to the Sikh soldiers. Hardinge declared the annexation of Kashmir to the Company but when Gulab Singh offered to pay the money, Kashmir was made over to him. This was how Hardinge paid the war expenses to troops of Khalsa army. Karl Marx, *Notes on Indian History*, Moscow, rpt., 1988, p. 142. For further details see K.M. Panikkar, *Maharaja Gulab Singh: Founder of Jammu and Kashmir State*, London, 1930.

3. The physical character of the region imposed a serious handicap on intensive farming and diversification of crops. This was because the land remained under snow for five months a year when no cultivation was possible at all. As a result after harvesting of *kharif*, crops in late September/October, very little time was left for a peasant to sow another crop. The *rabi*, took four to five months in Kashmir. *Rabi* seeds were therefore sown only in such fields as had not been cultivated in *kharif* season. In fact, Kashmiri peasants had to content themselves with a one crop economy. Generally the peasants preferred the cultivation of rice. The improved varieties of cash crops such as cotton, wheat, oil seeds, and pulses were grown in very small quantities and therefore could afford only little scope for agro-based industries. The traditional crops like barley, maize, etc., apart from providing long-term yields were less competitive as marketable commodities. W.R. Lawrence, *Imperial Gazetteer of India, Princely Series, Jammu and Kashmir*, Calcutta, 1909, pp. 40-70. See also Hargopal Kaul Khasta, *Guldasta-i-Kashmir* (Urdu), Lahore, 1869, pp. 9-21. However, disregarding all these problems, the fundamental feature of the Dogra Raj and its hierarchical revenue machinery was the condition under which the extraction of surplus took place.
4. When the administration of Kashmir was handed over to Maharaja Gulab Singh the turbulent hill tribes of Hazara and Muzaffarabad rose in revolt. Due to ill-equipped troops of Hazara and Muzaffarabad, the Maharaja anxiously requested the British at Lahore to exchange territories of Hazara and Balkot with some portions of territory lying in the plains of river Jhelum. The British asked the Maharaja to reaffirm all jagirs, and muafis (charitable grants) which he had resumed. After issuing the orders for the reaffirmation of these grants a treaty was signed by Maharaja Gulab Singh with Lahore Durbar on 25 May 1847. Under this treaty the Maharaja received the districts of Munawar, Sujanpur, and Pathankot in exchange for the territories of Hazara and Balkot. After some time the Maharaja had to surrender the districts of Sujanpur and Pathankot and retained only a part of Munawar and districts of Kathua and Suchetgarh, 'Agricultural reports submitted by Hill Chiefs to

Henry Lawrence, Foreign Secret Consultations', File no. 1125 dated 26 December 1846, National Archives of India. According to Henry Lawrence this arrangement was made with the intention of paying Rs. 56,000 annually to the hill chiefs of Rajouri, Basoli, Jasrota, Ramnagar and Kishtwar, who preferred to live under British protection and not as the subjects of the Maharaja. See also *Lahore Political Diaries*, vol. III, Punjab Archives, Patiala, pp. 66, 148, 149.

5. The difference in these assignments of jagirs and *chaks* was done according to the nature and conditions attached to each one of them. The jagir and *chak* holders provided military and civil service to the state. Muafi grants were only for religious and charitable purpose. H.M. Lawrence, 'Report from Kashmir' (unpublished), 15 November 1847, Foreign Secret Consultations, File nos.1247-49. N.A.I. For details see Mirza Saif-ud-din, *Akhbarat*, vol. I, folios 2-6. The entire set of 14 volumes is also available with the author in microfilm.
6. The jagirdars of Khatai, Duppatta, and Muzaffarabad paid an annual revenue of Rs. 9,000 and also maintained 5,000 armed retainers. The Khaka chiefs of Buniar, Kotti, Donna and Uri had to maintian two armed troops and also pay an annual revenue of Rs. 4,000. 'Taylor's Report' (unpublished), 27 September 1847, Foreign Political Consultation, File nos. 1243-7, N.A.I.
7. Secret Political Consultation, General Department, File no. 76, of 1896, entitled: 'Levy of Cesses and reassessment of Jagirs in the state and validity of pattas granted' (unpublished), Jammu Archives. The officials like chief record keeper, chief treasurer, chief physician, Diwan of Province, chief kotwal, chief toshkhana and chief wazir were also the army jagirdars, Mirza Saif-ud-din, *Akhbarat*, vol. I, folios 2-6, vol. V, folios 21 and 23.
8. See R.L. Hangloo, 'Magnitude of Land Revenue Demand in Kashmir', *Social Scientist*, no. 133, June 1984.
9. H.M. Lawrence, 'Transfer of Government'.
10. A. Wingate, 'Preliminary Land Settlement Report in Kashmir' (unpublished), Lahore, 1889, Jammu Archives. In spite of all these assessments it was not until the second half of twentieth century (when the land reform took place in Kashmir in 1950) that a genuine effort was made to avoid the confusion, secure confidence, and attach peasants permanently to their holdings when a fair distribution of produce between the peasant and state took place.
11. The various officials connected with the work of assessment were Diwan-i-jine, tahsildar, thanedar, kardar, sazowul, patwari, lambardar, shiqdar, harkar, muqadam and tarazudar. All these officials not only neglected to undertake steps to improve agricultural production and thereby ameliorate the condition of peasantry but equally ignored the increasing corruption in states revenue department. R. Thorp, *Kashmir Misgovernment*, London, 1870, pp. 2-21. And also see Mirza Saif-ud-udin, *Akhbarat*, vol. I, folio 6, and Charles Girdlestone, *Memorandam on Kashmir*, pp. 8-10.

12. A. Wingate, 'Preliminary Land Settlement Report in Kashmir', p. 49.
13. The kardars and chakladars were always bent upon collecting from the peasant as much as they could without looking into the revenue paying capacity of the peasant. Revenue officials always preferred the collection in kind because the cash payment would have reduced their share in produce. Even after the settlement of Lawrence the situation continued to worsen. Diwan Kripa Ram, *Gulzar-i-Kashmir* (Persian), Lahore, 1877, W.R. Lawrence, *Imperial Gazetteer,* pp. 417-18.
14. W.R. Lawrence, *Valley*, p. 417.
15. W.R. Lawrence, *Imperial Gazetteer of India*, pp. 60-7. In these circumstances both state and peasant had to suffer losses but between the two the peasant suffered more. He was left with as little as was perhaps sufficient to keep his body and soul together. See also R.L. Hangloo; 'Magnitude of Land Revenue in Kashmir', *Social Scientist*, June 1984.
16. W.R.Lawrence, *Assessment Report of Ich Nagam Tehsil*, 1891, Jammu Archives, pp. 2-6.
17. In pargana Dansu the peasant had paid the revenue in full for the period in 1880-8 still Rs. 31,747 were shown as outstanding against them. The mustajir had paid the state demand in full but at the same time succeeded in taking from treasury an equivalent sum in the form of agricultural loan on behalf of peasants. In actual practice it was never advanced to peasants but only entered against each peasant on paper, *Mujmui-Report, Jammu-Va-Kashmir and Tibet*, pp. 21-2.
18. A.Wingate, 'Preliminary Land Settlement Report in Kashmir', pp. 60-2. The various kinds of *chaks* included *istihari*, *ahalikari*, *mukararee* and *zar-naiar.*
19. Ibid.
20. Report of W.R. Lawrence regarding the condition of cultivating classes in Kashmir, 1890, N.A.I. In fact by the first half of the twentieth century more than half the area in Kashmir was under *chaks* held by revenue officials as absentee landlords.
21. For example a tahsildar cast his eyes upon a fine village within his charge near Srinagar. There were 14 acres of land which had been abandoned by peasants because of the oppression of revenue officials. He got it allotted as a *chak* and was to pay Rs.12 per year on wet land and 6 *annas* on dry land. But he got the records forged and declared all lands as dry. A. Wingate, 'Preliminary Land Settlement Report in Kashmir'.
22. Maharaja Pratap Singh, 'Diary of an Inspection to Gilgit' (unpublished), 1896, Jammu Archives.
23. Lawerence, *Valley*, p. 414, once the peasant rendered himself landless he could easily escape from *begar* often moving out of his village to another part of the country. In fact, this can also be construed as the non-violent path of the protest on the part of the peasant.
24. Mir Sarif-ullah, 'Tarikh Nama-i-Kashmir', Persian manuscript, 1806-66.

25. At this time the average landholding in some parts of the valley has been worked out at about 4 acres with average debt rate of Rs. 9, 6 *annas* and 4 paise per acre. *Note on the Review of Six Tahsils of the Valley*, published by Jammu and Kashmir Government, 1909. For details also see W.H. Brailsford, *Kashmir Today Through Foreign Eyes*, Bombay, 1948.
26. Pandit Hargopal Koul Khasta, *Guldasta-i-Kashmir* (Persian), Lahore, 1889, pp. 225-6. Although Maharaja issued instruction to his officials to return immediately whatever extra they exacted from the peasants in that particular year but once Maharaja left, the officials got annoyed and instead of acting on the instructions of Maharaja, searched the homes of peasants and took what was left with them.
27. M.D. Fauq, *Kalam-i-Fauq,* vol. I, Lahore, 1912 (melu).
28. Ibid.
29. *Kalam-i-Mahjor*, published in Kashmir by Kashmir Cultural Academy, vol. I, 1982.
30. The Kashmiri Anjuman at Lahore was started before 1909 and it was later renamed as Muslim Conference in 1909. Dr. Sir Mohd. Iqbal became its first General Secretary, ibid. But it was finally in April 1930, that the Reading Room Party was formed in Srinagar which grouped together various newly educated Kashmiri Muslims, who had been influenced by the pan-Islamists . . . in Aligarh during their study. In 1931 All India Kashmiri Committee was founded in Punjab. Rashid Tasir, *Tarikh-i-Huryat-Kashmir* (Urdu), vol. I, Srinagar, 1968, pp. 77, 140-5.
31. At this stage one of the important links remains unexplored because the leaders would have emerged from among the peasants but in case of Kashmir there is complete absence of this phenomenon.
32. The leaders of Muslim Conference were always alert to ensure that the movement does not come under the cloud of communal influences. In the presidential addresses at the annual sessions of Muslim Conference in 1935 and 1937, Choudhuri Ghulam Abbas of Jammu and Sheikh Mohd. Abdullah made 'Fervent Appeals' to non-Muslim subjects of the state to plunge into the struggle and ensure the protection of their rights. M.I. Khan, *Perspectives on Kashmir*, Srinagar, 1980.

The Social Background of People's Movement in the Jammu and Kashmir State, 1846–1931

MOHAMMAD ISHAQ KHAN

The political unification of Jammu, Kashmir, and Ladakh comprising what is now known as the Jammu & Kashmir State was achieved by Gulab Singh, the Dogra Raja of Jammu, as a result of the Treaty of Amritsar concluded with the British in 1846. Notwithstanding the seeming political unity under the Dogras, the period extending from 1846 to the close of the last century saw a strong feudalization of the state machinery the like of which can rarely be found in the eighteenth century Kashmir when, in spite of political instability, the rulers did not enjoy the optimum degree of direct access to the land. With the sale of Kashmir by the British to Gulab Singh, Kashmiri society underwent a deep-rooted change. The pattern of new agrarian relations began to emerge when the Dogra rulers declared themselves to be the absolute owners of the soil. A specific state concept survived repeatedly to play a powerful role throughout the Dogra period from 1846 to 1947. The new rulers often invoked the Treaty of Amritsar to establish their legitimacy and to perpetuate the notion of their superior ownership of land.[1] Not only that, the treaty was also invoked to thwart the British machinations of establishing a Residency in the state. It is no wonder that Maharaja Pratap Singh drew on the treaty in moments of despair to legitimate and consolidate his authority. His letter to his Chief Minister is worth quoting:[2]

> As you are already aware of the proprietary rights in all the lands of Kashmir belong to the ruling chief exclusively, for the simple reason that the territories of Kashmir, were purchased by my late lamented grandfather, Maharaja Gulab Singhji and hence any sale of such land by any one else is illegal.

It is hard to deny that the Treaty of Amritsar conferred both dejure and de facto rights on the Dogra Maharajas to regard Kashmir as their personal property.[3] In fact, the treaty was understood to imply that Gulab Singh had purchased against cash payment all lands, rivers, forests, mines, natural products,[4] and indeed, everything including even the skill of weavers of the famous shawl industry. It is this Dogra concept of superior ownership which so pathetically reflects in both Kashmiri and Urdu literature produced during the Dogra rule. Thus Allama Mohammad Iqbal in one of his Persian compositions remarks:

O breeze, if you happen to go Geneva way, carry a word from me to the Nations of the whole world. A land and people, its streams and forests all were sold. In fact the whole nation was sold and fancy at how cheep a price.

Although the recognition of the Dogra rulers' superior ownership of land formed the basis of the government's policy, throughout the period extending from 1846 to 1931 or so, the Dogra administration worked directly to create a class of landed aristocracy comprising the Dogra Rajputs[5] and large number of Kashmiri Pandits,[6] mostly concentrated in the city of Srinagar. The latter were the state officials. They were in small number of the entire population of Kashmir, but having common landed interests, they were interrelated and functioned in part through their direct relationship to institutions which expressed or symbolized society as a whole.

The use of land grants in the form of jagirs[7] and *chaks*[8] may be mentioned as a major device for ruling-class support. What the foundation of the Dogra rule brought about was a new class of agrarian exploitation, with a parasitical urban growth based upon it. The new polity combined political authority with economic power more fully than either of the preceding classes had united before, vesting the control over the bulk of the surplus produced by the peasants in the hands of a ruling class. The relationship of the peasants to the land was epitomized in the deriding remark *gama hakhur*, meaning village bull. Though many aspects of this ridicule are worthy of full investigation and comment such as the context[9] in which it first appears, it can, none the less, be taken as a byword of basic social relations which bound the peasants to the soil and to the master. The growth of the closed village economy was thus an essential element in the changed situation.[10] It is, not therefore, surprising that as late as the beginning of the present century salaries were unheard of in Kashmir.[11] The Dogra rulers' frequent attempts at changing currency[12] besides showing how unstable was the economy, also points to the decline of trade and industrial production resulting in the dependence of a vast number of people on the land.[13] As compared to the numismatic traditions of Kashmir of the eighteenth century, the coins of the nineteenth century show progressive debasement of metal and stylistic degeneration.[14]

Closely connected with the creation of the landed aristocracy is the system of forced labour (*begar*) which remained until the beginning of this century as the most prominent features of Kashmir administration.[15] After 1846 the magnitude of forced labour grew not only due to military expeditions sent to Gilgit and adjoining border areas of Kashmir, but also owing to the emergence of an organized landed aristocracy and the weak functioning of an exchange economy, especially in the agrarian set-up characterized by localism. The destruction of the Kashmiri peasants' proprietary rights under the institution of *begar* and the reduction of peasants to a state close to 'serfdom' are thus two marked features of the agrarian economy.[16]

It is now time to focus on the concentration of artisan labour in Srinagar, the chief urban centre of the Jammu and Kashmir State. The highest concentration of labour in the shawl industry at the end of the eighteenth century and the beginning of the nineteenth century has led Tchitcherov to conclude that 'there emerged enterprises which possessed a number of important features typical of capitalist manufactures'.[17] With the emergence of organized aristocracy after 1846, the landed aristocracy exercised its exploitation of the artisans of shawl industry not only through a ramified and diversified system of taxation,[18] but also by various forms of political and economic control,[19] feudal restrictions,[20] monopolies,[21] etc. This included widely practised direct plunder[22] and coercion[23] of artisans. Gulab Singh in order to ensure a constant income from the manufacture of shawls that he even promulgated an ordinance which bound the weaver to his master and forbade him to give up his operations.[24]

From the foregoing discussion, it would be clear why until the 1920s the Muslims of Kashmir remained in political backwaters as compared with their co-religionists in the rest of India. Their political inertia may also be attributed to the ban on the formation of societies or even the publication of newspapers in the valley. As late as 1921 the Dogra government hesitantly gave permission to the formation of an association whose object was the teaching of the Koran and ordered the police 'to watch that the Anjuman does not take part in political matters'.[25]

However, it should not be supposed that there was total absence of social consciousness among the Muslims of Kashmir. If on the one hand, they had developed a fatalistic outlook owing to oppression, exploitation and misery, on the other, they had tended to show spirit of revolt against intolerable conditions. The shawl weavers agitation demanding the reduction of various kinds of taxes such as *baj*, *nazrana*, etc., in 1847,[26] their demonstration in the streets of Srinagar in 1865,[27] peasants' protest against the high-handedness and corrupt practices of the landed aristocracy in 1877,[28] submission of two petitions by some eighteen Muslims to the Viceroy of India and the Resident in Srinagar in 1886 for the appointment of a Settlement Officer in Kashmir,[29] submission of petitions in 1907 and 1909 imploring the British Government to take effective measures for the propagation of education among Muslims,[30] submission of a memorial to Lord Reading during his visit to Srinagar in 1924 by some prominent members of Muslim community, and the silk factory riots in 1924, all point to the social tensions inherent in the emerging politics of Kashmiri Muslims.

A far-sighted observer like Sir Albion Bannerji deplored such a state of affairs. He resigned the post of the Foreign and Political Minister which he had held for over two years disgusted with the unimaginative mind of the rulers. On 15 March 1929 he made certain remarks regarding the political, social and economic conditions prevailing in the state in a press interview:[31]

> The Jammu and Kashmir state is labouring under many disadvantages, with a large Mohammedan population absolutely illiterate, labouring under poverty and very low economic conditions of living in the villages and practically governed like dumb driven cattle. There is no touch between the Government and the people, no suitable opportunity for representing grievances and the administrative machinery itself requires overhauling from top to bottom to bring efficiency. It has at present little or no sympathy with the people's wants and grievances.
>
> There is hardly any public opinion in the states. As regards the press, it is practically non-existent, with the result that the government is not benefited to the extent that it should be by the healthy criticism.

The observations of the trained British civil servant produced a deep effect on several Muslim young men,[32] fresh from universities in India, particularly Aligarh, where they had come into contact with Muslim leaders and propagators of pan-Islamism. They had organized themselves into a group holding frequent meetings at the Muslim Reading Room in Srinagar. It is the members of the group, including Sheikh Mohammed Abdullah, who initially created problems for the Maharaja's government with the help of Mir Waiz of Kashmir. However, it was not until the foundation of the All Jammu and Kashmir Muslim Conference founded by Abdullah in 1932, that the movement for the establishment of a responsible form of government in the state took definite roots.

During 1930-2 when Kashmir witnessed the flogging and mass killing of Muslim agitators, politics in Kashmir remained under the virtual control of the Punjabi Muslim leaders. The Ahrars launched a people's movement in Kashmir and carried on an intense propaganda in the form of a press campaign, meetings, processions of the Kashmiri labourers and the celebration of the Kashmir day against the state.[33] In June 1931, the Ahmediyas in their bid to gain a firm foothold in Kashmir sent Sayyid Wali Shah Zain-ul-Abidin and Chaudhari Bashir Ahmad to Srinagar for the guidance of emerging Kashmiri Muslim political leaders.[34] Even Sheikh Abdullah did not lose sight of the contribution of the Muslims of Punjab and Sind. In the early 1930s he presided over the first session of the Jammu and Kashmir Muslim Conference in October 1932. In his presidential address the Sheikh thanked them all for all that they had done for Kashmiri Muslims.

However, from the very beginning of the movement, Sheikh Abdullah was convinced of the hollowness of the idea of a religious conflict against the Dogra oligarchy. This also explains that notwithstanding Abdullah's use of mosques and shrines for effective mobilization of the people, the aims and objects of the Muslim Conference remained secular in principle. In spite of this, the urban leadership of Kashmiri Pandits who had vested interests in land, did not support the demand for responsible government. Thus, the daily *Mertand* which represented the minority point of view in Kashmir often described the Muslim Conference as a communal organization. Although credit can hardly be denied to the *Mertand* for focusing the attention of the government on certain social and economic issues, none the less, it left no stone unturned in casting doubts on the secular aspirations of the Muslim Conference.[35]

On the other hand, the papers run by Pandits like Prem Nath Bazaz, Gawash Lal Koul, and Kashyep Bandhu played a significant role in creating a favourable climate for uniting the Hindus and Muslims against the Dogra regime under a single party. Thus *The Kashmir Times* stood for the foundation of such an organization which had a common flag, common slogans, common programme, and a common goal (7 August 1937). Earlier on 20 March 1937, *The Kashmir Times* in an editorial heading Kashmir should Lead wrote:

> A large section of the people of Kashmir is already demanding a responsible form of government in the State. The minorities in the state have never opposed this demand but what they want is safeguards. The cry for responsible government cannot be deferred too long. Thwarting the way, progress of the country and the nation was never conceived by any school of patriotism. This is high time, therefore,

that various communities in the Jammu & Kashmir State should sink their differences and evolve a common formula so that Kashmir may be able to give a lead to the other Indian States.[36]

The lead, of course, was given. The Muslim Conference was converted into the National Conference in 1939. Commenting on the conversion of the Muslim Conference into the National Conference, *The Statesman* dated 11 July 1946 remarks:[37] 'The change gave fresh impetus to the movement. The occasion was unique. Never had any other communal organization in India achieved this amazing conversion. Large-heartedness seemed to have combined with far-sightedness to bring about this consummation.'

The conversion of the All Jammu and Kashmir Muslim Conference into the All Jammu and Kashmir National Conference considerably changed the tone of the press, and brought politics into the foreground of discussions. The more important papers like *The Hamdard*, *The Khidmat*, *The Khalid*, *The Kesari*, *The Desh*, etc., now sought to educate the public in the political ideal of the National Conference. But papers such as the *Islah*, *The Albarq*, and *The Millat* criticized the political ideal of the National Conference as chimerical and were definitely hostile to it. Sheikh Abdullah was vigorously opposed by the most powerful sections of the Muslim League and the Muslim Conference, but he could carry on easily because he had a mass appeal and a vest following. While most papers of the Srinagar press were guided by a robust spirit of nationalism, *The Mertand* was very critical of the radical land reforms envisaged by the National Conference. Not often, the nationalism of the National Conference came in for harping criticism in its editorial columns so much so that it nursed the fear of the establishment of Muslim rule in Kashmir should Muslims succeed in their struggle for responsible government. Realizing that a very insignificant number of Kashmir Pandits stood by the National Conference, Pandit Jawaharlal Nehru appealed them to join the National Conference. Nehru was conscious of the sad reality that 'impelled by a desire for self-production' the Kashmiri Pandits had organized themselves as a 'communal group' after the rise of what he characterized Kashmiri Muslims struggle as the 'popular mass movement'. He, therefore, warned his 'own people' not to 'fall into the trap into which minorities so easily fell and urged them to join the National Conference which under Sheikh Abdullah's leadership had steered the mass movement but of the narrow waters of Communalism into the broad sea of nationalism'.[38]

Although the emerging nationalism of the Muslims of Kashmir was not centred round the symbols of Islam or past Muslim supremacy, yet it was labelled as Muslim nationalism by urban Pandits with vested interest in the land. But notwithstanding the role played by Pandits like Prem Nath Bazaz and Kashyep Bandhu in championing the causes of Muslim peasants, a section of the Srinagar and Jammu press was very critical of Sheikh Abdullah for undermining the cause of Muslims of the Jammu and Kashmir state laying the foundation of a nationalist party. For instance, *The Albarq* saw in the conversion of the Muslim Conference into the National Conference the conspiracy of the Kashmiri Pandits against this change. This was also noted in *The Pasban* of Jammu. It was highly critical of Sheikh Abdullah and attributed the Muslim Conferences conversion into the National Conference mainly due to the influence of Gandhi and Nehru on him.[39]

Some broad issues may be raised in the context of foregoing discussion:

(1) The struggle for responsible government in the Jammu and Kashmir State was mainly the concern of Kashmiri Muslims notwithstanding the contribution of an insignificant number of Kashmiri Pandits and Dogras to the movement;
(2) It needs to be probed why so long as Muslims remained in political backwater, the Kashmiri Brahmins did not raise the Hindu-Muslim question. Did the Pandits feel a great challenge to their age-long supremacy? Did the Pandits who formed the only middle class intelligentsia of Kashmiri society, direct all their energies towards safeguarding their unique identity under the influence of outside forces like the Hindu Mahasabha, etc?
(3) It remains to be seen why a man like Bazaz who played an important part in laying the foundations of secularism in Kashmir, later turned to be an arch-enemy of the National Conference;
(4) Was the abolition of the Big Landed Estates Act of 1952, the main cause behind removing Sheikh Abdullah in 1952 as Prime Minister of Jammu and Kashmir State?
(5) Should we describe the people's struggle for responsible government in the state of Jammu and Kashmir as a nationalist movement considering the undertones of a defeatist Muslim nationalist mentality characterizing Sheikh Abdullah's autobiography (*Aatish-i-Chinar*) ?

There are several other questions related to the struggle for responsible government in Kashmir in the pre-partition period. But considering the fact that for the last 12 years or so my field of academic interest has centred round towards promoting dynamics of an objective understanding of the processes of Islamization in the valley during the fourteenth and eighteenth centuries, I would therefore seek answers for such questions from future research scholars.

NOTES

1. For detailed discussion, see Ishaq Khan, *Perspectives on Kashmir: Historical Dimensions*, Srinagar, 1983, pp. 68-96.
2. JKA, File no. 191/H-75, Bloc C of 1906.
3. Walter Lawrence describes Kashmir of the 1880s as an Absolute Monarchy. *The Valley of Kashmir*, London, p. 2. The Soviet and English Marxist historians have amply shown that the absolute monarchy is a form of feudal state. 'The Transition from Feudalism to Capitalism (A Symposium)', 1957, 1st edn., Patna, p. 75.
4. Mirza Muhammad Afzal Beg, *On the Way to Golden Harvests: Agricultural Reforms in Kashmir*, 1951, Jammu, pp. 22-3.
5. The Dogra Rajputs who were given land grants in Kashmir were mainly the kith and kin of the Dogra rulers.
6. Though a great mass of the people of Kashmir accepted Islam during the fifteenth-eighteenth centuries, a sizeable section of the Hindus were not converted to the new faith. This well-knit group whose members are now popularly known as Kashmiri Pandits has always struggled to maintain its identity. Demographically the Pandits formed approximately less then 7 per cent of population of Kashmir at the Dogra occupation of Kashmir, but they were a highly urbanized group and despite their overall numerical insignificance their demographic distribution was such that they were located in numbers in the city of Srinagar, the Center of Power, which was sufficient to remind both their rulers and their Muslim compatriots constantly of their presence.
7. The jagirs of the Dogra period should not be confused with the Mughal jagirs. While the Dogra jagirdar enjoyed unlimited powers and considered himself to be the virtual owner of the landed estate, the Mughal jagirdar was a mere functionary of the Government.
8. *Chaks* were the landed estates mainly under the possession of the Pandit officials of the Dogra Government. Lawrence, *The Vally of Kashmir*, p. 414.
9. In all probability, the term seems to have originated in the nineteenth century when Kashmiri literature developed a satirical style of its own.
10. More than three-fourths of the revenue of the Kashmir state was drawn from land and the cultivating classes, NAI/Foreign, [Pol.] Feb. See File no. 295.
11. In his preliminary report on the settlement operations in Kashmir in 1888, Wingate writes that prices were non-existent in the valley. Quoted in Lawrence, *The Vally of Kashmir*, p. 243. Lawrence also observes that when he

started his settlement operations in Kashmir in 1889 money prices did not exist. Salaries were paid in grain (ibid).

12. Pir Hasan Shan, *Tarithi Kashmir* (Persian text), II, Research and Publication Department, Jammu and Kashmir Government, not dated, pp. 833-4; 853-69.
13. The decline of the shawl trade in the seventies of nineteenth century, for example, forced some shawl weavers of the city of Srinagar to take to agriculture. See NAI/Foreign Sec. E, Pros., Feb. 1890, nos.106-10, KW, no. 3; also Foreign Sec., Feb. 1891, Sec. E, nos. 295-326, p. 28.
14. The observation is based on a comparative study of the coins of the eighteenth and nineteenth centuries Kashmir, made by the author of this paper, in the numismatic section of the Sri Pratap Singh Museum at Srinagar.
15. For greater details on the system of forced labour in Kashmir, see Ishaq Khan, 'Some Aspects of Begar in Kashmir', *Research Biannual*, vol. I, no. II, Srinagar 1971, pp. 58-71.
16. This question has been discussed at some length in Ishaq Khan, *Perspectives on Kashmir: Historical Dimensions*, Srinagar, 1993.
17. No evidence has been quoted by A.I. Tchitcherov to support his argument that 1,00,000 women were simultaneously engaged in the spinning of shawl wool and that 90,000 of this number sold yarn the market to earn their livelihood. Even if the learned Russian historian had furnished evidence, we would have doubted the authenticity of his statement considering the simple fact that the population of Srinagar never exceeded 1,25,000 number in the nineteenth century. A.I. Tchitcherov, *Economic Development in the 16th-18th Centuries*, Moscow, 1971, p. 217.
18. Ishaq Khan, *History of Srinagar: A Study in Socio-Cultural Change,* Srinagar, 1976, pp. 59-63
19. Ibid.
20. The system under which the shawl weavers were not allowed to leave Kashmir was known as *rahdari.*
21. For a detailed discussion on the monopolistic control exercised by the Dogra rulers over shawl industry, see Ishaq Khan, *History of Srinagar*, p. 62.
22. Ibid., pp. 56-63.
23. Armed with the authority of the rulers, the officials of the shawl department subjected the poor weaver to a great deal of tyranny which, in turn, often led to the extensive migration of the shawl weavers to the Punjab. But even deserting their own families did not assuage the troubles of the shawl weavers. This was because their escape was made difficult by the high mountain passes which were guarded. And even if they succeeded in managing their escape, the members of their families were not left in peace. See for greater details, ibid., p. 62.
24. K.M. Panikkar in his bid to prove the ameliorating zeal of the greedy and rapacious Gulab Singh says that as a result of new regulations, announced by the Maharaja, the shawl weaver become free and that he was no longer serf, Maharaja Gulab Singh. *Founder of Jammu and Kashmir*, London, 1930,

p.139. However, the evidence furnished by the contemporary Persian historian of Gulab Singh and corroborated by the travellers accounts belies Panikkar's argument. In fact, the shawl weaver was tied to his master, and was not allowed to work for another master. See, Hasan, *Tarikh-i-Kashmir*, I, p. 364; Andrew Wilson, *The Abode of Snow*, London, 1876, p. 398; Robert Therp, *Cashmere Misgovernment*, Gadru, Kashmir Papers, p. 67.

25. Kashmir Government Records (General), File no. 66/102/c of 1921. The Government also accorded permission to Sanatan Sabha to open its branch in Srinagar in 1923 on the distinct understanding that the Sabha will take no part in politics. Ibid., no. 46/G39 of 1923.
26. *Lahore Political Diaries, 1847-49*, vol. VI, p. 48; also Panikkar, 'Maharaja Gulab Singh', p. 139.
27. *Cashmere Misgovernment*, typed copy in the J & K Archives, pp.18-19; Mir Saifullah, *Tarikh-nama Kashmir*, Ibn-i-Mahjoor's collection, pp.100-1; Khalil Mir Janpuri, *Tarikh-i-Kashmir*, vol. II, MS, no. 800 (Research Library, Srinagar) p. 910; Pir Hasan, *Tarikh-i-Kashmir* (Urdu tr.), III, p. 577.
28. Hasan, *Tarikh-i-Kashmir* (Persian text), II, pp. 860-61, see also Pandit Hargopal Khasta, *Guldasta-i-Kashmir*, Lahore, 1883, pp. 222-4.
29. NAI/Foreign Sec., Oct. 1886, nos. 235-300, p. 20; J.C. Bose, *Cashmere and its Prince*, Calcutta, 1889, p. 3.
30. NAI/Foreign Sec., Feb. 1907, nos. 163-4.
31. Quoted in Prem Nath Bazaz, *The History of Struggle for Freedom in Kashmir*, New Delhi, 1954, pp.140-1.
32. Sir Albion Bannerji's words produced a stir in the young minds. He may fitly be said to have awakened from the slumber. The political awakening owes its origin to his openness, wrote the Resident of Kashmir. See *The Eastern Times*, 18 Feb. 1932. See also Jalali's note 'Wither Kashmir', in *J.L. Jalali's Collections*, Jammu & Kashmir State Archives, Srinagar.
33. NAI/Home, Pol., File no. 150 of 1934; see also *Civil and Military Gazette*, 4 Feb. 1932.
34. Rashid Ta Sir, *Tahreek-i-Hurriyat-i-Kashmir*, I, p. 95.
35. See Ishaq Khan, *History of Srinagar*, p.181.
36. Quoted in ibid.
37. Ibid.
38. Ibid.
39. Ibid.

People's Movement in the Princely State of Gwalior

MAYANK KUMAR

The history of national movement of India remains incomplete without an analytical study of the role played by the people residing in the Princely States. Whereas abundant literature has been produced on various aspects of the Freedom movement, no one has so far attempted a comprehensive work on their role in the Princely States of Hyderabad, Jamnagar, Kashmir, etc. There is a relative scarcity of literature as far as the state of Gwalior is concerned. An attempt is thus being made in this article to document the dynamics of the people's movement in the Princely State of Gwalior. However, before dwelling into the issue it is necessary to bring out the differences between Indian national movement and movements originating in the Princely States. What was the difference between 'British India' and 'Indian India'?

The answer to this question lies in the line of questions; what were that Indian states? What was their locus standi in relation to the British Government represented by Crown and with the British Indian provinces? And what was the nature of ruling elite in their respective states, etc?

The variegated pattern of the British conquest of India and the different stratagems, through which the various parts of the country were brought under colonial rule, had resulted in two-fifths of the subcontinent being ruled by Indian princes. The common feature was that all of them recognized the paramountcy of the British Government. Sir William Lee Warner wrote that 'A native state was a political community that occupied defined boundaries within India, subject to a common and responsible ruler who was actually enjoyed and exercised, as belonging to him in his right duly recognised by the supreme authority of the British Government, any of the function and attributes of sovereignty.'[1] In other words, the British guaranteed the princes against any threat to their autocratic power. In Princely States the absolute power was concentrated in the ruler or his favourites and administration was run as unmitigated autocracies. The burden of land tax was usually heavier. The rulers had unrestrained power over the state revenues which sustained ostentatious living and waste. This necessitated a heavier burden of land tax on the peasantry. Along with such conditions we find less of the rule of law and civil liberties. The states were usually bastions of economic, social, political, and educational backwardness.[2]

Not only the native rulers but also the British Government was responsible for such a situation. Since the Revolt of 1857, these princes were gradually developed by British Government as 'bulwarks of reaction'.[3] Their significance grew as the national movement strengthened. In return these were guaranteed against any threat to their autocratic power, even if forged internally by the natives of the state only. It was a relationship between the paramount power of British rule and subordinate Princely State.

The relationship between the paramount British Government and the Princely States was based on a peculiar understanding which kept on shifting according to the realities of time, being described by the Butler Committee as 'shifting necessities of time'.[4] Newer meanings were provided to this relationship to serve the imperial interests. The Butler Report represented that 'Paramountcy must remain paramount', but explicitly stated that it was not automatically transferable from the Crown to any future self-governing centre enjoying dominion status. Paramountcy would be exorcized by the Viceroy directly, not by the Governor-General in Council—a clear attempt to remove relations with the princes away from the orbit of a possible Congress dominated central government.[5]

Similarly the Government of India Act of 1935 had a provision, according to which the transfer of relations between the Crown and Indian states to the Crown representative—in practice, the Viceroy himself but functioning not through responsible ministers but via the purely official political department, local residents and political agents.[6] Through the various reports and acts British Government had deliberately tried to maintain the difference between British India and Indian India. Later Congress criticized even the Cabinet Mission Plan for not providing for elected members from the states for the Constituent Assembly.

British Government had established a working economic and political unity within British India with the Princely States, particularly in the economic field and to the extent dictated by imperial interests, welding the country into a composite and integrated unity. At the same time, it thwarted the unification of India by driving a wedge between the two parts of the county, i.e. British India and Indian India. This division was most wanted in the fields of social and political awakening. While British India progressed with the spread of 'English Education', newspapers, and the railways and in the early years of eighteenth century, sympathetic Englishmen, the Indian Princely States continued to be under the control of autocratic despots without any awakening for social and political causes.

The emergence and development of the national movement in British India, and the accompanying increase in political consciousness about democracy, responsible government, and civil liberties had an inevitable impact on the people of the states as well. The political activities of the Indian National Congress, the All India Muslim League, and other parties made the state's people conscious of their political rights. The events abroad such as the Russo-Japanese war and the principle of 'national self determination' as enunciated by Lenin during the Bolshevik Resolution in Russia also infused awakening in the people of the states. A much more powerful influence was exercised by the Non-Cooperation and Khilafat movements launched in 1920; around this time and under its impact, numerous local organizations of the states' people came into existence.

The emergence and development of state's people's movement was greatly influenced by the internal socio-political conditions in the respective states. States where the government was liberal and encouraged social awakening, educational opportunities, and even representative bodies witnessed less of such development as the basic thrust of state's people's movement was to secure a participatory government. The economic conditions of the states was also an important factor. States which encouraged industrial development, railways, etc., were able to cater to the demands of their people.

In this respect, Gwalior presents a picture of a liberal 'state' and hence we find very restrictive development of people's movement. In Gwalior, Praja Mandal was set up soon after the establishment of the All India State's People Conference, but for two reasons the freedom struggle mostly remained dormant and subdued. Firstly the administration happened to be somewhat broad-based and their rulers enlightened, comparatively speaking, Maharaja Madhav Rao Scindhia had established two bodies—Majlis-i-Am and Majlis-i-Kanoon for a better and representative governance.[7] Such arrangements satisfied the need for constitutional development for the time being. Demand for reform and for the responsible government were, no doubt, made but since the efforts were not backed by the masses as such, it was not followed by a popular agitation of the kind we witnessed in numerous other states.

Popular opinion was further softened by the Maharaja of Gwalior conceding diarchy in 1945, whereby certain departments were entrusted to the care of popular ministers, the reserved ones being administered by the ruler through his own nominee. Secondly in Gwalior, the Praja Mandal movement was largely confined to the educated sections of the society.[8] It could never percolate down to the lower strata.

Gwalior had a long tradition of national political awakening. People were very much influenced by the Swadeshi movement. In 1905, a small exhibition on swadeshi was organized. Initially the Gwalior government opposed any such political activity. The first political case was filed in 1908. Dr. Haribau Diwakar and Madhorav Desai were among the first thirty convicts of the case. They were convicted for rigorous imprisonment. Apparently this conviction had checked the political activities in the state.[9]

The Non-Cooperation movement also influenced the political atmosphere of the region. In an attempt to curb any kind of opposition to the visiting Prince of Wales to Gwalior, leaders like Lala Bawa and Siremal Dugar were imprisoned and Dugar was exiled later on.

Trisumbak Damodar Pustake constituted the first organized political party. He established the Sarvjanik Sabha, Ujjain. It was later on registered with the broad principles of social service through education, health, and by pressurizing the state for these reforms.[10]

In Gwalior there were some prominent public leaders, notably Vijayvargiya and Takhtmal Jain, who were widely respected, but it would be no exaggeration to say that they were as much amenable to the Maharaja as to the rank and file of their own organization.[11] Therefore, even during the ten years preceding independence Gwalior hardly experienced any large-scale turbulence.

Although legislatures, in the modern sense, did not exist in the former Gwalior State, the rulers of the state had adopted certain measures from time to time, to associate people in the framing of laws and in other matters of administration. The first step in this direction was taken as early as 1877 when the first municipality was constituted in the state. In 1906 a nominated body with ten members, called the Majlis-i-Khas, was created with the primary object of advising the ruler in the matters of legislation. Later in 1912, another nominated body called Majlis-i-Kanoon, was formed which consisted of all the members of the Majlis-i-Khas and any number of additional members, officials, and non-official representing various classes and interests such as jagirdars, landowners, bankers, mill-owners, etc. A similar boost was given to the movement by the formation of first panchayat in 1912 to extend the administrative experience to the rural people.[12]

A further step was taken in 1921, when another body called the Majlis-i-Am was constituted. It was composed, among others, of all the members of Majlis-i-Kanoon[13] and 63 non-official members, the latter having a majority over the official members who had no vote. All the non-official members except those representing the graduates were indirectly elected by various institutions representing diverse interests such as District Boards, Municipalities, Wakaf Committees, Association of Jagirdars and Money-lenders, Chamber of Commerce, etc. The Majlis-i-Am could express its views, in the form of resolutions on bills referred to it by government but the resolutions had to be submitted to the ruler, who was not bound to accept them.[14]

The real impetus for representative government developed only after the enactment of the Government of India Act of 1935. It was during 1938 that the Sarvjanik Sabha of Ujjain, being a registered association was extended/projected as a state level organization by establishing numerous branches all over state. It later on became the State Congress.[15]

Due to the efforts made by the leaders, the Maharaja inducted the three non-official members of Majlis-i-Am in the administrative reforms committee. Another scheme put forward by the State Congress aimed at ensuring the establishment of a responsible government within five years.

The report of the Administrative Reforms Committee was finalized unanimously and submitted to the king. However, when the king declared the provision of administrative reforms, the State Congress felt that there had been a dilution in report. Hence the State Congress opposed it by boycotting the Franchize Committee. Later on the king was forced to revise his proposal, but even these could not satisfy the State Congress.

Despite the opposition of the State Congress, the government went ahead with their programme of creation of a bicameral legislature, to be known as Praja Sabha and Samant Sabha. In an attempt to provide representation to various sections of the society, the state was divided into two kinds of constituencies, viz., special and territorial. The former representing various interests such as trade and commerce, industries, jagirdars, etc., and the latter, which was further divided into urban and rural, representing the people of the state. However, in total the Franchize was extended only to 20 per cent of the adult population. The election to the Praja Sabha and Raj Sabha could be held only in 1945. The Praja Sabha had the strength of 90 members, of whom 55 were directly elected while the remaining 35 were nominated. The Raj Sabha was composed of 40 members, out of whom half were directly elected and rest were nominated. The members of the State Congress won the majority in the election despite various hindrances.[16]

Political opposition to the Britishers continued in the meantime. In response to the call for Quit India movement, there were witnessed numerous disturbances all over the state of Gwalior. Strikes were organized to oppose the imprisonment of national leaders. Colleges and schools were closed due to political disturbances. The Central Committee of the State Congress sent a resolution asking the king to sever its relations with the British Government and demanded representative government. It declared 30 August as the deadline for the king to accept the resolution failing which a Non-Violent movement was to be initiated. However, the government in an attempt to check any unforeseen circumstances started imprisoning leaders and political activists from 26 August.

Later, on 29 and 30 June 1943 an agreement was signed and all the political prisoners were released. It was in June 1946 that the State Congress as a formal association at Shivpuri session redefined its demand and asked the state government to constitute a popular Constitutional Committee to frame the Constitution for the state. The creation of an interim government was recommended as a short-term measure. In response, the state offered two seats in the Council of Ministers and their intention to move towards representative form of government. However, in November, the State Congress demanded the implementation of their demand by 31 December. Later, on the request of AIPSC the Direct Action Programme was postponed. Meanwhile in June 1947, an agreement was signed, whereby the State Congress sent its nominated minister to the Council of Ministers and also agreed to participate in the Administrative Reforms Committee.[17]

The declaration of Indian Independence changed the whole scenario. The first question, now was to determine the legal position of the Gwalior State in relation to independent India. The Congress had already criticized the Cabinet Mission Plan for not providing for elected members from the states. Nehru presided over the Gwalior session (April 1947) and declared that refusing to join the Constituent Assembly would be treated as hostile.

However, the above description very clearly highlights the following tendencies prevalent in the state of Gwalior. Initially in Gwalior the political demand was to secure a responsible government. A government is responsible for the social welfare of its subjects. The notion of welfare state was in a very nascent stage at the time. The prime concern of the common man was to ask for economic development of the state. The coming of railways must have satisfied the demands of the common man to a great extent. However, the coming of railways had also opened the floodgates of political activities in the state.

Gradually, the demand for a representative form of government got momentum and replaced the demand for a responsible government. The movement was to secure constitutional monarchy where the Constitution would provide the guiding principle.

At another plain, the struggle was to secure independence from foreign rule. In this struggle, help from monarchy was sought time and again, strengthening the argument that the ideal of people's movements in Gwalior was to secure a participatory form of government with monarchy at its top. Similarly the very fact that Nehru had made a declaration at Gwalior points out that there were certainly tendencies towards the integration with an independent India which was to be governed democratically.

NOTES

1. Ranjana Kaul, *Constitutional Development in the Indian Princely States*, New Delhi, 1998, p. 1.
2. Mridula Mukherjee, 'The Freedom Struggle in the Princely States', in Bipan Chandra, Aditya Mukherjee et al. (eds.), *India's Struggle for Independence*, New Delhi, 1988, p. 356.
3. Ibid.
4. R.L. Handa, *History of Freedom Struggle in Princely States*, New Delhi, 1968, p. 37.
5. Sumit Sarkar, *Modern India*, New Delhi, 1983, p. 265.
6. Ibid., p. 337.
7. V.S. Krishnan, ed., *Gazetteer of India, Madhya Pradesh, Gwalior*, Bhopal, 1965, p. 40.
8. R.L. Handa, *History of Freedom Struggle in Princely States*, 1968, p. 279.
9. Bhagwan Das Kela, *Deshi Rajyon ki Jan Jagrati*, Allahabad, 1948, p. 280.
10. Ibid., p. 281.
11. Ibid., p. 280.
12. V.S. Krishnan, ed., *Gazetteer,* p. 40.
13. Michael H. Brown, *Gwalior Today*, Bombay, 1940, p. 20.
14. V.S. Krishnan, *Gazetteer*, p. 341.
15. Bhagwan Das Kela, *Deshi Rajyon ki Jan Jagrati*, p. 280.
16. Ibid., p. 283.
17. Ibid., p. 285.

People's Movement in the Princely States of Orissa in the Wider Context of the Nationalist Movement: A Case Study of the Nilgiri State

ATUL CHANDRA PRADHAN

Nilgiri which now forms a subdivision of the Balasore district was, at the time of Independence, a 'B' class feudatory state, belonging to the Eastern States Agency. Bounded on the north and north-east by the Mayurbhunj State and on the west and south by the Moghulbundi district of Balasore, it was a small state, being about 281 sq. miles in area.[1] Its population, about 75,000 in 1947,[2] consisted of two main elements, Hindus (including caste Hindus and Untouchables) and the aborigines. The aborigines, belonging to such tribes as Kolbha, Munda, Santhal, and Bathudi, constituted 15 per cent of the total population,[3] and the Hindu Untouchables formed nearly 10 per cent.[4] Educationally, the Nilgiri State was very backward. According to the *Annual Report of the Nilgiri Durbar for 1943-4*, there were 33 schools in the state, out of which 24 were Lower Primary Schools, 8 Upper Primary Schools, and only one M.E. School.[5] Till 1946 there was no High School in Nilgiri.[6]

Like many other Princely States Nilgiri suffered from the misrule of arbitrary chiefs. The system of taxation was unjust and oppressive. The ordinary land revenue was much higher than that of the British ruled areas. In Nilgiri in 1939, the rent per acre of land was Rs. 5 which was quite high rate as compared with the cost of living of those days.[7] Besides the high rate of revenue, the people were subjected to such illegal exactions as *magan* (forced levies on ceremonial occasions), *salamies* (presents) and *rasad* (cesses collected for the provision of British officials and troops assessing through the state).[8] Major portion of the revenue collected from the people, legally or illegally, was appropriated to the coffer of the ruler. As it was found by the States Inquiry Committee, in Nilgiri, in 1938, although according to the state budget, the annual domestic expenditure of the palace was Rs. 50,000 out of the net income of Rs. 1,50,000 the ruler practically managed to spend more than half of the state's income for his private domestic purposes. This could be possible because there was no clear-cut demarcation between the public treasury and the ruler's private privy purse.[9]

Besides the unjust financial system narrated above, the people of Nilgiri also suffered from the following handicaps, arising out of an arbitrary system of government:

(1) it was not possible for the public to secure authentic and adequate information regarding the administration, moral and material progress, as well as the social, economic, and political conditions prevailing therein;
(2) there was no rule of law, even proper codification of laws was absent;
(3) no fundamental rights of citizenship were recognized, civil liberty was crushed, and the people were daily oppressed causing danger to the security of life and property of the people;
(4) the peasants had no rights in agricultural land. They could neither sell, nor mortgage, nor transfer it without the permission of the authorities. High mutation fees were levied, even when permission was granted for the transfer. The cultivator was a mere tenant-at-will liable to be ejected at the whim of the ruler or the state authorities;
(5) *bethi* or forced labour for *shikar* excursions and *kheda* (catching of elephants with its attendant—evils such as the wastage of the peasant's time at the time of sowing and harvesting, and wastage of crops) were also prevalent in Nilgiri;
(6) interference by the state authorities in the social and religious life of the people and the exercise of wide powers of control over them through caste panchayats and ecclesiastical courts impeded the march of progress and served as agencies of oppression;
(7) there was no security of tenure for public services. Nepotism was widespread in matters of recruitment;
(8) there were hardly any local self-government institution worth the name, civic amenities were, therefore, non-existent;
(9) the judiciary was entirely dependent upon the ruler and the impartial administration of justice was, therefore, not easily available;
(10) 'nation-building departments' were systematically starved. The quality of what little work they produced was very poor.[10]

Thus the people were not only oppressed by the Raja but also exploited by the *sarbarakars* (rent-collectors), the *lakhrajdars* (those who enjoyed rent-free lands and constituted the aristocracy of the state) and the moneylenders.[11]

According to Banamali Das, who himself belonged to a family of the *lakhrajdar*, the poor aborigines used to pay to these privileged classes heavy interests for loans, free labour and vegetables free of cost.

The last ruling chief of Nilgiri during whose time the process of transition from feudalism to democracy started and attained a successful culmination was Kishor Chandra Mardaraj. A product of the Ajmer College, the Raja twice visited England. According to Banamali who was politically active against him, the Raja was a patron of arts, sports, and music, but he made himself thoroughly unpopular by openly indulging in drunkenness and debauchery with tribal women.[12]

The growth of nationalism in the Balasore district whose headquarters, the Balasore town, was only 15 miles away from Raj Nilgiri, the headquarters of the state, had its repercussion among the people of Nilgiri. Consequently, from the beginning of the Gandhian nationalist movement, some people from Nilgiri became involved in it. During the Non-Cooperation movement, from Nilgiri, Khirodananda Devagoswami, Lakshmidhar Misra, and Pranabandhu Agasti associated themselves with the Congress activities.[13]

As the 1920s advanced, the increasing political consciousness arising out of the Gandhian movement, tended to give a new direction to the people's latent resentment against the unjust rule of the chiefs. Consequently, it was found that some conscious people whose number increased with the passage of time simultaneously fought against the Raja's oppression and also took part in the nationalist movement. However, with the joining of Harekrushna Mahtab, an young Congress leader from Balasore district, the Nilgiri affairs got radically changed from the beginning of the Gandhian movement.

At the beginning of 1928, about 1,000 people, protesting against the injustice of the Raja, left Nilgiri and came to Balasore. Their main grievance was that the chief was repeatedly compelling them to give *bethi* or forced labour for the *kheda* or elephant-catching operation.[14] Their another complaint was the collection of *magan* for the marriage of the chief's daughter.[15] In this unrest the Congress workers sympathized with the fugitive rebels from Nilgiri by providing them food and shelter.[16] Mahtab published an anonymous booklet, called *Nilgiri Atyachar* (oppression in Niligiri) and its distribution roused the ferment among the people. He also wired to C.F. Andrews, the Christian missionary and philanthropist, to intervene.[17] Andrews came to Nilgiri in February 1928.[18] Through the arbitration of Andrews and the intervention of the Political Department, a settlement was arrived at and the fugitives went back to their houses.[19]

From among the people of Nilgiri, Hadibandhu Raj played an important role in this movement. As Banamali Das pointed out, Raj was sentenced to imprisonment for one year by the Raja on the charge of having played an important role in this movement.

Mahtab has made the following eulogistic remark about this movement: 'To leave homes and go on self exile as a technique of Satyagraha was widely known all over India after the Bardoli Satyagraha of 1930. . . . The people of Nilgiri and Orissa may justly feel proud of the fact that they had learnt and implemented the technique earlier.'[20]

By 1930, revolutionary consciousness had further spread in Nilgiri. The people who had agitated against the injustice of their ruler also took active part in the Civil Disobedience movement against the British Raj. An emotional link was established between the agitation against the oppressive native chief and the movement against British Raj which gave protection to the chiefs. In the spectacular Salt satyagraha which took place in the seashore of Balasore, a number of people from Nilgiri took part. Mentioned below are the names of the people of Nilgiri who took part in the Civil Disobedience movement, viz., Bipracharan Mohapatra, Daityari Prasad Rath, Gajendra Nath De, Golak Nath De, Hadibandhu Sa, Jagannath Rana, Kalicharan Parida, Kasinath Mahapatra, Meheshwar Pradhan, Nimai Charan Chowdhury, Pranabandhu Agasthi, and Pranabandhu Parida.[21] Golak Nath Del whose name has been mentioned above was a pleader by profession. His pleader license was cancelled by the high court for his revolutionary activities. He was the Secretary of the Balasore District Congress Committee and also a member of the Pradesh Congress Committee. He was a volunteer in the first batch of Salt satyagrahis.[22]

By 1931 an attempt was made by Sarangadhar Das, the leader of the popular unrest against the Dhenkanal Durbar, to channellize the popular resentment in all the Princely States of Orissa into one organization. He organized the Praja Sammilani at Cuttack with the help of the Congress leaders like Nabakrushna Choudhuri and Malati Choudhuri in 1931. This Sammilani, also known as the Orissa States People's Conference, was held under the presidency of Pattabhi Sitaramayya.[23]

However, this organization remained dormant till 1937-8. It was in 1937-8 that the people's movement in the several Princely States of Orissa, specially Nilgiri, entered into a critical and decisive phase because of the second Orissa State People's Conference and the Constitution of the State

Inquiry Committee to collect evidences from the states' people and prepare report on their grievances. The second Orissa States People's Conference was held at Cuttack on 23 June 1937 under the presidency of Patttabhi Sitaramayya. Sitaramayya appealed to the Orissa States' people to form the Congress Committee and fall in line with their fellow countrymen in British India. This conference called upon the rulers of the Orissa States to confer upon their subjects rights of occupancy on their holding and fundamental rights of citizenship. This conference also urged them to abolish the evil practice of extracting *rasad*, *magan* and *bethi*.[24]

In this Conference a committee consisting of Satish Chandra Bose, Balwantray Mehta, Braja Sundar Das, and Sarangadhar Das (Convener) was appointed to investigate and report on the illegalities in the states. This conference also authorized its delegates to form 'people's sabhas' in their respective states.[25]

The committee, mentioned above, was reconstituted by the Working Committee of the Orissa States People's Conference on 6 June 1938 with the following members—Harekrushna Mahtab, Lalmohan Patnaik, and Balwantray Mehta.[26] Mahtab was elected as the Chairman of the Committee on 20 June 1938. The committee began its work and People's Associations were formed in different states.[27] In Nilgiri the Praja Mandal was formed under the presidency of Kailas Chandra Mohanty, a lawyer.[28] The Congress and socialist leaders patronized the agitation in the states. In June 1938 Sarangadhar Das organized a party of volunteers to carry on propaganda in Nilgiri.[29]

The all-Orissa State Enquiry Committee and the local Praja Mandals became the channels for ventilating the accumulated discontent of the people of the states. They could now feel that they could voice their grievances in a forum instead of crying in wilderness as they had done earlier. The people, in hundreds, came forward to give evidences before the States Inquiry Committee, but the chiefs not only refused to comply with the communications from the committee but also adopted repressive measures towards those who came forward to give evidence. At this time, the ruler of Nilgiri created a tense situation in his state by imposing heavy fines on people for the alleged 'offence of intending on a social occasion'.[30] The Nilgiri ruler's repressive policy added fuel to the flame. As pointed out by Mahtab, thousands of people spontaneously came forward and held meetings and processions to protest against the repressive policy of the Durbar. Meetings and processions were banned by the Durbar. Those who organized the meetings were fined, flogged, and imprisoned. But the Durbar found it difficult to collect the fines, because if anybody's property was confiscated, thousands of people surrounded his house and the police could not dare to remove his property. The Darbar asked for police help from the government of Orissa, but the Congress ministry refused to give police help for the alleged oppression of the people. Thereafter, the Political Agent, Major R.L. Bazelgette brought police from the Mayurbhanj State. Bazelgette was astonished to see the discipline and unity of the revolutionary mob.[31]

On 5 July 1938, 116 Praja Mandal agitators were arrested in Nilgiri.[32] Due to the harassment by the Durbar, the Praja Mandal agitators found it difficult to maintain their headquarter in Nilgiri. They made a village of the Balasore district on the border of Nilgiri their headquarter. From that village trained volunteers were sent to Nilgiri by their leader, Gour Chandra Das, a Congress socialist.[33]

Early in July 1938, an attempt for compromise between the Durbar and the Praja Mandal agitators was made through negotiations between the Political Agent and the Diwan of Nilgiri on one hand and the President and Secretary of the Nilgiri Praja Mandal on the other. But the negotiations ended in failure.[34]

The movement in Nilgiri became particularly intense after the arrest of Banamali Das, the Secretary of Nilgiri Praja Mandal, on 10 August 1935.[35] Banamali Das was a popular young leader, twenty years old at that time and had recently passed the Matriculation Examination from the Balasore Zilla School. On 10 August, also, the police lathi-charged and fired upon the agitators, as a result of which some were wounded.[36] Being infuriated over this incident, the people declared the Raja's family ex-communicated.[37] In the final stage of the agitation, Kailas Chandra Mohanty gathered a mob of eight to ten thousand people to launch the Civil Disobedience movement against the Durbar. At this stage, Mahtab, the Chairman of the States Enquiry Committee, intervened. The Political Agent, Major Bazelgette and the Collector of Balasore, Solomon also made efforts to restore normalcy. After much discussion among Kailas Chandra Mohanty, the Diwan, and Mahtab, a settlement was finally made. As a result, the rebellious people withdrew the ex-communication of the Raja's family and the Raja released those whom he had arrested and imprisoned.[38] The people were granted civil liberties and the right to ventilate their grievances before the ruler in a constitutional manner.[39] According to Banamali Das, as a result of this agreement, the practices like *bethi* and *maqan* were abolished. But the Raja did not concede the Praja Mandal's demand for the formation of a state assembly and the popular control over the state budget.[40]

The 1938 movement in Nilgiri was a success. As found by the States Enquiry Committee whose work was completed by 18 July 1939, in only two states of Orissa, people enjoyed civil liberties like the freedom of speech and association. They were Nilgiri and Mayurbhanj.[41] Banamali Das observed that the successful agitation of 1938 strengthened the position of the Praja Mandal which hereafter took an upper hand in the affairs of the state.

By 1938, as a result of the interaction and coordination between the Praja Mandal and the National Congress, the Praja Mandal movement became a part of the nationalist movement. As Mahtab pointed out, some of the Praja Mandal leaders themselves were also Congressmen. The Official report of 4 November 1938 made the following observation about the link between the nationalist movement and the Praja Mandal movement:

> A noticeable feature of most, if not all, these meetings is the fact that the British Government is described as the root of the trouble. The economic condition of the States tenants appears to be forgotten and the whole agitation is apparently considered a part of the general struggle against the British imperialism.[42]

The States Enquiry Committee also observed:

> that most of the States border on one or more sides of the districts in the province of Bihar or Orissa were adjoining. The messages of the great national leaders of the Indian National Congress like Mahatma Gandhi, penetrated into the forest-bound hinterland of the States and kindled the hearts of the States' people to deal with the problems confronting them. The agrarian legislation of the popular cabinets also reached them....[43]

The Nilgiri Praja Mandal endorsed the Congress party's demand for freedom on the outbreak of the Second World War in September 1939. Kailas Chandra Mohanty took an active part in the Individual Civil Disobedience movement. He delivered an anti-war lecture at Ambodia Hat and was sentenced to six months' rigorous imprisonment.[44] Besides Mohanty, Bhagaban Puhan, and Chintamani Naik from Nilgiri also took part in the Individual Civil Disobedience movement.[45]

The Quit India movement of 1942 had a remarkable impact upon the people of Nilgiri, for which they suffered repression by the Durbar. According to the annual report of the Durbar for 1943-4, the number of convicts in jail increased because of their participation in the Quit India movement.[46] Batakrushna Sarangi, Hadibandhu Raj Kshetramohan Behera, Madhu Das, and Chintamani Naik, etc., took active part in the 1942 movement.[47] In the Tudigadia mob uprising which took place in

September 1942 the people from Nilgiri took part and in this uprising some Santhals of Nilgiri were killed.[48]

From 1942 to 1946, the ruler of Nilgiri remained out of power on account of his inability to provide an administration to the state.[49] Full powers were restored to him a few months before Independence. But the government was well aware of his unpopularity and the fact that he would have to face agitation from Congressmen and state agitators of Orissa in his state. In an interview in July 1946 H. J. Todd, the Resident of Eastern States Agency, told the Raja about his inability to counter such an agitation effectively.[50] Soon after the complete restoration of powers, the Raja started the move to counteract the Praja Mandal party by forming a party of his own, consisting mostly of aborigines. He also recruited a number of Gurkha armed guards in his Police Force from the eastern states joint Police Force and also two platoons of the Punjabi Muslims.[51]

On the other hand, as the country was heading towards Independence, the Praja Mandal party began to make preparations for wresting power from the ruler and establish a provisional government on the border of the state. They began to capture the officers and other state officials. They also captured grain shops and resorted to picketing and social boycott of the state officials.[52]

In the meantime, the first session of the Orissa and C.P. Regional Council of the All India State People's Conference was held at Cuttack on 1 March 1947. This meeting decided that democratic rule should be introduced in the states and that the states should act in collaboration with the neighbouring provinces. This meeting also elected ten delegates to the general council of the All India State's People's Conference which included the leader of the Nilgiri Praja Mandal, Kailas Chandra Mohanty. To direct the Praja Mandal movement of the states in a systematic manner, this meeting constituted a Working Committee under the presidency of Sarangadhar Das. Kailas Chandra Mohanty was also a member of this committee.[53]

Shortly before Independence, a local branch of the Communist Party had come to prominence in Nilgiri. Organized by Banamali Das, the first Secretary of the local Praja Mandal. Das had been expelled from the Praja Mandal in May 1940 because of his Communist ideas.[54] Das told that he had organized a secret and underground Communist Party in Nilgiri in 1940. The Communists played two roles simultaneously: (i) they joined hands with the Praja Mandal in fighting against the Raja; on the other hand, (ii) they championed the cause of the landless labourers, mainly tribals belonging to Kolha and Munda tribes, against the exploitation by the privileged classes.

As Das pointed out, though the Praja Mandal leaders had fought against the Raja's oppression, socially many of them indulged in the exploitation of the weaker sections of the society, specially since 1938.[55]

While the Praja Mandal was carrying on its activities for the capture of power from the Raja, the pro-Raja tribal people began to take forcible possession of lands belonging to the non-aboriginal people, and moved about in the state with bows and arrows. They announced that the paddy fields belonged to them, and they would kill or injure anybody who dared to resist them. These loyalist tribals were led by a convicted criminal named Sandhya Singh, who had been released on 15 August 1947. According to the press communique of the Orissa Government, the Nilgiri State Police remained indifferent to the activities of the tribal people.

On 31 October 1947 when the District Magistrate of Balasore contacted the ruler of Nilgiri about the disturbance, the latter pleaded that he was unable to put down the disturbance with the small force at his disposal. On 29 October 1947, the Praja Mandal workers brought two dead bodies to the Balasore town, and also hospitalized two people who had been injured. A state of lawlessness and terrorism prevailed in Nilgiri since the end of October. The whole administration of the state was in a virtual state of collapse. Mail service of the state failed to function, even transport service between Balasore and Nilgiri was cut off.[56]

From the standpoint of the Praja Mandal and the Congress Government of Orissa, the tribals were instigated by the Raja against the Praja Mandal. The press communique of the Orissa Government pointed out that 'the just or fancied grievance of the aboriginal supporters of the ruler were exploited to put them in a rebellious mood and to induce them to imagine that the Praja Mandal party were responsible for all their shortcomings, for their inferior position in the economic and social life of the state and indeed for all wrongs done to them in the past'.[57]

On the other hand 'it was contended on behalf of the Rajah that the aborigines did not need any instigation from him; that their grievances were economic'.[58]

The Communist role in the clash between the Praja Mandal and the loyalist tribals made the situation more complicated. Though they were no supporters of Raja, yet ideologically they were sympathetic to the economic interests of the landless tribals, many of whom supported the

Raja. That was probably the reason why Mahtab held this about the Communists' role in the Nilgiri disturbances in his autobiography.

> In Nilgiri, the Darbar's policy and also that of the Communists towards the tribals put them in such a rebellious mood that the tribals set fire to the houses of the non-tribals and forcibly harvested paddy crops of the latter and the tribal uprising assumed serious proportions. The non-tribals left their villages and came to the nearby villages in the Balasore district. A tense situation prevailed. The Communist leader Sharat Pattnayak met me and discussed with me about this matter in the *Prajatantra* office. We discussed about solution. During conversation, I suggested, 'If the Rajah is removed, what might be the reaction?' He did not give due importance to this. Both of us agreed about the necessity to pacify the tribals, because if, they are excited, they become uncontrollable.[59]

Banamali Das believes that in 1947 the tribals were divided into three groups:

(1) the rich aborigines, mainly belonging to the Santhal tribe, supported the Praja Mandal;
(2) a section of the poor aborigines were anti-Raja, anti-British, and were opposed to their exploitation by the upper classes. These aborigines were under the influence of the Communists;
(3) another section of the aborigines were pro-Raja and were opposed to the Praja Mandal agitators whom the former regarded as social exploiters.

Mahtab holds that the tribals were so backward that they did not know much about politics and they only understood their economic interest on which the Raja conveniently harped and instigated them against the Praja Mandal.[60]

In any case, the Communists were opposed to the Raja for which they had a serious clash with the loyalist tribals on 12 November 1947. According to Banamali Das, in this clash which was reported in the Orissa Government's press communique as one between the Communists and the tribals, on the Communists' side there were 150 armed tribal volunteers out of a total of 200 Communist volunteers. The Communist tribal volunteers raised such slogans in their language as '*Ara Taga Tainto*' (long live the red flag) and '*Rajren Dalalka Hese Kape Hese Kape*' (kill the loyalists).[61]

But Mahtab's contention was that the tribals in general had no understanding of the sophisticated ideology of the Communists. It may also be substantially borne out by this clash which was officially reported as one between the Communists and tribals.

In the meantime, the Praja Mandal party, in a meeting held on 1 November 1947 decided to serve an ultimatum on the Raja that if he failed to suppress the rising of aborigines within thirty-six hours, the Praja Mandal workers would take any action they deemed necessary for the establishment of peace and order, and that the people would take steps to place the administration in the hands of their representatives. It was also decided that the Praja Mandal party would form a provisional Azad (independent) Nilgiri Government under the leadership of Kailas Chandra Mohanty with effect from 4 November 1947. But at the instance of two members of the Board of Rulers of Eastern States Union of which Nilgiri was an acceding state, who visited Nilgiri on 3 November 1947, the Praja Mandal party entered into negotiation with the Durbar for the establishment of a responsible government. As a result of this negotiation the ruler of Nilgiri, by a public proclamation, invited Kailas Chandra Mohanty to form a popular government. It was decided that Mohanty would form a popular ministry on 14 November 1947.

But soon the events took a different turn and the ruler changed his earlier decision. On 12 November, the clash took place between the loyalist tribals and the Communists. Firearms were used and a number of persons were killed. On that day, the loyalist tribals plundered two villages and set fire to a number of houses. On 13 November, the Raja informed Kailas Chandra Mohanty that instead of heading the responsible government, he would be one of the three ministers, and the other two ministers would be selected by the Raja himself. At this, Mohanty broke off negotiations with the ruler. As a result, the disturbance once again started, and a large village in the disturbed area was gutted.[62]

Meanwhile, the Government of Orissa took serious note of the disturbance in Nilgiri and became apprehensive that the violent activities of the tribals of Nilgiri might excite the tribals in other areas to take resort to similar activities. The Government of Orissa, which was at that time headed by Herekrushna Mahtab, the veteran Congressman who had also played a key role in the Nilgiri disturbance of 1938, drew the attention of the state's ministry of the Dominion Government of India to which Nilgiri had become an acceding member, to the lawless situation in Nilgiri. About Government of India's concern for the tribal outbreak in Nilgiri. P.V. Menon, the Secretary of the States at that time, made the following observation in his autobiography later on:

The greatest concern to the Government of India was the possibility that outbreaks among the aborigines might spread to those neighbouring areas in which they formed a considerable proportion of the population. They are easily excited, and being accustomed to the use of bows and arrows, are difficult for the unarmed plainsmen to withstand. Troubles with the aborigines had often broken out in the past and had cost considerable effort and expense to put down. It appeared that the time had come to take firm and immediate action if chaos was to be prevented.[63]

Following a discussion between Sardar Vallabhbhai Patel, the Home Minister of India and H.K. Mahtab, the Prime Minister of Orissa,[64] the Government of India, authorized the Government of Orissa, by its telegram, dated 8 November 1947 to take over the administration of Nilgiri and restore law and order.

However, in view of the negotiations between the Praja Mandal party and the ruler, the Government of Orissa deferred its intervention in Nilgiri. The failure of the negotiation and the prevailing chaotic situation finally compelled Orissa Government's intervention. On 14 November, the District Magistrate of Balasore proceeded to Raj Nilgiri with an adequate force to take over the administration of the state.[65] Mahtab gives the following description of the takeover of Nilgiri by the Orissa Government in his autobiography:

On 14 November, as per the earlier plan, under the command of Senapati, Orissa Military Police marched to Nilgiri. On the way the villagers gave them overwhelming ovation. The Communists extended full cooperation. The fugitive non-aborigines were following the police force. The aborigines went to the Rajah. The Rajah contacted the police of Eastern State Federation, but they replied that they had received no order from their Inspector General of Police. Moreover, they did not possess adequate arms. The Dewan and the police Sub-Inspector of the Rajah were on leave. All the officials of the ruler were absent. Giving prior intimation, Senapati met the Rajah, described to him the chaotic condition of Nilgiri and showed some photographs of non-aborigine villages. The Rajah looked surprised. Then Senapati hinted that under the prevailing circumstances it would be good for the Rajah as well as his subjects, if the Orissa Government took over the administration of the state. After a little thinking, the Rajah agreed....[66]

There was no armed resistance from the Raja. He peacefully handed over the administration to the Government of Orissa and issued a proclamation, expressing therein his gratitude to the Government of India for the decision to take over the administration of his state and asking all the state officials to extend their fullest support and cooperation to the new administration. The Collector of Balasore, in a statement prepared according to the instruction of the Government of Orissa, promised to administer the state with 'strict impartiality', 'to dole out justice to all sections of the public and all citizens without fear or favour', and to give special attention to the grievances of aborigines.[67] Afterwards, the merger of Nilgiri in Orissa was legalized by the passing of the Extra Provincial Act in the dominion parliament and the merger plan of the states ministry, which was finally implemented on 14 and 15 December 1947.

In conclusion, we may identify some redeeming features of the political movement in Nilgiri. First, since the beginning of the Congress movement under Gandhian leadership, some politically conscious people of Nilgiri simultaneously carried on their fight on two fronts; they fought with the Raja for civil rights within the state and they responded to the clarion call of the Congress and fought against the colonial rule. Secondly, unlike the political movements of the other states, the movement of Nilgiri in 1938 was a substantial success. Thirdly, the movement in Nilgiri was mass-based and well organized. Even the Political Agent, Major Bazelgette, was astonished to see the discipline and unity of the rebellious mob. That was most probably due to the training and guidance provided by the Congress party. Quite a number of the political leaders in Nilgiri suffered imprisonment and physical torture for the cause of democracy. Finally, in the last phase of the Praja Mandal movement, an unpleasant situation was created by the Raja's policy of recruiting a body of tribal loyalists and the tribals' susceptibility to easy instigation and violence. The Communists, with their ideological sympathy for the landless tribals some of whom had been instigated by the Raja, found themselves in an imbroglio which was resolved by the timely political and military action of the Governments of Orissa and India.

NOTES

1. H.K. Mahtab, *Beginning of the End*, Cuttack, 1972, Appendix XXXII, p. 253; Orissa Government's Press Communique, 15 November 1947.
2. Ibid.
3. V.P. Menon, *The Story of the Integration of the Indian States,* Orient Longman, 1956 (rpt. 1969), p. 146.
4. This information was verbally gathered from Banamali Das, the noted Praja Mandal leader and ex-MLA of Nilgiri.
5. *The Annual Administration Report of the Nilgiri State (Eastern State Agency) for the year 1943-44*, publishhed under the authority of the Nilgiri Durbar, p. 29.
6. Verbal statement of Banamali Das.
7. *Report of the States' Enquiry Committee*, 1939, p. 8.
8. Ibid., pp. 15-17, 55.

9. Ibid., pp. 9-11.
10. Ibid., pp. 53-6.
11. This information was collected from Banamali Das.
12. Interview with Banamali Das.
13. See *Who's Who of Freedom Workers in Orissa, Mayurbhanj, Keonjhar and Balasore Districts,* published by the State Committee for Compilation of 'Who's Who' of Freedom Workers in Orissa.
14. Mahtab, *Dasha Varsar Odisa (1920-30)*, 1st published in 1935, rpt., Cuttack, 1977, p. 70.
15. Mahtab, *Sadhanar Pathe*, vol. I, *(1899-1950)*, Cuttack, 1972, p. 120.
16. Mahtab, *Dasha Varsar Odisa*, p. 71. See the extract from C.F. Andrews' *India and Simon Commission.*
17. Mahtab, *Sadhanar Pathe*, vol. I, pp. 120-1.
18. *Utkal Dipika*, 25 February 1928.
19. *Report of the Orissa State Enquiry Committee*, p. 6 and also Mahtab, *Dasha Varsar Odisa*, p.121.
20. Mahtab, *Dasha Varsar Odisa*, p. 71.
21. See *Who's Who of Freedom Workers in Orissa, Mayurbhanj, Keonjhar and Balasore Districts*, published by the State Committee for Compilation of 'Who's Who' of Freedom Workers in Orissa.
22. Ibid., p.124.
23. N.K. Sahu, Sarangadhar Das (1887-1957) in *Dictionary of National Biography*, vol. I, [ed.] S.P. Sen, Calcutta, 1972, p. 361.
24. *Indian Annual Register*, 1937, vol. I, pp. 356-7.
25. Ibid., p. 358.
26. *Report of the Orissa State Enquiry Committee*, p. 1.
27. Ibid., p. 358.
28. Mahtab, *Sadhanar Pathe*, p. 185.
29. *Diary of Political Events in Orissa, 1 April 1936 to 15 August 1947*, [ed.] Sushil Chandra De, published by the Committee for Compilation of 'Who's Who' of the Freedom Movement, Bhubaneswar, 1964, p.18.
30. Radhanath Rath, 'The Story of Freedom Movement in Orissa States', in M.N. Das, *Sidelights on History and Culture of Orissa*, [ed.] M.N. Das, Cuttack 1977, p. 286.
31. Mahtab, *Sadhanar Pathe*, pp. 185-6.
32. *Diary of Political Events in Orissa, 1 April 1936 to 15 August 1947,* p.19.
33. Mahtab, *Sadhanar Pathe*, pp.185-6.
34. *Diary of Political Events in Orissa, 1 April 1936 to 15 August 1947*, p.19.
35. Ibid., p.19.
36. Ibid.
37. *History of the Freedom Movement in Orissa*, vol.V (Supplement), [ed.] Prabhat Mukherjee, Sushil De and Sudharkar Patnaik, published by the Secretary, State Committee for Compilation of History of the Freedom Movement in Orissa, 1959, p. 123.

38. Mahtab, *Sadhanar Pathe*, pp. 186-8.
39. Rath, 'The Story of Freedom Movement', p. 286.
40. *Diary of Political Events in Orissa, 1 April 1936 to 15 August 1947*, p. 19.
41. *Report of the States Enquiry Committee*, p. 54.
42. *History of Freedom Movement in Orissa*, vol. IV, Govt. of Orissa Publication, p. 19.
43. *Report of State Enquiry Committee*, p. 578.
44. Balasore Records 1940-2, ACC no. 60, WWCC, BCSCA, Move File of 1940 (Orissa State Archives), Letter no. 698/C, dated 16 December 1940 from the Collector of Balasore to the Chief Secretary, Orissa.
45. See *Who's Who of Freedom Workers in Orissa, Mayurbhanj, Keonjhar and Balasore Districts*.
46. *The Annual Administration Report of the Nilgiri State for the year 1943-4*, pp. 14-5.
47. See *Who's Who of Freedom Workers in Orissa, Mayurbhanj, Keonjhar and Balasore Districts*.
48. Balsore Records, 1942, ACC no. 57, WWCC, Confidential letter from Collector Balasore to the Chief Secretary, Orissa, dated 25 September 1942.
49. Mahtab, *Beginning of the End*, Appendix XXIII, D.O. no. 1017, dated 15 November 1947 from T. Satyanarayana, Officer on Special Duty, Eastern States Agency to C.C. Desai, Additional Secretary to the Government of India, Ministry of States, New Delhi.
50. Ibid., Appendix XXI, p. 250.
51. Ibid., Appendix XXII, Orissa Government's Press Communique, dated 15 November 1947.
52. See Orissa Government's Press Communique, dated 15 November 1947.
53. Rath, 'The Story of the Freedom Movement', pp. 292-3.
54. Balasore Records 1940-2, ACC no. 60, WWCC, BCSCA, Move File of 1940 (Orissa State Archives), letter from the Collector of Balasore to the Commissioner, dated 13 May 1940.
55. All the above information were collected from Banamali Das through interview.
56. See Orissa Government's Press Communique, dated 15 November 1947.
57. Ibid.
58. Menon, 'The Story of the Integration of the Indian State', p.146.
59. Mehtab, *Sadhanar Pathe*, p. 326.
60. Interview with Mahtab.
61. Interview with Banamali Das.
62. See Orissa Government's Press Communique, dated 15 November 1947.
63. Menon, The Story of the Integration of Indian State', p.147.
64. Mahtab, *Sadhanar Pathe*, p. 326.
65. See Orissa Government's Press Communique, dated 15 November 1947.
66. Mahtab, *Sadhanar Pathe*, p. 328.
67. See Orissa Government's Press Communique, dated 15 November 1947.

Freedom Struggle in the Banaganapalle State

K. MADDAIAH

No account of the Indian national movement would be complete without a reference to the struggle that the people in the Princely States carried on against the oppressive rule of their chiefs. By 15 August 1947, all the native states (five hundred and sixty-two in total) with the exception of a few like the Banaganapalle State had signed the Instruments of Accession.

LOCATION OF BANAGANAPALLE STATE

Banaganapalle[1] was a small and the only Muslim native state in the erstwhile Madras Presidency, with an area of 275 sq. miles. It is now in Kurnool district of Andhra Pradesh.[2] It was one of the five native states in the Presidency which had political relations with the Madras Government.[3] It lies between 15^{0} 29^{0} N and 77^{0} 59^{0} and 78^{0} 22^{0} E on the table-land of the southern Deccan, at a height of about 800 feet above the sea level. It was bound on the north by Ramallakota (now Dhone) and Nandyal taluqs, on the east and south by Nandyal and Koilkuntla taluqs and on the west by Pattikonda and Koilkuntla taluqs. In its heyday, Banaganapalle had 64 villages. The population of Banaganapalle mandal, according to the 1991 census was 74,823. Majority of the population were Hindus. The Muslims and the Christians came next. The Muslims were mostly sunnis, though the Nawab himself was a shia. Telugu and Urdu were the principal languages of the state.[4]

BRIEF HISTORY

When Banaganapalle was ceded, along with other territories to the British Government, as a part of the subsidiary alliance, by the Treaty of 12 October 1800, it was agreed, in accordance with the stipulation of the Nizam who represented that the jagir was the 'sole means of subsistence of a numerous family', to allow Banaganapalle to remain in jagir to Asad Ali

Khan (Muzaffar-ul-Mulk) and Ghulam Ali Khan (Mansur-ud-Daula) and their family, subject to the permanent authority and control of the East India Company as sovereigns of the whole of the Nizam's late possessions south of Tungabhadra and Krishna rivers below their junction. The family which ruled Banaganapalle traces its descent from Ghulam Ali Khan who survived his uncle Asad Ali Khan. In 1920, the Government of India conferred on the Nawab, the honorary rank of the Second Lieutenant and a permanent salute of nine guns.[5] On 8 February 1921, when the Chamber of Princes, also known as Narendra Mandal was inaugurated at Delhi by the Duke of Connaught, the Nawab of Banaganapalle became one of its members.[6]

It may be mentioned here that Mir Fazle Ali Khan was installed on the *gaddi* of Banaganapalle by Lord Wellingdon, the Governor of Madras on 6 July 1922. Owing to certain administrative differences between Nawab Mir Fazle Ali Khan, Diwan Humayun Mirza,[7] and the British Resident, the Nawab was persuaded to relinquish his powers. The British Government administered the state from 1939 to 1947 through their Resident at Mysore.[8]

After World War II, the Government of India reviewed the situation in Banaganapalle and decided to restore the powers to Nawab Mir Fazle Ali Khan on 26 June 1947. The title His Highness was conferred on the Nawab and gun salutes of the state was increased from nine to eleven.[9]

REVOLT OF SANJAMALA, 1897-1898

It is interesting to note that a non-tax campaign was organized at the Sanjamala village in Banaganapalle State during 1897-8 against the irregular and heavy taxation of lands levied by Nawab Syed Fateh Ali Khan. This campaign was led by Belgaum Ismail Saheb, Golla Yenganna, Nallappa Reddy, Nagi Reddy, and other ryots. Initially, it was a peaceful satyagraha but the Nawab's henchmen provoked the people to take up arms. The Nawab got an opportunity to invoke the aid of armed police from the Collector of Kurnool who was the Political Agent of the state. The leaders of the movement were arrested and sentenced to imprisonment ranging from one year to life. By 1906, four of these prisoners were still in Banaganapalle jail. Two of them were life convicts. J.C. Molony who was appointed as the Assistant Political Agent of Banaganapalle State on 1 February 1905, reviewed their cases and decided to pardon them as he felt that the offences committed by them were largely due to ignorance and that they had been adequately punished.[10] However, information on the political activity, for that matter even on the general political situation in Banaganapalle between 1905 to 1947 is not available. It was only after the entry of Swami Hamsananda, Nivarthi Venkata Subbaiah, and Pendekanti Venkatsubbaiah in the affairs of the State and raising the demand for its merger with the Indian Union, that the Banaganapalle political affairs came to light.

FORMATION OF BANAGANAPALLE STATE CONGRESS COMMITTEE

Banaganapalle State Congress Committee (hereafter BSCC) was formed on 25 March 1947 with 11 members. The State Congress elected J. Satyanarayana as the President, S. Krishnamurthy as the General Secretary and I. Narasimham of Koilakuntla as the Office Secretary and Nukala Ramaiah as the Treasurer.[11] Under instructions from and as per the Constitution of the All India State's Peoples' Conference (hereafter AISPC), New Delhi[12] it had been affiliated to the Mysore State Congress (hereafter MSC)[13] and Mysore Regional Council (hereafter MRC).[14]

ACTIVITIES OF THE STATE CONGRESS

On 25 March 1947, J. Satyanarayana organized a meeting at Banaganapalle to highlight the high-handedness of the state authorities. The state police immediately arrived on the scene and arrested him and threatened the gathering with lathi-charge. J. Satyanarayana was released the next day on furnishing a security of Rs. 500. Again, on 5 April 1947, when he tried to organize a meeting at Kothapeta, he was arrested and released after a few hours with a severe warning. There was rumour that his entry into the state had been banned and that he was likely to receive a notice to this effect.[15]

PUBLIC MEETING AT KOILKUNTLA

Congress leaders and workers of Kurnool district met at Koilkuntla 5 mile beyond Banaganapalle State borders on 22 May 1947 to consider certain matters connected with the administration of the state. The Nawab of Banaganapalle had warned the people through a *tom tom*, not to attend the meeting. The police unleashed repression all over the state and the people were terror-stricken. In spite of police repression, the meeting was held and was presided over by G. Rami Reddy, the President of the Kurnool District Congress Committee[16] (hereafter KDCC). A total number of 160 delegates from all over the Kurnool district and 13 delegates from

Banaganapalle State attended the meeting. Addressing the meeting M. Venkatasubba Reddy, a prominent leader of the Koilkuntla Taluq Congress Committee said that the people of the state were very backward economically and were not enjoying the minimum civil liberties. Whatever liberties were enjoyed by the people, they were taken away by the officials of the state. J. Satyanarayana, the President of the BSCC said that the Durbar had served orders on him, externing him from the state. He also announced the election of K.V. Krishnamurthy Rao as the organizing Secretary of the State Congress. Y. Ramachandraiah, Secretary of the Kurnool Town Congress Committee and R.K. Ramalinga Reddy also spoke. K.Veerachari, a prominent Youth Congress leader assured the support of the youth for the State Congress. Hosur Sreeramulu, Dornala Venkatratnam from Pattikonda, Bysani Satyam and Yekkali Ramaiah from Giddalur and Yerragonlapalem also participated in the meeting. It was resolved at the meeting to start a branch office of the State Congress at Koilkuntla and to lead a deputation to the Diwan in regard to the matters connected with the state administration. P. Ramanatha Sastry advised the delegates to meet the Nawab instead of the Diwan. But G. Rami Reddy ruled out any meeting with the 'despotic Nawab'.[17]

Later in the evening, a public meeting was organized in the Edward Reading Room at Koilkuntla under the presidentship of K. Anki Reddy, the Secretary of the Kurnool District Congress. C. Bali Reddy, a prominent kisan leader stressed the need to unite the agricultural labourers for the welfare of the country and appealed to the delegates to extend all help to the people of the state. After the meeting was over, a burra katha, entitled Azad Hind Fauj was enacted by the Youth from Bheemunipadu village. A sub-committee was formed to take necessary steps for establishing popular government in the state. The members of the sub-committee were: (1) Four MLAs and one MLC from Kurnool district; (2) President and Secretary of the Kurnool District Congress Committee; (3) President and Secretary of the Banaganapalle State Congress; (4) M.Venkatasubba Reddy; (5) Iskapalli Narasimham; and (6) K.V. Narayana Rao.[18]

As per the directive of the AISPC, R.Venkata Rao toured the villages in the state for five days. He met the Kurnool district, taluq and village Congress workers and discussed with them the problems of the state. He also met a cross-section of the people of the state—men, women, young, old, rich poor, businessmen, and farmers. He also had a separate meeting with the Muslims of the state. He said that all were unanimous that the dictatorial rule of Syed Imam, the Diwan, should be put to an end. He also said that the Diwan had raised the walls of the boundaries of the state to prevent the State Congress leaders from entering. He said that the same Diwan permitted the sale of illicit liquor though there was total prohibition in Kurnool district. He was glad to note that the people of the state were politically conscious and that they were ready to sacrifice everything for the merger of the state. He also said that the future of the state was linked with the political developments in Kurnool district. He appealed to the Congress workers in the district to utilize this opportunity and support the struggle launched by the people. He said that the tyrannical and indifferent attitude of the Diwan, corruption among the officials of the state, disrespect shown to women were some of the factors for this open rebellion. He warned that the flames of the revolt would devour everyone—whether high or low. He hoped that the Nawab would realize his responsibility towards the people. He thanked K.V. Krishna Murthy, Secretary and M. Benkata Subba Reddy, Executive Member for extending their cooperation during his tour. Later, R. Venkata Rao left for Delhi.[19]

FORMATION OF STATE EXECUTIVE COUNCIL

It may be recalled here that on 1 July 1947, at a Durbar held in Banaganapalle, the Nawab announced the formation of the State Executive Council and the future constitution of Banaganapalle, giving the people a large share in the administration of the state. The Nawab also promulgated the Banaganapalle State Council Act which came into force immediately. The Act provided for a State Executive Council consisting of 3 members: State Diwan as the president, one official member, and one non-official member. The Nawab inivited Pendekanti Venkatasubbaiah to be the non-official member of the Executive Council. Pendekanti Venkatasubbaiah declined the offer and Medum Subbaiah was nominated to the post. The State Executive Council exercized all the powers vested in the Durbar under all the enactments, rules, and regulations and orders which were in force. According to it, all the official correspondences, between the state and the Government of India was to be carried on by the Diwan President. The Nawab also announced his decision to join the Indian Constituent Assembly.[20]

HOISTING OF THE TRI-COLOUR FLAG AT KOTHAPETA

On 26 July 1947, Nivarthi Venkatasubbaiah, MLA, was invited for a discussion with Nazir Hussain, Revenue Minister of the Banaganapalle State about the proposed public meeting on 27 July 1947. Nivarthi

Venkatasubbaiah said that he would not postpone the meeting. In the evening, a conference of important officials of the state was held in the state headquarters and on the morning of 27 July 1947, the Revenue Minister and others interviewed the Nawab. At noon, Nazir Hussain and other officials arrived in Kothapeta and sent for J. Satyanarayana, the President of the BSCC, but he declined to go and meet them.[21]

The tri-colour flag was hoisted and the State Congress was inaugurated before a gathering of over 2,000 people on 27 July 1947 at Kothapeta in Banaganapalle State. Earlier, a huge procession led by a squad of volunteers from Bheemunipadu village carrying tri-colour flags with the photos of Mahatma Gandhi and other leaders was taken out terminating before the Congress office. Nivarthi Venkatasubbaiah said that the day opened up for the people of the Banaganapalle State, a new chapter of political consciousness and awakening. He assured the people that whatever might happen to them, he and other Congress workers would stand by them and undergo any amount of suffering and sacrifice, in their struggle to establish a democratic and popularly elected government in the state. Referring to the reforms announced by the Nawab at a Durbar held on 1 July 1947, Nivarthi Venkatasubbaiah said that, unsatisfactory though they were, they were certainly an improvement and hence he congratulated the Nawab. The object of the State Congress was the establishment of a popularly elected government consisting of representatives with progressive views, who would understand the needs of the people and safeguard their interests and asked the people of the state to work in that direction. After the flag was hoisted, the volunteers gave the salute. Mrs and Mr Rama Rao of the Hyderabad State Congress sang the 'flag song', eulogising the tri-colour flag. Later, Pendekanti Venkatasubbaiah of Sanjamala presided over the public meeting. Messrs Swamy Hamsananda Saraswathy, K.A. Narayana Rao, M. Venkatasubba Reddy, Ramasubba Reddy, Naganna later Municipal Chairman of Banaganapalle, Nagabhushana Rao, J. Satyanarayana, Narasimhaiah, and Nukala Kondaiah also addressed the meeting. A Narasa Rama Sarma, S. Kazam Ali, Naguri Chinna Basappa and Naguri Naga Basappa of Kothapeta, Goturu Venkatasubbaiah, and Goturu Subrahmanyam of Sanjamal also attended the meeting.[22]

The meeting passed a resolution welcoming the proclamation of the Nawab on 1 July 1947 announcing his decision to join the Constituent Assembly of the Indian Union and to set up a popularly elected representative government. It was resolved to appoint a sub-committee to prepare the draft of the Constitution. The members of the sub-committee were: Nivarthi Venkatasubbaiah, P. Venkatasubbaiah, M.Venkata

Subba Reddy, and Naga Basappa. It was also resolved to appoint another sub-committee to prepare comprehensive plans for the economic development of the state.[23]

INDEPENDENCE DAY CELEBRATIONS IN BANAGANAPALLE

The attainment of Independence on 15 August 1947 was received with great jubilation by the people of the Banaganapalle State. At the stroke of midnight on 14 August 1947, Nivarthi Venkatasubbaiah hoisted the Indian National Flag at Banaganapalle and appealed to the state authorities to understand the significance of the historic changes that were taking place in India consequent on the transfer of power, and urged that instead of making futile attempts to suppress popular movements and immediate steps were needed to be taken to hand over power to the elected representatives of the people. A huge gathering of over 2,000 persons was present in front of the Kanyakaparameswari temple. Earlier, a procession organized by the State Congress along with the photos of Mahatma Gandhi and other Congress leaders was banned by the Magistrate under Section 144 Cr. P.C. But Messrs. Nivarthi Venkatasubbaiah, M. Venkatasubba Reddy, Pendekanti Venkata Subbaiah, J. Satyanarayana, and K.A. Narayana Rao, followed by a volunteer squad of seventy people, defied the ban and they were placed under arrest. For five hours, they staged satyagraha by squatting on the road, refusing to give up the procession. Finally, they were set free and the procession was allowed to move to its destination.[24]

The procession stopped in front of the Kanyakaparameswari temple and a public meeting was held there. Balasubbaiah, a local advocate presided over the meeting. It is interesting to note that K. Balaswamy, a document writer who was seventy years old, distributed biscuits and water to the precesionists and quenched their thirst. Nivarthi Venkatasubbaiah congratulated the volunteers and the people on the first round of victory they had won that day. He was sure that they would very soon reach their goal of a completely responsible government. He appealed to the state officials to take immediate steps to instal a popular government. The meeting passed a resolution on the lines of Nivarthi Venkatasubbaiah's speech. It was also resolved to start a political school to train volunteers and to invite Kala Venkata Rao, Revenue Minister to inaugurate the same.[25]

RESOLUTIONS OF THE STATE CONGRESS

The Central Committee of the Banganapalle State Congress met at Kothapeta on 2 September 1947 under the presidentship of J. Satyanarayana.[26] On behalf of the State Congress, Nivarthi Venkatasubbaiah, Y. Ramachandraiah, P. Ranga Reddy, Member, Provincial Congress Committee, J. Satyanarayana, P. Venkatasubbaiah, K. Narayana Rao, and M. Venkatasubba Reddy went to Madras and met the two ministers—Kala Venkata Rao and B. Gopal Reddy in September 1947. They discussed with the ministers the political and economic matters of the state. They also brought to the notice of the ministers the manufacture, sale, and export of illicit liquor from the state headquarters. They appealed to the ministers to take stringent action against the Nawab. The ministers subsequently assured the delegates that they would look into the problems.[27]

An executive meeting of the State Congress was held on 17 November 1947, under the presidentship of J. Satyanarayana; Nivarthi Venkatasubbaiah and M. Venkatasubba Reddy attended the meeting as special invitees. The meeting warned the Nawab not to ignore the opinion of the State Congress and not to implement the reforms in a hurry. The meeting reiterated its resolve to sacrifice everything for the establishment of a responsible government. The meeting also appointed a sub-committee to hold talks with the Nawab.[28]

ROLE OF SWAMY HAMSANANDA SARASWATHI

Like Swamy Ramananda Tirtha of the Hyderabad State Congress, the people of the Banaganapalle State Congress were fortunate to be guided by Swamy Hamsananda Saraswathi. He was born on 14 August 1859 at Varanasi and died on 31 January 1980 at Banaganapalle. His original name was Nitya Gopal.[29] But he was locally known as 'Kasaiah' since he came from Kasi. It is said that he was an Arya Samaj activist in the beginning. Later, he became a disciple of Swamy Ramakrishna Paramahamsa and Swamy Vivekananda. He had close contacts with several religious and political personalities of the time like Swamy Sharaddhananda, M.K. Gandhi, T. Prakasam, V.D. Savarkar, Aurobindo Ghosh, Pandit Madan Mohan Malavya, C. Rajagopalachari, Jayaprakash Narayan, Sardar Vallabhbhai Patel, and others.[30] He founded the Swasthi Ashram at Banaganapalle which became a centre for discussing the affairs of the state.[31] Prominent leaders like Nivarthi Venkatasubbaiah, Pendekanti Venkatasubbaiah, J. Satyanarayana, M. Venkatasubba Reddy, and others were taking his counsel. It is stated that Jayaprakash Narayan and his wife were the guests of the Swamy during one of their visits. For his role in the struggle against the Nawab, Swamy Hamsananda Saraswathi was externed. But he did not give up his fight. With his headquarters at Tadpatri in Anantapur district, he continued his fight against the Nawab. He went to Delhi and appealed to Sardar Patel to end the atrocities of the Nawab and his Diwan and to take over the administration of the state at the earliest.[32]

MERGER OF THE BANAGANAPALLE STATE: PROVISIONS OF INSTRUMENTS OF ACCESSION, 1948

According to the agreement made between the Governor-General of India and Nawab Syed Mir Fazle Ali Khan,[33] in February 1948, the Nawab of Banaganapalle ceded to the Union Government his 'full and exclusive authority, jurisdiction and powers in relation to the governance and administration of the state to the Indian Dominions with effect from 20 February 1948.

Article 2 of the this agreement entitled the Nawab to receive from the revenues of the state annually for his privy purse the sum of Rs. 53,900 free of taxes. This amount was intended to cover all the expenses for the ruler and his family including expenses on account of his personal staff, maintenance of his residences, marriages and other ceremonies, etc., and would neither be increased nor reduced for any reason whatsoever.

According to Article 3 of the agreement, the Nawab was entitled to the full ownership, use, and enjoyment of all private properties (as distinct from state properties) belonging to him on the date of the agreement.

According to Article 4, the Nawab, his wife the Begum, the mother of the Nawab, the son of the Nawab, the heir-apparent, and his wife were entitled to all personal privileges enjoyed by them whether within or outside the territories of the state, immediately before 15 August 1947.

Under Article 5, the Dominion Government guaranteed the succession according to law and custom, the *gaddi* of the state and to the Nawab's personal rights, privileges, dignities, and titles.[34]

It may be mentioned here that on 23 February 1948, a special function was organized in the Durbar Hall of the mango-shaped Banaganapalle Fort.[35] M.P. Bangara, District Collector of Kurnool took over the administration of the state, as per the orders of the Madras Government. As the Nawab and the Diwan were away in Delhi, Khwaja Nazir Hussain, Revenue Minister of the State handed over the administration.[36] V.N.

Kudwa, Member, Board of Revenue of the Madras Government, Kurnool district officials and prominent citizens from the state attended the function. The Malabar Special Police conducted a march past and presented the guard of honour. Kala Venkata Rao, Revenue Minister, in his message, expressed happiness over the merger of the Banaganapalle State and assured that the Madras Government would take steps for the economic development of the people, without any religious discrimination. The message was read out by Nivarthi Venkatasubbaiah.[37]

After the function, V.N. Kudwa hoisted the tri-colour Indian national flag within the premises of the fort. Later, a public meeting was also held which was presided over by Nivarthi Venkatasubbaiah; M.P. Bangara and V.N. Kudwa also attended the meeting. Nivarthi Venkatasubbaiah explained the significance of the administrative changes and said that the states' people would also enjoy equal rights like other Indian citizens. He also said that there would be total prohibition in the state and that the taxes would be reviewed. He expressed the hope that both Hindus and Muslims would enjoy equal rights like other Indian citizens and would show their allegiance to the Indian Government. G.Venkata Reddy, MLA, and others also spoke. A resolution was passed expressing happiness over the merger of the state and also that the people would be loyal to the Indian Federal Government.[38] In its Gazette Extraordinary, the Madras Government declared that the administration of the Banaganapalle State was handed over to the Madras Government under section 4 of the Indian Government Extra Provincial Jurisdiction Act of 1947.[39]

The merger of Banaganapalle State in February 1948, was the culmination of the aspirations of the people of the state who were very much inspired by the wave of nationalism that swept across the country. The Indian National Congress also spread its activities to this native state. The people of this tiny state had a tradition of revolting against oppression even in the past. As early as 1898, they successfully opposed the indiscriminate enhancement of land tax by the then Nawab, Syed Fateh Ali Khan. The formation of the Banaganapalle State Congress in March 1947 was a milestone in the Congress development of national consciousness among the people. The State Congress catapulated several local leaders like J. Satyanarayana, M.Venkatasubba Reddy, Pendekanti Venkatasubbaiah,[40] Nivarthi Venkatasubbaiah, and others who were to play an important role later in public life even at the national level. Besides the State Congress leaders, the role of Swamy Hamsananda was highly responsible to get Banaganapalle State merged with the Indian Union.

NOTES

1. Banaganapalle derived its name from Bhanumukkapalle, a hamlet named after Bhanumurthy, an elderly goldsmith, see M.V. Rajagopal, *Andhra Pradesh District Gazetteers: Kurnool*, Hyderabad, 1974, pp. 242-3.
2. V.P. Menon, *Integration of the Indian States*, Madras, 1985, pp. 307-308.
3. The five native states which were having political relations with the Madras Government were: Travancore and Cochin (Kerala), Pudukkotai (Tamilnadu), Sandur (Karnataka), and Banaganapalle (Andhra Pradesh).
4. *The Imperial Gazetteer of India: Aragaon to Bardwan,* Oxford, 1908, vol. VI, pp. 371-8. See also R.P. Singh, *Census of India*, 1991, Series 2, Andhra Pradesh Paper I of 1991, Supplement, Provisional Population Totals, Hyderabad, 1992, p. 15. See also Amulya Ratna Nanda, *Census of India*, Series I, India Paper I of 1992, Final Population Totals, vol.1, New Delhi, 1993, p. 156.
5. C.U. Aitchison (Comp.), *A Collection of Treaties, Engagements and Sanads Relating to India and Neighbouring Countries*, Delhi, 1983, rpt., pp. 217-19.
6. Syed Ali Akbar Basha Qadri, 'State of Banaganapalle under British Rule from 1858 to 1948', unpublished M.Phil. thesis submitted to S.V. University, Tirupati, 1978, pp. 63-4.
7. Humayun Mirza (son of Ismail Mirza, Diwan of Mysore) was the Diwan from 1937 to 1940. H.S. Mandanna, a retired official from Coorg, was the Diwan from 1940 to 1943. Krishnamacharya, a retired administrator of Pudukkotai was the Diwan from 1943 to 1946. Syed Imam was the Diwan from 1946 till the merger of the state on 20 February 1948, *Krishna Patrika*, Machilipatnam, 16 November 1940, p. 16A. See also *Andhra Patrika*, 24 February 1948, p. 4, Saraswathi Niketanam, Vetapalem (hereafter SNV).
8. Nripendranath Mitra (ed.), *The Indian Annual Register*, Calcutta, 1940, vol. I, January-June 1940, p. 12.
9. Syed Ali Akbar Basha Qadri, 'State of Banaganapalle under British Rule', pp.101-4.
10. After the revolt, the lands were surveyed by T.E. Moir, the Special Settlement Officer and uniform taxation was followed in the State. After the merger of Banaganapalle State on 20 February 1948, Pendekanti Venkatasubbaiah convened a ryot's conference at Sanjamala. The conference was inaugurated by Kala Venkata Rao, Revenue Minister in the Madras Government. The place where the skirmishes occurred was named as Ismail Nagar in memory of Belgaum Ismail Saheb, the leader of the no tax campaign. See *Aindravathi*, 9 July 1948, pp. 3-5. My interview with Pendekanti Venkatasubbaiah, Ex-Governor of Bihar and Karnataka, at Hyderabad on 2 June 1992. Also see Syed Ali Akbar Basha Qadri, 'State of Banaganapalle under British Rule', p. 52.
11. Gamago, *Vismruta Karyakarta*, Kurnool, 1993, pp. 39-50; My interview with M. Venkata Subba Reddy, alias Gamago (an abbreviation of Gandhi, Marx, Gora), Ex-MLA, at Kurnool on 10 December 1991; Venkatasubba Reddy

was familiarly known as 'Gamago' with the first two letters in the names of Gandhi, Marx, and Gora; Gamago, 'The History of the Banaganapalle State Congress Movement' (unpublished manuscript), pp.19-20. My interview with Joshyam Satyanarayana at Panyam on 9 December 1991. S. Krishnamurthy settled down in Kurnool as a journalist and hence resigned his post. In his place, Pendekanti Venkatasubbaiah of Sanjamala, who later became a union minister of the State for Home Affairs and the Governor of Bihar and Karnataka, was elected. As the head office of the State Congress Committee was shifted from Koilkuntla to Kothapeta into the State boundaries, I. Narasimham of Koilkuntla resigned his post of Office Secretary. In his place S. Kazam Ali was elected.; For details, see Letter dated 4 May 1947 from J. Satyanarayana, President, BSCC to the President, MSC.

12. For details, see Letter RC. no. 7-1/825 dated 5 August 1947 from Dr B. Pattabhi Sitaramayya, Working President, AISPC to the Secretary to the BSCC. The office bearers of the AISPC, New Delhi in 1947 were: Sheikh Mohammed Abdullah (President), Dr Pattabhi Sitaramayya (Working President), Balwantrai Mehta (Vice-President), Pandit Hira Lal Shastri, Sarang Dhar Das, T.M. Varghese and Jainarain Vyas (all General Secretaries) and Seth Kamalnayan Bajaj (Treasurer). See also Letter RC. no. 7 January 1938 dated, 23 August 1947 from M.P. Bhargava, Office Superintendent, AISPC, New Delhi to the Secretary, BSCC.
13. The Office bearers of the MSC were: K. Chengalraya Reddy (President), A.G. Ramachandra Rao (General Secretary), K.R. Madhava Rao (Joint Secretary) and S. Chennaiah (Treasurer). For details, see Letters RC. no. 903 dated 3 June 1947 from K.R. Madhava Rao, Joint Secretary, MSC to M. Venkatasubba Reddy of Koilkuntla.
14. The Office-bearers of the MRC were: S. Nijalingappa (President) and H.K. Veera Gowd (Secretary). For details, see Letter RC. no. 896, dated 18 January 1947 from the Office Secretary, AISPC, New Delhi to J. Satyanarayana President, BSCC.
15. See Letter dated 4 May 1947 from J. Satyanarayana, President, BSCC to the President, MSC.
16. *Amara Jyothi* (a Telugu Weekly from Kurnool), 31 May 1947, p. 3.
17. *The Hindu*, 28 May 1947.
18. *Amara Jyothi*, p. 3.
19. *Andhra Patrika*, 7 July 1947, p. 3 (SNV).
20. Syed Ali Akbar Basha Qadri, 'State of Banaganapalle under British Rule', pp. 101-4.
21. *The Hindu*, 1 August 1947.
22. Ibid.
23. *Andhra Prabha*, 7 August 1947, p. 6 (SNV).
24. *Notice dated 15 August 1947 from T.R. Krishnan, Munsiff Magistrate, Banaganapalle to J. Satyanarayana, President, BSCC Prohibiting the Meeting*. See also *Andhra*

Patrika, 18 August 1947, p. 5 (SNV). See also *Andhra Prabha*, 19 August 1947, p. 6 (SVN)

25. *The Hindu*, 23 August 1947. See also *Andhra Prabha*, 17 September 1947, p. 4 (SNV).
26. See *Resolutions of the Central Committee of the Banaganapalle State Congress Committee*, dated 2 September 1947.
27. *Andhra Prabha*, 29 September 1947, p. 5 (SNV).
28. *Andhra Prabha*, 2 December 1947, p. 6 (SNV).
29. G. Ramakrishna Sastry, *Sri Sri Sri Swamy Hamsananda Saraswathi Yatheendrula Sangraha Jeevitha Charithamu*, Banaganapalle, 1990, pp. 18-21.
30. Y. Rama Mohan Reddy, *Swasthi Ashram in Pendekanti Venkatasubbaiah Industrial Training Institute First Anniversary Souvenir*, Banaganapalle, 1984, n.p.
31. Prashanthathku Nilayam, *Swasthi Ashram* in *Seema Vaibhavaniki Anavallu: 186 Vasanthala Kurnool, Eenadu*, Special Supplement, Anantapur, n.d., p. 15.
32. Hamsa Dhwani, *Udayam*, Hyderabad, 14 February 1993, p. 16.
33. Nawab Syed Mir Fazle Ali Khan died on 1 July 1948 due to heart attack. He was succeeded by his only son Mir Ghulam Ali Khan who contributed to the dissolution of the Ruler's Union by resigning his membership from it. See M.V. Rajagopal (ed.), *Andhra Pradesh District Gazetteers: Kurnool*, p. 54.
34. Syed Ali Akbar Basha Qadri, 'State of Banaganapalle under British Rule', pp. 105-6.
35. K. Maddaiah, 'Renovation of Forts', *Indian Express*, Hyderabad, 20 November 1991, p. 6. See also K. Maddaiah, 'Ninnati Chartraku Addam: Banaganapalle Kota', *Andhra Prabha*, Hyderabad, 5 December 1991, p. 4. Also see A. Nagabhushanam, 'Banaganapalle Kota', *Telugu* (quarterly literary journal), Hyderabad, January-March 1980, pp. 119-24.
36. *Andhra Patrika*, 22 February 1948, p. 3 (SNV).
37. *Andhra Prabha*, 22 February 1948, p. 1 (SNV).
38. *Andhra Patrika*, 24 February 1948, p. 4 (SNV). See also *Andhra Prabha*, 25 February 1948, p. 6 (SNV).
39. *Andhra Prabha*, 14 March 1948, p. 7 (SNV).
40. It may be stated here that in 1949 Pendekanti Venkatasubbaiah of Sanjamala was nominated to the Madras Legislative Assembly to represent the merged states of Banaganapalle, Sandur, and Pudukkotai. Immediately after the merger, Banaganapalle was constituted into an independent sub-taluq of Kurnool district with G.S.S. Rama Murthy as the tahsildar. See *Aindravathi*, 27 February 1948, p. 6.

Bibliography

Abhayankar, G.R., *Work in England of the Deputation of Indian States People's Conference*, Bombay, 1928.

AISPC, *A Hand Book of the Chamber of Princes* (proceedings of AISPC), Simla, Govt. of India Press, 1943.

———, *What are the Indian States*, Allahabad, 1949.

Ahmad, Z.A., *Indian Federation*, K.M. Ashraf, Allahabad, 1938.

Aitchison, Charles U., *A Collection of Treaties, Engagements and Sanads relating to India and Neighbouring Countries*, Govt. of India Central Publication Branch Calcutta, 1909.

Alan Campbell-Johnson, *Mission with Mountbatten*, Jaico Publishing House, Bombay, 1951.

Alexander, K.C., *Peasant Organisations in South India*, New Delhi, 1981.

Ali, Moulvi Chirag, *Hyderabad under Sir Salar Jung*, 4 vols., Bombay, 1986.

Ali, Mir Laik, *Tragedy of Hyderabad*, Cooperative Book Society, Karachi, 1962.

Ali Yavar Jung Commemoration Volume, ed. Abul Kalam Azad Oriental Research Institute, Hyderabad, Bombay, 1983.

Alistair Lamb, *Kashmir: A Disputed Legacy, 1846-1990*, Hestingfordbury, 1991.

Appadorai, A., Maurice Goyer (ed.), *Speeches and Documents on the Indian Constitution, 1921-1947*, 2 vols, OUP, London, 1957.

Ashton, S.R., *British Policy Towards the Indian States, 1905-1939*, Curzon Press, London, 1982.

Baden Powell, B.H., *Administration and Land Revenue and Tenure in British India*, New Delhi, 1978.

Bakshi, S.R., *Kashmir Through Ages*, 5 vols., Sarup & Sons, New Delhi, 1996.

Bamzai, P.N.K., *Socio-Economic History of Kashmir, 1846-1925*, New Delhi, 1987.

Banerjee, Anil Chandra, *The Rajput States and British Paramountcy*, Rajesh Publications, New Delhi, 1980.

Banerjee, Anil Chandra. (ed.), *Indian Constitutional Documents 1758-1947*, vols. III and IV, Calcutta, 1961, 1965.

Barton William, Paton, *The Princes of India*, London, 1934.

Bawa, V.K., *The Last Nizam: The Life and Times of Mir Osman Ali Khan*, Penguin Books, New Delhi, 1992.

———, *The Nizam between the Mughals and the British, Hyderabad under Salar Jung I*, S. Chand, New Delhi, 1986.

Bazaz, Prem Nath, *Democracy Through Intimidation and Terror: The Untold Study of Kashmir Politics*, New Delhi, 1978.

———, *A Story of Struggle for Freedom in Kashmir: Cultural and Political: From the Earliest Times to Present Day*, Kashmir Publishing Co., New Delhi, 1954.

———, *Inside Kashmir*, Kashmir Publishing Co., Srinagar, 1941.

Bedford, Ian, 'Telangana Insurrection: A Study in the Cause and Development of Communist Insurrection in Rural India 1946-1951', unpublished Ph.D thesis, Australian National University, Canberra, 1967.

Benichou, Lucien D., *From Autocracy to Integration: Political Developments in Hyderabad State (1938-1948)*, Orient Longman, Hyderabad, 2000.

Bhagat, K.P., *A Decade of Indo-British Relations 1937-47*, Popular Book Depot, Bombay, 1959.

Bhargava, R.P., *The Chamber of Princes*, New Delhi, 1991.

Bhashyam, K.T., *The Mysore Struggle*, Dharwad, 1940.

Bingley, A.H., *Sikhs*, Patiala, 1970.

Brailsford, W.H., *Kashmir Today Through Foreign Eyes*, Bombay, 1948.

Bridge, Carl, *Holding India to the Empire*, New Delhi, 1986.

Briggs, H.G., *The Nizam: His History and Relations with the British Government*, 2 vols., London, 1961.

Brown, Judit, *Gandhi's Rise to Power: Indian Politics, 1915-1922*, Cambridge, 1972.

Burton, Sir William M., *The Princes of India*, London, 1934.

Caine, P.J. and A.G. Hopkins, *British Imperialism: Crisis and Deconstruction, 1914-1990*, London, 1993.

Cell, John W. Hailey, *A Study in British Imperialism*, Cambridge, 1992.

Chandra, Bipan (et al.), *India's Struggle for Independence 1875-1947*, Penguin Books, New Delhi, 1989.

———, *Nationalism and Colonialism in Modern India*, Orient Longman, New Delhi, 1981.

Chandrashekar, S., *Dimensions of Socio-Political Changes in Mysore 1918-40*, New Delhi, 1985.

Chudgar, P., *Indian Princes and British Protection: A Study of their Personal Rule, their Constitutional Position, their Future*, London, 1929.

Cohn, Bernard S., *Colonialism and its Forms of Knowledge: The British in India*, OUP, New Delhi, 1997.

Collins, Larry and Lapierre Dominic, *Freedom at Midnight*, London, 1975.

Communist Party (ed.), *Glorious Telangana Armed Struggle*, New Delhi, 1973.

Copland, Ian, *The British Raj and the Indian Princes: Paramountcy in Western India, 1857-1930*, Orient Longman, Bombay, 1982.

———, *The Princes of India in the Endgame of Empire, 1917-1947*, CUP, Cambridge, 1997.

Corfiled, Conrad, *The Princely India I know: From Reading to Mountbatten*, Indo-British Historical Society, Madras, 1975.

Coupland, R., *The Cripps Mission*, OUP, London, 1942.

______, *The Constitutional Problem in India*, 1944.

Dharma Kumar, *The Cambridge Economic History of India*, vol. II, Orient Longmans in association with CUP, New Delhi, 1982.

Daniel, D., *Struggle for Responsible Government in Travancore, 1938-1947*, Raj Publications, Madurai, 1985.

Das, Durga (ed.), *Sardar Patel Correspondence, 1945-50*, 10 vols., Ahmedabad, 1974.

Das, Tarakanth, *Sovereign Rights of the Indian Princes*, Madras, 1924.

Deo, N.G., *The Princes of India*, Bombay, 1921.

Desai, A.R. (ed.), *Peasant Struggles in India*, London, 1982.

Desai, Janardhan Rao, *The Hyderabad Reforms*, Hyderabad, 1946.

Devulapalli, Venkateswara Rao, *Telangana Prajala Sayudha Porata Charitra (1946-51)*, P.L. Publications, Hyderabad, 1988.

Fisher, Michael H., *Indirect Rule in India: Residents and Residency System 1764-1857*, New Delhi, 1991.

Fitze, K., *Twilight of the Maharajas*, London, John Murray, 1956.

Force H. Wilber, Bell, *The History of Kathiawad*, Ajay Book Service, New Delhi, 1980.

Frykenburg, Robert Eric (ed.), *Land Tenures and Peasants in South Asia*, New Delhi, 1977.

Gandhi, M.K., *The Indian States Problem*, Navjivan Press, Ahmedabad, 1941.

———, *Satyagraha*, Ahmedabad, 1958.

Ganguly, Sumit, *The Crises in Kashmir*, Woodrow Wilson Centre Press and CUP, New Delhi, 1997.

Gustafson, 'The Making of Model State, Mysore 1881-1902', unpublished Ph.D thesis, University of Wisconsin, 1969.

Gopalan, A.K., *Kerala, Past and Present*, London, 1959.

Govt. of India, 'White Paper on Hyderabad', New Delhi, August 1948.

______, 'White Paper on Indian States', New Delhi, 1950.

______, 'Whie Paper on Kashmir', New Delhi, 1948.

Guha, Ranajit, *Dominance Without Hegemony: History and Power in Colonial India*, OUP, New Delhi, 1998.

Gundappa, D.V., *A Memorial on the Position of Native States in the Empire*, Bangalore, 1918.

———, *The Problem of Indian Native States*, Bangalore, 1930.

Gurumukh, Nihal Singh, *Indian States and British India—Their Future Relations*, Banaras, 1930.

Halappa, G.S., *History of Freedom Movement in Karnataka*, 2 vols., Govt. of Mysore Publications, Bangalore, 1964.

Handa, R.L., *History of Freedom Struggle in Princely States*, New Delhi, Central News Agency, 1968.

Hasan, Mushirul (ed.), *Communal and Pan Islamic Trends in Colonial India*, Manohar New Delhi, 1985.

Hettene Bjorne, *The Political Economy of Indirect Rule: Mysore, 1881-1947*, Curzon Press, London, 1978.

History of Freedom Movement in Orissa, 5 vols., Govt. of Orissa Publication, 1959.

Hobsbawm, E.J., *Nations and Nationalism since 1870*, Canto, CUP, 1990.

Hudson, H.V., *The Great Divide*, Hutchinson of London, London, 1970.

Hurd, John, *Some Economic Characteristics of the Princely States of India, 1901-1931*, University of Pennsylvania, 1969.

Hussain, Fazal, *Kashmir-aur-Dograraj*, Srinagar, 1979.

Hussain, Syed Abid, *Whither Hyderabad*, B.N. Press, Madras, 1935.

Hutchins, Francis, *The Illusion of Permanence: British Imperialism in India*, Princeton, 1967.

Hyderabad State Congress, *At the Altar of Freedom*, 1948.

Hyderabad Struggle Committee (Socialist Party), *The Hyderabad Problem, The Next Step*, Bombay, 1948.

Imadi, Mohammud Abdul Kader, 'The Nobles of Hyderabad—A Study in Social Change', unpublished Ph.D thesis, Osmania University, 1977.

Iyengar, S. Kesava, *Rural Economic Enquiries in Hyderabad State, 1949-51*, The Govt. Central Press, Hyderabad, 1951.

———, *Economic Investigations in Hyderabad State 1929-30*, 5 vols., The Govt. Central Press, Hyderabad, 1931.

Jeffrey, Robin, *The Decline of Nayar Dominance: Society and Politics in Travancore*, University of Sussex, 1973.

Jeffrey, Robin, ed., *People, Princes and Paramount Power: Society and Politics in the Indian Princely States*, OUP, New Delhi, 1978.

John, Lord, *The Maharajas*, London, 1971.

Karaka, D.F., *Fabulous Mughal, Nizam VII of Hyderabad*, Derck Verschoyle, London, 1955.

Kashi Reddy, *Niyanta Nizam Nizarupam*, Hyderabad, 1992.

Kaul, Ranjana, *Constitutional Development in the Indian Princely States*, New Delhi, 1998.

Khalidi, Omar, *The British Residents at the Court of the Nizams of Hyderabad*, Wichita, Kangar, Hyderabad Historical Society.

Khan, Gulam Hassan, *Freedom Movement in Kashmir, 1931-40*, Light and Life, New Delhi, 1980.

Khan, M.I., *History of Srinagar: A Study in Socio-Cultural Change*, Srinagar, 1978.

———, *Perspectives on Kashmir: Historical Dimensions*, Srinagar, 1983.

Khan, Mohd. Fathullah, *A History of Administrative Reforms in Hyderabad State*, New Hyderabad Press, Secunderabad, 1935.

Khoude, Achyut (ed.), *The Peoples Movement in Hyderabad*, Nanded, 1947.

Khusro, A.M. *Economic and Social Effects of Jagirdari Abolition and Land Reforms in Hyderabad*, Osmania University Press, Hyderabad, 1958.

Koshy, M.J., *Genesis of Political Consciousness in Kerala*, Kerala Political Society, Trivandrum, 1972.

———, *The History of the Legislature of Travancore-Cochin up to 1956*, University of Kerala, Trivendrum, 1956.

Koul, Bamzai Premnath, *A History of Kashmir, Political, Social and Cultural: From the Earlist Times to the Present Day*, Metropolitan Book Company, New Delhi, 1962.

Krishnaswami, Mudiraj, *Pictorial Hyderabad*, 2 vols., Chakrakanth Press, Hyderabad, 1929, 1934.

Kulkarni, V.B., *The Future of Indian States*, Thacker, London, 1954.

Kusuman, K.K., *The Abstention Movement*, Kerala Historical Society, Trivandrum, 1976.

Law, John, *Modern Hyderabad (Deccan)*, Calcutta, 1914.

Low, D.A., *Eclipse of Empire*, Cambridge, 1991.

______, *Congress and the Raj: Facets of the Indian Struggle 1917-47*, Heinemann, London, 1977.

Lumby, E.W.R., *The Transfer of Power in India*, George Allen and Unwin Limited, London, 1954.

Lumby, E.W.R. and Manserg, *Transfer of Power*, vols. 1-8, His Majesty's Stationary Office, London, 1970-80.

Mallikarjuna Sarma, I, *The Role of Revolutionaries in the Freedom Struggle, A Critical History of the Indian Revolutionary Movements 1918-1934*, Hyderabad, 1987.

Mani Kamarkar, *British Paramountcy: British-Baroda Relations, 1818-1848*, Bombay, 1980.

Mankekar, D.R., *Accession to Extinction—The Story of the Indian Princes*, Vikas Publishing House Pvt. Ltd., New Delhi, 1974.

Manor, James, *Political Changes in an Indian State: Mysore 1917-1955*, Manohar, New Delhi, 1977.

Mansergh, Nicholas (ed.), *The Transfer of Power 1942-47, Constitutional Reforms Between Britain and India*, 12 vols., London, 1970.

Mathur, R.M., *Rajput States and the East India Company*, New Delhi, 1979.

Mehta, Balwantrai, *A Peep into Hyderabad Deccan*, Bombay, 1938.

Menon, P.K.K., *The History of Freedom Movement in Kerala*, 2 vols., Trivandrum, 1970.

Menon, Sreedhara, *Survey of Kerala History*, 4 vols., Kottayam, 1967.

Menon, V.P., *The Story of the Integration of the Indian States*, Orient Longman, Hyderabad, rpt., 1995.

———, *The Transfer of Power in India*, Orient Longmans, Calcutta, 1959.

Metcalf, Thomas R., *Ideologies of the Raj: The New Cambridge History of India*, vol. III, 4, New Delhi, 1996.

Mirza, F., *Pre and Post Police Action Days in the Erstwhile Hyderabad State, What I Saw, Felt and Did*, Paramount Press, Hyderabad, 1976.

Mirza, Muhmmad Afzal Beg, *On the Way to Golden Harvests, Agricultural Reforms in Kashmir*, Jammu, 1951.

Misra, S.C., *National Movement in a Princely State*, Pointer, Jaipur, 1993.

Moore, R.J., *End-games of Empire*, New Delhi, 1988.

Mosley, Leonard, *The Last Days of the British Raj*, Bombay, 1972.

Munshi, K.M., *The End of An Era*, Bharatiya Vidhya Bhavan, Bombay, 1957.

Muthanna, I.M., *History of Modern Karnataka*, Sterling Publishers Pvt. Ltd., New Delhi, 1980.

Namboodiripad, E.M.S., *Kerala: Society and Politics, An Historical Survey*, New Delhi, 1984.

Narayana, B.K., *Agricultural Development in Hyderabad State, 1900-1956*, Keshav Prakashan, Secunderabad, 1960.

Narendraji, Pt., *Arya Samaj in Hyderabad*, Janashakti Mudran Yantralaya, New Delhi, 1975.

Neogi, Ajit K., *The Paramount Power and Princely States of India, 1858-1881*, K.P. Bagchi & Company, Calcutta, 1979.

Nicholson, A.P., *Scraps of Paper, India's Broken Treaties, Her Princes and the Problem*, Ernest Benn, London, 1930.

Oren, A. Stephen, *Religious Groups at Political Organisations: A Comparative Analysis of three Indian States*, University of Columbia, 1969.

Ommen, T.K., *From Mobilisation to Institutionalisation: The Dynamics of Agrarian Movement in 20th Century Kerala*, Bombay, 1985.

Ouwerkerk, Louise, *No Elephants for the Maharaj: Social and Political Change in Travancore, 1921-1947*, Manohar, New Delhi, 1994.

Panikkar, K.M., *The States and the Constitutional Statement*, Institute of Pacific Relations International Secretariat, New York, 1942.

———, *An Introduction to the Study of Relations of Indian States with the Government of India*, London, 1927.

———, *The Evolution of British Policy towards Indian States, 1774-1858*, Lahiri and Company, Calcutta, 1929.

———, *The Indian Princes in Council: A Record of the Chancellorship of H.H. The Maharaja of Patiala 1926-31 and 1933-36*, OUP, London, 1936.

———, *Maharaja Gulab Singh: Founder of Jammu and Kashmir State*, London, 1930.

Parameswaran, G., *The Peasant Question in Kerala*, Bombay, 1951.

Patil, S.H., *The Congress Party: Princely States*, Bombay, 1981.

Pavier, Barry, *The Telangana Movement 1944-51*, Vikas Publications, New Delhi, 1981.

Pernau, Margrit, *The Passing of Patrimonialism: Politics and Political Culture in Hyderabad, 1911-1948*, Manohar, New Delhi, 2000.

Phadnis, Urmila, *Towards the Integration of Indian States 1919-1947*, Asia Publishing House, New Delhi, 1968.

Phatak, L.B., *Religious Disabilities of Hindus in Hyderabad State*, Secunderabad, 1931.

Philips, C.H., *The Evolution of India and Pakistan 1858-1947* (Select Documents), London, 1962.

Pole, D. Graham, *India in Transition*, 1932.

Punnaiah, M. Basava,, *Telangana Armed Struggle—Realities*, Vijayawada, 1972.

Puntambakar, S.V., *Paramountcy in Indian Politics*, Bombay, 1949.

Qureshi, A.I. *The Economic Development of Hyderabad State*, vol. I, Bombay, 1947.

Radhakrishnan, P., *Peasant Struggles, Land Reforms and Social Change: Malabar, 1836-1982*, New Delhi, 1989.

Raj, Sheela, *Medievalism to Modernism: Socio-Economic and Cultural History of Hyderabad, 1869-1911*, Popular Prakashan, Bombay, 1987.

Rajendra Prasad, H., *The Asif Jahs of Hyderabad: Their Rise and Decline*, Vikas Publishing House, New Delhi, 1984.

Raju, V.B., *Legislative Reforms*, Hyderabad, 1946.

Ramesan, N. (ed.), *Freedom Struggle in Hyderabad State*, vol. IV, *1921-1947*, Hyderabad, 1966.

Ramakrishna Reddy, V., *Economic History of Hyderabad State (Warangal Suba) 1911-1950*, Gian Publishing House, New Delhi, 1987.

Ramusack, Barbara, *The Indian Princes and their States, The New Cambridge History of India*, vol. 3, no. 9, CUP, Cambridge, 1992.

———, *The Princes of India in the Twilight of Empire: Dissolution of the Patron-Client System, 1914-1939*, Ohio State University Press, Columbus, 1978.

Ranadive, R.K., *Legal Rights of Indian States and their Subjects*, Good Companion, Baroda, 1950.

Rangaswami, Vanaja, *The Story of Integration: A New Interpretation*, Manohar, New Delhi, 1981.

Rao, D. Raghavender (ed.), *Misrule of the Nizam*, Madras, 1926.

Rao, V. Veerabhadra and V. Ramachander Rao, *India's Police Action Against Hyderabad*, C. Mallikarjuna Rao, Gadwal, 1949.

Ray, Bharati, *Hyderabad and British Paramountcy, 1858-1883*, OUP, New Delhi, 1988.

Ray, M.K., *Princely States and the Paramount Power 1858-1876*, Rajesh Publications, New Delhi, 1981.

Razvi, S.M. Javid, *Political Awakening in Hyderabad, Role of Youth and Students (1939-56)*, Hyderabad, 1985.

Reddy, Ravi Narayana, *Heroic Telangana, Reminiscences and Experiences*, New Delhi, 1973.

Regani, Sarojini, *Highlights of Freedom Movement in Andhra Pradesh*, Ministry of Cultural Affairs, Govt. of Andhra Pradesh, Hyderabad, 1972.

———, *Nizam-British Relations, 1724-1857*, Concept Pub., New Delhi, 1963.

Renu Chakravarthy, *Communists in Indian Women's Movement*, New Delhi, 1980.

Report of the Indian States Committee (Butler Committee Report), 1928-1929, London, 1929.

Report of the Royal Commission on Jagir Administration and Reforms, Hyderabad, 1356 F (1947).

Robinson, Andrew and Sumia Uchiyana, *The Spectacular Heritage of Princely India*, London, 1988.

Rushbrook William, L.F., *The Cultural Significance of the Indian States*, London, 1930.

Sever, Adrian (ed.), *Documents and Speeches on the Indian Princely States*, 2 vols., B.R. Publishing, New Delhi, 1985.

Sharma, Dewan Chand, *Kashmir Under the Sikhs*, Seema Publications, New Delhi, 1983.

Sharma, G.N., *Rajasthan Studies*, Lakshmi Narain Agarwal Educational Publishers, Agra, 1970.

———, *Rajput Polity*, Manohar, New Delhi, 1977.

Sharma, H., *Princes and Paramountcy*, New Delhi, 1978.

Sharma, S.K. and S.R. Bakshi, *Kashmir During British Rule*, Anmol Publishers, New Delhi, 1995.

Sharma, Usha and S.K. Sharma, *Kashmir and the World*, New Delhi, 1998.

Singh, Anita Inder, *The Origins of the Partition of India, 1936-47*, Oxford, New Delhi, 1995.

Singh, Ganda, *Modern Kashmir (Encyclopedia of Kashmir Series)*, Anmol Publishers, New Delhi, 1995.

———, *History of Freedom Movement*, Punjab University, Patiala, 1970.

———, *Shaik Abdullah and Kashmir* (Encyclopedia of Kashmir Series), New Delhi, 1995.

Singh, Hira, *Colonial Hegemony and Popular Resistance, Princes, Peasants and Paramount Power*, New Delhi, 1998.

Singh, Karani, *The Relations of the House of Bikaner with the Central Powers 1865-1949*, Munshiram Manoharlal, New Delhi, 1974.

Singh, Khushwant, *A History of the Sikhs*, 2 vols., Princeton, 1963-6.

Singh, L., *Political and Constitutional Developments in the Princely States of Rajasthan*, Jain Brothers, New Delhi, 1970.

Singh, Raghuvir, *Indian States and the New Regime*, Taraporewala, Bombay, 1938.

Singh, S.K.P., *The Indian Ruling Princes and the National Movement*, New Delhi, 1991.

Singh, R., *The Indian States under the Government of India Act 1935*, Taraporewala, Bombay, n.d.

Singh, Ravindra Pratap, *Geography and Politics in Central India: A Case Study of Erstwhile Indore State*, New Delhi, 1987.

Sitaramayya, P., *History of Indian National Congress, 1885-1935 and 1935-1947*, Padma Publications Ltd., Bombay, 1946 and 1947.

Stern, Robert W., *The Cat and the Lion: Jaipur State in the British Raj*, Leiden, 1988.

Sufi, G.S.D., *Kashmir (A History of Kashmir)*, Light and Life Publishers, New Delhi, 1974.

Sundarayya, P., *Telangana Peoples Struggle and its Lessons*, National Book Centre, Calcutta, 1972.

Syed, Khaja Abdul Gafoor, *Tribes, Tribal Welfare in Hyderabad*, Government Press, Hyderabad Deccan, 1953.

Syed, Mahdi Moulvi Ali, *Hyderabad Affairs*, 3 vols., Hyderabad, 1883.

Talbot, Philip, *Kashmir and Hyderabad in World Politics–I*, 1948.

Terence, Creagh Coen, *The Indian Princely Service: A Study in Indirect Rule*, London, 1971.

Thaper, Romesh, *Storm over Hyderabad*, Kutb Publishers, Bombay, 1948.

Thompson, Edward, *Making of the Indian Princes*, OUP, London, 1943.

Tirtha, Ramananda, *Memoirs of Hyderabad Freedom Struggle*, Popular Prakashan, Bombay, 1967.

Tomlinson, B.R., The *Indian National Congress and the Raj, 1929-42, The Penultimate Phase*, London, 1976.

———, *The Political Economy of the Raj: The Economic Decolonisation in India*, London, 1979.

Udayan, Abhyankar, *State Policy and Economic Development in Mysore State, 1887-1930*, University of London, 1930.

Vaikuntham, Y., 'Peasants in Colonial South India', *Proceedings of South Indian History Congress*, 1991.

———, 'Vandemataram Movement in Hyderabad State', *Journal of Indian History*, vol. LIX, 1981, pp. 335-45.

———, *State Economy and Social Transformation: Hyderabad State (1724-1948)*, Manohar, New Delhi, 2002.

———, 'Genesis of Hyderabad State Congress', *Osmania Journal of Social Sciences*, vol. I, 1986.

Varghese, T.V., *Agrarian Change and Economic Consequences: Land Tenures in Kerala, 1850-1960*, Delhi, 1970.

Veldurthi Manikya Rao, *History of Hyderabad Freedom Struggle*, Hyderabad, 1984.

Venkatarangaiya, M., *The Freedom Struggle in Andhra Pradesh (Andhra)*, 4 vols., published by The Andhra Pradesh State Committee for Compilation of A History of the Freedom Struggle in Andhra Pradesh (Andhra), Hyderabad, 1965-1974.

Warikoo, K., *Central Asia and Kashmir*, Gian Publishing House, New Delhi, 1989.

Warner, William Lee, *The Native States of India*, Macmillan, London, 1910.

Wood, John Ray, *Political Integration of British and Princely Gujarat: Historical-Political Dimensions of Indian State Politics*, University of Columbia, 1972.

Wingate, A., 'Preliminary Land Settlement Report in Kashmir', Lahore, 1889.

Yazdani, Zubeda, *The Seventh Nizam: The Fallen Empire*, Cambridge, 1985.

Index